New Canadian Readings

P9-EDZ-868

PERSPECTIVES ON CANADIAN ECONOMIC HISTORY

Edited by
Douglas McCalla

Copp Clark Pitman Ltd.
A Longman Company
Toronto

ISBN 0-7730-4679-8

Editing: Barbara Tessman
Design: Kathy Cloutier
Cover: Montreal — Harbour 1880; #4062 — Websters Canadiana
       Collection, New Brunswick Museum, St. John, N.B.
       Courtesy of The New Brunswick Museum
Typesetting: Compeer Typographical Services Limited
Printing and Binding: Webcom Ltd.

Canadian Cataloguing in Publication Data

Main entry under title:
Perspectives on Canadian economic history

(New Canadian readings series)
Bibliography: p.
ISBN 0-7730-4679-8

1. Canada — Economic conditions. I. McCalla,
Douglas, 1942–   . II. Series: New Canadian
readings.

HC113.P47 1987 ⁄ 330.971   C87-093701-4

_54825_

Copp Clark Pitman Ltd.
495 Wellington Street West
Toronto, Ontario
M5V 1E9

Associated Companies:
  Longman Group Ltd., London
  Longman Inc., New York
  Longman Cheshire Pty., Melbourne
  Longman Paul Pty. Auckland

Printed and bound in Canada.

FOREWORD

New Canadian Readings is an on-going series of inexpensive books intended to bring some of the best recent work by this country's scholars to the attention of students of Canada. Each volume consists of ten or more articles or book sections, carefully selected to present a fully-formed thesis about some critical aspect of Canadian development. Where useful, public documents or even private letters and statistical materials may be used as well to convey a different and fresh perspective.

The authors of the readings selected for inclusion in this volume (and all the others in the series) are all first-rank scholars, those who are doing the hard research that is rapidly changing our understanding of this country. Quite deliberately, the references for each selection have been retained, thus making additional research as easy as possible.

Like the authors of the individual articles, the editors of each volume are also scholars of note, completely up-to-date in their areas of specialization and, as the introductions demonstrate, fully aware of the changing nature of the debates within their professions and genres of research. The list of additional readings provided by the editor of each volume will steer readers to materials that could not be included because of space limitations.

This series will continue into the foreseeable future, and the General Editor is pleased to invite suggestions for additional topics.

J.L. Granatstein
General Editor

CONTENTS

Introduction[1]

In the 1960s, what its proponents termed the "new" economic history emerged and quickly became the dominant approach to American economic history. So bold were its claims, and so effectively made, that two of its leading practitioners, Robert Fogel and Stanley Engerman, achieved the unusual distinction for economic (or indeed any) historians of appearances in the pages of general interest magazines such as *Time* and *Newsweek*.[2] Such work was markedly iconoclastic and took aim at a number of historical myths, and perhaps some straw men. If there was less new to this than its most extreme advocates claimed, and if it did not always destroy its targets, it did reveal large gains in analytic clarity from explicitly applying neo-classical economics to history; and there was genuine invigoration of research, debate, and understanding of economic change in the past.[3]

In a Canadian context, E.J. Chambers and Donald Gordon captured the spirit of the new approach well when they boldly speculated on how per capita Canadian economic growth might have been reduced had the prairies been rock and the prairie wheat boom not occurred. The flavour of their analysis is nicely indicated in one of their general contentions, that "resource endowment has very little connection with income levels" (p. 212). This directly challenged one of the most hallowed of all Canadian clichés: the relationship between resources and Canadian wealth. Similarly, Peter George deployed the new style of thinking when he set out to estimate the appropriateness of levels of subsidy given to the CPR in its construction period (pp. 144–166). These, along with John Dales' critical analysis of the National Policy of tariff protection,[4] allow us to mark the mid-1960s as the beginning of an era of new Canadian economic history, or at least newer and in some ways qualitatively different work in the field. Considering the noise, controversy, and scholarly impact of the American debate, surprisingly little of it made its way into Canadians' understanding of their economic history, at least beyond the world of a modest group of specialists. That is, the work of the 1960s and after that challenged established views has not had the impact it should have on general historical scholarship in Canada, or on Canadian economics either.

The need for a survey of such new work has been increasingly marked. The last anthology of articles in Canadian economic history was W.T. Easterbrook and M.H. Watkins' *Approaches to Canadian Economic History*, published in the Carleton Library series in 1967. That it remains in print is an indication both of its merits and of the need for a book to take account of articles published in the almost twenty-five years since even its most recent articles were written. Remarkably, the thirty-year-old text by W.T. Easterbrook and H.G.J. Aitken, *Canadian Economic History*, also remains in print, evidence that it retains a considerable following, although two capable surveys of Canadian economic history have been published in recent years.[5] All four of these books are useful, but they need to be supplemented and extended; students and non-specialist scholars alike will benefit from direct access to some of the methodologies and argumentative styles of the discipline of economic history in Canada today.

What can only be described as the retardation in wider understanding of the last generation's research in Canadian economic history can be attributed to a number of factors. One that is particularly relevant to this volume is that the field falls at the frontier of two disciplines—at the "hard" edge of history and the "soft" edge of economics—and that, in recent years, it has not been very central to either. Canadian economic history has also lacked a strong institutional focus. Economic history of all kinds (i.e., not just Canadian) typically plays a consistent but only small, and rather marginal, part in the programs of the annual meetings of the Canadian Economics Association and the Canadian Historical Association. Nor is there a core journal in the field, unless it is the American-based *Journal of Economic History*, in whose frame of reference Canadian concerns can scarcely be central. By necessity, the articles below are drawn from eight different journals, five of them non-Canadian; and pertinent articles could have been drawn from at least as many more.[6] There are, of course, advantages to this diffusion, notably that researchers must meet solid, usually international, standards to have their work published, but the absence of a Canadian focus means that the cumulative impact of such research may well be diminished because few readers beyond the most dedicated specialists are likely to see more than a fraction of it. In fact, the principal institutional focus of the field in recent years has been the periodic (every eighteen months) meetings of the Conference on the Use of Quantitative Methods in Canadian Economic History, together with the regular research surveys conducted by the Committee on Economic History of the Canadian Economics Association. Both are valuable to practitioners, but they cannot in themselves convey key developments to the much wider audience that ought to hear important conclusions arising from new research, and be influenced by the methods of that new research.

If it has been institutionally diffuse, Canadian economic history was for a long time intellectually focussed in the staples tradition. Regrettably, this focus has begun to be as much a burden on inquiry as an advantage to it. Especially in the hands of what its Canadian proponents term the "political economy" approach —with its quasi-theological quality evidenced in its repetitious incantations of sayings of Harold Innis, and with its ideological, empirical, and methodological blind spots—it has tended to become self-contained and simply uninterested in a wide range of relevant and sophisticated scholarship on the history of the Canadian economy.[7] Thus, exponents of this tradition often cite it to evade threatening questions, rather than to engage in debate about new hypotheses, new evidence, and new models. This is depressingly illustrated by the recently "updated and expanded" *The New Practical Guide to Canadian Political Economy*,[8] in which only one of the articles included in the present volume is even mentioned — in a section prepared by Tom Traves, the article's co-author.

An irony of the self-proclaimed political economists' rejection of such recent work is that the political and wider social dimensions of Canadian economic history are very much addressed by the best of the new research, as the articles here amply demonstrate. Moreover, while a few of these papers include technical passages that will be obscure to non-specialists, all ultimately arrive at conclusions that are clear and comprehensible to those unversed in the nuances of economic theory and econometrics; some even support arguments of at least some of the "political economists." That the authors' arguments are logically and clearly presented does not, of course, mean that they are not debatable, or that the reader must agree with their assumptions, methods, or conclusions, which are in any case diverse; but serious students of Canadian history do need to come to terms with them, something that has not sufficiently happened. Hence this book, which is intended to bring lively, controversial, and methodologically sophisticated articles in Canadian economic history to the attention of a wider or different audience than they will have reached in their original journals. One paper, by Green and Urquhart (pp. 182–199), has not previously been published, though its data, fruits of a major long-term research project at Queen's University, have been reported at several conferences and further publications related to them are to be anticipated.[9]

A number of principles of selection, of varying degrees of arbitrariness, have gone into picking the articles below. (1) They are complete texts, not edited excerpts, in order to do fullest justice to each author's arguments. For similar reasons, and also because the scholarly paper is this field's usual form of publication, I have not taken excerpts from books. (2) The approaches and topics that can be included are necessarily limited by space constraints. Another editor would undoubtedly have chosen a somewhat different collection to represent so large a field, but I think these articles fairly represent what is new in our economic history in the past generation. (3) With regret, I have confined myself to works published in English, and considerable important work, particularly on the economy of Quebec, is thus omitted.[10] The bibliographical essay offers suggestions for those wishing to pursue the work further in French. (4) From the recent literature, much of which is addressed to a specialist readership, I have sought articles that are at least relatively accessible to non-specialists. Of course the articles can be read at a number of levels, according to the reader's background and interests. (5) Recognizing that this is an interdisciplinary field, I have sought to balance the work of authors whose links are with economics with those in history; there are important differences in style and approach between the two, and both have contributions to make to the progress of understanding. (6) I have sought to balance subject matter, periods, and regions as much as possible. As the collection shows, the largest proportion of work has focussed on the period from the 1860s to the 1920s, with an especially pronounced empirical and theoretical interest in the significance of the 1900–14 period. (7) I have tried to illustrate issues that have been controversial; where articles sparked explicit challenges, I have confined myself to the initial article, except for the response by Bertram (pp. 221–242) to Chambers and Gordon. Interested students will find leads to subsequent arguments in the bibliographical essay. (8) I have sought a mix of quite recent articles and "classic" articles of the 1960s and 1970s — by classic I mean articles that nicely embodied particular issues and approaches, that shaped productive discussions, and/or that offered summary statements of large and important research projects.

Some fields are not represented here, because somehow the articles in them did not quite fit one or more of the criteria just listed, or because articles did not exist at all, but also because space limitations precluded comprehensiveness. The bibliographical essay will, I hope, help the reader wishing to explore some of the field's other areas. Only one article is included here to represent the long, so-called pre-statistical era of Canadian economic history (i.e., the period before regular decennial census-taking began in 1851). Similarly, the coverage of the collection fades after the 1920s. There is material on the subsequent era written by economists, especially with policy issues of the Depression and post-war years in mind, but as the periodical literature of the last twenty years attests, the period from the Depression on has not lately attracted the attention of very many economic historians *per se*. No papers focus centrally on explaining the trade cycle, price history, demography, labour, money and banking, or urbanization, although these themes do play important parts in some of the articles. In light of my desire to give this volume an explicitly economic focus, I have found it necessary to omit material in the political economy tradition, at least as Drache and Clement define it; I assume that this approach is relatively better known to many students and non-specialists, and perhaps also in its argumentative style more immediately accessible to them. I have also had to omit quantitative social history, despite its evident relevance, and business history. The omissions I most regret are examples of some of the more sophisticated but empirical Marxist-influenced analysis (notably in the field of working-class history).[11] This has already contributed substantially to deepening our understanding of the character and timing of Canadian industrial development, for example.

It is not possible to review each article below individually, but some comments are in order on what readers may expect from them. While these papers offer new views, their virtues are by no means unique to the "new" economic history. Indeed, half of these papers are not avowedly in the "cliometric" style at all and derive from other approaches, such as France's *Annales* style (which helps inform Le Goff's article, pp. 10–36), the Kuznets-inspired national income accounting approach (e.g., pp. 182–199), and culturally influenced economic growth theory (e.g., pp. 58–80). In fact, the papers demonstrate the qualities of good economic history of any era. Students often see the approach as distinguished by quantification, but both before and after the numbers come imagination, theory, and logic. An essential element of this work is the care its authors take to discuss explicitly the methods and assumptions that are an integral part of any organized body of data or any argument. At least as much as it is an empirical field, then, Canadian economic history is a speculative one. I hope students will find this combination stimulating, even exciting.

The central theme of the discipline is economic growth, development, and change (and the welfare implications of these processes). The staples approach to Canadian economic history has essentially been an argument for unbalanced growth propelled by leading, export-oriented sectors. Much of the work below, however, argues or implies that balanced growth is the more relevant approach to Canada (e.g., pp. 58–80, 182–199), and even if not all the authors would entirely agree here, they do agree that the causes and character of Canadian growth need debate and specification that the staples tradition has not yet offered.[12] They carry understanding of the causation of development well beyond the typical general history textbooks with their standard list of staple products and undifferentiated lists of multiple causes. The gains from such analytic clarity are made abundantly clear, for example, in Norrie's careful dissection of what actually caused the prairie wheat boom (pp. 168–181).

The stories these papers tell are international. Despite the complaints of some nationalist critics that the abstractions of economics and the American origins of "new" economic history will subsume Canadian uniqueness into a continental or wider homogeneous economic and political universe, no author here assumes that Canada's was an economy identical to any other one in the world. Rather, all use international and comparative questions to inform their inquiry into evidence from the Canadian past. Canada was, after all, connected to the world in a variety of ways, through knowledge, credit networks, and price movements, for example, as well as such more familiar and visible links as migration and flows of capital and trade. Seeing how all these impinged on a specific country or region at a specific time is very much the task of the economic historian. When such case studies are done, they typically reveal complexities in Canada's actual international experience that are not anticipated in more abstract, often monocausal analyses (e.g., pp. 270–283).

These papers depend on and illustrate the use of a considerable variety of documentation. Those by Sager and Fischer (pp. 97–117) and Green and Urquhart are based on years of fundamental primary research by substantial teams of scholars and research assistants. Others derive from extensive research in manuscript sources, including the key census manuscripts, and/or offer the results of typically very substantial empirical research for doctoral theses. Others still are relatively more speculative and contribute in part by the application of theoretical insight to data from rather more familiar compilations such as the printed census. Whatever the data, the information needed to answer any of the questions we wish to pose in Canadian economic history was seldom gathered and kept in immediately usable form by anyone, especially before the creation of the Dominion Bureau of Statistics (now Statistics Canada) in 1926. Thus, research strategy and an understanding of the character and implications of one's evidence are fundamental. A number of important approaches and techniques are exemplified below, including the creation and use of national income accounts (pp. 182–199), time series analysis (pp. 10–36), sampling (pp. 37–57), cross-sectional structural analysis (pp. 37–57), data creation by controlled conjecture (pp. 144–166), the use of counter-factual reasoning (pp. 201–220), and the development of data in alternative ways when direct measurements of the phenomena being studied are wholly unavailable or simply intractable (pp. 58–80).

As already suggested, these papers are highly relevant to students of Canadian political and social history, and several explicitly test the significance of particular policies. But they do not begin with the assumption that research in policy documents can answer their questions or that economic change was simply or directly, if at all, a result of public policy. An important dimension of this work is thus its way of addressing economic reality in the past, studying economic behaviour and choices made by specific groups of economic actors. What did Atlantic shipowners actually do (pp. 97–117)? What did farmers grow and sell (pp. 37–57)? What went on inside the walls of a railway shop (pp. 118–143)? How was expansion of mining companies financed (pp. 270–283)? From such evidence emerges a much sharper sense of the shape and character of the Canadian economy than can be derived when we focus our research at the level of public policy or of commentary on economic life such as pamphleteers, social critics, or politicians had to offer. So, for example, Trevor Dick is able to estimate with considerable precision just how important, by comparison with essentially economic variables, the "manufacturing condition" (i.e., provincial prohibitions on export of unmanufactured logs) was to the migration of the North American newsprint industry to Canada (pp. 244–269).

One of the "new" economic history's key techniques in challenging established myths was its way of putting specific phenomena into more precise proportion (when joined with the ingenuity it used in developing data to accomplish this). But measurement was always essential to good economic history. No magnitude is significant in and of itself without reference to some standard of comparison. So the works here measure relative rates of change, rates of return, price levels, scale of specific sectors within the larger economy. Where precise data are lacking, orders of magnitude must sometimes suffice (pp. 10–36). Where estimates are involved, they are made explicit, tested for sensitivity to changes in the shaping assumptions, and not biased in favour of the "desired" conclusion (pp. 144–166). Given the importance of having standards of reference, it is difficult to overestimate the significance of the research of Green and Urquhart and their colleagues; their carefully constructed annual series for Canadian Gross National Product and its sectoral composition, for the whole period from 1870 to the beginning of the modern Canadian national accounts should be part of the working knowledge of every student of Canadian history, no matter what his or her particular research interests. It should also be said that the authors here use numbers but are not trapped by them. When, for example, they use statistical measures such as means, they are equally aware of the significance and the shape of variations from their measures of the normal (pp. 37–57, 81–95). If, as Le Goff aptly remarks, "the 'average' habitant is a fiction" (p. 31), this does not mean that numbers pertaining to habitants have nothing to say, as some critics of quantitative approaches have tried to argue over the years.

As with any good history, time is of the essence in this work. The sequence and the timing of developments say much about the processes of economic change. In the papers below, we meet careful discussion of changes hinged on very specific years and conjunctures, such as 1802 (pp. 10–27), the 1860s (pp. 81–95), 1921 (pp. 244–269), and so on. Both very short-term, essentially cross-sectional studies (e.g., pp. 37–57) and very long-term studies (e.g., pp. 244–269) have contributions to make. Time arises in other ways here, too, as in the careful use of results (*ex post* data) to infer something about causes and antecedents (*ex ante* situations) (pp. 144–166), or when discussions hinge, as they often do, on expectations, that is on economic actors' actual or probable perceptions of their future (e.g., pp. 168–181).

Like economics, economic history works at both micro and macro levels. We need to study both the overall economic system and also its more specific dimensions from the perspective of those within it. For the "pre-statistical" era, indeed, Le Goff argues convincingly that local and specific studies can open the way to understanding larger and otherwise highly abstract and unmeasurable processes of general, systemic economic change. In short, economic history can be fruitfully pursued at every level from the individual economic actor through sectors and regions to the national and the international economic system.

Whatever the perspectives we choose, there is enormous scope for new research, for much of the material life and economic development that Canadians actually experienced is as yet scarcely understood.[13] The new and more sophisticated Canadian economic history that we eventually build will depend significantly on these papers, and on the work of this and the next generation of students of Canadian economic history, who will, I hope, draw inspiration here. In their methods, their spirit of open debate and inquiry, their use of explanatory models, and their focus on basic structures and patterns, these papers represent a way of thinking that deserves the attention of all students of our past.

Notes

1. I have benefited greatly from discussions of this work with Michael Huberman; he is, of course, not to blame for any errors or biases in the volume.

2. E.g., "Massa's in de Cold, Cold Computer," *Time*, 17 June 1974, 56–60; "History by the Numbers," *Newsweek*, 20 Oct. 1975, 70. The attention focussed especially on their *Time on the Cross*, 2 vols. (Boston, 1974). For some of the criticisms that this book evoked, much of it from within the perspective of the new economic history, see Paul David et al., *Reckoning with Slavery* (New York: Oxford, 1976).

3. On the new economic history, a useful starting point is Robert Fogel's chapter in Fogel and G.R. Elton, *Which Road to the Past? Two Views of History* (New Haven: Yale, 1983), 1–70; see also Robert Fogel, "The Limits of Quantitative Methods in History," *American Historical Review* LXXX (1975): 329–50.

4. John H. Dales, *The Protective Tariff in Canada's Development* (Toronto: University of Toronto Press, 1966).

5. William L. Marr and Donald G. Paterson, *Canada: An Economic History* (Toronto: Gage, 1980); Richard Pomfret, *The Economic Development of Canada* (Toronto: Methuen, 1981).

6. Without wishing to offer a list that might be very long indeed, I would note that other articles that I considered including here are to be found in *Histoire sociale/Social History*, *Explorations in Economic History*, *Canadian Papers in Rural History*, *Agricultural History*, the *Revue d'histoire de l'Amérique française*, *Research in Economic History*, the *Journal of Canadian Studies*, *Acadiensis*, and *Labour/Le Travail*. See the bibliography for some of these articles.

7. It perhaps needs to be stressed that this is not a criticism of Innis, whose work obviously speaks for itself and can be directly debated and considered; it is the appropriation of the name and work for purposes of current academic partisanship that is the problem. Two thoughtful discussions of the Innis tradition are Robin Neill, "The Passing of Canadian Economic History" and Hugh G.J. Aitken, "Myth and Measurement: The Innis Tradition in Economic History" in *Journal of Canadian Studies* XII, 5 (Winter 1977): 73–82 and 96–105.

8. Daniel Drache and Wallace Clement, eds. (Toronto: Lorimer, 1985).

9. See, e.g., the forthcoming volume 51 of the National Bureau of Economic Research, *Studies in Income and Wealth*, for several examples.

10. One other debate is available in English and offers further perspective on themes raised here by Le Goff and Isbister. See Frank Lewis and Marvin McInnis, "The Efficiency of the French-Canadian Farmer in the Nineteenth Century," *Journal of Economic History* XL (1980): 497–514; their "Agricultural Output and Efficiency in Lower Canada, 1851," *Research in Economic History* IX (1984): 45–87; and McInnis's "A Reconsideration of the State of Agriculture in Lower Canada in the First Half of the Nineteenth Century," *Canadian Papers in Rural History* III (1982): 9–49. Critical of their analysis is Robert Armstrong, "The Efficiency of Quebec Farmers in 1851," *Histoire sociale/Social History* XVII (1984): 149–63.

11. See Allan Greer's criticism, in Marxist terms, of an older Canadian Marxist classic in "Wage Labour and the Transition to Capitalism: A Critique of Pentland," *Labour/Le Travail* XV (Spring 1985): 7–22; the work referred to is H.C. Pentland, *Labour and Capital in Canada 1650–1860* (Toronto: Lorimer, 1981). For samples of the newer work, see Gregory S. Kealey, *Toronto Workers Respond to Industrial Capitalism, 1867–1892* (Toronto: University of Toronto Press, 1980); Bryan D. Palmer, *Working-Class Experience: The Rise and Reconstitution of Canadian Labour, 1800–1980* (Toronto: Butterworth, 1983); both have excellent bibliographies. In general, see *Labour/Le Travail* (formerly *Labour/Le Travailleur*) for examples of such work and for further bibliographical leads.

12. See Edward Vickery, "Exports and North American Economic Growth: 'Structuralist' and 'Staple' Models in Historical Perspective," *Canadian Journal of Economics* VII (1974): 32–58.

13. See Douglas McCalla and Peter George, "Measurement, Myth and Reality: Reflections on the Economic History of Nineteenth-Century Ontario," *Journal of Canadian Studies* XXI, 3 (Fall 1986): 71–86.

SECTION 1

AGRICULTURE AND ECONOMIC CHANGE

THE AGRICULTURAL CRISIS IN LOWER CANADA, 1802–12: A REVIEW OF A CONTROVERSY†

T.J.A. LE GOFF

Historians for some time now have been aware that basic changes were taking place in the economy of Lower Canada in the first two decades of the nineteenth century. These changes in one way or another drastically reshaped a society which had up to then retained most of the economic structure of the pre-Conquest period. They are considered to have played a significant part in setting off and keeping alive the political conflicts which developed during these years, in which a new French-Canadian professional group, backed by the bulk of the Canadiens, fought for power against the alliance of English merchants and placemen in a struggle which finally exploded in the 1837–38 rising and the troubles of the 1840s. These economic transformations can be grouped under three heads. One is the decline of the northwest fur trade through Montreal, the St. Lawrence and the Great Lakes system. Another is the growth of the timber trade after 1807, when Great Britain, finding difficulty in obtaining timber from the Baltic because of Napoleon's Continental System, turned to Canada for its ship and other timber. Finally, there was the opening of the British market to Canadian and North American agricultural produce after the British entry into war with France in 1793.[1] Yet if historians agree that these were the principal transformations in the Lower Canadian economy, they are far from sure what the impact was of each of these changes.

This is especially true of the third phenomenon mentioned above: the change in the market for agricultural produce. In recent years a rather bitter polemic has been carried on by Fernand Ouellet on the one hand and by Gilles Paquet and J.-P. Wallot on the other over what happened to Lower Canadian agriculture at the turn of the century. Unfortunately, the debate over this question has been carried on in a rather confused fashion. Moreover, both parties to the discussion clearly believe that the answer to the question "What happened to Lower Canadian agriculture between 1800 and 1820?" has a larger political significance. This was not initially clear when Paquet and Wallot launched an attack on Ouellet's *Histoire*

†*The Canadian Historical Review* LV, 1 (March 1974): 1–31.

économique et sociale du Québec in 1967[2] but it has been made plain in a
recent article.[3] As for Ouellet, there was never any question that he saw
than purely economic consequences in the agricultural difficulties of Lower C_____a
at the turn of the century. At this time, he held, French-Canadian agriculture
began a long decline which, if its effects became more intense in the 1820s and
1830s, nevertheless had begun as early as 1803. It was then that Lower Canadian
agriculture failed to modernize and compete on international markets. This failure
of the only sector of the economy in the hands of the French Canadians to grow
and expand coincided with the rise of the first French-Canadian nationalism,
born of economic and cultural despair, but dressed up by the French-Canadian
professional bourgeoisie in the swaddling clothes of a liberal ideology which really
masked a conservative social ideal.[4] By taking issue with Ouellet's view of French-
Canadian agriculture, Paquet and Wallot clearly intended to lay part of the
groundwork for a larger interpretation of the political conflicts of the period.[5]
With this larger interpretation I shall take little issue here. Rather, this paper will
try to set out in a clear and simple fashion the arguments for and against an
"agricultural crisis" in the 1800s, and come to some conclusion about what was
really taking place.

Ouellet's notion of an agricultural crisis after 1802 was first developed in a
joint article with Jean Hamelin in 1963[6] and later expanded in his massive *Histoire
économique et sociale du Québec* (1966). Much of his argument is similar to one
appearing in two earlier articles by R.L. Jones, written in the 1940s,[7] but Ouellet's
treatment offered some statistical proof to back up Jones' impressions. The principal
sets of statistics which Ouellet presented were grain prices for Quebec and Montreal and figures for the volume of exports from the port of Quebec which, if
properly handled, Ouellet claimed, could be used to illustrate the fluctuations of
agricultural production.[8] Since the appearance of Paquet and Wallot's critiques,
Ouellet has published a set of tithe records for Lower Canada between 1774 and
1850 which, he maintains, bear out his original thesis.[9]

The broad outlines of Ouellet's "crisis" are simple. The British declaration of
war on France in 1793, the growth in British population, and the increasing
diversification of the British economy at the end of the eighteenth century meant
that Britain had to look beyond domestic agriculture and her usual sources in the
Baltic region for grain and flour. Lower Canada had only directed a small share
of its grain production towards exports in the best years of the French regime
and, although it grew in the 1770s, the Canadian agricultural sector was only
really drawn into the North Atlantic commercial economy during the 1790s.
Exports then boomed and grain prices rose in Canada, pulled up by the possibilities of sales on the British market and in the British West Indies. The Lower
Canadian government in 1795 prohibited the export of grain except to the empire
(previously there had been a small Iberian and Mediterranean export trade), and
this helped tighten the imperial bond.[10] The *habitants*, encouraged by grain merchants, tried to expand production to meet new demands of the British Isles:
"[The Quebec merchants] who, every year, send agents into the countryside to
buy up grain not needed for the subsistence of the habitants" — wrote one observer
quoted by Ouellet — "have inspired in them resourcefulness and a degree of
activity previously unimaginable."[11]

Production and exports rose, despite one bad year in 1795, and reached record heights in 1801–2. After this point, however, exports declined. Demand, Ouellet argues, remained strong in England and the British West Indies, but 1803 saw a fall in exports from Lower Canada, the harvests of 1804 and 1805 were poor, and the record levels of 1801–2 were never reached again. The figures for exports show only a part of this decline, for after 1802 a higher proportion of the grain and flour exported from Lower Canada was really American, allowed duty-free into British North America presumably by way of the Richelieu and from the Genesee Valley towards the upper St. Lawrence or Niagara.[12] This fall in exports, Ouellet maintains, though apparently of the order of 27 percent, really attained a drop of 40–48 percent.[13]

Why did this decline take place? There were some crop failures, for example the ravages made by the Hessian fly in 1805, but the basic cause, according to Ouellet, was the fall in total production and productivity per unit of land cultivated:

> If, from 1760 to 1802, yields were rather high on the average and if production rose, this was not the result of a transformation of agricultural techniques. An increase in production was primarily the result of an increase in land cleared. In other words, to produce more, the peasant cleared land and sowed more; as for his sons, they cultivated new land which for a certain time allowed greater productivity.[14]

Thus, for Ouellet, the decline of Lower Canadian agriculture was caused by the failure of the *habitants* to adopt modern agricultural techniques such as those being pioneered in England. Without a change in agricultural methods, any increase in production brought about by clearing more land was bound only to be temporary since the new soil was soon depleted and the older cultivated land was becoming less and less productive all the time. And, in fact, agriculture had changed little in its methods or crops since the French regime; all contemporary witnesses seemed to be in agreement, and so are the participants in the present-day controversy.[15]

If Ouellet and his critics agree on this question, however, it is certainly difficult to find other points in common between them. Since the appearance of Ouellet's pioneering work, Paquet and Wallot have taken issue with most of his findings in the course of trying to build a systematic model of the Lower Canadian economy in the years 1790–1812. Their critiques are far-ranging and their explorations often take them beyond the limits of a simple discussion of the agricultural sector. And yet, in reading them, it is often difficult to pin them down to a particular clearly stated counter-thesis on the existence and impact of the "agricultural crisis." It is possible, however, to extract an argument from their various criticisms which, I think, fairly summarizes their position.

Such a counter-thesis would run like this. There was no crisis in Lower Canadian agriculture in the 1790s and the 1800s. External demand for Canadian grain was not steady, but varied enormously, and Lower Canadian farmers produced more or less grain according to the variations in the prices offered on the market in Quebec and Montreal, prices which reflected the variations in world market prices. Thus, when Lower Canadian farmers did not export as much after 1802, they were not failing to produce enough to meet an insatiable foreign demand, but rather behaving like rational producers and, ultimately, gave up prod for an unstable export market on which they could not hope to gain. But don demand was steady, and the inhabitants produced for an expanding market ... the process, they bettered their standard of living as the economy became more diversified and demand for grain in the non-agricultural sector rose.[16] As for supply, the Lower Canadians were able to produce if they saw an advantage in doing so, and their methods of cultivation were well enough adapted to a North American environment; indeed, they diversified their agricultural production in these years.[17] Finally, they would argue, Ouellet's thesis is based on unsound postulates. Ouellet uses the methods of "serial history" — in which the historian builds long series of prices and quantities and then deduces from their ups and downs general conclusions about the expansion and contraction of the economy and the impact of these fluctuations on different groups of people living in that economy. Such an approach, Paquet and Wallot argue, lacks conviction in this particular case because it does not have a systematic overview of the interrelations of the prices and quantities employed by the historian and of the international context in which the Lower Canadian economy operated. If such a structural approach were taken, they suggest, the agricultural sector would not be seen to dominate in the Lower Canadian economy and the agricultural crisis, if there was one, would not appear as the overriding factor in the development of French-Canadian nationalism.[18] Let us take each of the elements of this argument and analyse them more closely.

External Demand

Paquet and Wallot argue that demand for Canadian grain on export markets was unsteady, and that Canadian producers responded to the variations in prices on the world market. Their argument on this point is in two parts. The first is based on a theoretical economic model developed by R.E. Caves for determining from movements of price and quantity schedules whether increased prices and/or quantity are demand-induced or supply-induced. Wallot and Paquet apply this model to Ouellet's local price and production data — that is, to his price and export figures, the export figures being made to represent production. The demonstration has a certain elegance (see table 1).

According to this analysis, since prices and quantities do not move in contrary directions in eleven out of the twenty years from 1792 to 1812, demand must also be a factor in inducing shifts in the supply schedule for wheat. For, their reasoning runs, if the supply schedule were unalterable, or nearly so, years in which quantity *and* price rose or fell concurrently would be rare.[19]

The second part of their criticism of Ouellet's description of demand is based on a study of corn-dealers' and estate-managers' correspondence. From this it emerges, as one might have expected, that the conditions in which grain merchants in Quebec had to work were difficult: they could not predict what European prices for their products would be because their shipments normally arrived in Britain after the European harvest was in; they had severe competition from the United States to reckon with and British prices sometimes were too low to permit profitable export.[20]

TABLE 1

Year	Increase (+) or Decrease (−) in Wheat Exports	Increase (+) or Decrease (−) in Wheat Price	Dominant Factor
1792–93	+	no change	increased demand
1793–94	−	no change	decreased demand
1794–95	+	+	increased demand
1795–96	−	+	fall in production
1796–97	+	−	rise in production
1797–98	+	−	rise in production
1798–99	+	−	rise in production
1799–1800	+	+	increased demand
1800–1	+	+	increased demand
1801–2	+	−	rise in production
1802–3	−	no change	decreased demand
1803–4	−	no change	decreased demand
1804–5	−	+	fall in production
1805–6	+	−	rise in production
1806–7	+	+	increased demand
1807–8	+	+	increased demand
1808–9	−	+	fall in production
1809–10	−	+	fall in production
1810–11	−	−	decreased demand
1811–12	+	+	increased demand

SOURCE: Paquet and Wallot, "Crise agricole," 200.

Now, what is interesting about this double criticism of Ouellet's work is that both parts of it cannot stand together. The second part — backed up as it is by extensive proof and confirmed by what we know of the operation of the grain trade in Europe — automatically cancels the first, in all logic. Because there is *no* direct connection between demand and supply in the *same* year, it is impossible to make a model like Caves' work for the agricultural sector in a pre-industrial economy. In such an economy there is no mechanism which will allow producers, once they have seeded their fields in the fall or early spring, to increase their output to meet foreign demand of which the dimensions are only known in the foreign countries themselves as the harvest grows nearer. Indeed, this is a problem which even modern agriculture has not solved. To carry out their analysis of the responsiveness of suppliers to demand with a higher degree of plausibility, Paquet and Wallot might have tried to correlate supply with price movements in preceding years. But it would be a waste of time in any case, if only because the figures which both Ouellet and Paquet and Wallot use for "production" are only export figures from Quebec, and in any case these figures are greatly distorted by American imports after 1802. When we add to this the knowledge that year-to-year prices reflect not only direct responses to the availability of grain from the supplier, but also the existence of slack and tension in the systems of grain transport and marketing caused by unpredictables such as hoarding, dumping, stupidity, bad weather, and shipwreck, the futility of such an enterprise can be seen. conclusion from all this, then, is that Lower Canadian producers were apparently having difficulty in competing on the market in the United Kingdom. Part of the trouble would appear to be that they were unable to adjust their level of production to suit the variations in British and world prices, but the extent to which Lower Canadians could compete on the British market after 1802 and the strength of demand on that market is a question which Paquet and Wallot, like Ouellet, leave unsettled.

Domestic Demand

Demand for grain on the domestic market, Paquet and Wallot argue, was steady, and the *habitants* were able to produce for an expanding domestic market. The population of Lower Canada, only 165,000 in 1792, rose beyond 300,000 by 1815, and the growth appears to have accelerated after 1807. This demand, say Paquet and Wallot, is relatively "integrated and firm." The inflationary push of prices after 1807 was due, they argue, to the increasing employment of people in towns or in non-agricultural pursuits, although external demand also played a role on occasion.[21]

If Paquet and Wallot's own analysis of the rise in prices after 1807 is to be believed, then

> with the rise of the timber trade and the profitability of this new sector there
> was a double effect of a rise in local demand and a reduction in the
> agricultural labour force. There is no doubt that, from 1807 onwards in
> particular, this is the principal reason for the rise in prices; the displacement
> of the demand curve towards the right [of a supply-and-demand diagram,
> that is, a rise in the prices consumers are willing to pay for grain at all levels
> of production] was however more considerable than the displacement of the
> supply curve towards the left [of a supply-and-demand diagram, that is,
> suppliers were able to put only reduced amounts on the market at each price
> level].[22]

In other words, inflation was induced principally by increased domestic demand caused by a shift in the population out of the agricultural sector rather than by a deficiency of supply. But the question here is whether increased demand can call out *increased* supply. What Paquet and Wallot are saying is that it cannot. As we shall see, there is good reason to believe that they are right—but such an explanation does not seem to fit in with their argument that the *habitants* were "rational" producers. It is true that this does seem to be a more plausible explanation of the shortages after 1807 than that offered by Ouellet, who put them down sometimes to a real downturn in production and sometimes to the activity of speculators.[23] But what was the impact of the rise in *total* population on demand and on prices? It is quite clear that both parties to the dispute are going on faith here, and are not at all clear about the quantities or changes involved in the domestic market during these years nor about the relative importance of domestic and international demand.

Supply

Paquet and Wallot agree with Ouellet that there was no real lack of land in the seigneurial settlements before 1812, if not before 1820; they also agree that agricultural techniques were backward by the standards of European and English agricultural commentators who visited the colony, or heard of it.[24] Their interpretation of the meaning of this backwardness, however, differs from that of Ouellet. Ouellet sees it as a psychological problem, a failing to innovate and seize the main chance which ultimately would be responsible for a failure of local production.[25] Paquet and Wallot point out, however, as Maurice Séguin once did, that the same methods of extensive rather than intensive cultivation were in use elsewhere in North America, and fitted into a system of agriculture in which the relative costs of yield intensification per unit of soil were higher than those of further land clearing. It made sense to be prodigal with the soil. This is a useful suggestion, especially when we compare Lower Canadian land use with that in, say, southeastern Pennsylvania, where a somewhat similar attitude prevailed.[26] However, one would like to know more about particular cases of farming methods used in Lower Canada, instead of summaries of travellers' impressions.

Why then was it that the *habitants* did not increase production, either by yield intensification or by more extensive cultivation? We know Ouellet's answer. Paquet and Wallot offer a more complicated reply. On the one hand, they say that it is not proven that production did not rise.[27] On the other, they suggest that the *habitants*, discouraged by the instability of the market caused by the intermittent repercussions on it of international shortages, made a rational decision not to increase their production and satisfied only the local market.[28]

In any event, the crucial question for this system of agriculture was: could it produce enough food for the population which depended on it? As neither party to the controversy has provided figures for overall domestic supply, no conclusions can be drawn from these statements.

The Problem of Economic Structures

Paquet and Wallot claim that Ouellet has failed to indicate rigorously the interrelationship of the prices and quantities which he cites, and that he fails, in effect, to put "weights" or, as they term them, "valences" — indicators of the relative significance in the economy — on his series of price and quantities. This is a telling point. As the French economic historian Jean Marczewski points out:

> *Serial* history . . . in fact is the first stage of quantitative history. Quantitative history uses not only vertical chronological series which represent the evolution of a single category of phenomena in time, but also horizontal accounting, which analyses the structures formed by phenomena belonging to a single period. Quantitative history, then, can be compared to a three-dimensional edifice, of which serial history makes up the "columns" and national accounts the "storeys." Serial history is the necessary and indispensable precondition of quantitative history. But serial history, without the horizontal synthesis furnished by quantitative history is only a piece of unfinished workmanship.[29]

Ouellet's *Histoire économique* bears the subtitle *Structures et conjoncture*, and it is certainly true that in this part of his long analysis Ouellet was unable to give a very rigorous description of the structure of the Lower Canadian economy.

This is perhaps not for lack of trying. There is a fundamental problem in carrying quantitative history beyond the serial stage in the analysis of "pre-statistical" economies: the absence of sufficient data to build reliable models of national accounting, or even of accounting within sectors of the economy. Lower Canada in the 1800s was barely into the statistical age, as were most Western countries at the time, and it is not surprising that it should be difficult to carry out this form of analysis. Is it possible, then, to take the description of the Lower Canadian agricultural sector beyond the serial stage?

If Ouellet cannot be said to have succeeded in this, it must be admitted that so far Paquet and Wallot have not been much more successful, though they have had the merit of calling attention to the gaps in Ouellet's analysis and publishing some highly useful material. There are, however, several serious defects in their own attempts at model-building.

First, one may ask whether, in their critique of Ouellet, Paquet and Wallot have sufficiently examined an important element of any model of a national economy which forms a part of a larger international system: namely, the relation between foreign trade, domestic trade, and the prices offered and quantities suppliable by foreign competitors — especially the United States — to the common external market, Great Britain and, to some extent, the British West Indies. After 1802, exports from Lower Canada fell, or at least did not continue to rise. Was this the fault of the Canadian producers, or was it because other countries' grain was cheaper in Britain after that point?

If the grain of other countries was cheaper in Great Britain, this might point to a failure of production or an increased demand in Lower Canada. But we know little about either. Up to now neither Ouellet nor Paquet and Wallot have been able to furnish us with indications of the quantities of agricultural production in Lower Canada. As we have just seen, Paquet and Wallot's analysis of supply and demand, which was based on price series and export figures, breaks down for the reason, among others, that agricultural production is *not* faithfully mirrored by export figures, themselves swollen by American and Upper Canadian shipments through the St. Lawrence. Even without the inflation of export quantities, export figures could tell us little about production.

If there is supposed to be an agricultural crisis in Lower Canada, it would be interesting to know why it had come about. Had the *habitants* decided not to compete on export markets, as Paquet and Wallot maintain, because they or their shippers judged those markets to be too risky, or were they simply unable to compete, as Ouellet maintains, without going into great detail, because something was radically wrong with Lower Canadian agriculture?

Even if we could arrive at figures for domestic production, how much of it reached the market? We do not know if the *habitants* were equally sensitive to markets all the time. If they were not, within a given year only a fixed amount of grain would be available for the market, regardless of the price buyers are willing to pay (on a supply-and-demand diagram, this kind of supply schedule would resemble S_1 and S_2 on graph 1). If, however, the *habitants* were sensitive to markets, then they would be willing to dip into supplies reserved for their own consumption if the price were high enough, and eke out their reduced grain supply with substitutes such as potatoes and lesser grains like barley and oats. This would produce a flexible grain supply which would increase in volume at higher prices (on a supply-and-demand diagram, this situation would resemble the supply schedules S_1 and S_2 in graph 2, which are sloped rather than vertical). One would suspect that the grain supply in Lower Canada was tending more and more to this second situation, but we do not know. If it were, then much of the increase in "production" shown by increased exports before 1802, and indeed the exports through all of the period, might simply represent shifts in patterns of consumption on the farm.

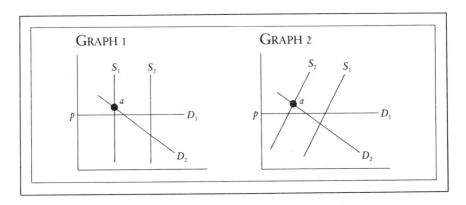

We do not know, either, the volume of domestic demand. It could hardly have been stable, since the population was rising. How much larger a share of production did the rising population demand? How could Lower Canadian agriculture meet this? Was the price rise after 1805 the reflection of a world grain price inflation, or the result of shortages at home? Here, in fact, is the key problem. Both parties to this controversy place great importance on international demand and the *habitants'* response to it. Yet neither seems to be able to assess its impact on the domestic market in anything more than an impressionistic and imprecise fashion. It will be my contention that it was not so much international as domestic demand which put new and insistent pressures on supply in Lower Canada, and which proved in fact too great for Lower Canadian suppliers to meet.

Finally, without statistics of production in Lower Canada, we cannot say much about the condition of people producing in the agricultural sector. It might be possible, if the statistics are available, to try and arrive, as Paquet and Wallot do, at a crude index of the terms of trade under which the agricultural sector as a whole operated, obtained by dividing an index of agricultural prices by an index of non-agricultural prices.[30] But as the population of the agricultural sector was increasing during these years, it is necessary to know whether production was increasing as well, and in what proportions; otherwise the index, while it might be statistically valid, might have no historical meaning. And we ought to have some idea how the revenues of the agricultural sector, whether increasing or decreasing in real terms, were divided up among the different economic strata of the *habitants*. Paquet and Wallot do not appear to have weighed these problems sufficiently before presenting us with an index of the terms of trade which, they claim, proves that the standard of living of the average *habitant* was improving. Nevertheless, the index which they do present is of importance, in that it does at least suggest that Ouellet's interpretation of the fate of farmers in Lower Canada at this time was mistaken. The methods used to obtain these potentially revolutionary conclusions thus deserve some careful examination.

I therefore propose to examine in the remainder of this article the competitive position of Lower Canada vis-à-vis the United States in the international grain market, then go on to take a fresh look at the supply side of Lower Canadian agriculture, and finally try to evaluate the claim of Paquet and Wallot that the agricultural sector and agriculturalists themselves were prospering by "profit maximization" in this period.

The competitive position of Lower Canadian agriculture in the international market appears to have grown steadily worse through the 1790s and the 1800s, especially after 1803. The evidence which can be offered for this is not complete, but it appears telling: it consists of price data for wheat in Great Britain,[31] the U.S. Atlantic ports,[32] and Quebec;[33] grain import figures for the United Kingdom;[34] partial export figures for flour from the United States;[35] and overall export figures for wheat from Lower Canada.[36] Unfortunately, we do not have lists for the West Indies of prices or of quantities imported, but this was of course a much smaller market than Great Britain.

One thing is clear: in nearly all these years there was a demand in Britain for foreign grain. In the 1790s and in the 1800s it was normal to import between 2.4 million and 4 million imperial bushels annually.[37] This demand, as far as Lower Canada was concerned, was virtually unlimited. In any given year the British would be able to buy any amount of grain that the Lower Canadians could produce — but only at the going price, which was determined in Britain by the interaction of their domestic demand, domestic supply, and supply from other countries such as the United States and the Baltic powers. The problem for the Lower Canadians was whether they could supply grain at that price. If the price in Lower Canada were higher, when shipping and handling costs were added there would be no advantage to shipment abroad, and such a higher domestic price might indicate that Lower Canadian producers were not feeding their own population adequately (on a supply-and-demand diagram, British demand, as far as Lower Canada was concerned, could be represented, as in graphs 1 or 2, as a horizontal line D_1. This represents the willingness of British purchasers to buy unlimited quantities of wheat at a given price p. This line intersects a domestic demand curve D_2. The market price in Lower Canada is then determined by the intersection of the local supply curve S_1 or S_2 with the combined D_1 and D_2 curve. If the local supply curve resembles S_2, it is impossible to meet foreign demand because of the inadequacy of local supply, and this failure is reflected by a price a above the price British buyers are willing to pay p. If the supply curve in Lower Canada is at S_1, then foreign demand can be met and it is profitable to export).

GRAPH 3

Wheat Prices: Quebec, Philadelphia, United Kingdom (in $U.S./Winchester bushel)

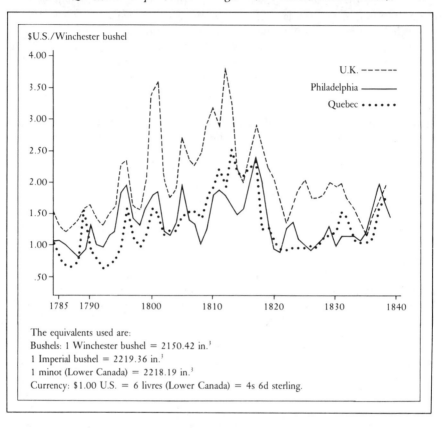

$U.S./Winchester bushel

U.K. ------
Philadelphia ———
Quebec • • • • •

The equivalents used are:
Bushels: 1 Winchester bushel = 2150.42 in.³
1 Imperial bushel = 2219.36 in.³
1 minot (Lower Canada) = 2218.19 in.³
Currency: $1.00 U.S. = 6 livres (Lower Canada) = 4s 6d sterling.

Could Lower Canada, then, compete with its neighbours in the British trade? By reducing British, Quebec, and Philadelphia prices for the years from 1783 to 1838 to a common unit, the Winchester bushel, and a common value, the United States dollar, we can trace the changes in the relative positions of Lower Canada and the U.S. on the British grain market.[38] Graph 3 shows that in the 1780s and the 1790s, Lower Canada may have enjoyed a favourable position in comparison to American prices, if we assume that transatlantic freight rates from U.S. ports and Quebec were about equal (actually, they appear to have favoured the American shipper). And, in fact, an estimate prepared in 1793 by the Canadian merchant J. Walton indicated that the normal price of wheat and flour in the port of Quebec was less than the normal price of wheat and flour in American ports.[39] In these circumstances, wheat shipped from Quebec probably enjoyed an advantage over American grain in the British market.

After 1805, however, the two price series, Philadelphia and Quebec, part company. In every year thereafter, down to 1817, Philadelphia wheat was cheaper than Quebec wheat. This inversion of the price curves of Canadian and American grain is largely confirmed by a glance at the monthly prices for Quebec from 1805 to 1812, published by Paquet and Wallot,[40] and Philadelphia and New York monthly prices. What the rise in Lower Canadian prices relative to American prices implies is that, on balance, the domestic situation in Quebec wheat production is tending to the point where Lower Canadian prices attract wheat from Upper Canada and the United States, but still rise relative to American prices (this would be represented by the point a on graphs 1 and 2).[41]

It might be objected that the rise in the price of Canadian grain relative to American after 1805 was somehow the result of a change in the British Corn Laws which, by protecting colonial grain, might have discouraged U.S. shippers and helped keep U.S. prices down by eliminating foreign demand as far as they were concerned. G.S. Graham, for example, suggested that "Small colonial preferences beginning in 1804, and culminating with the famous British Corn Law of 1815, helped to balance transportation costs [for Canadian shippers]."[42] Actually, preferential treatment for British North American grain dates from at least 1791, but neither the 1791 act nor the 1804 act appears to have been of much help to the Lower Canadian shippers. The 1791 act may have given an occasional slight advantage — in 1791, 1793, 1798 perhaps — to British North American shippers.[43] As for the 1804 act, it was undoubtedly ineffective, since it accorded preference to the colonies only when British grains sold between 53s. and 63s. a quarter. This did not happen again until 1821. The Americans, then, enjoyed a real price advantage over the Lower Canadian shippers from at least 1805 onwards at the latest, and this, as Paquet and Wallot themselves have found, was resented by the Quebec corn-merchants.[44]

Small wonder, then, that much of Lower Canadian exports after 1803 should have been in American grain! No doubt there were additional problems for grain shippers in Quebec because they had a harder time communicating with Great Britain than did their American colleagues. No doubt the lateness of the Quebec harvest, as Paquet and Wallot assert, made it harder to guess market trends at home and abroad.[45] Nevertheless, the principal difficulty for Lower Canadian merchants and farmers competing in the British market (or the West Indian market, for that matter) was simple: Quebec wheat cost too much.

One might argue that the rise in Quebec wheat prices was due to a virtual monopoly by Canadian suppliers of grain shipments from North American to Britain after the U.S. embargo in December 1807 on trade with the belligerents, followed in 1809 by the Non-Intercourse Act. If such a monopoly was held by Quebec shippers, it was only held for a single year, 1808, and then never completely. Normally, Great Britain imported anywhere from three to ten times as much grain from the United States as from British North America, but in that year the American embargo seems to have caused imports from the U.S. to Britain to fall to 102,000 bushels, as against 148,000 bushels imported from the colonies.[46] Even then, the Americans were not cut off from the British market entirely. In addition to the 102,000 bushels mentioned above, grain also filtered through to Britain from the United States through Nova Scotian and New Brunswick ports opened to unlimited trade in American or British bottoms, and also through the interior, by way of Lake Champlain and the Genesee Valley. In the winter, the forbidden commodities travelled by sledge; in the summer, according to Graham, "gigantic rafts loaded with the produce of forest and farm and guarded by armed men were floated down the Lake Champlain route from Vermont north,"[47] with sharpshooters picking off curious U.S. customs men as they passed. In any event, the abnormal situation created in 1808 ended in the succeeding year when, despite the new Non-Intercourse Act, American wheat flooded into Great Britain again in quantities vastly superior to Canadian exports. Thus, the year 1808 is the only one before 1812 in which legislation of one kind or another can be said to have given Lower Canadian suppliers an "artificial" advantage over Americans in the British market and pulled up prices in Quebec as a result. The reasons for the deficiencies of Lower Canadian suppliers have to be sought elsewhere.

In fact, the more we examine the behaviour of Canadian grain prices between 1805 and the end of 1807, and then in years like 1808, 1811, and 1812, when imports into Britain were, for one reason or another, practically non-existent, the more we are compelled to ask whether in fact the Lower Canadian farmers were simply unable to produce enough to feed the rapidly growing population of the province, let alone the British Isles. In short, is the failure of Lower Canadian farmers to produce for the export market after 1804 due, not to fears that they might be caught out in the dicey speculations of overseas trade, but rather to a radical inability to satisfy the growing wants of their own customers and families at home?

It is in answering this question that a systematic economic model, which Paquet and Wallot rightly reproach Ouellet with failing to use, might be helpful. How, then, did domestic demand grow in these years? What was the importance of domestic consumption in relation to the exportable surplus? Unfortunately, Paquet and Wallot only provide us with some of the materials of a model, not the model itself. I have therefore constructed from their material and some other sources three theoretical models of domestic and foreign wheat consumption and local production in Lower Canada. The purpose of these models is not to represent the exact situation of Lower Canadian wheat production in any given year, but rather to indicate the general trend of its evolution and the order of size of production and consumption. I have chosen to work with wheat production, not only because it is the agricultural product for which statistics of production and prices are the most abundant, but above all because it was the staple element of the diet of the overwhelming majority of persons, and the largest single element of production in the agricultural economy of Lower Canada, as indeed in most countries in the commercial world of the Atlantic in the eighteenth century. If we can understand the evolution of wheat production and the reasons for it, we can interpret the changes in production in other parts of the agricultural sector.

How much wheat was produced in a normal year in Lower Canada? Paquet and Wallot cite a merchant's estimate of the amount necessary for the subsistence of the inhabitants of Lower Canada in the 1790s: 2 million *minots*. (One *minot* equals approximately one imperial bushel and 1.03 Winchester bushels.)[48] This is a rough figure indeed, but it does not seem unreasonable. We know that, for instance, in 1784 the total sowing of wheat amounted to 383,349 minots.[49] The seed-yield ratio towards the end of the French regime (1739) derived by

R.C. Harris for a total of twenty seigneuries was 1:5.8;[50] if we round this up to 1:6 or 1:7, we have an annual production of 2.3 to 2.6 million *minots*, probably an excessively optimistic estimate, but nevertheless sufficient to give us an order of size. However, in 1827 the total wheat crop was 2.9 million bushels (for the moment, we can consider the bushel and the minot as roughly equivalent), plus 363,000 bushels of barley and 863,000 bushels of "other grains." If we reckon the yield per unit of soil cultivated of barley and other grains at the excessively optimistic estimate of three times that of wheat, the total crop in 1827, if all the grain land had been planted in wheat, would have been about 3.3 million bushels.[51] In 1831, a good year, it amounted to the equivalent of 4.4 million bushels of wheat.[52] By this time, land under cultivation had increased vastly. So it seems that 2 million *minots* or bushels for an average year in the 1790s is probably an overestimate, if anything. As for the estimate of four million minots average production made by the Duc de Rochefoucauld-Liancourt,[53] an agricultural enthusiast who never in fact came to Lower Canada, it must be classed, like many of the speculations of the eighteenth-century agronomists, as pure fantasy.

How much of this production of two million bushels was necessary for the subsistence of those inhabitants of Lower Canada who did not live on farms or from agriculture? According to Paquet and Wallot, the non-agricultural population consumed about 300,000 *minots* around 1790 and 750,000 near 1800. They do not explain how they arrived at this figure: perhaps it is related to the percentage of the population living in towns plus an increment for landless workers, traders, widows, civil servants, clergy, professional men, lumberjacks, and so forth in the countryside.[54] Of the two million minots of the minimum crop necessary for subsistence, then, there remained about 1.7 million *minots* around 1790 and perhaps 1.25 million *minots* around 1800 for consumption and sowing in the agricultural sector.

The surplus, when there was one, was exported in the crop year or in the succeeding one. I have estimated the average surplus for the period from 1793 to 1799 by taking an average of the real export volume, which comes to 282,000 *minots* a year.[55] So, if we add the average exportable surplus to the minimum subsistence crop, we have an annual average production of 2,282,000 *minots* a year for the period from 1793 to 1799.

The disadvantage of this calculation is that it gives us only a static estimate of production and consumption. Yet the population of Lower Canada was rising during this time and, presumably, agricultural production must have risen, at least somewhat. How can we tell what increase occurred in production and what increase in consumption?

Fortunately, for wheat production we have some figures recently reproduced by Fernand Ouellet for tithe yields. Ouellet produces nine sets of tithes for different parishes of Lower Canada.[56] In some ways, the solidity of these series seems better than similar records which have been used recently in France.[57] The *curé* collected his own tithe and was backed by the force of law after the Quebec Act in 1774. It is true that the *habitant* himself delivered the product of his field to the *curé*, and that the priest was thus to some extent at the mercy of his parishioner. But, in any case, these series at least give us a quantitative indication of the direction in which production evolved, and it is possible to correct for underestimation.

TABLE 2

Index of Wheat Production, Lower Canada (9 parishes).
Base: Average 1784–1799 = 100

Year	Index	Year	Index	Year	Index
1784	65	1796	122	1808	71
1785	82	1797	84	1809	109
1786	99	1798	98	1810	139
1787	107	1799	106	1811	83
1788	93	1800	111	1812	129
1789	87	1801	150	1813	98
1790	89	1802	179	1814	105
1791	108	1803	114	1815	116
1792	128	1804	109	1816	122
1793	111	1805	109	1817	146
1794	95	1806	107	1818	120
1795	118	1807	89	1819	137

SOURCE: Derived from Ouellet "L'agriculture bas-canadienne," passim.

I have calculated an index of wheat production from Ouellet's figures, by taking the unweighted arithmetical average of the indices of the nine series, using the average of production in the period 1784–99 as a base period for each series equal to 100 (see table 2). The use of the unweighted arithmetic average rather than a geometrical average makes it likely that the estimation of the rise in production will be generous, if anything, and the tithe returns are numerous enough for the 1790s and the 1800s to be used as a hypothesis for the evolution of production in these years. If we take the average year's production in the 1790s as 2,282,000 *minots* for the reasons which have just been explained, we can then use the index of production to see how this quantity, which we can make equal to base 100, evolved.

But what of the evolution of consumption? Here, we are relatively fortunate in that the Canadian Census of 1871 gives global census figures for 1790 and figures for the increase of the Roman Catholic population by localities for each successive year. I have combined these tables to produce the figures given in table 3, showing the evolution of the urban and rural population. (Although this is only based on the natural increase of the Roman Catholic population, the non-Catholic population of the province at this time was insignificant and, in any case, its omission, and the omission of urban immigration, will help make estimates of consumption conservative.) These figures of population growth were then converted into indices of population growth. If we reckon that this population required a minimum of 2 million *minots* for its needs in the 1790s, we can use the indices of population growth to estimate the evolution of that consumption.

We are now in a position to put together the figures of the volume of production and the volume of domestic consumption for the period around the turn of the century. Using the results which have just been worked out, I have built two models of the growth of production and domestic consumption, the first based on an urban population consuming 300,000 *minots* out of 2 million in 1790,

TABLE 3

*Estimated Evolution of the Roman Catholic Population of
Lower Canada*

Year	Urban Population*	Rural Population	Year	Urban Population	Rural Population
1786	32,000	114,502	1803	35,810	184,403
1787	32,531	117,123	1804	35,980	188,237
1788	32,792	120,798	1805	36,291	193,442
1789	32,995	124,493	1806	36,672	199,503
1790	33,213	128,098	1807	37,069	205,496
1791	33,217	130,707	1808	37,459	211,718
1792	33,350	133,849	1809	37,951	218,044
1793	33,590	137,954	1810	38,291	223,647
1794	33,790	141,865	1811	38,405	227,819
1795	34,031	146,301	1812	38,917	234,069
1796	34,246	150,939	1813	39,386	241,279
1797	34,381	155,504	1814	39,526	246,603
1798	34,574	159,676	1815	39,700	252,327
1799	34,930	164,337	1816	40,074	259,414
1800	35,149	169,765	1817	40,568	267,614
1801	35,430	174,863	1818	41,042	274,763
1802	35,608	179,469	1819	41,626	283,433

*Quebec, Montreal, Trois-Rivières.
SOURCE: Derived from *Census 1870–71*, IV and V (based on natural increase).

and the second, probably less realistic, based on an urban population consuming 750,000 *minots* in 1800, taking my estimates of urban consumption from Paquet and Wallot. In both tables (4a and 4b) the amount available for export, if the rate of consumption of wheat was strictly proportionate to the increase in population (the "theoretical exportable surplus"), has been calculated.

Of the two models, probably the first (table 4a) comes closer to measuring the real situation, since the figures in table 4b indicate a theoretical exportable surplus after 1802 which is rather higher than the real one. But what is important here is not so much the exact exportable surpluses shown, but the idea that these tables give us of the relative impact of the rise in consumption, caused by population growth, on the available stock of wheat. If table 4a is an approximate indication of the evolution of production and consumption, then internal consumption, given the rise in population, had to go up by about 50,000 *minots* a year. Even if it rose by as much as 20 percent less in any given year, such a rise was still about one-seventh of the amount exported in an average year from Lower Canada in the years before 1800. Any slackening in the growth of output, let alone a fall in production, would put tremendous pressures on producer and consumer alike. And we know that this was what happened to production. It was not so much that wheat production had declined after the record highs of 1801–2, it was simply that it stagnated after this date near its earlier levels while population continued to rise, steadily and inexorably.

TABLE 4a

Wheat Production and Consumption in Lower Canada—Model 1
(thousands of minots*)*

Year	Total Production	Domestic Non-Agricultural Consumption	Domestic Agricultural Consumption	Theoretical Exportable Surplus	Real Exports
Pre-1800 averages	2282	300	1700	282	282
1790	2031	300	1700	31	
1791	2465	300	1734	431	
1792	2921	300	1768	853	
1793	2533	303	1836	394	542
1794	2168	306	1887	25	483
1795	2693	306	1938	449	449
1796	2784	309	2006	469	25
1797	1985	312	2057	− 384	101
1798	2236	312	2125	− 101	139
1799	2419	315	2176	− 72	201
1800	2533	318	2261	− 46	318
1801	3423	321	2329	773	663
1802	4084	321	2880	1383	1151
1803	2396	324	2448	− 376	438
1804	2944	324	2499	171	273
1805	2601	327	2567	− 293	115
1806	2327	330	2652	− 655	152
1807	3126	336	2720	70	334
1808	2442	339	2805	− 632	399
1809	3172	342	2890	− 60	
1810	3606	345	2975	286	
1811	1940	348	3026	− 1434	
1812	2350	351	3026	− 1027	
1813	2214	357	3111	− 1254	
1814	2716	357	3281	− 922	
1815	2617	360	3349	− 1092	
1816	2784	363	3451	− 1030	
1817	3332	366	3553	− 587	
1818	2438	372	3638	− 1372	
1819	3126	375	3757	− 1006	

The same phenomenon can be observed in a rather different model of wheat production (table 4c), which shows the per capita amount of wheat available in Lower Canada after seed for sowing has been deducted and before and after exports. I have introduced this third model here because the amounts which Paquet and Wallot allot to "agricultural" and "non-agricultural" consumption seem rather arbitrary, especially the figure of 750,000 *minots* for the period after 1800.

TABLE 4b

Wheat Production and Consumption in Lower Canada—Model 2
(thousands of minots)

Year	Total Production	Domestic Non-Agricultural Consumption	Domestic Agricultural Consumption	Theoretical Exportable Surplus	Real Exports
Pre-1800 averages	2282	750	1250	282	
1800	2533	750	1250	533	318
1801	3423	758	1288	1377	663
1802	4084	758	1325	2001	1151
1803	2396	765	1363	268	438
1804	2944	765	1388	791	273
1805	2601	773	1425	403	115
1806	2327	780	1475	72	152
1807	3126	788	1513	825	334
1808	2442	803	1563	76	399
1809	3172	810	1600	762	
1810	3606	818	1650	658	
1811	1940	818	1675	− 553	
1812	2350	833	1725	208	
1813	2214	840	1775	− 401	
1814	2716	840	1813	63	
1815	2617	848	1863	− 94	
1816	2782	855	1913	14	
1817	3332	863	1975	494	
1818	2738	878	2028	− 165	
1819	3126	885	2088	153	

Two sets of calculations have been made, the one allowing for a seed-crop ratio of 1:5; the other, probably too optimistic, for a ratio of 1:6. Since the amount a farmer sows is more a function of what he normally expects to harvest rather than what he actually harvested in a given year, I have taken the amounts needed for sowing as a moving average of the three previous harvests, divided by one-fifth or one-sixth. Two figures of grain available per capita in each year are given for each of these ratios, the one for wheat available before exports, and the other for wheat available after exports (after 1802, the latter figure has little value, because of the influx of American grain into the St. Lawrence for re-export). As in tables 4a and 4b, the object is not to present a tableau of the exact situation of the wheat economy in a given year, but to indicate the general evolution of supplies available.

Again, the results seem to confirm a pessimistic view of the possibilities of Lower Canadian agriculture in a grain economy. Before 1802, per capita production was sufficiently high to permit exports; after this point, it does not seem to have been possible to export much, except for wheat sent through from the

TABLE 4c

Model 3: Per Capita Production Available, Lower Canada (in minots*)*

A: Assumed Ratio of Seed to Crop 1:5

Thousands of *minots*								
Year	Production	Seeding Requirements	Remainder	Exports	Remainder	Population	Supply Available Per Capita Before Exports	Supply Available Per Capita After Exports
1792	2921	494	2427			167	14.5	
1793	2533	527	2006	542	1464	172	11.7	8.5
1794	2168	508	1660	483	1177	176	9.4	6.7
1795	2693	492	2201	449	1752	180	12.2	9.7
1796	2784	510	2274	25	2249	185	12.3	12.2
1797	1985	497	1488	101	1387	190	7.8	7.3
1798	2236	467	1769	139	1630	194	9.1	8.4
1799	2419	443	1976	201	1775	199	9.9	8.9
1800	2533	479	2054	318	1736	205	10.0	8.5
1801	3423	558	2865	663	2202	210	13.6	10.5
1802	4084	669	3415	1151	2264	215	15.9	10.5
1803	2396	660	1736	438	1298	220	7.9	5.9
1804	2944	628	2316	273	2043	224	10.3	9.1
1805	2601	529	2072	115	1957	230	9.0	8.5
1806	2327	525	1802	152	1650	236	7.6	7.0
1807	3126	537	2589	334	2255	243	10.7	9.2
1808	2442	526	1916	399	1517	249	7.7	6.1
1809	3172	582	2590			255	10.2	
1810	3606	615	2991			261	11.5	
1811	1940	581	1359			266	5.1	
1812	2350	526	1824			273	6.7	
1813	2214	434	1780			280	6.4	
1814	2716	485	2231			286	7.8	
1815	2617	503	2114			292	7.2	
1816	2784	541	2243			299	7.5	
1817	3332	582	2750			308	8.9	
1818	2438	570	1868			316	5.9	
1819	3126	593	2533			325	7.8	

United States. If a very rough and optimistic estimate of the amount of wheat necessary per capita in a population and economy like that of Lower Canada is six to ten bushels a year (eighteenth-century Pennsylvanians consumed an average of thirteen bushels, apparently),[58] it can be seen how near the margin production in Lower Canada was by the later 1800s, and how the province would have been in real need if all the grain exported after 1802 had in fact come from the region.

Thus, while Ouellet has asserted that production fell after 1802, and Paquet and Wallot have pointed out that 1801–2 were anomalous years and that production after that point seems not to have fallen, both parties are in fact missing

Model 3: Per Capita Production Available, Lower Canada (in minots)

B: Assumed Ratio of Seed to Crop 1:6

Thousands of *minots*							Supply Available Per Capita Before Exports	Supply Available Per Capita After Exports
Year	Production	Seeding Requirements	Remainder	Exports	Remainder	Population		
1792	2921	418	2503			167	15.0	
1793	2533	440	2093	542	1551	171	12.2	9.1
1794	2168	423	1745	483	1262	176	9.9	7.2
1795	2693	411	2282	449	1833	180	12.7	10.2
1796	2784	425	2359	25	2334	185	12.8	12.6
1797	1985	415	1570	101	1469	190	8.3	7.7
1798	2236	389	1847	139	1708	194	9.5	8.8
1799	2419	369	2050	201	1849	199	10.3	9.2
1800	2533	399	2134	318	1816	205	10.4	8.9
1801	3423	465	2958	663	2295	210	14.1	10.9
1802	4084	558	3526	1151	2375	215	16.4	11.1
1803	2396	550	1846	438	1408	220	8.4	6.4
1804	2944	524	2420	273	2147	224	10.8	9.5
1805	2601	441	2160	115	2045	230	9.4	8.9
1806	2327	437	1890	152	1738	236	8.0	7.4
1807	3126	447	2679	334	2345	242	11.1	9.7
1808	2442	439	2003	399	1604	249	8.0	6.4
1809	3172	486	2686			256	10.5	
1810	3606	512	3094			262	11.8	
1811	1940	484	1456			266	5.5	
1812	2350	439	1911			273	7.0	
1813	2214	361	1853			281	6.6	
1814	2716	404	2312			286	8.1	
1815	2617	419	2198			292	7.5	
1816	2784	451	2333			299	7.8	
1817	3332	485	2847			308	9.2	
1818	2438	475	1963			316	6.2	
1819	3216	494	2632			325	8.1	

the point that it was not enough for Lower Canadian agriculture to stand still in a time of rapid demographic growth in the province; it had to increase its production. The results of this failure — which no doubt have much more to do with the quality of the new soil and the exhaustion of the old than with failure to show entrepreneurial ability — began to be felt, and the shortages of foodstuffs and the rise in food prices around Quebec in 1808 and after were the direct result of this stagnation of production.

In fact, it is likely that in these years the *habitants* were giving up an increasing proportion of their wheat crops to the market. In effect, this is the period in which Lower Canadian farmers began to increase production of subsidiary crops:

oats, barley, potatoes, and hay, and to put more emphasis on livestock production.[59] However, even with this limited substitution and shift in farm consumption patterns, it is unlikely that they produced in anything like the quantities required, since their efforts had no appreciable effect on the price of wheat. One would expect wheat prices to fall at least to the American level if sufficient amounts of substitute cereals and alternate food resources were developed. And, after 1805, no such fall in prices took place; the continued rise and the reversal of Quebec and American price curves after this date, then, represent a real agricultural crisis.

So, then, there was a crisis in the agricultural sector. But what of the farmers themselves? This is a separate question, of course, though it is not clear that the participants in the controversy always realize this. After all, price rises have been known to benefit producers of a commodity in short supply.

Paquet and Wallot offer two ways of answering this question which, to be fair, Ouellet never tackled himself. One is to present a series of "parish revenues" — apparently collections and charity funds — and seigneurial revenues for several seigneuries.[60] The "parish revenues" approach, unfortunately, has the severe defect that we know little of the conditions in which these revenues were collected. We do know that this was a period in which the church was commonly considered to be strengthening its hold over the population somewhat, though the extent of this renewal has been questioned.[61] If the parish priest was zealous, one would expect revenues to go up. If the population was rising, they ought also to rise. If we could deflate these revenues by the growth in population in the areas from which they came, they might well show stagnation, if not a downturn. I have tried this with two of the parishes Paquet and Wallot have cited, using the index of the overall rural population growth, and the result in one is stagnation, in the other, some increase. But this does not take us very far.

This "demographic" argument would also seem to be a valid reason for questioning the significance of at least some of the revenues included in the rising seigneurial revenues which Paquet and Wallot cite, to prove that farmers had more revenue to dispose of. A rise in population would presumably lead to an increase in the volume of land transfers, and this, in turn, would increase, for example, the revenue of the *lods et ventes*. Not all of the increase can be explained away in this fashion, of course, because some of these seigneurial revenues are the equivalent of pure rent. But one would expect the seigneurs to try and squeeze more revenue out of their *censitaires* in a period of high agricultural prices. This is generally supposed to have happened during this period.[62] So, in their figures of rising seigneurial revenues, Paquet and Wallot may be merely measuring in part a seigneurial reaction and in part a rising number of land transfers.

Using a different approach, Paquet and Wallot have tried to calculate a standard-of-living index for *habitants*, civil servants, and workers from an aggregate series of wages of town workers and civil servants, a series of agricultural prices, and a series of consumer prices.[63] Presumably, for the civil servants and workers, the standard-of-living index was derived by dividing the consumer price index by an index of wage rates. For the *habitants*, the index of consumer prices must have been divided by the index of agricultural prices, providing in theory a measure of their real purchasing power.

The index for the *habitants*, according to Paquet and Wallot, indicates "amelioration." I would be more inclined to call the curve which they have reproduced "stagnation." But this is not really to the point. The problem with their index is that it is little more than one index of agricultural prices divided by another index of agricultural prices. Thus, on the Quebec index, wheat, oats, eggs, and butter are present in both indices; the difference is caused by the presence of firewood, peas, charcoal (presumably the sense of *charbon* here — how many *habitants* bought this, one wonders?), pork, beef, rum, and oil in the consumer price index. Of these, only charcoal, rum, and oil, and perhaps firewood, are really non-agricultural. Similarly, for Montreal, the only non-agricultural products included in the consumer price index are salt, charcoal, and firewood. It is not surprising that the quotient from the division of these two indices by each other should oscillate rather closely around unity! Although these cost-of-living indices may have validity for urban living standards, they tell us nothing about the *habitant*'s standard of living at all.

Parenthetically, it might be noted that the proper approach to this problem would be to multiply indices of the quantities of foodstuffs not consumed on farms by indices of their prices, and divide the result by the product of an index of agricultural population multiplied by indices of a reasonable number of non-agricultural prices. Failing this, one could multiply indices of all agricultural prices by production and divide by indices of population and non-agricultural prices. But in the present state of our knowledge, neither operation is possible.

A final attempt at answering the question of what was happening to the standard of living of rural people in Lower Canada during this period of transition might have been made indirectly, by using demographic sources. The trends they reveal, however (see table 5), seem to indicate no change for the better in rural society during the period. The rural birth rate was slowly falling. The rural marriage rate in the 1800s was on the whole lower than it had been in the 1790s, and fell markedly from 1805 to 1810; the rural death rate rose dramatically from 1800 to 1802, fell away until 1809, and then rose again. What this means in a population growing as rapidly as Lower Canada's is anyone's guess; it certainly does not seem to signal any drastic betterment of the lot of the rural people. Taken together with all the other evidence, or lack of it, it must be admitted that a rise in the prosperity of the "average" *habitant* is certainly not proven.

Thus the debate appears to have reached a dead end. The main reason for this seems to be that if we now have fairly accurate data on prices and wages in Lower Canada during this period, thanks to the patient research of Ouellet, Paquet, and Wallot, it is doubtful whether we shall ever enjoy the same certainty about the evolution of overall production, and even less certain that we can obtain overall figures which will give us some notion of the distribution of the revenues of that production among the population of the colony.

For the "average" *habitant* is a fiction. How many *habitants* really grew enough grain to put it on the market? How many of them joined the work force, either by migrating to the towns or working in the countryside, and thus benefiting from that "restructuring" of the rest of the economy which permitted, apparently, a revolution in the living standards of labourers and the professional classes? Only answers to questions such as these can permit us to say whether the dead

TABLE 5

Estimated Birth, Death, and Marriage Rates in Lower Canada, Urban and Rural (per 1000)

Year	Death Rate Urban	Death Rate Rural	Birth Rate Urban	Birth Rate Rural	Marriage Rate Urban	Marriage Rate Rural
	Urban	Rural	Urban	Rural	Urban	Rural
1790	22.0	27.2	22.1	47.5	3.2	8.1
1791	21.0	30.4	25.0	54.5	3.9	9.5
1792	17.2	25.3	24.3	56.0	3.9	9.9
1793	19.1	24.5	25.0	52.8	3.9	9.0
1794	18.6	22.7	25.5	53.9	3.8	10.9
1795	19.3	24.9	25.6	56.6	4.1	9.6
1796	20.7	23.9	24.6	54.2	3.4	8.4
1797	19.1	27.0	24.8	53.8	3.7	9.0
1798	15.4	24.2	25.7	54.7	3.6	9.0
1799	18.5	22.4	24.7	54.2	4.5	7.9
1800	20.1	23.5	28.1	53.6	4.4	8.9
1801	21.3	26.8	26.3	53.1	4.4	9.3
1802	22.7	28.0	28.4	55.5	4.5	9.6
1803	24.0	32.3	28.8	53.1	4.4	9.6
1804	21.5	27.5	30.2	55.2	4.2	9.1
1805	19.8	22.2	30.3	53.5	4.1	8.0
1806	20.2	22.3	31.0	52.3	3.9	8.0
1807	20.6	21.7	31.2	52.0	4.3	8.4
1808	18.6	21.1	31.7	50.9	5.4	8.9
1809	23.1	24.6	32.1	50.3	6.0	8.5
1810	31.7	31.5	34.7	50.2	5.6	8.6
1811	24.1	22.4	37.5	49.9	6.9	9.1
1812	24.9	19.9	36.9	50.7	5.6	10.1
1813	32.6	27.5	36.1	49.6	4.0	7.8
1814	31.2	26.0	35.6	49.2	5.6	9.0
1815	28.0	23.4	37.4	51.5	8.4	9.7
1816	28.6	19.2	41.0	50.7	8.2	7.9
1817	28.4	21.9	40.1	48.7	7.7	7.8
1818	29.6	19.9	43.8	55.5	7.6	8.5
1819	32.8	22.5	44.5	51.2	6.3	8.9

SOURCE: Derived from *Census 1870–71*, V: 217–29 and table 1 above (based on natural increase).

weight of an archaic system of agriculture prevented the betterment of the mass of the population in these years. The most fruitful solution to this problem probably lies in the direction of local studies of social structure and economic change within small, well-defined regions — the route, in short, which historians of other pre-statistical economies have taken when confronted by the inadequacy of the macro-economic evidence available to them.

In the meantime, we can only go on the material available to us, and it ought to be evident that many of the figures and models advanced in this article are rather artificial, and it would be unwise to put more weight on them than they will bear. Taken at their lowest, they are merely an attempt, in a fairly rough-and-ready fashion, to test what the existing data produced by the two sides in this controversy can tell us. They do seem to prove that, if there may not have been a thoroughgoing disaster in Lower Canadian agriculture after 1802, there was certainly no boom either. After 1802, the agricultural sector was less and less able to meet internal demand as populations rose faster than production. It was this overall population growth, rather than a shift of the labour force away from the agricultural sector, which drove up prices, making exports less possible. Insofar as Lower Canada did continue to export after 1802, it seems that this was because the *habitants* cut back on their consumption. It would appear at least plausible that the farmers fell back on the more productive but much less remunerative lesser grains to feed themselves and their animals, and ultimately on potatoes and on an increase in livestock. But even such cutbacks could not assure that grain would be available on domestic markets at the price levels of former days.

This diversification, however, does not seem to have been a rational investment choice except in the sense that it prevented people from starving. Prices rose, to be sure, but too much of domestic consumption appears to have been committed to sowing and the subsistence of rural people for the *habitants* to profit by them, given their inability to increase production. At least the figures adduced by Paquet and Wallot do not succeed in shaking this hypothesis, which remains the most reasonable explanation of the fate of the rural people. It may be that they managed to make a little money from part-time employment outside the agricultural sector, in logging and mills, and thus eke out their apparently stagnating agricultural revenues; it may be that they did not. As agriculturalists, in any event, they do not appear to have been successful. The beginnings of a diversification of agricultural production — which, in the long run, was to provide a partial solution to the problems of Lower Canadian agriculture — seem to have been a solution adopted by producers who were, if not despairing, at least pessimistic; who, like the Irish peasants, turned to productive and cheap foods like the potato as a solution to a food crisis brought on by population growth, a food crisis that the traditional rural economy was incapable of solving.[64] Rural people did not willingly shift from wheaten bread to oats, peas, and potatoes, no matter how nourishing by modern standards, anywhere else in the western world; they were only forced to do so, and accepted it with the greatest reluctance, because of population pressure. It would be surprising if Lower Canada proved to be an exception to this rule.

What this limited analysis means for the larger question of the economic and social background to the first French-Canadian nationalism is not completely clear. No doubt it is difficult to associate the long-term maturing of an ideology and class-consciousness with a short period of economic history, and it is probably true, as Paquet and Wallot point out, that manifestations of national or political consciousness among the French majority had already occurred in Lower Canada before the 1790s; perhaps it is too restrictive to make this nationalism the child of economic distress. At the same time, it is hard to see how the interpretation can be reversed and how this nationalism can be made a by-product of agricultural prosperity, especially if there was no such prosperity. Evidently, Professors Paquet and Wallot intend to show in their forthcoming book that this was so; it should be interesting to see how they manage it.

Notes

1. The classic treatments are D.G. Creighton, *The Commercial Empire of the St. Lawrence, 1760–1850* (Toronto, 1937), and F. Ouellet, *Histoire économique et sociale du Québec 1760–1850* (Montreal/Paris, 1966).

2. G. Paquet and J.-P. Wallot, "Aperçu sur le commerce international et les prix domestiques dans le Bas-Canada (1793–1812)," *Revue d'histoire de l'Amérique française* (hereafter *RHAF*) XXI (1967): 447–73.

3. G. Paquet and J.-P. Wallot, "Crise agricole et tensions socio-ethniques dans le Bas-Canada, 1802–1812: éléments pour un ré-interprétation," *RHAF* XXVI (1972): 185–237.

4. Ouellet, *Histoire économique*, 169–74, 180–8, 196–212.

5. Paquet and Wallot, "Crise agricole," 234–37.

6. F. Ouellet and J. Hamelin, "La crise agricole dans le Bas-Canada, 1802–1837," *Canadian Historical Association Report* (1962): 317–33.

7. R.L. Jones, "French-Canadian Agriculture in the St. Lawrence Valley, 1815–1850," *Agricultural History* XVI (1942): 237–48; "Agriculture in Lower Canada, 1792–1815," *Canadian Historical Review* (hereafter *CHR*) XXVII (1946): 33–51.

8. Graphs in Ouellet, *Histoire économique*, 603, 609.

9. F. Ouellet, "L'agriculture bas-canadienne vue à travers les dîmes et la rente en nature," *Histoire sociale/Social History* IV (1971): 5–44.

10. G.S. Graham, *Sea Power and British North America* (Cambridge, Mass., 1941), 139.

11. Ouellet, *Histoire économique*, 153.

12. Graham, *Sea Power*, 201–4.

13. Ouellet, *Histoire économique*, 180.

14. Ibid., 155.

15. For example, Paquet and Wallot, "Crise agricole," 201–4, 217–21.

16. Ibid., 197–200, 205–16.

17. Ibid., 231–34.

18. Ibid., 185–96 and by the same authors, "Le Bas-Canada au début du XIXᵉ siècle: une hypothèse," *RHAF* XXV (1971): 39–61; "International Circumstances of Lower Canada," *CHR* LIII (1972): 371–401; "Aperçu sur le commerce international," 447–50, 471–73. Paquet and Wallot also raised some doubts about Ouellet's price statistics in "Aperçu sur le commerce," 459–70, but these do not seem relevant here, since the tendency of Ouellet's series and those published by Paquet and Wallot is roughly the same. See Ouellet, "L'agriculture bas-canadienne," 6–8.

19. Paquet and Wallot, "Crise agricole," 195–201.

20. Ibid., 205–11.

21. Ibid., 211–16.

22. Ibid., 215.

23. Ouellet, *Histoire économique*, 185–87.

24. Paquet and Wallot, "Crise agricole," 226–34; cf. also M. Séguin, *La Nation canadienne et l'agriculture (1760–1820)* (Trois-Rivières, 1970), 131–44.

25. For example, *Histoire économique*, 222.

26. J. Lemon, *The Best Poor Man's Country: A Geographical Study of Early Southeastern Pennsylvania* (Baltimore/London, 1972), 150–233.

27. Paquet and Wallot, "Crise agricole," 218–19.

28. Ibid., 214–15.

29. J. Marczewski, *Introduction à l'histoire quantitative* (Geneva, 1965), 48.

30. That is, the indication of the change in the purchasing power of a given "basket of goods" sold by the agricultural sector. It should be noted that Paquet and Wallot's "agricultural basket" does not vary according to fluctuations in agricultural output.

31. B.R. Mitchell and P. Deane, *Abstract of British Historical Statistics* (Cambridge, 1962), 488–89; cf. also 484–87 and D.G. Barnes, *A History of the English Corn Laws* (London, 1930, 1961), 297–98.

32. A.H. Cole, *Wholesale Commodity Prices in the United States, 1700–1861: Statistical Supplement* (Cambridge, Mass., 1938).

33. Derived from Ouellet's graph in *Histoire économique*, 603. It is regrettable that Professor Ouellet has not been able to publish his figures for these prices. The series of prices published in Paquet and Wallot, "Aperçu sur le commerce," 461–68 unfortunately covers only the period 1805–12.

34. Barnes, *English Corn Laws*, 300; W.F. Galpin, *The Grain Supply of England During the Napoleonic Period* (Philadelphia, 1925), 238–56.

35. T. Pitkin, *A Statistical View of the Commerce of the United States of America*, 120.

36. The best series is Ouellet, "L'agriculture bas-canadienne," 10, where wheat and flour exports are combined.

37. Barnes, *English Corn Laws*, 300. The figures for flour and corn imports are (thousands of quarters):

Year	Imports	Exports	Year	Imports	Exports
1791	469	71	1807	405	25
1792	22	300	1808	85	98
1793	490	77	1809	456	31
1794	328	155	1810	1567	76
1795	314	19	1811	336	98
1796	879	25	1812	291	46
1797	462	55	1813	559	?
1798	397	60	1814	853	111
1799	463	39	1815	384	228
1800	1265	22	1816	332	122
1801	1425	28	1817	1090	318
1802	647	149	1818	1694	59
1803	374	77	1819	626	45
1804	461	63	1820	996	95
1805	921	78	1821	707	200
1806	310	30			

(One imperial quarter = 8 imperial bushels)

38. The equivalents used are:
Bushels: 1 Winchester bushel = 2150.42 in.[3]
1 Imperial bushel = 2219.36 in.[3]
1 *minot* (Lower Canada) = 2218.19 in.[3]
Currency: $1.00 U.S. = 6 *livres* (Lower Canada) = 4s. 6d. sterling.

39. Graham, *Sea Power*, 133, n. 11.

40. "Aperçu sur le commerce," 461–68.

41. The failure of American suppliers to ship to Lower Canada in sufficient quantities to bring down the price to the American level can only be explained either by transport costs or by the greater attraction of the British market and the relative smallness of the Lower Canadian one.

42. Graham, *Sea Power*, 140.

43. The 1791 act gave British North American grain preferential treatment over American when British port prices were between 48s. and 50s./quarter and between 52s. and 54s./quarter. In the first case, American grain paid 21s. 9d./quarter more than British North American; in the second, 2s./quarter more. In fact, since the second case gave only a derisory advantage of 3d./bushel, only the first mattered. This judgment is based on national average prices, and prices for Eton and Winchester Colleges and Exeter

published in Mitchell and Deane, *Abstract*, 487–88. In addition duty-free import of grain was allowed by Parliament as an emergency measure from 1795 to 1797 and again in 1800–1. On the legislation, see Barnes, *English Corn Laws*, 66–98.

44. "Crise agricole," 206, n. 60.

45. Ibid., 205–11.

46. On the difficulties of trade, see F. Crouzet, *L'économie britannique et le blocus continental* (Paris, 1958), which resumes the earlier studies and is the classic treatment. Import figures are given as a graph in ibid., 901, and in figures in Galpin, *The Grain Supply of England*, 238–45. Wheat imports to Britain from the U.S. and British North America respectively were as follows (in 'ooo quarters):

	U.S.	BNA		U.S.	BNA
1800	77.6	21.3	1808	12.8	18.5
1801	245.4	67.6	1809	170.9	18.8
1802	79.4	75.2	1810	98.3	24.2
1803	109.1	43.2	1811	18.0	.4
1804	4.3	21.2	1812	10.8	23.7
1805	13.5	2.3	1813	.8	.001
1806	79.8	9.8	1814	.001	.1
1807	249.7	27.3			

47. Graham, *Sea Power*, 203 and generally, 197–204.

48. "Crise agricole," 206, n. 60.

49. *Census of Canada, 1870–71* (Ottawa, 1873), IV: 74.

50. R.C. Harris, *The Seigneurial System in Early Canada* (Madison, 1966), 153.

51. *Census, 1870–71*, IV, 96. The estimate of the relative productivity is based on the ratio of wheat prices in the 1800s to those of lesser grains. This is probably an overestimate, to judge from Lemon's figures for Pennsylvania in *The Best Poor Man's Country*, 155–56, which suggests yields of 10–15 bushels/acre as against 5–12 bushels/acre for wheat in the last half of the eighteenth century.

52. *Census, 1870–71*, IV: 109.

53. Cited in Ouellet, *Histoire économique*, 151.

54. In effect, the last figure (750,000) appears exaggerated. The estimates are from "Crise agricole," 211.

55. Derived from Ouellet, "L'agriculture bas-canadienne," 10. Before 1803, these figures represent Lower Canadian produce almost exclusively.

56. Ibid., 14–15, 18–19.

57. J. Goy and E. Le Roy Ladurie, eds., *Les fluctuations du produit de la dîme* (Paris/La Haye, 1972).

58. Lemon, *The Best Poor Man's Country*, 155. I arrived at the average given here by comparison with French figures for Paris in the eighteenth and nineteenth centuries in R. Phillippe, "Une opération pilote: l'étude du ravitaillement de Paris au temps de Lavoisier" in J.J. Hémardinquer, *Pour une histoire de l'alimentation* (Paris, 1970), 60–67 and J.P. Aron, *Essai sur la sensibilité alimentaire* (Paris, 1967). A large proportion of Parisians lived on a mixed diet, consuming less bread than labouring people, and the chances are that Parisian figures underestimate the needs of Lower Canadians. However, I have taken a daily per capita ration of 1 to 1½ *livres* of bread as an average. If this bread is made of wheaten flour, a ration of this size requires 6.2 to 9.5 bushels of wheat a year. This, of course, is only a gross approximation, and the whole question of rural and urban diet in Canada still awaits its historian. Compare also J.-C. Toutain, "Le produit de l'agriculture française de 1700 à 1958. I: Estimation du produit au XVIIIe siècle," *Cahiers de l'Institut de Science Économique appliquée*, série AF, (5 July 1961) 1: 82 (8.7 to 10.3 bushels/year per capita).

59. "Crise agricole"; cf. Jones, "Agriculture in Lower Canada."

60. "Crise agricole," 229–30.

61. J.-P. Wallot, "Religion and French-Canadian Mores in the Early Nineteenth Century," *CHR* LII (1971):51–94.

62. For example, Séguin, *La nation "canadienne,"* 153.

63. "Crise agricole," 213, 224, 226, 231–34.

64. L.M. Cullen, "Irish History Without the Potato," *Past and Present* XL (1968):72–83.

MARKETABLE SURPLUSES IN ONTARIO FARMING, 1860†

MARVIN McINNIS

Background and Motivation

It is now commonplace to acknowledge that self-sufficiency never really existed in North American farming. From the earliest years of settlement farmers had some degree of orientation to the market. Even on the frontiers of most recent settlement, farms generally could not be characterized as being of a wholly subsistence nature. Nor was there some mystic moment when agriculture shifted from self-sufficiency to commercialization. The real issue is the extent of commercialization at any time and place. One way of examining that is to determine the extent to which specialization and resort to the market was feasible, through assessing the magnitude of marketable surpluses. How much did farms typically produce over and above the consumption needs of their own households, and how did that vary according to circumstances?

Commercial orientation has been especially emphasized in the historical accounts of farming in Canada, particularly in Upper Canada — the province that was to become Ontario. From the earliest years of settlement, wheat farming is thought to have predominated in Ontario. Indeed, the most widely accepted account of Canadian economic development — the "staples hypothesis" — makes the production of wheat for export markets the motivating force behind the settlement and development of Ontario. Frequent references are made in the literature to "wheat mining." All of this conjures up an image of highly specialized and commercially oriented agriculture. There has been little, however, in the way of detailed examination of the available evidence of farming in Ontario to verify that this portrayal is borne out.

In this article a sample of data for individual farms from the 1861 *Census of Canada* is used to investigate the extent of marketable surpluses in Ontario and

†*Social Science History* VIII, 4 (Fall 1984): 395–424. Someshwar Rao provided much appreciated assistance in the original assembly of the Canada West Farm Sample. James Nugent contributed valuably to the organization and handling of the computer files of the data. Much of the analysis for the present article was done with the assistance of Heather Tremble. The financial support of the Social Sciences and Humanities Research Council of Canada is gratefully acknowledged.

to explore some of the factors associated with variation in it. The data sample matches in date, and a number of other characteristics, the widely cited Bateman-Foust sample of farms in the northern United States in 1860. This date is of considerable interest to the study of Canadian agricultural development, for it comes at the end of a little over a decade of transformation and development in the agriculture of Ontario.[1]

The period before the mid-1840s is generally thought of as the pioneer era in Ontario farming, a period dominated by land settlement and the clearing of forests; a period in which agriculture is supposed to have had a simple orientation toward wheat. By the time the census of 1860 was enumerated, the extension of agricultural settlement in Ontario had virtually come to an end. Many new farms were established in the course of the preceding decade, but it was more a process of filling in behind the frontier than of settling whole new districts. An increasing complexity of agriculture, diversification of marketed products, and a considerable overall increase in prosperity have been portrayed as the foremost characteristics of agricultural development in the 1850s. Jones,[2] the preeminent historian of Ontario agriculture, refers to the period as the "Grand Trunk Era," although he makes clear in a chapter devoted to this period that there was more than just the first spate of railway building at work in spurring the development of agriculture in Ontario. Soaring world demand for wheat, in part as an outcome of the Crimean War, increased access to the U.S. market, partly as a result of the Reciprocity Treaty of 1854, a rapidly growing urban market in Canada, and the beginnings of mechanization all came to bear on Canadian agriculture in this period.

What, then, was the state of agriculture in Ontario in 1860? How common and how extensive were substantial marketable surpluses? These are questions that have not even been addressed in quantitative terms, let alone answered.

To deal with these questions I turn to the manuscript enumerations of individual farms in the Canadian census of 1861. The census data on crops and livestock are used to make estimates for each farm of the likely level of net output. To obtain that aggregate, estimates are made of the net production of each of the principal field crops and livestock and animal products. The sample has farm and personal data linked so the age and sex of each person in the farm household can be combined with plausible assumptions about per capita consumption of farm products to generate an estimate of total consumption for each household. The extent to which estimated production exceeds or falls short of estimated consumption can then be gauged. These marketable surpluses are then examined in relation to a number of variables that might be expected to influence them. Mainly these variables are farm size, recency of settlement of the district in which the farm is located, and access to markets and transport facilities.

This article was written with the express purpose of comparing results with those obtained by Atack and Bateman[3] in a similar effort directed at agriculture in the northern United States at the same juncture of history. For that reason I endeavour to stick closely to the assumptions and procedures of Atack and Bateman. I pay less attention than they to the geographical location of farms per se. That is because I am examining what is geographically a fairly homogeneous region, in contrast to their consideration of the whole of the northern United States. The sample I use includes farms that are widely distributed throughout

Ontario, but location, in and of itself, is less important than features such as the recency of settlement of the districts, wherever located, or their proximity to urban areas or transport routes. I try to take these factors into account directly rather than to sort things by geographic location.

The Canada West Farm Sample, 1861[4]

The Canada West Farm Sample was originally drawn and tabulated in 1972 in connection with historical demographic research that is reported in McInnis.[5] It is rich in information relating to farm production, however, and invites examination of many aspects of the nature of farming in early Ontario. Although a brief account of the characteristics of this sample is given here, a fuller description is available from the author.[6]

The sample is quite modest in size, including only 1100 farms and farm households.[7] That is barely one-tenth the size of the Bateman-Foust sample of the northern United States and admittedly may be at the lower bound of reliable sample size for its purpose. The greater homogeneity of Ontario than of the whole of the northern United States in 1860, however, makes a smaller sample more feasible. Initially, a sample size of 1200 was arrived at as the solution to a formal exercise of solving for the sample design and size that would minimize certain key variances, given the limited resources available at the time to carry out the job. The upshot was a stratified, two-stage random sample, The townships of Ontario were first stratified into groups according to settlement date so as to assure that adequate representation would be given to both recently settled and early settled farms.[8] The sampling then proceeded in two stages. A random sampling was made of the townships within each settlement date stratum; then a random selection of farmers was made within each selected township. There are 148 townships in the sample and seven or eight farmers randomly selected within each township. The sample design thus called for 1131 farms. After editing, a sample of 1096 farms underlies the results reported in this article; however, one of the issues motivating the original sample design was to explore what could be done with a small, special-purpose sample. In another paper,[9] the matter of the quality of the sample is discussed more fully.

For present purposes it may be sufficient to have some assurance that, on the whole, the Canada West Farm Sample tests out reliably. The estimated standard errors of most of the variables are sufficiently low to permit testing for significance of differences in values of variables of as little as three or four percent. The sample replicates closely the published census distributions of crops and livestock numbers. When the sample is split in half on a random basis, the values of almost all variables in the two subsamples are not significantly different. The single variable that turns out to be most problematic is one of the most basic — the average occupied acreage of the farms. The difficulty here is that the published census includes a sizable number of small plots that were not really farms. The Canada West Farm Sample was deliberately designed to exclude those units. Nevertheless, it is possible that the sample may have a slight upward bias in farm sizes. In particular, the proportion of large farms included in the sample may be slightly high.

The Canada West Farm Sample began with a random selection from the manuscript enumerations of the Canadian 1861 census of population of heads of households who gave their occupation as farmer. The agricultural schedules were then manually linked. In addition to the data from the census, other variables reflecting characteristics of the township in which each farm is located have been added to the file. These take on the same value for each of the seven or eight farms in a given township. They include such variables as the date of first settlement in the township, proximity to transport through being located on the lake or river front or on a rail line, and the proportion of land that is of high quality, as judged by twentieth-century soil surveys.

A final point to be noted about the Canada West Farm Sample is that a small number of the persons in the sample gave their occupations as farmer and were enumerated as occupying farms but had only unimproved land. They reported no crop output or any livestock. This is plausible. The process of initial settlement was still under way and we should expect to find a few farmers who were just starting up. These farms are included in all of the calculations reported in this article. This has only a minor effect on the calculated averages and is unlikely to alter any of the conclusions. It would be a relatively simple matter to retabulate the sample to exclude these "new" farms. I have retained them here because, realistically, they were a part of the system. Numerically, though, this does have the effect of introducing a few large deficits into the tabulation.

Estimates of Net Farm Production

The census itself provides no aggregate of net production or sales for each farm. It records the acreage and output of each crop and the number of livestock of various types and gives some record of production of butter, cheese, packed pork and beef, and homemade cloth. Several components of farm production are missing entirely from the record. There is no count of poultry and eggs and only an intermittent and probably inaccurate reporting of orchard and garden production. It also should be kept in mind that forest products — ashes, barrel staves, saw logs, and shingles — were an important part of farm production in many areas of Ontario at this time. Nevertheless, information is included on the most important components of farm production — enough to allow at least a rough calculation of marketable surpluses. The reported output of individual crops or products can be compared with estimates of consumption by the farm household. The latter are averages, however, varying across households only to the extent that numbers and composition of the households vary. It would be attractive to aggregate as much as possible, implicitly allowing as much substitution between products as possible. To do that, an estimate of the value of net production was made for each farm in the sample.

The method used to estimate net production for each farm is a modification of the procedure followed by Lewis and McInnis[10] to estimate agricultural output for small areas such as parishes and townships in Lower Canada. This procedure is described in fuller detail elsewhere.[11] In its essentials, it consists first of a tally of all measurable output of the farm, including feed crops that would be consumed largely on the farm. Estimates of seed requirements are deducted from the production of each crop. At this stage, the procedure provides estimates of production, net of seed, of crops such as wheat and potatoes that enter primarily into human consumption, either on the farm or elsewhere. The next step is to add the estimated value of production of livestock and animal products. Here the Canadian census itself is skimpy. Quantities of butter and cheese produced on the farm were recorded, but they represent only processed dairy output and make no allowance for milk consumed in fluid form. Furthermore, the reported butter production appears to be quite deficient. It aggregates across the province to a figure that is far too skimpy to be a reliable indication of local consumption. One gets the impression that many farms may have reported only butter sold, not all butter produced. The situation is even more problematic for meat. Cured pork and beef in barrels were enumerated, but that was only a fraction of production. An alternative approach is necessary. Production — or at least possible production — can be inferred from the number of each type of livestock, but that assumes a constant relationship across all farms of production to stocks of livestock. The average production relationships are based on assumptions about slaughter ratios and weights of animals at slaughter that are drawn from an extensive reading of the contemporary literature on farming.

This approach to estimating the output of animal products has the obvious disadvantage of making no allowance for any variation between farms in the efficiency and intensity with which livestock were utilized. That may not be so severe a limitation as first appears. If animal products are thought of as essentially upgraded feedstuffs, then actual production of animal products should bear a reasonably close relationship to the quantities of feed produced on each farm. That is borne out reasonably well by the estimates from the Farm Sample.

The essential point involved can be developed further to make the basis for a more reliable estimate of the overall net output of the farm. I first made a fixed coefficient estimate of animal product output, as outlined above. Then I added an estimate of the value of all crops — feed crops as well as those for human consumption and sale — and made a fixed coefficient estimate of animal feed requirements. The procedures followed for that are explained immediately below. The point to be made at this juncture, however, is that the deviations between actual animal product output and actual animal feed and the amounts estimated by applying fixed coefficients to each farm are largely (although not entirely) offsetting. Consequently, the resulting estimate of the net output of the farm is more reliable than the initial estimates of either feed or animal products. This estimate of net production can be compared to the aggregate value of farm consumption implied by application to the farm household of a fixed set of average per capita consumption coefficients. The procedure allows for substitution of individual products on both the output and the consumption sides. The resulting net difference should be the best estimate that can be obtained of the marketable surplus of the farm. Estimated differences between production and consumption for individual commodities are of a more qualified sort.

The animal feed requirements are made in a way that is fairly analogous to the estimates of human consumption, with one additional twist. The contemporary agricultural literature was scoured to obtain indications of typical feeding practices. These tended to lean toward "better practice" and would imply a national aggregate of feed crop output considerably in excess of what was actually recorded. The feed coefficients for each type of animal were therefore decreased proportionally to make the feed bill commensurate with the available supply of feed crops in Ontario in 1860.

The components of farm production and of feed requirements are aggregated in value terms, the quantities of each crop weighted by market prices. Thus the quantities of feed required, on average, by each type of animal are aggregated into a feed bill expressed in dollars. Similarly, the quantities of all crops produced — both feed and market crops — are weighted by prices and aggregated to a total value of production, to which is added the total value of livestock and animal products, including an estimated value of so-called surplus horses available for sale. This last component is based on a comparison of the number of horses reported by each farm with an estimate of the required number of draft animals. The availability of oxen is taken into account in the calculation. It is a potentially important adjustment, given that the raising of horses for sale was one of the most profitable and clearly commercial activities in the agricultural community. To leave it out would be to miss an important element of commercial orientation in the agriculture of the time. For the purposes of estimating net production it does not matter whether the "surplus" horses were being sold or were added to the capital stock of the farm. That distinction cannot be made, although it is important for the calculation of marketable surpluses.

Estimates of Household Consumption

The estimates of household consumption of farm products are of the fixed coefficient type. They are computed by assuming the same average consumption per head of each product across households. In that sense, they are undoubtedly unrealistic and should be taken as only the roughest indicators of consumption. They have two main components: estimated quantities of yearly per capita consumption of each commodity per adult male, and the age and sex structure of the household. A range of estimates has been examined, but the results reported here are based on fairly modest assumptions about consumption.

The starting point for the assumptions about annual consumption of food products per adult male is a set of national average per capita consumption estimates made for 1870 as part of a forthcoming research project by McInnis and Urquhart. Those estimates were based on national domestic disappearance of the products as estimated from census and trade statistics. The 1870 values are averages of both farm and nonfarm populations and have been reduced by six percent to allow for some growth of per capita food consumption over the 1861–71 decade. Food consumption of farm families is typically higher than that of urban families, and these estimates were national averages of both farm and nonfarm families. The figures were raised by ten percent in recognition of the usually higher levels of consumption on farms. That is almost certainly a minimum differential. The consumption allowances were then adjusted further in two ways. One was to raise potato consumption as a substitute for wheat flour. Reported potato production was quite abundant. It is difficult to estimate likely consumption, given that we know there was waste in the potato crop and some part would also have

TABLE 1

Adult Male Equivalent Consumption of Major Food Items

Commodity	Quantity Per Year
Wheat (as flour)	7 bu.
Potatoes	14 bu.
Beef	62.5 lbs.
Pork	95 lbs.
Mutton	20 lbs.
Butter, cheese & milk (as butter)	52 lbs.

been fed to animals. I followed the presumption that farm families would obtain their carbohydrate consumption from potatoes to the greatest extent possible and market their wheat. Even so, the resulting marketable surpluses of potatoes appear to be rather high. The assumption seems to be a reasonably safe one.

The other modification is to hold beef and pork consumption to fairly modest levels and to go rather higher on milk and dairy products. On the whole this seems reasonable. It implies a level of butter and/or milk consumption in Canada well above the level that Atack and Bateman[12] use for the United States. Early twentieth-century estimates of butter consumption in Canada point to figures well above those of the United States. The nineteenth-century estimates made by McInnis and Urquhart are considerably higher than the estimates for the United States reported in Bennett and Pierce.[13] Again, the ethnic background of the population of Ontario — predominantly British and especially northern Irish — points to fairly heavy consumption of milk by farm families. The overall caloric value of the diet assumed in this article is very close to that used by Atack and Bateman for the United States at the same date, but I am assuming that the Canadian farmers consumed more wheat flour and less corn meal, more potatoes, less meat, and more dairy products than did people in the United States.

The assumed consumption standards would provide an adult male with almost 3200 calories per day of the foods included in the calculation, but it must be kept in mind that only part of the diet is included. If one raises the figure of 3200 calories by the ratio of the caloric value of included to total items in early twentieth-century diets, the figure would imply a daily average of 5300 calories per adult male.[14] This seems to be a reasonable figure for active, hard-working farm men and is about the same as assumed by Atack and Bateman for the United States. The actual consumption of each product that implies is listed in table 1.

One other aspect of this diet that is dubious is the allowance for mutton or lamb. The Canadian population, like that of the United States, is not noted for consumption of lamb or mutton. Nevertheless, Canadian farmers in 1861 raised a great many sheep. It is not clear what should be assumed about their use for meat consumption. Undoubtedly these sheep were primarily for wool production. Nevertheless, their numbers imply a supply of meat that would at least be available and may have been consumed to a greater extent than is ordinarily believed. Canadian farmers were producing a substantial number of sheep; whether they

TABLE 2

Food Consumption by Sex and Age as a Proportion of the Consumption of Adult Males

Age Class	Males	Females
Less than 5 years	0.40	0.40
5–9 years	0.55	0.55
10–14 years	0.80	0.75
15–59 years	1.00	0.80
60 years and over	0.85	0.75

SOURCE: R. M. Woodbury, "Economic Consumption Scales and their Uses," *Journal of the American Statistics Association* XXXIX (1944): table 1, based primarily on F.M. Williams and J.E. Lockwood, *An Economic Study of Food Consumed by Farm and Village Families in Central New York*, Bull. 502 (Ithaca: New York Agricultural Experiment Station, 1930).

were consuming them on the farm is another matter. At this stage we do not have sufficient information.[15]

The second element in the estimates of household consumption is to weight the individuals in the household according to their sex and age, given that average food consumption varies considerably by sex and age. Numerous surveys over the years have provided the basis for consumption scales; several of these are summarized by Woodbury.[16] Although there is scope for considerable disagreement, the weights given in table 2, a synthesis of the more plausible figures given by Woodbury, seem to be as suitable as any. The main features of this set of consumption scales are that it provides for infants at a relatively high level, it sets a relatively low ratio of adult women's to adult men's consumption, and it recognizes the decline in food consumption at older ages.

Calculated Marketable Surpluses

With all of the assumptions explained above and the procedures generally outlined, we can now consider the potentially marketable surpluses of farms in Ontario in 1861 and relate these to levels of both farm production and farm household consumption. Both perspectives are useful. The value of net output of the average farm in Ontario in 1861 was $384[17] (see table 3). The average marketable surplus was $210, a figure that amounted to 55 percent of net output.[18] Looked at in another way, the average marketable surplus was 21 percent greater than the value of average household consumption of the commodities covered. Typically, then, Ontario farms in 1861 were well beyond what can be described as essentially self-sufficient or subsistence agriculture. Nevertheless, the average marketable surplus was not very large, even in relation to what was then still a low level of farm production. Each farm household was producing a surplus that would have provided for the consumption of at most two nonfarm households.

TABLE 3

Per Farm Marketable Surpluses and Their Distribution,
Ontario, 1861

	Value of Marketable Surplus
Average for all farms in sample	$210
Average for farms with positive surplus only	$280
First quartile: value exceeded by 75% of farms	$ 20
Median	$149
Third quartile: value exceeded by 25% of farms	$324
Value exceeded by 10% of farms	$639
Value exceeded by 5% of farms	$830
Percent of farms with deficit	16
Percent of farms with surplus in excess of consumption requirements of 3 households	16

For an economy that is supposed to have been strongly oriented toward the production of wheat for export, that level of marketable surplus seems rather meager.

The distribution of marketable surpluses across the farms in the sample is shown in table 3. Only 16 percent of farms did not produce enough to provide for the consumption of their own households. Considering that almost 4 percent of farms in the sample were estimated to have negative net output, and that some of the farms were very small, it seems remarkable that so few produced less than their estimated household consumption. On the other hand, the size of the surpluses was typically small. One-quarter of all farms produced marketable surpluses of less than $20, and half of all farms produced no more than $150 — a bit more than the consumption requirements of one other family. Large surpluses were produced by only a small proportion of the farms. Only 5 percent of farms, for example, produced more than $830 worth of output above and beyond their consumption needs. In a rather arbitrary way, we might define "substantially commercial" farms to be those with marketable surpluses of more than three households' consumption. By that criterion, only 16 percent of farms were "substantially commercial."

The distribution of marketable surpluses is shown in figure 1, where I have interpolated between the points that came routinely out of the computer analysis.[19] Figure 1 shows quite clearly that most farms produced only modest surpluses, and that relatively few farms turned out the really large surpluses. Also seen in figure 1 is that the slope of the line is relatively flat in the vicinity of the point where farms produce surpluses rather than deficits. The proportion of farms with food deficits is not sensitive to the assumptions made about average

FIGURE 1

Marketable Surpluses: Ontario Farms, 1861

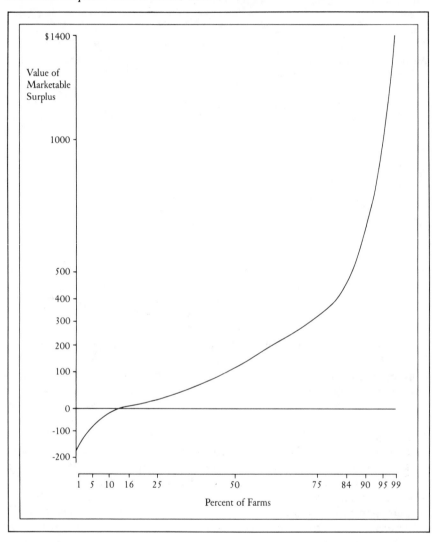

consumption. Surpluses would be small for the bottom half of the distribution of farms over a wide range of assumptions about per capita consumption. The large surpluses are found only in the upper tail of the distribution and are primarily a reflection of the amounts of production rather than what is assumed about consumption.

There are numerous characteristics of farms with which we might expect the size of marketable surplus to be associated. To keep this article within reasonable bounds, only three factors are examined. One obvious influence should be size of farm. That might be measured in several alternate ways. Here I use the most straightforward measure: the number of acres of land occupied. A second factor examined is the duration of settlement of the township in which the farm is located. This is measured in decades from the period of first recorded settlement in the township. Two conflicting hypotheses might be considered. One is that surpluses are likely to be greater in longer-settled communities where a larger market would have developed in connection with a greater complexity of non-agricultural activity. Alternatively, we might expect newly settled regions to have a higher proportional, if smaller absolute, marketable surplus as farmers initially direct their attention to the wheat staple as a means of financing the development of their farms. A third factor is access to transport. That is analyzed in terms of a simple binary categorization according to whether the townships in which farms were located fronted on the lake and river system that provided the principal water transport route or had railways passing through them, or, in contrast, were one or more townships distant from the transport system. Access to transport and duration of settlement are, of course, interdependent factors, given that the lake and river-front townships were the first to be settled.

Four size classes of farms are considered[20] (see table 4). The size classes deliberately bracket the modal acreage of farms in each class. One shortcoming of published census tabulations and much other work on farming is that size classes are set so that the class boundaries split large concentrations.[21] The size classes used here are based on an examination of the distribution of the sample farms by individual acreages, and the boundaries are placed at sizes of minimum frequencies. It should not be surprising that marketable surplus rises more than output as farm size increases. What may be surprising is that it does not rise even more steeply. Thus for large farms the average marketable surplus was 61 percent of net farm output, whereas for standard, 100-acre farms it was 55 percent. A much higher proportion of large farms, however, had surpluses of more than three times household consumption: 39 percent as compared with only 14 percent for standard-sized farms. It is interesting to note, however, that even in the largest size class 12 percent of farms had deficits. On the other hand, even in the smallest size class some farms averaged a surplus, although almost half of the smallest farms had deficits.

Occupied acreage is a conventional but probably not very good way to classify farms by size. In further research on this topic it would be useful to explore the implications of alternate measures of farm size. Several possibilities are available. The estimated net output would be one obvious choice. The data file also included the value of the farm as reported on the census. Even improved acreage might be preferable to occupied acreage. Farms in the smallest size class typically had practically all of their land under cultivation, whereas many large farms were relatively new and had only a few acres, quite often less than 30, in actual use. This explains, for example, why as many as 12 percent of large farms had deficit production.

The distinction between farms according to duration of settlement of the districts in which they are located ultimately is of consequence only for the most recently settled districts. The duration of settlement categories mean roughly the following: The earliest-settled districts were those in which first settlement had occurred

TABLE 4

Marketable Surpluses by Farm Type, Ontario, 1861

Farm Type	Estimated Surplus	Net Farm Output	Surplus as % of Net Output	% of Farms with Deficit	% of Farms with a Large Surplus
	$	$			
Whole Sample	210	384	55	16	16
Earliest Settled Region	251	429	58	12	27
Mid-Period	224	486	46	19	17
Recently Settled	123	237	52	32	4
Very Small Farms (1–31 acres)	41	120	34	46	0
Small Farms (32–69 acres)	116	260	45	23	5
Standard Farms (70–169 acres)	203	378	55	17	14
Large Farms (170 acres+)	402	661	61	12	39
Adjacent to Transport	264	511	52	14	28
Not Adjacent	194	292	66	31	12

before 1815 and the most recently settled districts were opened after 1840. Farmers in the most recently settled districts would consist almost entirely of the generation of farmers who actually carried out the settlement. These are the real frontier farms. Their average marketable surplus is barely half that of farms in earlier-settled regions, but their farm output is a great deal lower as well. What is perhaps surprising is that their marketable surplus averages as much as half of the net output of the farms. That proportion is not much less than the 58 percent seen in the earliest-settled districts. Considerably more of the frontier farms, though, had deficits of food production and scarcely any had large surpluses.

Farms in townships that were adjacent to the transport system had substantially larger marketable surpluses than those in more remote townships. The difference in average net output per farm was even greater, however, so we get the rather anomalous result that farms in the townships not adjacent to transport had a higher ratio of surplus to net output than in the more advantageously situated districts. A much larger proportion had no surpluses.

What emerges from this study is that the distinction between self-sufficiency and commercialization is not very important. The great majority of farms in a wide range of circumstances was producing an excess over household consumption needs. Conversely, substantial surpluses were much less common. Only a small fraction of farms was producing a marketable surplus great enough to provide for more than just the local nonagricultural population. It is these large surpluses that are most notably found on large farms, in the longest-settled districts, and in localities that have closer access to the transport system.

Marketable Surpluses of Individual Products

Differences between production and consumption of several individual commodities can be examined at the individual farm level, although, as has already been noted, these measures have to be viewed as less reliable than the aggregate consumption/production relationship. The method used here permits no variation between farms in per person consumption except for that introduced by variations in the composition of farm households. No provision can be made for substitution in consumption between commodities. Similarly, the only variation of individual commodities allowed on the production side is that resulting from variation in the numbers of livestock. The situation is least problematic in the case of wheat. There are widely repeated contemporary statements of what was presumed to be a reasonable average level of consumption of wheat flour. The actual yields were reported in the census. Wheat could be fed to animals, and in some cases undoubtedly was, but there is good reason to believe that wheat was predominantly sold off the farm.

Potatoes are surely more problematic. We can make only a crude guess about the likely level of consumption. Potato yields were reported less reliably, if for no other reason than that in the absence of a commercial transaction the production was less likely to be measured. They were more commonly fed to animals. Also, with potatoes there was considerable waste. Meat and dairy products require even cruder guesses. Imposing fixed proportions of pork and beef on each household is especially restrictive. Nevertheless, it is worth a look at the results of the calculations to see what they indicate about possible levels of marketable surplus of each of these products. These are summarized in table 5.

Wheat was the preeminent marketable commodity. It was the only commodity of which the average farm was producing enough to support more than one additional household. In addition, wheat was a much larger component of the marketable surplus of agriculture than it was of net agricultural production. For the farms in the sample, the value of the marketable surplus of wheat was almost 70 percent of the total surplus. This reinforces the confidence we might have in the reliability of the estimates of aggregate marketable surplus because wheat is the commodity most reliably estimated. Moreover, a wider range of farms produced surpluses of wheat than produced surpluses of the other commodities. Although most farms may have produced small surpluses of pork and beef, substantial commercial production appears to have been the domain of only a small fraction of farms. Dairy production seems especially slim. The results reported here concur with the number of milk cows reported in the Canadian census of 1861. At least six cows would have been required to produce a substantial marketable surplus of dairy product, such as the quantity required to feed three nonfarm households. By that criterion, less than 8 percent of farms in Canada West had enough dairy cattle to mount even a modest commercial dairy operation.

The profiles of the distribution of marketable surpluses of wheat and beef are compared graphically in figure 2. The overall impression is not greatly different. Very large surpluses are concentrated in only a small proportion of the farms. The curve for wheat, however, crosses the line between deficit and surplus well

Table 5

Estimated Marketable Surpluses of Individual Commodities, Ontario, 1861 (all farms)

Commodity	Mean Household Consumption	Mean Surplus or Deficit	Ratio of Surplus to Consumption	Surplus or Deficit at		
				Q1	Q3	.95
Wheat (bu.)	35	150	4.3	22	212	542
Potatoes (bu.)	69	56	0.8	− 18	102	265
Beef (lbs. liveweight)	563	475	0.8	17	746	1708
Pork (lbs. liveweight)	620	320	0.5	− 73	571	1463
Mutton (lbs. liveweight)	99	111	1.12	− 36	179	774
Dairy product (in lbs. butter equivalent)	258	77	0.3	− 53	151	510

to the left of that for beef. The 5 percent or 10 percent of farms with the largest surpluses of beef, however, have relatively greater surpluses than is the case for wheat. For wheat, the 95th percentile is six times the median; for beef it is eight times the median.

In table 6 the estimated marketable surpluses of each commodity are related to farm size, duration of settlement, and access to transport. It should not be surprising that potato crops show the least sensitivity to these factors. Marketable surpluses of wheat may have been relatively more important in recently settled districts rather than in the longer-settled districts. The size of those surpluses was smaller in the recently settled districts, but farm output was lower as well. Whereas net farm output in the recently settled districts averaged a little over half that in the longest-settled districts (table 4), the marketable surpluses of wheat were almost two-thirds. Pork and dairy production appear to have been the most deficient in the frontier areas.

It is striking that the gradient of the marketable surplus of wheat rises less than proportionally with the size of farm. Doubling occupied farm acreage is associated with less than a doubling of the marketable surplus of wheat. That is not what we might have expected. The gradients of marketable surpluses of pork and dairy products rise much more steeply with size of farm. Wheat was the ubiquitous crop, as was the potato, but that mostly for subsistence use. Commercial specialization in livestock and dairy products — especially pork and dairying — was not only a more notable feature of the longer-settled regions but was associated with larger farms as well. Again, access to transport made the most difference for pork and dairy production.

So far I have treated feed crops as though they were used entirely on the farms on which they were raised and have looked at wheat and potatoes as the only crops likely to be sold off farms. There was a market for oats and hay in both the cities and the lumber camps. Draft animals used in construction and in transport had to be fed. Some amount of barley, rye, and corn was sold to breweries and distilleries. Barley and oats were both exported. It would be instructive if estimates could be made of marketable surpluses of feed crops as well. That is greatly complicated by the procedure used to estimate net farm output. There is no way to distinguish between surpluses of feed crops and greater than average production

FIGURE 2

Marketable Surpluses of Wheat and Beef: Ontario Farms, 1861

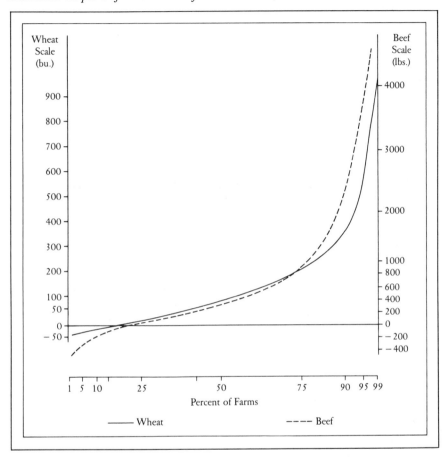

of dairy products and meat through higher than average rates of feeding. Indeed, apparent small surpluses of feed crops would more likely indicate higher levels of output of animal products. About all that can be done is to put an arbitrary upper limit on the extent to which above-average feed crop production is likely to have been transformed into greater dairy and livestock production. A feed surplus of one-third might be a reasonable cut-off and 45 percent would probably be an upper limit. Only 10.5 percent of farms in the Canada West Farm Sample had feed crop production in excess of 1.33 times the feed bill required to provide for the farm's livestock at average rates of feeding; only 6 percent of farms had feed crop surpluses in excess of 45 percent of the feed bill. Thus, even for the purpose of interfarm sales, the census evidence does not point to widespread marketable surpluses of feedstuffs.

TABLE 6

*Average Marketable Surpluses of Selected Commodities,
by Farm Types, Ontario, 1861*

Farm Type	Wheat	Potatoes	Beef	Pork	Dairy
	bu.	bu.	lbs.[a]	lbs.[a]	lbs.[b]
Whole Sample	150	56	475	320	77
Earliest Settled					
Region	154	56	519	319	112
Mid-Period	171	65	504	418	76
Recently Settled	97	37	318	112	5
Very Small Farms					
(1–31 acres)	28	37	− 107	217	11
Small Farms					
(32–69 acres)	87	40	287	172	41
Standard Farms					
(70–169 acres)	148	56	566	389	80
Large Farms					
(170 acres +)	270	81	1028	780	213
Adjacent to					
Transport	178	60	542	412	106
Not Adjacent	115	51	390	203	42

a. Liveweight basis.
b. Butter or equivalent.

A final aspect of marketable surpluses that should be considered is the production of horses for sale. Horses were the most highly valued type of livestock, and horse breeding was a relatively specialized art that took both skill and substantial capital. The rewards were high, however, and the raising of horses for sale may have been the single most profitable activity open to mid-nineteenth-century farmers. In estimating net farm output it was important to take the production of horses for sale into account, given that the proceeds from even a pair of horses would amount to a sizable fraction of the net output of the average farm. Because the marketable surplus of horses was estimated in the course of making estimates of farm net output, it is worth looking separately at that item. These estimates overstate the frequency and importance of sales of horses as the estimates are strictly ones of surpluses available for sale. Additions to the stock of farm capital are not distinguished from actual sales. Because agriculture was expanding at this time, some of the surplus horses on farms would be just home-produced capital accumulation. From the point of view of the estimation of farm net output, it does not matter whether horses were sold or added to the capital stock of the farm; the treatment is equivalent. The number of horses actually being raised for sale would typically be smaller than this calculation indicates.

Only 23 percent of farms show any surplus horses. Most farms either have only the complement of draft animals needed to work a farm of their size or were getting by with something less. Of the 23 percent of farms with surplus horses, the average value of that surplus is $187, which at a market value per horse of $72 implies somewhat more than two and a half horses per farm potentially available for sale. Commercial production of horses was evidently highly concentrated on a few farms; only 5 percent had a value of surplus horses greater than $172. These specialized horse-rearing establishments were not necessarily large farms. Except for the category of tiny (under 32 acres) farms, the proportion of farms with surplus horses varies only a little across the size distribution of farms from 21 percent of small farms to 28 percent of large farms.[22]

Some Comparisons with Farming in the Northern United States

The marketable surpluses in Ontario farming in 1861 can be compared with those estimated by Atack and Bateman[23] for the northern United States at the same date. They use similar census microdata, although from a considerably larger sample. In many respects, the procedures they follow are similar to those used in this article, although they have a different basis for estimating the production of dairy and meat products. The levels of food consumption assumed for the farm population amount to similar levels of caloric intake, although the Ontario farmers are presumed to be consuming more potatoes and dairy products and less pork. That is consistent with both contemporary observations and later diet comparisons.

The single greatest difference between farming in Ontario and farming in the northern United States was the minor role of Indian corn in Ontario. Except for a few counties in the southwest area of the province, corn could not be relied upon to ripen in Ontario because of a cooler, shorter growing season. In the twentieth century the introduction of hybrid varieties of corn and the widespread practice of growing corn for ensilage have meant that corn has come to play a much greater role in Ontario agriculture. In the middle of the nineteenth century, however, corn was a minor crop in Ontario. Its place was taken by peas and oats. The inability to ripen corn meant that the relative cost of fattening livestock was higher. That partly accounts for the lesser role of pork in Ontario.

The composition of both production and consumption differed between Canada and the United States, reflecting adaptation to local conditions. Overall, however, there is considerable comparability to the result for the two countries. The average marketable surpluses were lower in Ontario, but average farm production was probably lower as well. The average net surplus of $210 for Ontario farms is well below the $360 figure that Atack and Bateman obtain for all farms in their sample. It is a little closer to the $331 figure for farms in the Old Northwest, the region of the northern United States with the closest affinity to Ontario. The differential in average marketable surplus between regions that differ in recency of settlement seems to have been more pronounced in Ontario, but that may be because there is a sharper gradation of settlement periods in the Ontario sample. That access to transport was important for integration into the market system is borne out by the strong differential in marketable surplus in relation to transport access, a differential that is relatively similar in the two countries.

Two points of qualification should be noted. One is that Atack and Bateman use a different scale of age and sex weights for relative food consumption than underlie the present article. In particular, they assign a lower weight to very young children. Second, I have assumed a substantially higher level of consumption of dairy products than have Atack and Bateman. They assume an annual average consumption of dairy product in all forms of 35 pounds of butter, or equivalent, per adult male; I have put the figure for Canada West at 52 pounds. The Atack and Bateman figure corresponds closely to the estimate of Bennett and Pierce[24] for the United States as a whole in 1879. Dairy consumption was probably higher than average in the North, and I think that dairy products especially were an item where farm family consumption would have been higher than the average for the whole population. Hence Atack and Bateman may have understated probable dairy consumption. By contrast, I would expect the Canadian average to be higher than that in the United States. Estimates I have made in a work done jointly with Malcolm Urquhart[25] would put Canadian average consumption in 1870 and 1880 above the levels estimated for the United States by Bennett and Pierce. For 1870 we estimated about 30 pounds per capita of butter and cheese consumption alone before any provision is made for fluid milk. For 1861 Canada West it would seem to be conservative to assume 52 pounds per capita of butter equivalent, applying to the farm population only, because that figure is the national average estimated for 1870. Perhaps that has turned out to be on the high side. I am surprised at how meager the estimated marketable surpluses of dairy product appear to be in the 1861 Canada West Farm Sample. It is in dairying that the greatest contrasts appear between Canada West and the northern United States as estimated by Atack and Bateman.

In other regards the results for Canada and the United States are more closely comparable. In general, marketable surpluses were modest on the average and largely concentrated on a small fraction of the farms. Both sets of data, however, indicate that marketable surpluses rose less than in proportion to farm size measured by occupied acreage. Within the more confined area of Canada West there does not exist the extent of regional differentiation revealed by Atack and Bateman for the northern United States. Location did make a difference, in that marketable surpluses were larger in districts with closer access to the transport system and in earlier-settled districts. Those findings are hardly surprising. What should be emphasized, however, is that at least in the case of Ontario, the larger marketable surpluses in earlier-settled regions and in districts with closer access to transport are attributable to considerable extent to the higher values of farm output to be found in those areas rather than to much higher ratios of marketable surplus to net farm output. That raises the interesting question of the direction of causation that cannot be pursued here. Was larger farm output induced by the profit opportunities found in closer access to more extensively built-up markets, or did the larger farm output in the longer-settled districts merely reflect a process of farm development through clearing of land and building up of stocks of livestock that had gone on for a longer time?

Conclusions

Some of the more interesting conclusions have already been dealt with in the foregoing comparison of findings for Canada West and the northern United States. Now let me direct attention to two matters, one methodological and the other substantive.

The methodological question concerns whether census data at the individual farm level can be manipulated to reveal more about the likely extent of specialization and commercialization in mid-nineteenth-century farming than we have been able to learn in the past from other sources. If the results are treated with due caution, the exercise would seem to have been rewarding. Little comes out that could be thought of as strikingly anomalous. More might be done to test the sensitivity of results to the many bold assumptions that have to be made. Most of the conclusions, however, are unlikely to be highly sensitive to variations in the assumptions. The results often reflect closely what one might infer from simple counts of animals or the tallying up of acreages. The important step was to go to the microdata. Even the simple counting of animals per farm requires that, and published tabulations for census districts often present a misleading picture. We are much less interested in whether farms in general typically had marketable surpluses than in establishing which farms had surpluses, and what the magnitudes of those surpluses were.

The substantive finding of greatest import is the great prevalence of marketable surpluses in the agriculture of Ontario. The evidence presented in this article could be interpreted as another, to put it in the words of Fowke,[26] "convincing demonstration of the unreality of the concept of agricultural self-sufficiency." It makes us able to agree readily with Atack and Bateman[27] that agriculture in Ontario like "northern agriculture in the United States had moved beyond self-sufficiency to market dependency by 1860." I am inclined, however, to read the evidence in a more qualified way. Although one can be impressed by how widespread was the existence of marketable surpluses over and above the consumption needs of farm households, I am impressed by how modest those surpluses were for most farms and for most commodities. In any locality only a few farms had become substantially specialized producers for the market. The surpluses they turned out were sufficient to give a general impression of specialization and exchange. The majority of farmers, however, produced a variety of products that were essentially an extension of the self-sufficient production of the farm. They required, and mainly catered to, a local market provided by the nonagricultural population of nearby towns, villages, rural craftsmen, and functionaries. This is a modified view of market dependency. It is consistent with what we know about the structure of the economy. Farm productivity was still relatively low, and the farm population made up half or more of the total.

Another impressive result is that it appears possible to have provided for the food consumption of a reasonably large farm family with the output of a small farm. Families with only 25 or 30 acres of land were able to produce more than what was needed for family consumption at average standards. Real poverty is unlikely to be widespread under such conditions. Also, there was a lot of scope for increased agricultural production in a community like Ontario where the average farm had 100 acres of land, at least two-thirds of which would have been cultivable. The real importance of markets, and of the expansion of markets, may have lain in the inducements offered to utilize more intensively the resources at hand. Inherently, this farming economy had considerable scope for economic development.

Notes

1. F. Bateman and J.D. Foust, "A Sample of Rural Households Selected from the 1860 Manuscript Censuses," *Agricultural History* XLVIII (1974): 75–93.

2. R.L. Jones, *History of Ontario Agriculture, 1613-1880* (Toronto: University of Toronto Press, 1946), chaps. 11 and 12.

3. J. Atack and F. Bateman, "Marketable Farm Surpluses: Northeastern and Midwestern United States," *Social Science History* VIII, 4 (1984): 371–93.

4. A clarification of nomenclature may be called for. The area under study is the southern part of the present Canadian province of Ontario. Prior to 1842 it was the British North American province of Upper Canada. After 1842, and at the time of the census of 1861, the name of the territory was Canada West. That name, although strictly correct, often causes confusion because the area would not now be thought of as part of western Canada.

5. R.M. McInnis, "Childbearing and Land Availability: Some Evidence From Individual Household Records" in *Population Patterns in the Past*, edited by R.D. Lee (New York: Academic, 1977).

6. R.M. McInnis, "The Canada West Farm Sample, 1861" (unpublished paper, Queen's University, 1984).

7. This amounts to 0.85% of the total number of farms in Ontario in 1861.

8. Townships were small, rural administrative areas averaging about 40 square miles in extent.

9. McInnis, "The Canada West Farm Sample."

10. F. Lewis and M. McInnis, "The Efficiency of the French-Canadian Farmer in the Nineteenth Century," *Journal of Economic History* 40 (Sept. 1980): 497–514, and "Agricultural Output and Efficiency in Lower Canada, 1851," *Research in Economic History* 9 (1984).

11. Lewis and McInnis, "Agricultural Output and Efficiency in Lower Canada, 1851"; McInnis, "The Canada West Farm Sample."

12. Atack and Bateman, "Marketable Farm Surpluses."

13. M.K. Bennett and R.H. Pierce, "Change in American National Diet, 1870–1959," *Food Research Institute Studies* 2 (May 1961): 95–119.

14. That probably biases the comparison upward to some extent. The items included here in the calculation are probably from the more calorie-intensive segment of the diet. Fruit and garden vegetables have been left out, as have poultry and eggs.

15. It may be the case that farmers in Canada consumed more beef and less mutton than is assumed here. That would make at least some farmers even more committed to the market for the sale of sheep and lambs than is assumed in the calculation here.

16. R.M. Woodbury, "Economic Consumption Scales and their Uses," *Journal of the American Statistics Association* 39 (1944): 455–68.

17. Goods have been priced in the Canadian dollar, which until after the outbreak of the Civil War was equivalent in value to the U.S. dollar. The output measure is net of intermediate products such as feed used on the farm.

18. Recall that neither the output nor the consumption figures are comprehensive. They leave aside poultry and eggs, vegetable garden and orchard products, for which we do not have census data on production, and the consumption estimates exclude such items as tea and sugar that would have been

purchased. More correctly, then, we should speak of measured net production and the estimated marketable surplus of products entering into that measure of production amounting to 55 percent of net production.

19. The univariate procedure of the SAS.

20. The original plan was to look at three farm sizes — small, medium, and large, so to speak. The standard farm occupied a 100-acre lot. Half of all farms had about 100 acres. Large farms might be taken to be those with two or more lots. Small farms would be those with a half-lot, typically, but the sample contained an assortment of even smaller farms that were more in the order of rural residential plots rather than actual farms. It seemed wise to segregate these tiny farms from the more ordinary small ones.

21. For example, the published tabulations of the 1861 *Census of Canada* make the size classes "50 acres and less than 100, then 100 acres to 200 acres." The standard farm lot was 100 acres, and 40 percent of all farms had exactly 100 acres of land.

22. That difference would not be statistically significant at a .95 level of confidence.

23. Atack and Bateman, "Marketable Farm Surpluses."

24. Bennett and Pierce, "Change in American National Diet."

25. This work is not yet published.

26. V.C. Fowke, "The Myth of the Self-sufficient Canadian Farmer," *Transactions of the Royal Society of Canada* 56 (series 3, section 2, 1962): 23–37.

27. Atack and Bateman, "Marketable Farm Surpluses."

AGRICULTURE, BALANCED GROWTH, AND SOCIAL CHANGE IN CENTRAL CANADA SINCE 1850: AN INTERPRETATION†

JOHN ISBISTER

French Canadian society has been unique in North America: founded in feudalism, rooted in the soil, conquered by a commercial race, devoted to the church, and committed to the conservative goal of survival. English Canadian society has been quite similar to, although not identical with, the dominant cultures in the United States: commercial, capitalist, secular and ambitious in its goals, mobile and acquisitive in its style.[1] Both societies have undergone the principal economic transformation of the modern era, from agriculture to industry as the prime locus of productive activity. The paths by which they achieved this transformation have been quite distinct, however.

Prior to the twentieth century, the French Canadian agricultural sector in Quebec generally achieved only a subsistence level of production; it was poor and commercially isolated. In contrast, from the latter part of the eighteenth century when it was first settled by English-speaking farmers, the Ontario agricultural sector produced surplus food for sale and was intimately involved in trade and commerce. This essay documents the contrast in agricultural development in the two provinces since approximately 1850 and shows how Quebec's industrial sector was able to develop at a relatively rapid rate without the support of a dynamic agricultural sector. The fundamental effects of the two different patterns of agricultural development are shown to lie not so much in the economy per se as in the realms of social structure and ideology. In the second section of the essay the argument is made that the differences in the rural cultures of the two provinces have been largely responsible for the differences in urban social stratification and political mores.

It is illuminating to present the aggregate data for the two provinces in the framework of the theory of balanced growth, a theory which highlights the role of agriculture in the economic development of preindustrial societies.[2] The first

†*Economic Development and Cultural Change* XXV (1976–77): 673–97. This essay was written while the author was a visitor at Scarborough College in the University of Toronto. He would like to thank Donald E. Campbell, R. Marvin McInnis, Nadja M. Stanchfield, and the members of the Santa Cruz Seminar on Comparative History.

section demonstrates that, while Ontario's experience has been a very model of balanced growth, Quebec's economic development has been distinctly unbalanced.

The theory of balanced growth directs its attention to the interrelationships between economic sectors and the potential of these interrelationships for the creation of bottlenecks, on the one hand, and for the mutual reinforcement of growth on the other. The contribution of the agricultural sector may be considered within at least three categories. (1) *Labor transfer:* The agricultural sector may be the principal source of manpower for expanding nonagricultural activities. (2) *Commodity exchange:* The agricultural sector may provide food for a growing nonagricultural labor force and markets for industrial production. (3) *Exports:* Expansion of agricultural exports may provide the foreign exchange required as increased incomes induce imports of both consumer and capital goods. Additional connections are possible, but these are the ones usually stressed.

Economic growth may proceed without any of these intersectoral connecting links; if so the nonagricultural sector is a pure enclave, and the sectors are so separate that it is not useful to consider them as together constituting a single economy. Development may proceed with only the first link, that of labor transfer. In such a case, one may properly speak of an economy, but it is unintegrated, without much potential for mutual support of the sectors. The second link, that of commodity exchange, lies at the heart of the balanced growth prescription; an economy with both the first and the second links is well integrated, with the potential for autonomous, self-reinforcing growth. The third link, exports, is not a necessary feature of the balanced growth pattern, but in Canadian history it has played a role of unusual importance as one staple export has succeeded another, inducing and stimulating domestic economic activities.

Patterns of Economic Growth in Ontario and Quebec Compared

There are conflicting opinions in the literature about the comparison of economic growth in Ontario and Quebec. One view holds that Quebec's economic development has lagged seriously behind Ontario's, another that growth in the two provinces has proceeded in a parallel fashion.[3] The most comprehensive statistical analysis of the issue is by André Raynauld,[4] who comes down predominantly in the latter camp: since the second half of the nineteenth century, he shows, growth rates in agriculture and in manufacturing have been identical in the two provinces, and in mineral production Quebec's growth has been slightly faster. Raynauld's conclusions about the manufacturing sector appear to be beyond reproach; table 1, in which his data are converted to a constant-dollar basis, demonstrates the highlights.[5] Quebec's manufacturing output has fluctuated around 60 percent of Ontario's since 1870; in the nineteenth century there was no persistent trend in the ratio, and in the first half of the twentieth century Ontario's growth was somewhat faster. The ratio of productivity per employee has shown no long-run trend; it remained 15 percent higher in Ontario, with Quebec temporarily filling the gap early in the twentieth century. The ratios in the measures of value added in manufacturing per labor force member and per capita fell gradually if not regularly over the period, reflecting Quebec's faster population growth (the lower ratio of value added per capita is the result of the higher proportion of children in Quebec and consequent lower labor force participation rate). Since 1915, when annual data became available, inflection and turning points in the manufacturing series have been the same in the two provinces in all but three years.

In sum, Quebec's lag in manufacturing has been real but marginal; what seems remarkable, in view of the widespread discussion of Quebec's industrial backwardness, is the speed of its growth. Both provinces have enjoyed sustained increases in manufacturing production, since at least the last third of the nineteenth century.

There have, however, been profound differences between the two provinces in the very nature of their agricultural sectors, particularly in the nineteenth century. Raynauld's agricultural statistics, while not incorrect, are misleading. He estimated that over the whole period 1870–1955, and over the subperiods 1870–1934 and 1934–54, the growth rates of agricultural output in the two provinces were almost the same. He found this result, and the similar result in the other two sectors studied, to be unsurprising, since in a market economy the movement of goods, capital, and population between regions can be expected to equalize levels of development.

The theoretical problem with Raynauld's argument is that in the nineteenth century the greater part of Quebec's agricultural sector was only barely if at all connected to the market economy. His data themselves indicate a faster rate of growth in Ontario agriculture in the period 1870–1900: 0.017 per annum versus 0.013 in Quebec. The case that Quebec's agriculture was qualitatively different from Ontario's cannot be well established by comparing aggregate growth rates, however; in the remainder of this section the two sectors are examined in greater detail from the perspective of the balanced growth model.

In the first link of the model, the labor transfer process, the historical data show little appreciable difference between the two provinces; both agricultural sectors contributed to the growth of manpower in the secondary and tertiary sectors. Table 2 shows that the growth of gainfully employed in the primary sector slowed considerably in the first forty years of the twentieth century in Quebec and ceased in Ontario. Before mid-century, the number was declining in both provinces. The number of nonagricultural workers grew continuously; by the 1891 census they outnumbered agricultural workers in both provinces, and the gap has widened regularly since that time. Net migration out of agriculture began at least as early as 1881 in both provinces. The push factors were particularly important in this migration: the scarcity of good land made it ever more difficult to establish farmers' sons on new farms, and attempts at colonization of wilderness areas in both provinces in the nineteenth century met with only limited success. The rate of migration out of agriculture was usually greater in Quebec than in Ontario; this was the logical consequence of the higher rates of fertility and natural increase among the rural French Canadian population. Nathan Keyfitz has calculated that from 1871 to 1951, in a quite regular pattern, approximately one half of the farm boys coming of age in Quebec left the farm between the ages of fifteen and thirty-four.[6]

TABLE 1

Value Added in Manufacturing, Quebec and Ontario, 1870–1955

Year	Value Added (in 1,000,000 Constant 1935–39 Dollars)		Average Annual Growth Rates of Value Added		Ratio of Quebec to Ontario			
	Quebec	Ontario	Quebec	Ontario	Value Added	Value Added per Manufacturing Employee	Value Added per Labor Force Member	Value Added per Capita
1870	40.9	62.1	...	...	.658	0.867	0.955	.896
1880	58.6	93.1	.036	.040	.630	0.870	0.961	.892
1890	99.5	166.2	.053	.058	.599	0.852	0.962	.850
1900	114.8	165.5	.014	.000	.693	1.017	1.053	.918
1910	212.1	359.5	.061	.080	.590	0.891	0.886	.743
1920	245.9	389.9	.015	.008	.631	1.015	0.898	.783
1930	424.3	688.1	.055	.057	.617	0.924	0.808	.736
1940	552.5	931.9	.026	.030	.593	0.875	0.725	.674
1950	834.9	1,424.4	.041	.042	.586	0.851	0.749	.664

SOURCES: Value added, manufacturing employment, and labor force: Raynauld, *Croissance et structure économiques de la province de Québec* (Quebec: Ministère de l'industrie et du commerce, 1961), 569–70 and 597–98. Price index: M. C. Urquhart and K. A. H. Buckley, eds., *Historical Statistics of Canada* (Toronto: Macmillan of Canada, 1965), series J34. Population: Canada, *Census of Canada 1870–71*, 5 vols. (Ottawa: I. B. Taylor, 1872–78); Canada, *Census of Canada 1880–81*, 4 vols. (Ottawa: Maclean, Roger, 1882–85); Canada, *Census of Canada 1890–91*, 4 vols. (Ottawa: S. E. Dawson, 1893–97); Canada, *Fourth Census of Canada 1901*, 4 vols. (Ottawa: S. E. Dawson, 1902–6); Canada, *Fifth Census of Canada 1911*, 6 vols. (Ottawa: C. H. Parmelee, 1912–15); Canada, Dominion Bureau of Statistics, *Sixth Census of Canada 1921*, 5 vols. (Ottawa: F. A. Acland, 1924–25); Canada, Dominion Bureau of Statistics, *Seventh Census of Canada 1931*, 13 vols. (Ottawa: J. O. Patenaude, 1936–42); Canada, Dominion Bureau of Statistics, *Eighth Census of Canada 1941*, 11 vols. (Ottawa: Edmond Cloutier, 1944–50); Canada, Dominion Bureau of Statistics, *Ninth Census of Canada 1951*, 11 vols. (Ottawa: Edmond Cloutier, 1953–56).

TABLE 2

Workers Gainfully Occupied and Out-Migration, Agricultural Sectors of
Quebec and Ontario Gainfully Occupied (in 1,000s)

| | Quebec | | Ontario | | Decade Rate of Migration out of Agriculture | |
Year	Agriculture and Other Primary	Non-agriculture	Agriculture and Other Primary	Non-agriculture	Quebec	Ontario
1851	78	57	87	79	...	...
1861	108	90	134	106	...	...
1871	161	128	229	167	...	...
1881	202	159	305	232	.066	− .043
1891	217	233	345	385	.269	.129
1901	205	307	319	436	.344	.302
1911	226	427	338	653	.230	.139
1921	237	544	313	804	.189	.173
1931	256	766	335	1,011	.256	.136
1941	304	885	315	1,140	.141	.264
1951	249	1,223	245	1,640	.506	.416

SOURCES: Gainfully occupied: censuses of Canada. Migration rates: for Quebec calculated from data in Keyfitz; for Ontario calculated by author using Keyfitz's method no. 2.

There is not a precise correspondence between migration out of agriculture and into nonagricultural activities, because of the high level of international migration Canada has experienced during most periods. There was net emigration out of Canada during the last four decades of the nineteenth century; many of the young people who left rural Quebec and Ontario journeyed, not to Montreal or Toronto, but to New England or Chicago.

Nevertheless it is clear from the gross data that the agricultural sector made a major contribution to the nonagricultural labor force, as it has in most industrializing countries. Most important to the interpretation advanced in this essay, there was no substantial difference in the labor transfer process between the two provinces.

The striking contrast between the two provinces lies in the area of the second link, the commodity exchange process. In both provinces, the great majority of farmers have produced a mixture of products, almost exclusively food and feed.[7] In order to engage in exchange relationships outside the agricultural sector, such farmers must produce a surplus of food over and above their own family requirements. Production of surplus food for exchange has been a prime characteristic of Ontario farms since the earliest days of settlement — but it has been an attribute of the average Quebec farm only in the twentieth century.

Table 3 contains estimates of food production, expressed in terms of calorie or energy equivalents, from 1850 to 1970. The construction of table 3 is described fully in the appendix. The use of calories rather than prices as a common denominator has the advantage that, since the caloric requirements of human

TABLE 3

Food Production, in Millions of Calories per Day, Quebec and Ontario, 1850–1970

Year	(1) Calories Produced		(2) Requirements of Farm Population		(3) Farm Rate of Surplus Production [(1) − (2)] ÷ (2)		(4) Requirements of Provincial Population		(5) Provincial Rate of Surplus Production [(1) − (4)] ÷ (4)	
	Quebec	Ontario	Quebec	Ontario	Quebec	Ontario	Quebec	Ontario	Quebec	Ontario
1850	1,311	3,511	1,710	1,586	−0.2	1.2	2,289	2,488	−0.4	0.4
1860	1,897	6,939	1,866	2,094	0.0	2.3	2,858	3,648	−0.3	0.9
1870	2,133	5,623	2,108	2,734	0.0	1.1	3,063	4,235	−0.3	0.3
1880	2,360	9,158	2,461	3,132	0.0	1.9	3,492	5,035	−0.3	0.8
1890	2,410	8,859	2,588	3,107	−0.1	1.9	3,843	5,614	−0.4	0.6
1900	3,237	11,621	2,501	2,772	0.3	3.2	4,274	5,864	−0.2	1.0
1910	4,585	10,498	2,672	2,732	0.7	2.8	5,193	6,820	−0.1	0.5
1920	5,874	9,601	2,281	2,378	1.6	3.0	6,143	7,886	0.0	0.2
1930	4,210	9,592	2,000	2,157	1.1	3.5	7,563	9,332	−0.4	0.0
1940	4,656	12,113	2,193	1,920	1.1	5.3	8,941	10,465	−0.5	0.2
1950	5,080	11,757	2,020	1,875	1.5	5.3	10,658	12,420	−0.5	−0.1
1960	5,923	11,503	1,517	1,400	2.9	7.2	13,837	16,585	−0.6	−0.3
1970	7,116	13,247	905	1,045	6.7	11.7	16,411	20,983	−0.6	−0.4

populations are known within broad limits, the aggregate surplus or deficit of food production relative to those requirements can be estimated.

The contrast in the food production performance of the two provinces is evident from column 1. Production was greater in Ontario than in Quebec by a factor of three or four in the nineteenth century, and about two in the twentieth. These are much greater differences than can be accounted for by the somewhat larger size of the agricultural labor force in Ontario shown in table 2.

The food requirements of the farm population in column 2 were calculated on the assumption that the average adult consumed 3,000 calories per day (3,500 for men, 2,500 for women) and that the average child ten years of age or less consumed half this amount. These standards are somewhat higher than the FAO allowances for the "reference" man and woman, namely, 3,200 and 2,300 calories per day, respectively.[8] The FAO reference man and woman are, however, engaged in occupations which require standing but only occasional hard work. Durnin and Passmore estimate that male farmers in Scotland use 3,550 calories of energy per day, and female bakery workers 2,510 calories. These seem to be the appropriate levels to use for Canadian farmers and their wives.

Column 3 indicates the rate of surplus food production on farms, over and above family requirements. When positive, this may be thought of as the number of nonfarm families whose food requirements can be met by a single farm family. It is in column 3 that the contrast between the two provinces becomes clearest. From the time of the earliest reliable census data, in 1850, Ontario farmers were producing and selling a sizeable surplus. Throughout the nineteenth century, they were sufficiently productive to support from one to two nonfarm families in addition to their own — and in the twentieth century their productivity increased far beyond these levels.

In Quebec, on the other hand, there was very little surplus food available for sale on the market in the nineteenth century. Before 1900 the surplus rate hovered around zero and appears upon occasion to have been negative. The column 3 figures are averages, and doubtless conceal some diversity. It is known, for example, that some farmers, especially those of English and Scottish descent in the Eastern Townships and in the vicinity of Montreal, did produce surplus food for sale in urban markets.[9] The rate of surplus food production was calculated, for 1860 and 1870, in seven Eastern Township counties with concentrations of English-speaking descendants of the United Empire Loyalists, namely, the counties of Brome, Compton, Missisquoi, Richmond, Shefford, Sherbrooke, and Stanstead. The surplus rate, of 0.3 in both years, was positive and higher than Quebec's average, although not as high as Ontario's. To offset such pockets of surplus production, the nutritional standards on many Quebec farms may have been less than ideal. The populations of most present-day Third-World countries subsist on significantly fewer than 3,000 calories per person per day, even when deductions are made for the lesser needs of children: in 1964–66, average per capita consumption was 3,043 calories in developed countries and 2,097 calories in less developed countries.[10] It is quite possible, therefore, that surplus production on some Quebec farms was balanced by a certain amount of hunger, malnutrition, excess infant mortality, weight and height shortfalls, and the like. A similar explanation can be made of the negative average surplus rates in column 3; they indicate, not that Quebec farms were purchasing food, but that the nutritional standards of the average Quebec farm family were inadequate, at least in the light of modern norms.

Part of the difference in the ability of the Quebec and Ontario farms to produce a surplus is accounted for by the size of the average farm family in the two provinces. The French Canadian birthrate was significantly higher than the English Canadian in the nineteenth century, and until quite recent years it fell more slowly. As a result, in the mid-nineteenth century, the average size of a farm family was 7.1 in Quebec and 6.2 in Ontario.[11] Family sizes fell in both provinces to the 1930s, rose in the postwar baby boom, and fell again thereafter. Throughout the period the differential was maintained and even widened; in 1971 farm family-sizes were 5.5 in Quebec and 4.1 in Ontario. The effect of the family-size differences on the surplus-producing abilities of the two farm sectors was fairly small in the nineteenth century and greater in the twentieth. Quebec's farm food requirements in column 2 were recalculated, assuming Quebec's farm families to be the same size as Ontario's. Under the extreme assumption that if Quebec farms had had fewer children only consumption and not production would have been reduced, hypothetical surplus rates were calculated. According to these calculations, which are biased in the direction of indicating a larger than accurate effect of family size, the gap between the Ontario and Quebec surplus rates of column 3 would have been reduced by 5–10 percent in the nineteenth century and by an average of about 33 percent in the twentieth century.

The greater part of Ontario's superior performance, particularly in the nineteenth century, is to be explained therefore in terms of its higher productivity per farm. Table 4 contains estimates of calories produced per day per farm in the two provinces. In the nineteenth century Ontario farms were about two-and-one-half times as productive as Quebec farms; in the twentieth century the differential decreased. Particularly important in the nineteenth century was the superior performance of the Ontario farms in the field crops, principally wheat and potatoes. Lower Canadian[12] farmers had concentrated upon wheat, but the ravages of wheat midge and rust were severe in the province; by 1850 Lower Canadian wheat producers were in very serious difficulty and were forced to turn in subsequent years to other grains and to dairy and meat products.[13] While the wheat midge caused damage in Upper Canada also, the consequences were not nearly as serious there.[14] Farm productivity was least divergent in dairy products: Ontario's productivity exceeded Quebec's by only about 50 percent in the nineteenth century, while in the twentieth century the provinces were roughly even. In the last half of the nineteenth century, the dairy industry was responsible for the greater part of the increase in Ontario's farm productivity and for almost all of the increase in Quebec's. The contrast is that, while in Ontario dairy products and meat were added to a substantial base of field crops, in Quebec dairy products substituted for a level of crop production which was inadequate for domestic needs. In Ontario crop production alone would have provided a farm surplus; in Quebec it would not.

Column 3 of table 3 indicates, in sum, that Quebec's agricultural sector must

TABLE 4

Food Production per Farm, in Thousands of Calories per Day, Quebec and Ontario, 1850–1970

Year	Total		Grain and Potatoes		Meat		Poultry and Eggs		Dairy Products		Fruit, Vegetables, and Others	
	Quebec	Ontario	Quebec	Ontario	Quebec	Ontario	Quebec	Ontario	Quebec	Ontario	Quebec	Ontario
1850	13.7	35.1	8.8	26.2	2.9	5.6	0.1	0.1	1.6	2.7	0.3	0.6
1860	18.0	52.6	11.8	42.5	3.2	5.8	0.1	0.2	2.3	3.3	0.4	0.9
1870	18.1	32.6	10.9	22.5	3.4	5.4	0.2	0.3	3.1	3.4	0.5	1.0
1880	17.1	44.2	9.3	31.7	2.9	5.0	0.2	0.4	4.0	5.6	0.7	1.6
1890	16.6	41.0	7.6	26.1	3.1	6.8	0.3	0.5	4.8	6.6	0.8	0.9
1900	23.1	57.0	8.9	35.2	3.9	9.2	0.4	0.7	9.1	9.7	0.9	2.1
1910	30.6	49.5	12.0	25.1	6.4	12.4	0.4	0.8	10.9	9.9	0.9	1.5
1920	42.7	48.5	25.2	25.0	5.9	10.4	0.4	0.7	10.4	10.5	0.8	2.0
1930	31.0	49.9	11.1	25.1	5.9	9.8	0.6	1.2	12.7	12.3	0.8	1.5
1940	30.1	68.0	7.3	30.2	8.5	19.0	0.9	1.9	17.5	14.9	0.9	2.0
1950	37.8	78.4	6.0	32.2	11.7	21.8	1.3	3.0	17.3	18.6	1.5	2.9
1960	61.9	94.8	8.2	27.0	16.5	28.4	2.6	5.7	31.7	28.1	2.9	5.5
1970	116.2	139.9	12.5	37.2	32.2	47.9	8.7	8.8	56.8	37.9	6.0	8.1

have been very different from Ontario's in the nineteenth century. It produced little surplus food and can therefore have made little contribution to urban non-agricultural production through the provision of food or the purchase of industrial output. It was for the most part a subsistence sector, economically isolated, not integrated into the wider market system. Ontario's agriculture, on the other hand, possessed the capability to make an important contribution to balanced economic development. In the first half of the twentieth century Quebec's agricultural sector began to produce a surplus, and by mid-century the data in table 3 indicate that the sector had been transformed.

The contrast between Ontario and Quebec farm productivity in the nineteenth century is attributable largely to cultural differences. Differences in the natural resource endowments of the two areas — in soil and climate, for example — probably did leave the Quebec farmers at some disadvantage. The disadvantage was relatively modest, however: the most recent data in table 4 show that with the use of advanced technology Quebec farms were able to pull within 20 percent of the productivity of Ontario farms. The much greater gap in the nineteenth century was the result of a different culture, a different attitude toward the farming life. The Quebec *habitant* was a peasant, poor and self-sufficient, not a man of business. To assert that cultural rather than natural-resource differences were the principal cause of the gap in productivity is to make no judgment about inferiority in any broader sense or about inherent characteristics. In many human ways the French Canadian rural culture was more attractive than the English Canadian. Furthermore, there is reason to presume that English-speaking authorities, both public and private, bear some responsibility for having encouraged and supported the distinctively French Canadian way of life.

By the middle of the twentieth century, however, the French Canadian peasant had become a commercial farmer, somewhat less productive and prosperous than his Ontario colleague, but clearly engaged in the same type of business. That the transformation eventually occurred is perhaps not surprising. More noteworthy, in the North American context, is that it occurred so late, well after other sectors of the Quebec economy had grown and modernized.

It is axiomatic that an agricultural sector such as Quebec's, which produced little surplus food in the nineteenth century, could contribute little to the foreign exchange earnings of the economy. Ontario's agriculture could and did. Settlers in Upper Canada in the early part of the century shipped cereals through Lower Canadian ports to England; by 1850 the wheat trade had reached such proportions as to be appropriately referred to as a staple.[15] By mid-century the growth of United States cities began to establish an important new market, in particular for dairy products and meat. While the English-speaking farmers of Quebec's Eastern Townships participated in the trade with the United States, the principal beneficiaries were the Ontario farmers. The Ontario agricultural sector also competed for the urban markets of Quebec, along with local and American producers.

It has not been possible to develop very precise statistical indicators of the magnitude of agricultural exports from the two provinces in the nineteenth century. Series of exports from Canada by province do exist;[16] they indicate, however, the province from which the goods were finally exported, not in which they were produced. Since a high proportion of Ontario's exports was shipped to

Europe via Montreal, these data overestimate Quebec's exports at the expense of Ontario's. Furthermore, there are no available series for interprovincial trade, which in the case of Quebec and Ontario was probably quite significant.

Table 3 does contain data which may be interpreted as the minimal requirements for agricultural trade in the two provinces. The column 4 calorie requirements of the total population have been calculated on the same basis as the column 2 farm sector requirements. Column 5 shows the proportion by which provincial food production fell short of or exceeded total provincial requirements. In the most recent decades of the twentieth century, both provinces were in a deficit position; relatively highly specialized in urban industrial and tertiary activities, they imported much of their food from the western provinces and from abroad. In the nineteenth and early twentieth centuries, however, their positions were not similar: Quebec was always in deficit while Ontario produced a surplus. Until the end of the century, Quebec produced only 60–70 percent of her requirements, with the result that at least the remainder and probably more (since there were some known exports) had to be imported. Even when the province was in the very earliest stages of industrialization, therefore, its food sector was a net user, not provider, of foreign exchange. By contrast, in the nineteenth century Ontario farms consistently produced a surplus over and above the requirements of the provincial population. The surplus fluctuated but was generally quite large; it declined only as the great wheat-producing prairies in the west were settled and brought into production after the turn of the century. Until that time, the agricultural sector provided Ontario with a large and important source of foreign exchange.

Aggregate agricultural data have been used in this section to challenge what is at least an implication of Raynauld's presentation, also based upon aggregate data, that the two farming sectors were fundamentally alike. The position argued here is consistent, however, with the views of a considerable number of previous writers whose findings were based upon archival research or contemporary reports. For example, Fowke's careful study of the history of Canadian agricultural policy insists upon the contrast; from the settlement of the first Loyalists, Upper Canada was a commercial exporting region, while French Canadian farmers at that time and after were self-sufficient. Expansion of English Canadian settlement constituted a frontier for investment by the manufacturing and transport sectors, claimed Fowke, while expansion of French Canadian settlement did not. The primitive nature and poverty of nineteenth-century French Canadian agriculture was documented particularly fully by R.L. Jones. "In the 1850's," he wrote, "the defects of French Canadian farming were what they had long been — poor preparation of the soil, little or no fertilizing, no crop rotation, no clearing out of weeds by hoed crops or even by summer fallowing, no underdraining, and defective care of livestock."[17] Travelers in the 1870s and 1880s reported much the same: farm implements, methods, and knowledge were primitive. Many sociologists have noted and described the subsistence, self-sufficient peasant society typical of rural Quebec in the late nineteenth century.[18] It is true that the principal agricultural chapter in Jean Hamelin and Yves Roby's major study of the Quebec economy 1851–96 concentrates upon the changes in farming, for example, the development of the dairy industry.[19] The authors readily admit, however, that agricultural progress was difficult and that it is often not possible to generalize from specific instances of change and innovation. They are most persuasive in documenting that some structural changes were occurring throughout the latter half of the century and that by the end of the century a genuine transformation in the mode of farming was underway — both assertions being compatible with the data of tables 3 and 4. In Ontario, on the other hand, the literature reports that the agricultural methods were those common to the farmers of New England, New York, and the Old West. The Ontario farmers produced for sale, and their production choices were informed by market signals.[20] Mechanization began early in the nineteenth century and continued apace, with particularly rapid changes in the 1850s. Increasingly sophisticated inventions were applied to all aspects of farming — mechanical reapers, binders, threshers with separators, grain drills, disc harrows, steam tractors, cream separators, and many more, as the farm implements industry developed and equipment prices fell.

The contribution of this section is therefore antirevisionist — it shows that aggregate comprehensive data confirm rather than deny the findings of researchers using less quantitative methods. In brief, Ontario's experience of economic development is a classic example of the balanced growth doctrine, with a vigorous commercial agricultural sector providing manpower, food, markets, and foreign exchange for even more vigorously expanding nonagricultural sectors. Quebec's experience was quite different. The rural-urban labor migration permits one to call the Quebec geographical area an economy, but in the nineteenth century it was a singularly unintegrated one. The agricultural sector contributed little in the way of market stimulation to the growth of urban industry. Quebec's agricultural backwardness may bear some responsibility for the small lag in her manufacturing production behind Ontario's;[21] of greater interest is the fact that it had such little retarding effect. Quebec's urban industrial sector grew rapidly, but without the support and reinforcement of its agricultural sector in the nineteenth century and with lower levels of such support than Ontario received in the twentieth.

Quebec's industrial sector developed in the early years as a quasi-enclave, seeking markets in Ontario and in the United States and importing food for its workers. In a large country, such a pattern might have produced bottlenecks, with subsequent inflation or stagnation — as the Latin American structuralist school has argued. In a relatively small region, and especially in one which was surrounded by productive, commercial agriculture, there was no such effect. The composition of the industrial sector was affected, but the rate of growth was hardly influenced. Quebec has simply specialized in those goods for which she has had a comparative advantage given national tariff policies. In the mid-twentieth century these were primarily resource-intensive industries, such as pulp and paper and lumber, and what Dales calls "cheap labor" industries, such as textiles and tobacco. Interestingly but unsurprisingly, Quebec's agricultural implements industry was almost nonexistent. Ontario, in comparison, concentrated on heavy production, capital equipment, and consumer durables.[22]

Implications of the Different Growth Pattern

The strictly economic consequences of Quebec's agricultural lag were less serious than might be expected from a naïve reading of the theory of balanced growth. As Alexander Gershenkron has convincingly demonstrated, there are few immutable preconditions to industrialization: the absence in country B of what appeared to be a precondition in country A may call for innovation and substitution, but need not relegate country B to stagnation. This is not to say that the consequences were negligible in a context broader than the strictly economic — for as Gershenkron also has shown, different paths to industrialization may imply differences of great significance in social structure and ideology.[23] It is these broader implications that this section explores — tentatively, with no pretense of providing proof.

Among the many differences between Ontario and Quebec societies, there have been at least two whose origins may be traced in large measure to their respective agricultural sectors. First has been the pronounced ethnic stratification in Quebec industry, with English speakers in the controlling positions and French speakers in the work force.[24] Second has been the weaker commitment in Quebec than in Ontario to democratic governance and civil liberties.

It was natural that Quebec's enclave-type industrial sector should be guided, in its entrepreneurship and management, by an elite with strong external ties. This elite was English speaking: at the beginning an outpost of the British empire, but by the 1920s a mixed group including a large proportion of United States capitalists and managers. United States capital invaded Ontario too, of course, but there it confronted an indigenous elite. The causes of the ethnic stratification in Quebec industry are manifold[25] — they include positive discrimination on the part of English-speaking managers, as well as the ascendant place of the English language in the North American business world. Not until the 1960s, however, did French Canadians begin seriously to challenge the inferiority of the positions to which they had been consigned. This delay was associated, in large measure, with the slow development of the agricultural sector. The low level of agricultural productivity implied a weak domestic market, and therefore knowledge of provincial conditions was of less importance in Quebec than in Ontario. The relative poverty of such a large mass of residents made it more difficult for Quebec financial institutions to generate sufficient capital to exert more control.

Most important was the perpetuation of a noncommercial value structure among a substantial majority of Quebec's population. There are frequent references in the literature to the conflict between rural and urban values in Quebec,[26] but more revealing labels for the dichotomy would be traditional-modern or subsistence-commercial. The alleged conflict between rural and urban values is much less noted in Ontario than in Quebec, and for good reason: the secular, market-oriented commercialism of the Ontario farmer posed little handicap when he or his children attempted to move up the urban social ladder. The problem for the *Québécois* was not his farming background per se, but his unfamiliarity with and at times profound mistrust of the market mechanism and modern technology. In a revealing series of interviews with French- and English-speaking industrial entrepreneurs in Quebec in the 1950s, Norman W. Taylor found that the French Canadians tended to accord less prestige to a career in business than did the English, that their policies were more oriented toward security, conservatism, paternalism, and the family, and that they were reluctant to expand or to commit themselves fully to the market.[27] These attitudes, which certainly handicapped the growth of French Canadian businesses and the rise of French Canadians through corporate hierarchies, are similar to the values in the traditional rural communities. The structure which reinforced them was to a large extent the same in both countryside and city — the church.

For centuries, the church was the leading institution in the Quebec countryside and the clergy the principal elite group. Although the land tenure system was formally feudal during the French regime and under British rule until 1854, the *seigneurs* were generally men of modest means and did not constitute an important rural upper class. The central social unit was the parish, not the *seigneurie*. The status and authority of the church was consciously buttressed by the British administration after the conquest of 1759 in a largely successful attempt to secure the loyalty of the population.

A major paradox of Quebec's modern history is that the old rural elite, the clergy, were not displaced but instead were strengthened during the province's massive industrialization. The clergy were quick to grasp the rules for survival in the modern world. They came to a tacit understanding with the English-speaking capitalists; in return for the provision of jobs required by their flock, they assured the stability of labor markets, combating industrial unionism and socialist ideology which would have been as disruptive to their own positions of authority as to corporate profits. The church provided for the whole range of necessary urban services, including youth groups, co-operatives, unions, hospitals, and, most importantly, schools. It thus retarded the development of secular values and generated a professional class whose loyalty was assured.[28]

The 1960s witnessed a revolt of the urban *Québécois* against clerical authority, this revolt constituting part of the larger change in values and attitudes which has been labeled the "quiet revolution." Again, the existence of such a revolt in an industrialized society is not surprising; what requires explanation is why it was delayed so long, why generations of Quebec workers were willing to accept the pact between capital and clergy. The clue is likely to be found back in the rural parishes, where their world views had been formed over centuries. There was nothing inconsistent in the rural parish between the conservative moral precepts of the church and the requirements of daily life. The subsistence peasant, largely isolated from the technological world, existing close to the margin of life, was almost required to be conservative and to respect his traditions if he was to survive. The daily work routines, the hierarchy of the family, the teachings of the church, and the practical advice of the *curé* together formed a culture of strength and integrity, a culture whose material foundation was hardly challenged until the twentieth century. "The life of the peasant," wrote A.R.M. Lower of the French Canadian,

> is a series of ritual occasions, planting and harvesting, being born, coming of age, begetting, dying. . . . All are one family, interrelated if not in this

generation, in the last or the next. All give unquestioned obedience to the great mother goddess, the earth-mother, who can easily be made to wear a Christian dress. . . . His religion is among the simplest and oldest of all creeds, Catholic almost by accident.[29]

Cultures change as material requirements change, but not quickly, automatically, or painlessly. For perhaps several generations the urban migrant would work in the factories, but he would respect his *curé* and would not easily adapt to the mores of commercial, individualist America.[30] To the stability of the traditional rural sector, therefore, can be attributed much of the failure of French Canadian city dwellers to attempt to rise to the heights of their technological society.

"Historically, French Canadians have not really believed in democracy for themselves," wrote Pierre Elliott Trudeau in 1958, "and English Canadians have not really wanted it for others." Trudeau argued that when the French Canadians were accorded some representative institutions by the British in 1791 they had no preparation for them: New France had been an authoritarian, paternal society. In consequence, French Canadians learned to use representative institutions only as weapons, to protect their nationality and to ensure their survival, but they developed no real belief in them as a way of life. The clergy denied the relevance of democracy and self-determination for the French Canadian people and actively opposed the radical, democratic *rouge* tendencies in the nineteenth century. The results were a cynical, make-believe attitude toward democratic politics and a lack of concern for civil liberties. Only in such a political climate could the regime of Maurice Duplessis (1936–39 and 1944–60) have survived.[31]

The English Canadian political tradition is quite different. Writers whose concern has been to illuminate the differences between English Canadian and American politics have stressed the persistent tory and monarchical components in English Canadian society and consequently the slower and less complete acceptance of individualistic liberal democratic politics north of the border.[32] The distinction is valid, and yet a vast gap remains between the predominant French and English Canadian conceptions of politics. Although in English Canada liberal democracy has confronted and continues to confront more organic, communal conceptions of society, from both right and left, nevertheless it has emerged victorious. English Canadian politics, especially in Ontario where socialism has been relatively weak, have been predominantly if not exclusively bourgeois and liberal. The tory oligarchy of the first half of the nineteenth century, the Family Compact, was defeated by the reform movement for responsible government. That defeat has been permanent, if not total — and not even the post-Confederation Conservative tradition of Sir John A. Macdonald challenged the ultimately democratic nature of its mandate.

A remarkable feature of French Canadian political culture has been the relative absence (until recently) of change. In order to explain the politics of the 1950s, Trudeau ranged back to 1763, 1791, 1837, and 1917, citing those dates not as important turning points in the evolution of a doctrine, but rather as exemplary illustrations of an unchanged attitude. Louis Hartz claimed that this phenomenon of continuity is not exceptional at all, but rather is typical of new societies founded by European settlers. In his view, European social change produced fundamental struggles between classes and ideologies—but the new societies (the United States, Latin America, Australia, South Africa, and Canada) were settled merely by "fragments" of the full European society. Each fragment was relatively homogeneous—removed from the turbulence of European struggle it was permitted to grow, but was not required to change in any important way because it confronted no significant opposing ideology.[33]

Hartz's "consensus" thesis is controversial, and its applicability in English Canada and other areas has been effectively questioned by Horowitz. In the case of French Canada, however, the thesis is most suggestive: that French Canada was an authoritarian fragment, formed directly (after 1663) by the *ancien régime* monarchy and essentially unchallenged until the most recent decades.[34] And yet the paradox in such an interpretation is immediately apparent, for French Canada has been engaged in continuous struggle since the conquest of 1759. Surrounded by alien rulers and hostile philosophies, and eventually constituting merely a minority of the population in a diverse country, French Canada's fight has been for survival itself. In the southern United States, another conflict between competing ways of life resulted in a violent explosion. In French Canada there was no such battle. The conflict was confined for the most part to the boundaries of the society, where it could be engaged in by politicians, leaving the political and cultural mores of the people barely affected. Such issues as the hanging of Louis Riel in 1885 and the conscription crises of the two world wars touched the spirit and emotions of French Canadians, but not their way of life. Although French-speaking minorities outside Quebec had to be abandoned to assimilation, the majority, inside the province, was protected. To what shall this success be ascribed?

The question is not an easy one, but fundamental to the answer, I would argue, lies the agricultural sector, the one sector that was isolated and protected from struggle for so long. In the rural parish there was little to confront the authority structure of the family and the church, no fertile ground of economic innovation from which could spring challengers to the old elite, fighting to break the fetters of tradition and secure the forms of liberty. No new class of entrepreneurs was spawned to embrace and embody the doctrines of individual freedom. Although the agricultural sector became a minority of the population by the end of the nineteenth century, it remained at the core, constantly sending its off-spring to the cities and, not incidentally, retaining a majority of the seats of the legislative assembly until well into the twentieth century. The urban capitalists, on their part, had no incentive to challenge the exercise of arbitrary authority, for as shown above they benefited materially from the perpetuation of the rural political culture.

It would be a mistake to identify the achievement of democratic government in Ontario and English Canada exclusively with the victory of a single sector or class. Most Upper Canadian farmers did not join William Lyon Mackenzie's abortive rebellion against the Family Compact in 1837, and even the later, more moderate reformers could not count upon the automatic allegiance of the agrarian sector. Nevertheless it is clear that farmers provided the most important center of support for a liberal political system in the nineteenth century. In the first half of the century, the Family Compact oligarchy were primarily men of commerce whose fortunes, however elusive, were thought to depend upon securing for the

St. Lawrence system the trade of the United States' hinterland. Their interests were usually hostile to those of the farmers, who sought protection from the Americans, and this conflict of interest constituted an important basis for political competition. In the second half of the century, when the vision of an empire of the St. Lawrence had been dissolved, capital was increasingly directed to manufacturing and to the exploitation and processing of natural resources. The resource industries sought the services and protection of the provincial government, in a perpetuation of the tory tradition and to the detriment of democratic accountability.[35] In this context as well, the farmers favored liberal democracy, although their commitments to the Crown and to established authority were such as to prevent any unanimous or radical political expression. In short, the small-scale, commercial, innovative Ontario farmer was in large part, although not exclusively, responsible for the achievement of political democracy, an achievement less spectacular than in the United States, but far more secure than in Quebec.

The association between agricultural traditionalism and political reaction, on the one hand, and between agricultural transformation and democracy, on the other, is the theme of Barrington Moore's seminal work, *The Social Origins of Dictatorship and Democracy;*[36] the Quebec-Ontario comparison casts some interesting light upon this theme. Moore argued that the transformation from feudal to commercial agriculture in England was bloody and violent, but that it was the necessary prerequisite for peaceful and democratic social and economic change. It destroyed the traditional authority structure by fatally weakening the power of the landed aristocracy. The bourgeoisie and commercial farmers fought to secure civil liberties and political rights for themselves, over and against the Crown, the aristocracy, and the peasantry — and in so doing they in fact created the very structure of liberal democracy which was later expanded with the franchise. In contrast, in Germany and Japan the agricultural aristocracy was not overthrown: the traditional rural elites themselves directed and controlled the great increases in agricultural productivity which supported industrial development. There was no crisis in the German agricultural sector; rather, the traditional authorities retained and supported the rural social structure, expropriated its surplus, and used that surplus to industrialize and enhance their own power. The price to be paid for avoiding the violent transformation of rural society was therefore fascism.

Moore restricted his attention to large countries — but in some ways Ontario is similar to his English example, and Quebec to his German-Japanese. Ontario knew no violent rural revolution, of course, but its farmers were the descendants of the revolutionaries of a different time and place, the English Puritans, and in a muted way they recreated that revolutionary movement in their struggle for responsible government. Quebec's agriculture was similar to Germany's in that there was little change in its social structure until recently. One contrast is that Germany's agricultural productivity grew substantially in the late nineteenth century, while Quebec's farm output was stagnant at close to a subsistence level. While such stagnation would likely have prevented the economic development of a large country, in Quebec it had no such effect. That being the case, the effects of rural traditionalism upon political culture in the two societies bear some similarity. The patterns are not identical: in Quebec the traditional authorities merely collaborated with the new capitalists, while in Germany the industrialists were a part of the old power structure. Nevertheless, in both cases the old elites were freed from constraints and strengthened by industrialization because no rival agrarian groups arose to challenge them effectively. While it would be a libel to call Quebec's politics fascist without qualification during the period when the world experienced extreme fascism, there were some disturbing similarities, among them the contempt shown by the governing party for electoral procedures and for the decorum of the legislative assembly, a movement for corporatism as a mode of industrial organization, considerable racial chauvinism and romanticism, a certain degree of anti-Semitism and impatience with civil liberties, and some sympathy for the Axis powers. In 1933 the editors of *Canadian Forum* wrote, "It is becoming increasingly clear that Quebec, with the open connivance and approval of the government of that province, is openly becoming a center of Fascist infection and of the blackest kind of reaction."[37] If the Quebec population had not been a minority in a country whose majority was more committed to democratic governance and individual liberties, the tendencies toward fascism might have progressed further.

This essay argues, therefore, that Quebec's rural sector was qualitatively different from Ontario's in the nineteenth century. While the latter was a commercial farming sector, the former was a subsistence peasant sector which was slowly transformed only in the twentieth century. Contrary to what might be expected from the balanced-growth literature, this difference did not seriously impede the growth of Quebec's nonagricultural manufacturing industries. Quebec's manufacturing found an alternate path of developing in its early years, exporting much of its output and importing food staples. The existence of a subsistence agricultural sector did have important effects on the general development of Quebec's society, however. On the one hand it was a unique cultural system, a system which imparted a strong and cherished world view to its participants and which for many other French Canadians offered a memory, a symbol, and at times even a program. On the other hand it so skewed the development of modern industrial society in Quebec that traditional elites were reinforced rather than replaced, a class structure external to French Canada came to dominate the urban proletariat, and a pattern of authoritarian undemocratic politics was prolonged. In Ontario, balanced economic development proved to be consistent with the balanced development of a predominantly liberal society. Commercial farming helped to create and reinforce values, social relationships, and politics that supported a pattern of free-enterprise industrial capitalism.

The eventual transformation of Quebec's agricultural sector may have had an important influence upon the timing of her quiet revolution. Horowitz has argued that the existence of a genuine conservative tradition in English Canada in a sense encouraged the growth of a socialist movement, with the result that the political spectrum is broader in English Canada than in the United States. If so, then a much broader spectrum can be expected, and indeed already recognized, in Quebec, as that province's agricultural sector undergoes a real transformation with genuine struggle between classes and ideologies representing very different ways of life.

Appendix

The appendix reports, in sufficient detail to allow replication, the procedures by which tables 3 and 4 were constructed. In order to fill some gaps in the coverage of the agricultural censuses, frequent advantage was taken of research done on the agricultural sector of the United States by Strauss and Bean and by Towne and Rasmussen.[38]

Grains and Potatoes[39]

(a) Wheat: Following Strauss and Bean, it was assumed that 85.5 percent of the wheat crop was available for human consumption, the remainder being used for feed and seed. (b) Potatoes: The Strauss and Bean ratio of 83 percent available for human consumption was used. (c) Coarse grains: Some are directly consumed in one form or another by humans. The 1861 census of manufacturing shows that about 1 percent of the oats crop was delivered to oatmeal factories. This proportion was doubled, to 2 percent, to account for home use; throughout the whole period, therefore, it was assumed that 1 pound per bushel of oats was used for human consumption. Based on the Strauss and Bean estimates it was assumed that 20 percent, or 10 pounds per bushel, of barley was used for conversion to spirits for human use. For peas and beans a ratio of 25 percent was used. Corn for human use was counted as a vegetable.

Meat[40]

(a) Beef and veal: On the basis of slaughter-to-stock-in-following-year ratios in subsequent censuses, a ratio of 0.20 was assumed for 1850 and 1860, in both provinces. The 1921 calves-to-total-cattle-sold-or-slaughtered ratio of 0.47 was used in the earlier censuses in both provinces.

From 1920 to 1960, there was almost no change in the average cold-dressed weight of beef cattle and of veal calves in Canada: 500 pounds and 100 pounds, respectively.[41] Strauss and Bean suggest that there was no change in the average live weight of beef cattle in the United States from 1870 to 1930. It was assumed, therefore, that the dressed weights were constant throughout the whole period in Canada. There is evidence, however, of a weight differential by province. Table 5 gives the ratio of the Ontario value per head to the Quebec value per head in various groups of years. Such persistent differentials can likely be accounted for only by supply factors, in particular differences in weights. A constant differential of 25 percent was assumed: 550 pounds for cattle and 110 pounds for calves in Ontario, 440 pounds and 88 pounds, respectively, in Quebec. (b) Mutton: Ratios of 0.55 in Ontario and 0.45 in Quebec were used in 1850 and 1860. The average dressed weight per slaughter in the twentieth century was 54 pounds.[42] From table 5 a 25 percent differential by province was assumed: 47 pounds in Ontario and 38 pounds in Quebec. (c) Pork: The assumed slaughter ratio was 0.9 in both provinces in 1850 and 1860. The average weight per slaughter is 130 pounds[43] with no differential by province.

TABLE 5

Value per Head of Livestock: Ratio of Ontario to Quebec,
1868–1965

Years	Cattle	Sheep	Pigs
1868–99	1.30	1.15	0.98
1920	1.48	1.33	1.01
1908–15	1.26	1.28	0.97
1916–25	1.24	1.27	0.90
1926–35	1.22	1.25	0.86
1936–45	1.21	1.32	0.99
1946–55	1.26	1.34	1.08
1956–65	1.28	1.37	1.11

SOURCES: 1868–89, *Sessional Papers*; 1920, *Sixth Census of Canada,
1921*; 1908–65, *Handbook of Agricultural Statistics*, 6.

Poultry and Eggs[44]

(*a*) Eggs: Production of eggs was reported first in the 1901 census, but stock of
chickens is available in 1891, so 1890 egg production could be estimated. The
estimated ratio of eggs produced to total population in 1890 was 18.4 dozen in
Ontario and 9.2 dozen in Quebec. As a guess, it was assumed that egg production
was negligible in 1840 and that there was a constant increment in production
per capita each 10 years to 1890. Eggs were evaluated at 1.5 pounds per dozen.[45] (*b*)
Poultry: Since no information is available prior to 1890, the ratio of poultry
slaughters to egg production was held constant at the 1890 level. The dressed
weight per slaughter was taken to be 4.0 pounds (somewhat higher than the
weight per chicken,[46] because turkeys, geese, and ducks are included as well).
Since poultry and eggs were only a very small part of total food production until
the most recent decades, errors in this category do not affect the overall results
greatly.

Dairy Products[47]

Separate estimates are made for fluid milk, butter, and cheese production. Statistics Canada estimates that 23.4 pounds of milk convert to 1 pound of butter; for
cheese the conversion factor is 11.2. For the years 1920 to 1970 the same
procedures were used. Data are available by province for total milk produced on
farms and butter and cheese produced in factories. Using the conversion factors,
these yield estimates of milk available for fluid use, feed, butter and cheese
production on farms, and other manufactured uses. Estimates of allocation of
milk among these latter uses are available only for the country as a whole; these
ratios were used for Ontario and Quebec.

Prior to 1920 the available information is less complete. Extrapolating from
the later data, it was assumed that the proportion of milk used for feed was 12
percent until 1900 and 10 percent in 1910. In the 1911 census there are figures
for the production of total milk on farms, cheese and butter on farms, and cheese

and butter in factories, by province. Using the conversion ratios, these yield a residual of fluid milk. In 1901 and prior years, there are no estimates in the census of total milk production. Strauss and Bean do show fluid milk as a proportion of total milk use in the United States from 1869. For 1910 the Canadian ratio is significantly lower than the U.S. ratio. Hence the whole series was lowered for Canada as follows: 1850, 0.50; 1860, 0.50; 1870, 0.48; 1880, 0.42; 1890, 0.38; 1900, 0.40. The 1881 and 1891 censuses of manufacturing give only the value of output in creameries and cheese factories, but in the 1901 census both physical and value figures are available. Therefore production was estimated in 1880 and 1890, deflating with the Strauss and Bean price series. In 1850, 1860, and 1870, farm production of cheese and butter is taken to be the total.

Fruits, Vegetables, and Other Products[48]

The coverage of fruits and vegetables in the official statistics has increased over time. In 1850 and 1860 only carrots were reported. In 1870 apples, grapes, and other fruits were added. In 1890 and again in 1900 coverage of fruits was expanded, and in 1920 vegetables production was first reported in detail. While these gaps are regrettable, nevertheless each commodity was produced in relatively small amounts the first time it was reported. Hence the omissions probably do not affect the totals very much, and no attempt was made to estimate the missing data. The principal other products included in this category were honey and maple sugar.

The estimates of food produced by weight were converted to calorie equivalents using U.S. Department of Agriculture tables.[49]

Census data on number of farms in each province were taken from the adjusted figures in Urquhart and Buckley,[50] with a deduction of 30,000 in Quebec in 1891.[51] The population living on farms was reported first in the 1931 census. The original census manuscripts for 1851, 1861, and 1871 are available on microfilm in the Public Archives in Canada. For each province in each year, the author drew a random sample of 150 households, the head of which was described as farmer, yeoman, *cultivateur*, or *fermier*. The average household sizes were statistically indistinguishable in successive censuses: 7.1 in Quebec and 6.2 in Ontario. From the same samples, the proportions of the farm populations under 10 years of age were 0.30 in Quebec and 0.28 in Ontario. These proportions were used in the calculation of equivalent adult consumers. In the rural Quebec population of 1921, the proportion under 10 was 0.29, only slightly less than 0.30; therefore it was assumed that the age distribution and the average farm family size in Quebec remained constant to 1911, fell slightly to 1921, and continued falling until the farm family was measured at 5.7 in the 1931 census. In rural Ontario the 1921 proportion under 10 was 0.22, significantly below 0.28 — a constant decline in proportion under 10 and in average farm family size was assumed from 1881, until the latter reached 4.2 in 1931.

Notes

1. For a provocative discussion of this contrast, see A.R.M. Lower, "Two Ways of Life: The Primary Antithesis of Canadian History," *Canadian Historical Association Report* (1943): 5-18.

2. Among many, see W. Arthur Lewis, "Economic Development with Unlimited Supplies of Labour," *Manchester School of Economic and Social Studies* 22 (May 1954): 139-91; and Bruce F. Johnston and John W. Mellor, "The Role of Agriculture in Economic Development," *American Economic Review* 51 (1961): 566-93.

3. For a survey of the literature, see René Durocher and Paul-André Linteau, *Le Retard du Québec et l'infériorité économique des Canadiens français* (Montreal: Boréal Express, 1971).

4. André Raynauld, *Croissance et structure économiques de la province de Québec* (Quebec: Ministère de l'industrie et du commerce, 1961), chap. 1.

5. A rather more detailed compilation is in Gordon W. Bertram, "Historical Statistics on Growth and Structure of Manufacturing in Canada, 1870-1957," in *Conference on Statistics 1962 and 1963*, Canadian Political Science Association (Toronto: University of Toronto Press, 1964). It differs in some respects, but not importantly.

6. Nathan Keyfitz, "Population Problems," in *French Canadian Society*, vol. 1, edited by Marcel Rioux and Yves Martin (Toronto: McClelland & Stewart, 1964).

7. Among the exceptions to this rule have been horses raised for sale, wood, and tobacco.

8. J.V.G.A. Durnin and R. Passmore, *Energy, Work and Leisure* (London: Heinemann Educational Books, 1967).

9. Robert Leslie Jones, "The Agricultural Development of Lower Canada, 1850-1867," *Agricultural History* 19 (Oct. 1945): 212-24.

10. U.S. Department of Agriculture, Economic Research Service, *The World Food Situation and Prospects to 1985*, Foreign Agricultural Economic Report no. 98 (Washington, D.C., 1975), 49.

11. See the appendix to this article.

12. Before 1867, Quebec was known as Lower Canada, Ontario as Upper Canada.

13. Jones, "The Agricultural Development of Lower Canada, 1850-1867," and "French Canadian Agriculture in the St. Lawrence Valley, 1815-1850," *Agricultural History* 16 (1942): 141-48.

14. Robert Leslie Jones, *History of Agriculture in Ontario 1613-1880* (Toronto: University of Toronto Press, 1946); Vernon C. Fowke, *Canadian Agricultural Policy, Historical Pattern* (Toronto: University of Toronto Press, 1946).

15. Fowke, ibid.

16. Canada, *Sessional Papers* (Ottawa, 1868-99).

17. Jones, "The Agricultural Development of Lower Canada, 1850-1867," 220.

18. See, for example, the papers by Gerin, Miner, Hughes, Fortin, and Guindon in Rioux and Martin, *French Canadian Society*.

19. Jean Hamelin and Yves Roby, *Histoire économique du Québec, 1851-1896* (Montreal: Fides, 1971).

20. Fowke; Jones, *History of Agriculture in Ontario, 1613-1880*; and D.A. Lawr, "The Development of Ontario Farming, 1870-1914: Patterns of Growth and Change," *Ontario History* 64 (Dec. 1972): 239-51.

21. This suggestion was made in J.H. Dales, "A Comparison of Manufacturing Industry in Quebec and Ontario, 1952," in *Canadian Dualism*, edited by Mason Wade (Toronto: University of Toronto Press, 1960), 203-21.

22. Dales, ibid.

23. Gershenkron, *Economic Backwardness in Historical Perspective* (Cambridge, Mass.: Belknap Press, 1962).

24. Non-French-speaking ownership is greatest in the mining and manufacturing sectors of Quebec and, within each sector, firms controlled by French speakers tend to be the smallest. Canada, *Report of the Royal Commission on Bilingualism and Biculturalism*, vol. 3A (Ottawa: Queen's Printer, 1969).

25. For a review of the literature, see Durocher and Linteau, *Le Retard du Québec*.

26. See, for example, many of the papers in Rioux and Martin, *French Canadian Society*.

27. Norman W. Taylor, "The French-Canadian Industrial Entrepreneur and His Social Environment," in Rioux and Martin, *French Canadian Society*.

28. This paragraph is based principally upon Hubert Guindon, "The Social Evolution of Quebec Reconsidered," *Canadian Journal of Economics and Political Science* 26 (Nov. 1960): 533–51.

29. Lower, "Two Ways of Life."

30. For a detailed account of the cultural conflicts faced by French Canadian migrants to urban industrial jobs, see Everett C. Hughes, *French Canada in Transition* (Chicago: University of Chicago Press, 1943).

31. Pierre Elliott Trudeau, "Some Obstacles to Democracy in Quebec," *Canadian Journal of Economics and Political Science* 24 (Aug. 1958): 297–311. For a similar analysis, see Herbert F. Quinn, *The Union Nationale: A Study in Quebec Nationalism* (Toronto: University of Toronto Press, 1963).

32. See, among many, A.R.M. Lower, "The Origins of Democracy in Canada," *Canadian Historical Association Report* (Ottawa: Department of Public Archives, 1930), 65–70; and G. Horowitz, "Conservatism, Liberalism, and Socialism in Canada: An Interpretation," *Canadian Journal of Economics and Political Science* 32 (May 1966): 143–71. The outstanding recent expression of conservative social and political philosophy in Canada is George P. Grant, *Lament for a Nation: The Defeat of Canadian Nationalism* (Toronto: McClelland & Stewart, 1965).

33. Louis Hartz, *The Founding of New Societies* (New York: Harcourt, Brace & World, 1964).

34. Kenneth D. McRae, "The Structure of Canadian History," in Hartz, ibid.

35. H.V. Nelles, *The Politics of Development; Forests, Mines and Hydro-electric Power in Ontario, 1849–1941* (Toronto: Macmillan of Canada, 1974).

36. Barrington Moore, Jr., *Social Origins of Dictatorship and Democracy, Lord and Peasant in the Making of the Modern World* (Boston: Beacon Press, 1966).

37. Quoted in Henry Milner and Sheilagh Hodgins Milner, *The Decolonization of Quebec: An Analysis of Left-Wing Nationalism* (Toronto: McClelland & Stewart, 1973), 125. Chapter 6 of this book contains an illuminating account of Quebec fascism in the 1930s.

38. Frederick Strauss and Louis H. Bean, *Gross Farm Income and Indices of Farm Production and Prices in the United States 1869–1937*, U.S. Department of Agriculture, Technical Bulletin no. 703 (Washington, D.C., 1940); Marvin W. Towne and Wayne D. Rasmussen, "Farm Gross Product and Gross Investment in the Nineteenth Centurys," in *Trends in the American Economy in the Nineteenth Century*, National Bureau of Economic Research, Conference on Research in Income and Wealth, vol. 24 (Princeton, N.J.: Princeton University Press, 1960).

39. Sources: 1850–1900, censuses of Canada; 1910–60, Canada, Dominion Bureau of Statistics, *Handbook of Agricultural Statistics*, pt. 1, *Field Crops 1908–63* (Ottawa: Queen's Printer, 1964); 1970, Canada, Statistics Canada, *Canadian Statistical Review* (Ottawa, 1971); Canada, Statistics Canada, *Coarse Grains Review* (Ottawa, 1971); Canada, Dominion Bureau of Statistics, *Wheat Review* (Ottawa, 1970–71).

40. Sources: 1850–1930, censuses of Canada; 1940–60, Canada, Dominion Bureau of Statistics, *Handbook of Agricultural Statistics*, pt. 6, *Livestock and Animal Products 1871–1965* (Ottawa: Queen's Printer, 1966); 1970, Canada, Statistics Canada, *Livestock and Animal Products Statistics* (Ottawa, 1971).

41. Urquhart and Buckley, *Historical Statistics*, ser. L233–L236.

42. Ibid., ser. L239–L240.

43. Ibid., ser. L237–L238.

44. Sources: 1890–1930, censuses of Canada; 1940–70, Canada, Statistics Canada, *Production of Poultry and Eggs* (Ottawa, various dates).

45. H.A. Innis, ed., *The Dairy Industry in Canada* (Toronto: Ryerson Press, 1937).

46. Urquhart and Buckley, *Historical Statistics*, ser. L241–L242.

47. Sources: 1850–1910, censuses of Canada; 1920–60, Canada, Dominion Bureau of Statistics, *Handbook of Agricultural Statistics*, pt. 7, *Dairy Statistics 1920–68* (Ottawa: Queen's Printer, 1970); 1970, Canada, Dominion Bureau of Statistics, *Dairy Statistics of Canada* (Ottawa, 1971).

48. Sources: 1850–1910, censuses of Canada; 1920–60, Canada, Dominion Bureau of Statistics, *Handbook of Agricultural Statistics*, pt. 5, *Vegetables and Fruits* (Ottawa: Queen's Printer, 1969); 1970, Canada, Statistics Canada, *Fruit and Vegetables Crop Reports* (Ottawa, 1971–72).

49. Bernice K. Watt and Annabel L. Merrill, *Composition of Foods, Raw, Processed, Prepared*, U.S. Department of Agriculture, Consumer and Food Economics Research Division, Agricultural Handbook no. 8 (Washington, D.C., 1963).

50. Urquhart and Buckley, *Historical Statistics*, ser. L2.

51. Ibid., 342.

THE MECHANIZATION OF REAPING IN NINETEENTH-CENTURY ONTARIO: A CASE STUDY OF THE PACE AND CAUSES OF THE DIFFUSION OF EMBODIED TECHNICAL CHANGE†

RICHARD POMFRET

The objective of this paper is to explain the rate of diffusion of the mechanical reaper in Ontario. The historical importance of the question lies in the relationship between reaper diffusion and a period of rapid Canadian economic development.[1] The broader intention of the work is to lend insight into the general question of the pace and the causes of the diffusion of embodied technical change. The reaper in Canada provides an especially appropriate case study for this question since the basic invention was available some thirty years before it was widely adopted. Thus it is possible to concentrate on the economic decision to innovate with an available invention rather than on isoquant shifts caused by inventions.

I

The history of mechanical reapers goes back at least to the start of the nineteenth century, but the first patents suitable for commercial production were not available until the 1830s. In the United States there was a slow, limited diffusion for twenty years, then a rapid burst of production in the 1850s. The invention was available almost as early in Canada and in the 1840s some American reapers were imported. In the late 1840s several Canadian producers started operations and by the second half of the 1850s they dominated the market to such an extent that a commentator in 1860 could say: "an American machine is now as great a rarity as a Canadian one was a few years ago."[2] Between the 1861 and 1871 censuses the value of Canadian annual output of agricultural implements rose from $413,000 to $2,685,000 (that is, by 550 percent). In the next two decades the value of the industry's output continued to expand, but more slowly

†*Journal of Economic History* XXXVI, 2 (June 1976): 399–415. I am grateful to D.J. DeVoretz and C.G. Reed for their comments on earlier versions of this article. A draft was presented at the 1974 Cliometrics Conference in Madison and I benefitted from comments made there. Editorial comments from N. Rosenberg and a referee were also helpful.

(by 64 percent and 70 percent). The rapid expansion in the 1860s appears to have been concentrated in Ontario; the 1871 census reports 36,874 reapers and mowers in use in Ontario; and 5,149 in Quebec. These conclusions regarding the timing and location of reaper introduction are also supported by available evidence from newspapers and the reports of agricultural societies which consider reapers as commonplace in Ontario by the early 1870s.[3] On a graph where the abscissa measures time and the ordinate measures the proportion of farms using the reaper, Canadian reaper diffusion would be represented by the well-known S-shaped pattern.

II

The model which will be used is formally set out in this section and is based on Paul David's concept of a threshold farm size.[4] The principal extension to David's work is the explicit consideration of the whole farm-size distribution rather than just the average farm size. The importance of this extension will soon become apparent.

David's behavioral assumption is that a farmer will purchase a reaper if its annual cost to him is less than the reduction in his annual wage bill following the introduction of the reaper. The threshold farm size,[5] S_T is then defined as that size of farm where the farmer is indifferent between purchase and no purchase, that is, where the following condition holds:

$$c = L_s \cdot w \cdot S_T \tag{1}$$

where c = annual cost to the farmer of a reaper, L_s = man-days of labor saved by using a reaper, per acre harvested, w = wage rate to the farmer of a man-day of harvest labor. Farmers with acreage greater than S_T purchase reapers, others do not.

If the threshold size and the frequency distribution for small-grain acreage per farm, $f(x)$, are known, then the proportion of farms using reapers, R, is given by:

$$R = \int_{S_T}^{\infty} f(x) \cdot dx \tag{2}$$

For a normal distribution equation (2) can be represented graphically (see Figure 1). In this model the proportion of farms using reapers is determined by the two exogenously determined factors, $f(x)$ and S_T. This approach can be criticized on two grounds. The availability of reapers may have provided the incentive for farmers to increase the size of their farms, and if there was any co-operative purchasing of reapers then there would be no uniform threshold size. Although the arguments are logically sound, they have little quantitative significance for the present study; the dominant causes of changes in small-grain acreage in mid-century Ontario were reduced land-clearing costs and increased grain prices, while there is no evidence of co-operative purchases.

FIGURE 1

Proportion of Farms Using Reapers

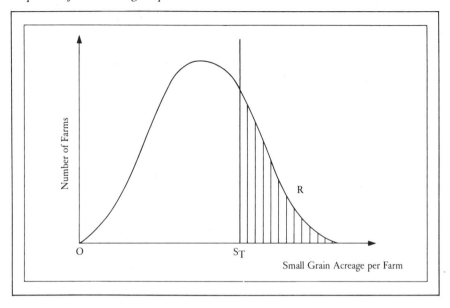

Some idea of how unlikely this type of reverse causality was, can be gained by comparing the changes in expected production costs of small grains due to reaper availability with the exogenous changes in grain prices and land-clearing costs. The rational farmer would have brought an extra acre into small-grain production if the discounted stream of expected profits were greater than the cost of clearing the land. Premechanized harvesting operations required 1.03 hours of labour per bushel of wheat. Of the harvesting labor requirements, reaping and raking took less time than binding and stocking, thus the absolute maximum that the reaper could have saved was half an hour's labor per bushel of wheat. The reaper, however, still required some labor and incurred a capital cost. Assuming that the reaping and raking costs per bushel of wheat with a mechanical reaper were the equivalent of a quarter of an hour's labor and assuming a ten-hour work day, then using the wage rates in table 1 we find that these costs fell from $0.5 \times 12.5 = 6.25$ c. in 1850 to $0.25 \times 15 = 3.75$ c. in 1870, that is, a reduction of 2.5 c. per bushel. Meanwhile Toronto wheat prices increased by more than a dollar per bushel and the price received by most farmers increased by even more after the building of railways between 1850 and 1870. There were also major reductions in clearing costs following the introduction of patented stump-pullers in the 1850s. Assuming that expectations did not diverge widely from the actual figures, the conclusion is that the quantitative significance of reverse causality between reaper availability and small grain acreage in Ontario between 1850 and 1870 was minor.[6] Furthermore, since the advantage in lower production costs enjoyed by reaper owners was small compared to the other variables entering the sowing decision,

TABLE 1

Summary of Data for Ontario, 1850–70

	1850	1860	1870
L_{s_1}	1/3	1/3	1/3
L_{s_2}	—	—	5/12
C	140	130	130
d	0.1	0.1	0.1
r	0.06	0.06	0.06
$c = (d + .5r)C$	18.2	16.9	16.9
w	1.25	1.25	1.5
c/w	14.56	13.52	11.26
$S_{T_1} = \dfrac{c}{L_{s_1} \cdot w}$	43.68	40.56	33.8
$S_{T_2} = \dfrac{c}{L_{s_2} \cdot w}$	—	—	27.04
A	1,290,528	2,253,989	3,592,331
N	99,906	131,983	172,258
μ_x	12.92	17.08	20.85

Notes: L_{s_1} = number of man-days of labor dispensed with by the hand-rake reaper, per acre harvested; L_{s_2} = the same for the self-rake reaper; C = the purchase price of a reaper; d = the technological rate of depreciation = the reciprocal of the life of a reaper; r = the rate of interest; c = the annual money cost of a reaper to the farmer; w = the wage rate; S_{T_1} = the threshold farm size for the hand-rake reaper; S_{T_2} = the same for the self-rake reaper; A = total small grain acreage; N = the number of farms; μ_x = average small grain acreage per farm = A/N.
SOURCES: See appendix.

reaper availability did not provide great incentive to consolidate land holdings (thus changing the shape of f(x)).

If farmers co-operated in purchasing reapers, then the fixed cost of a reaper would not be the same for all farmers and a model based on a uniform threshold size would not be applicable. In the absence of any evidence that co-operation in the purchase of reapers was actually taking place in Ontario, I must assume that the practice was uncommon.[7] My estimates based on this assumption will thus understate the pace of reaper diffusion to the extent that they ignore all reaper purchases by co-operating sub-threshold-size farmers. My analysis of the causal factors behind reaper diffusion will, however, only be affected by the existence of co-operation if the motivation of co-operating purchasers is different from that of individual purchasers.

Specification of f(x) permits estimates of the number of reapers, which can be compared to the actual pattern of reaper diffusion outlined above. If the model succeeds in capturing this pattern then it can provide insight into the question of the causes of the rapid diffusion of the 1860s. I can ask counterfactual questions such as what would the number of reapers have been if factor prices had not

TABLE 2

Distribution of Farms by Total Acreage, Ontario, 1850–70

	1850	1860	1870
Number of farms of 10 acres and under	9,746	4,424	19,954
Number of farms of 10–20 acres	2,671	2,675	
Number of farms of 20–50 acres	19,143	26,630	38,882
Number of farms of 50–100 acres	47,427	64,891	71,884
Number of farms of 100–200 acres	17,515	28,336	33,984
Number of farms above 200 acres	3,404	5,027	7,574
Total number of farms (N)	99,906	131,983	172,258

SOURCES: Canadian censuses: (a) 1851–52, vol. 2, 60–62; (b) 1860–61, vol. 2, 90–92; (c) 1870–71, vol. 3, 49.

changed? The answers to these questions will give some idea of the relative importance of the explanatory variables. These explanatory variables are factor prices (c,w), technical change (reflected in L_S) and the farm-size distribution.

III

The data used to calculate the threshold sizes in the years 1850, 1860 and 1870 are given in table 1. An important modification to the original hand-rake reaper was the introduction in the 1860s of the self-rake reaper which required one operator instead of two, thus increasing the amount of labor saved by purchasing a reaper and reducing the threshold farm size. The subscripts 1 and 2 refer to the hand-rake and self-rake reapers respectively. The threshold size fell from 43.68 acres in 1850 to 40.56 acres in 1860 to 27.04 acres in 1870.

Between 1850 and 1870 average small-grain acreage per farm increased from 12.92 to 20.85. Thus, approximately one third of the reduction of the gap $S_T - \mu_X$ is due to increased acreage and two thirds is due to falling threshold size. Even if the effect of the self-rake reaper on S_T were omitted, changes in factor prices are more important than increased farm size on the gap-reduction criterion. These results are similar to those obtained by David in his study of Illinois between 1849–50 and 1859–60.

No data are available for small grain acreage per farm, but the decennial censuses do give the distribution of farms by total acreage (see table 2). These distributions are clearly skewed and several theoretical frequency functions were fitted to them. The best approximation was given by a three-parameter lognormal distribution whose lower bound, δ, was set at 10 acres. On this basis it was assumed that the small-grain acreage distributions could also be represented by three-parameter lognormal distributions, and the parameters of these distributions were obtained by assuming that all farmers had the same ratio of small-grain acreage to total acreage.[8] The mean of the distributions, μ, rose steadily through the period 1850–70, but the standard deviation, σ, remained constant.

FIGURE 2

Effects on Reaper Adoption of Equal Changes in μ_x or S_T with Alternative Farm-Size Distributions

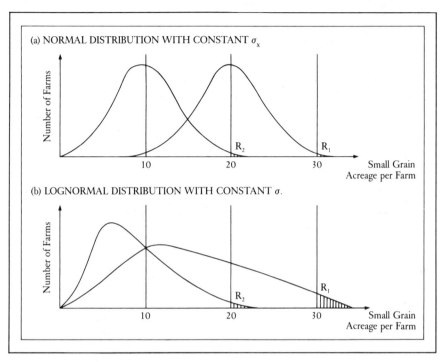

NOTES: In an initial situation of $\mu_x = 10$ and $S_T = 30$, the proportion of farms greater than the threshold size, R, is negligible in both cases. If μ_x increases by ten acres so that $\mu_x = 20$ and $S_T = 30$, then the proportion of farms above S_T is R_1. If instead S_T falls by ten acres so that $\mu_x = 10$ and $S_T = 20$, then the proportion of farms above S_T is R_2. In the normal distribution case $R_1 = R_2$, that is, the effect on reaper adoption of a ten-acre increase in μ_x is identical to that of a ten-acre reduction in S_T. In the lognormal case $R_1 > R_2$, that is, the effect of a ten-acre increase in μ_x is greater than that of a ten-acre reduction in S_T.

The farm-size distributions in table 2 reveal the weakness of David's method of determining the relative importance of the explanatory variables. The gap-reduction criterion implicitly assumes a symmetrical farm-size distribution with constant standard deviation, which was not the case in Ontario. If the farm-size distribution is not symmetrical, then it is not generally true that a reduction of S_T by k acres is equivalent in its effect upon reaper adoption to an increase in μ_x of k acres, even if σ_x remains constant. If farms are, for example, lognormally distributed, then an increase in μ_x does not just shift the distribution to the right, but alters the shape of the distribution.[9] In the lognormal case, if average farm size increases by the same amount as the threshold farm size falls, the former will have a greater effect on reaper adoption (see figure 2 (b)). The failure to take account of the skewed farm-size distribution would lead to underestimation of the importance of increased farm sizes using the gap-reduction criterion. Since the census farm-size data for Illinois is similar to that for Ontario, I can only conclude that David's hypothesis regarding the pre-eminent role of factor prices in determining the pace of reaper adoption in Illinois must be considered not proven.

The first statement of the stock of reapers in Ontario is in the 1870–71 census, which gives the total number of reapers and mowers as 36,874. Since this includes mowers, the figure represents a maximum value for the number of reapers, but the prevalence of combined reaper-mowers by this time implies that the number of reapers would have been close to this figure. Annual investment in agricultural implements rose by 550 percent in the 1860s (see section I above). In view of the continual increase in the rate of investment 1850–70, the 1870 *stock* of implements would have been an even greater multiple of the 1860 stock. Thus in 1860 there were less than 5,000 reapers in Ontario. No domestic output data are available for 1850, but the number of reapers in Ontario in 1850 must have been small.

The estimates obtained from the calculated threshold sizes and the farm-size distributions are given in table 3. The element representing the 1850 threshold size and farm-size distribution, that is, 270, is the estimated number of reapers in 1850. Similarly 2,283 and 30,080 are the estimates for 1860 and 1870 respectively. All the other elements of table 3 represent counterfactual estimates.

IV

The 1870 estimate is 18 percent below the census figure. This is a considerable variation, but the estimate is sensitive to small changes in the value of some of the variables.[10] The major triumph of the model is that the estimates do follow the S-shaped diffusion pattern. If we refer to the values of c/w and average farm size, μ_x, in table 1, it is clear that predictions based on either of these two variables alone could not have foreseen the actual rate of diffusion. In sum, while our estimates of the number of reapers in Ontario cannot be considered accurate predictions in the strict statistical sense of the word, they do form a diffusion pattern similar to that which actually occurred, which is more than any unicausal explanation or linear regression based on factor prices and/or average farm size could have done. This primarily follows from the introduction of the farm-size distribution into the analysis. The success of our model in predicting the diffusion pattern suggests that it can provide a useful explanation of Canadian reaper adoption.

If my model is a useful explanation of Canadian reaper adoption, then the explanation of the increased pace of farm mechanization in the 1860s lies in the three sets of variables in the model, that is L_s, c/w and f(x). The counterfactual estimates enable us to say something about the relative importance of these variables; in interpreting this aspect of table 3, I feel that three points stand out.

The introduction of the self-rake reaper, increasing L_s, accounts for half of the increase in reapers between 1860 and 1870. Much of the literature on diffusion of technical change has been concerned with explaining the "lag" between invention and innovation. This emphasis may be misplaced, however, because of the imperfection of most inventions. Only after one or more improvements do they

TABLE 3

Estimated Number of Reapers in Ontario, 1850, 1860 and 1870, and
Counterfactual Estimates

Farm Sizes	1850 f(x)^a	1860 f(x)	1870 f(x)
Threshold Size	($\delta = 1.31, \mu = 2.1$, $\sigma = 0.6$)	($\delta = 1.69, \mu = 2.4$, $\sigma = 0.6$)	($\delta = 2.22, \mu = 2.7$, $\sigma = 0.6$)
1850 S_{T_1}^{b}	270	1,658	6,671
1860 S_{T_1}	397	2,283	8,742
1870 S_{T_1}	956	4,770	15,946
S_{T_2}^{c}	2,515	10,524	30,080

a. f(x) = the frequency distribution of small grain acreage per farm; f(x) is assumed to be a three-parameter lognormal distribution.
b. S_{T_1} = threshold farm size for using a hand-rake reaper.
c. S_{T_2} = threshold farm size for using a self-rake reaper.
SOURCE: Values of S_T are taken from table 1.

become practical, and, as in this case, there may be no lag between an improvement and its introduction. Thus, emphasis on the "eureka" stage of a new technique, although traditional, may not have much economic significance, unless we also have an explanation of why subsequent improvements occur.[11]

The introduction of the self-rake reaper in the 1860s had a dramatic effect, but other factors were also important in determining the rate of reaper diffusion. Even without the self-rake reaper, the increase in the number of reapers 1860–70 would have been sevenfold; even if the self-rake reaper had existed in 1850 the number of reapers operating then would have been small. Comparison of the relative importance of changes in factor prices (which reduced S_T) and in scale of operations (reflected in μ) can be made from the square matrix formed by the first three rows of table 3. For example, changes in farm size alone induced an increase of 6,401 in the number of reapers between 1850 and 1870, whereas changes in factor prices alone led to an increase of only 686 reapers in the same period. Since the elements northeast of the main diagonal are greater than those to the southwest of it (and by large amounts), this gives support to the contention that scale of operations was more important than factor prices in stimulating the adoption of more capital-intensive techniques.[12]

The effects of changes in factor price or total acreage are not linear. Thus the 1850–70 change in factor prices leads to a far greater absolute change in the estimated number of reapers when acreage is held constant at the 1870 level than if it is held at the 1850 level (see columns 1 and 3 of table 3). Similarly, the change in acreage has greater effect on the estimated number of reapers if factor prices are held at their 1870 ratio rather than their 1850 ratio (see rows 1 and 3 of table 3). In sum, there is a critical region within which changes in either factor prices or farms' acreage have greater effect on the choice of technique than they had earlier. This non-linearity arises from postulating a non-rectangular distribution of innovating units, which is clearly a reasonable assumption. It is the same non-linearity which produced the S-shaped diffusion pattern dealt with above.

These results highlight the importance of introducing the whole farm-size distribution into the analysis. Without knowledge of the shape of the distribution it is impossible to determine the quantitative significance of an increase in S_T or reduction in μ_x on the number of farms above S_T. In contrast, the fully specified model permits numerical estimates of the predicted number of reapers, and these estimates can be compared with the actual situation. Introduction of the farm-size distribution also provides a simple explanation of the S-shaped diffusion pattern. Finally, consideration of the shape of the distribution permits unbiased estimates of the relative importance of the explanatory variables. The conclusion that factor prices were more important than increased farm sizes, which was arrived at by comparing the changes in S_T and μ_x between 1850 and 1870, is reversed when changes in S_T are compared with changes in the whole farm-size distribution.

V

Since the increased rate of mechanization of Canadian agriculture was associated with a period of rapid economic development and may itself have been an important component in that development,[13] knowledge of the causes of this phenomenon increases our understanding of the general pattern of economic change in modern Canada. The proximate causes of the increased diffusion rate were, in order of importance, (1) the development of the self-rake reaper, (2) increased grain prices and reduced costs of clearing land, which led to increased small-grain acreage, and (3) a change in relative factor prices following an increase in agricultural wage rates. The picture is one of a series of simultaneous external stimuli to mechanization, for example inventions which were imported from the United States (the self-rake reaper, stump-pullers) and the American Civil War, which affected the grain market and possibly the labor market. These stimuli had a powerful effect, however, only because Canadian agriculture was at the critical region mentioned in section IV. Thus the pattern of causation was complex, because changes in the 1850s (and earlier), when the price of reapers fell and grain prices rose, were essential prerequisites for the increase in the rate of reaper adoption in the 1860s. A conclusion, based on the 1860s, that supply effects were pre-eminent has to be changed when the 1850s are included.

This case study also raises some conjectures about the general process of diffusion of technical change. The first problem raised is semantic, but very important. If technical change is defined as anything that alters the shape of the isoquant map, then the development of the self-rake reaper was clearly technical change. It was, however, closely related to the hand-rake reaper which preceded it and it appears foolish to treat the two as completely separate phenomena. One of our findings is that this improvement was significant in increasing the rate of reaper adoption and we know that it increased the capital-labor ratio, but we have no explanation of why the improvement occurred when it did, and there is nothing in the diffusion literature to help us on this point.

Microeconomic theory, including the literature on induced technical change, has traditionally emphasized the role of factor prices in determining factor proportions. Our results suggest that the criticisms of Young and Kaldor, who consider the scale of operations to be more important in practice than factor prices, are well founded in this particular case. The tools of this study should be applicable to other cases of technical change whose introduction involved an element of fixed cost, and it would be a useful exercise to test the generality of this conclusion about the importance of scale considerations.

Finally, this model provides a satisfactory explanation of the S-shaped diffusion pattern. The basis for this explanation is the introduction of the size distribution of adopting agents into the analysis. The S-shape would be obtained from many unimodal theoretical frequency functions. Lognormal functions were fitted to the farm-size distributions in the present study and they produced an S-shape whose slope closely resembled that of the actual diffusion path. Analysis utilizing the size distribution of innovating units sheds new light on the diffusion process and, in view of the fact that firms in many industries are lognormally distributed, this method of analysis has potentially wide applicability.

Appendix

In the appendix the sources of the data in table 1 are outlined.[14]

Labor Saving

L_S is the number of man-days of labor dispensed with by mechanization, per acre harvested:

$$L_S = \frac{m - q}{n}$$ where n = number of acres cut by a reaper in a day,
m = number of men needed to cradle n acres in a day,
q = number of operators per reaper.

With this formulation we follow David in considering the only private economic benefit from the adoption of a reaper to have been a saving of cradling labor.

In the 1850s McCormick reapers were said to cut 15–20 acres per day, but this was working full speed and with a change of horses at noon.[15] Assessing the fairly extensive U.S. evidence for the period (including the 1860 Census), Rogin concludes that the average performance in a twelve-hour day of both the hand-rake and self-rake reapers was 10–12 acres.[16] There is little evidence to suggest that reaper performance in Canada was much different. Denison states that Wood's Reaper as made by Massey "could cut twelve to fifteen acres of grain a day," but it is not clear whether this represents a maximum or a normal performance.

Rogin's summary of U.S. evidence on cradling, mainly taken from the eastern states, was that "There appears . . . to have been a norm of performance for the country as a whole which approximated two acres (per man day)."[17] This seems to emphasize the lower estimates quoted by him, but since these are from New York they may be the most applicable for southern Ontario. Also, since the stand of wheat was relatively heavy in Ontario, the lower estimates are again the more probable. If $m = \frac{n}{2}$, then:

$$L_S = \frac{1}{2} - \frac{q}{n}$$

The self-rake reaper, introduced in 1854 but first produced commercially in Canada in 1861 by Massey, had no effect on n, but reduced the number of operators from two to one. Thus, if we introduce subscripts, 1 referring to hand-rake reapers and 2 to self-rake reapers, then $q_1 = 2$ and $q_2 = 1$. If $n = 12$, then:

$$L_{S_1} = \frac{1}{2} - \frac{1}{6} = \frac{1}{3}, \quad L_{S_2} = \frac{1}{2} - \frac{1}{12} = \frac{5}{12}$$

The Annual Cost of a Reaper

Data on the purchase price of a reaper (C) are scattered and not necessarily uniform; prices in any year could vary for different farmers depending upon the particular model bought, distance it had to be transported and the arrangements made for payment. Paucity of data prevents us from being scrupulous about these conditions. First let us summarize the Canadian prices quoted in the literature. In 1855 the Manny hand-rake reaper produced by Massey "sold for $130 with steel cutter bar, $120 with wood, and included as extras one set of knives, two blades, two guards, one pinion and one wrench."[18] In 1857 domestically produced McCormick-style machines were selling in Canada for $125–130, while McCormick's own product was offered there at $160.[19] In the 1862 Massey catalogue both Wood's self-rake and the Manny hand-rake were offered at $130.[20] At the 1876 Select Committee of the House of Commons Inquiry, F.T. Frost of Frost & Wood gave the price of a combined reaper at Prescott with twelve months credit as $125.[21] The overall impression is one of a pretty stable price of $125–130. Since the years 1873–76 saw generally falling prices, we will use $130 as the value of C for both 1860 and 1870. Since there were no Canadian producers in 1850, this year provides some difficulty. According to David the price of McCormick reapers in the United States was about $20 less in 1850 than in 1857, which in conjunction with the 1857 price given above suggests a Canadian selling price of $140. We will use this *faute de meilleur*, but it should be borne in mind that an unknown quantity of reapers was available at lower prices in Canada as a result of dumping following the U.S. patent wars.[22]

In the 1850s reapers had "an average life of nine or ten years,"[23] the larger figure presumably applying to good care and normal use: "With good care the reaper would harvest one hundred acres per year for ten years."[24] There is some doubt as to whether "good care" was prevalent; American farmers tended to leave reapers where they were last used regardless of weather conditions[25] and it is unlikely that Canadian farmers of the time were any more careful. Potentially more damage to the threshold hypothesis would be caused if the reapers' life could be extended by less intensive use, but there is no evidence to suggest that this was the case. It is assumed that the life of a reaper was ten years in the 1850s and that this did not vary significantly with care or use. This expected life span obtained through to the 1870s: ". . . a machine even at that time (the 1870s) lasted very close to ten years."[26] Thus, the annual straight-line depreciation rate, d, through the period 1850–70 was 0.1. There is no evidence that machines were abandoned before the end of their physical lives, at least not until the advent of the harvester in the 1870s. Thus the economic rate of depreciation or obsolescence was no greater than the physical rate.

An appropriate rate of interest to use would be the charges made by the reaper companies for credit. Even if the farmer could earn a higher return elsewhere, this represents the farmers' opportunity cost since he could buy the reaper on credit and then invest the freed capital in the more lucrative avenue. Unfortunately, however, we have no data on what this rate was in Canada. McCormick charged 6 percent through the 1850s,[27] and this is the rate used by David in his American study. To use this rate for Ontario 1850–70 begs many questions about the general trend of interest rates in Canada. The interest rate on government bonds was 5.4 percent in 1868,[28] but this may have been a peak, since it declined to 3.8 percent by 1885. As an approximation we use r = 0.06, but this rate may be too high.

The Wage Rate

Agricultural wage rates are quoted in many of the county reports in the appendices to the annual reports of the Ontario Commissioner of Agriculture of the early 1870s (in *Ontario Sessional Papers*). Here there is a great deal of uniformity in summer daily wage rates, which are quoted at $1.50 except in some counties in the extreme east (notably Glengarry where the quoted rates are $1.00 to $1.25). In 1867 the Immigration Agent at Kingston reported farm labor scarce even at $1.25 to $1.50 a day.[29] These sources suggest that in 1870 farmers hiring cradlers by the day would have to pay a rate of around $1.50.

As we go back in time data become less plentiful. For 1860, we will use an 1859 observation that "expert cradlers were plentiful at $1.25 a day."[30] This accords with the general impression that the 1860s were a period of rising wages in agriculture.[31]

Jones, in summarizing the scattered references to wages in mid-century, concludes that from the 1820s until the late 1850s "the worker by the day received from 50 cents to $1.00, or $1.25 if he was an expert cradler."[32] It is unlikely that this specific rate would apply to every year, but in view of the pioneer nature of Ontario agriculture to 1850 the concept of a regional labor market is much more hazy than in 1860 or 1870 and it would be unrealistic to expect a standard provincial wage rate anyway.

Small-Grain Acreage per Farm

The decennial censuses provide data on the total area in farms, improved land under crops; and, for 1850 and 1860, acreage sown for individual crops. These figures are given in table 4, where the bottom line gives total acreage under the principal small grains (=A). For 1870, A was estimated on the assumption that small-grain acreage represented the same proportion of improved land under crops as it had in 1860.

Table 4

Area in Farms and Total Acreage Under Small Grains, Ontario, 1850–70

	1850	1860	1870
Total area in farms	9,825,915	13,354,907	16,161,676
Improved land under crops	2,282,928	4,101,902	6,537,438
(1) wheat	798,275	1,386,366	
(2) oats	413,058	678,337	
(3) barley	30,129	118,910	
(4) rye	49,066	70,376	
$\Sigma(1) - (4)$	1,290,528	2,253,989	

SOURCES: *Census, 1851–52*, vol. 2: 60–62; *Census, 1860–61*, vol. 2: 90–92; *Census, 1870–71*, vol. 3: 49.

From the same sources we find that the total number of occupied farms in Ontario was 99,906 in 1850, 131,983 in 1860, and 172,258 in 1870. These figures provide upper bounds for the number of farms growing small grains, N, and assuming that all farms grew some small grains, they are approximate measures of N. Under this assumption average small-grain acreage per farm, $A/N = \mu_x$, is easily calculated. For the years 1850, 1860, and 1870 μ_x is equal to 12.92 acres, 17.08 acres, and 20.85 acres respectively.

Notes

1. This is the "revisionist" view of Canadian development. The older view held that 1860–96 was a period of "secular depression," but Firestone's GNP estimates (in NBER, *Studies in Income and Wealth* XXIV (Princeton, 1960), 230) suggest higher per capita growth rates for 1867–96 than for the 1867–1967 period as a whole and he concludes that an industrial revolution took place in Canada in the 1860s with the introduction of the factory system. Since agriculture was the largest sector of the economy and one place where the introduction of the factory system was occurring was the agricultural implement industry, this latter view would make the mechanization of agriculture an important aspect of Canada's economic development.

2. R.L. Jones, *A History of Agriculture in Ontario 1613–1880* (Toronto, 1946), 102.

3. For examples of the former, see quotations from the *Canadian Farmer* in W.G. Phillips, *The Agricultural Implement Industry in Canada: A Study in Competition* (Toronto, 1956), 40, and F. Landon, "Some Effects of the American Civil War on Canadian Agriculture," *Agricultural History* VII: 168. The latter reports are contained in *Ontario Sessional Papers*.

4. P. David, "The Mechanization of Reaping in the Ante-Bellum Midwest," in *Industrialization in Two Systems: Essays in Honor of Alexander Gerschenkron*, edited by H. Rosovsky (New York, 1966), 3–28; and P. David, "The Landscape and the Machine: Technical Interrelatedness, Land Tenure and the Mechanization of the Corn Harvest in Victorian Britain," in *Essays on a Mature Economy: Britain after 1840*, edited by D.N. McCloskey (London, 1971), 145–205.

5. To be precise we should say "threshold small-grain acreage." Throughout this paper farm size is measured by acreage under small grains unless otherwise stated.

6. For fuller treatment of this question see R.W.T. Pomfret, "The Introduction of the Mechanical Reaper in Canada 1850–70" (Ph.D. dissertation, Simon Fraser University, 1974). The estimates of premechanized labor requirements are for the northeastern United States (W.N. Parker and J.L. Klein, "Productivity Growth in Grain Production in the United States 1840–60 and 1900–10," NBER, *Studies in Income and*

Wealth XXX (Princeton, 1966): 523–80). The data on grain prices are from K.W. Taylor and H. Michell, *Statistical Contributions to Canadian Economic History*, II (Toronto, 1931).

7. The assumption of indivisibility in David's Midwest study has recently come under criticism in A. Olmstead, "The Mechanization of Reaping and Mowing in American Agriculture, 1833–1870," *Journal of Economic History* XXXV (June 1975): 327–52. Neither the present author's own research, nor discussion with other Canadian historians has brought to light documentary evidence of contracting or sharing of reapers in Canada comparable to the evidence which Olmstead provides for the Midwest. A tentative explanation of the lack of co-operative purchases is given in Pomfret, "The Introduction of the Mechanical Reaper," chap. 3. Samples of the spatial distribution of farms in three Ontario counties indicated that potential co-operators' farms were seldom adjacent, which, given the cumbersome nature of the early reapers, suggested high costs of moving reapers between co-operators' farms. Olmstead specifically rejects the argument that transport costs were high in the American Midwest (Olmstead, "The Mechanization of Reaping and Mowing," 339), but it should be borne in mind that geographical conditions in Ontario were more irregular than in the Midwest and hence less amenable to the movement of machinery (Pomfret, "The Introduction of the Mechanical Reaper," 33–35).

8. The final assumption is heroic, but is not crucial. Changing the parameters of the distribution does not alter our conclusions regarding the pattern or the causes of reaper diffusion (the more reasonable assumption that small-grain acreage was more concentrated than total acreage would even make our 1870 estimate closer to the census figure). What is crucial is the assumption of lognormality, or more generally the assumption of skewness, since a symmetrical distribution would have produced different results (Pomfret, "The Introduction of the Mechanical Reaper," chap. 6).

9. J. Aitchison and J.A.C. Brown, *The Lognormal Distribution* (Cambridge, 1963), 10.

10. This is especially true of the rate of interest. The rate used is 6 percent (see appendix), but there is no Canadian evidence to support this. Even a small adjustment like the use of 5 percent as the relevant rate of interest would raise our estimate above the census value.

11. An exception to the general tendency to ignore improvements is N. Rosenberg, "Factors Affecting the Diffusion of Technology," *Explorations in Economic History* X (Jan. 1973): 3–33. Olmstead has recently ascribed a major role to technological improvements in explaining the diffusion of reapers in the American Midwest (Olmstead, "The Mechanization," 344–52).

12. Although this contention is contrary to the usual emphasis in economic theory, it has a long history going back to Adam Smith; see A. Young, "Increasing Returns and Economic Progress," *Economic Journal* (1928): 529–42; and N. Kaldor, "The Irrelevance of Equilibrium Economics," *Economic Journal* (1972): 1237–55.

13. See note 1.

14. For a more detailed examination of the data and for consideration of some problems omitted here see Pomfret, "The Introduction of the Mechanical Reaper," chap. 5.

15. W.T. Hutchinson, *Cyrus Hall McCormick*, vol. 1 (New York, 1930), 336.

16. L. Rogin, *The Introduction of Farm Machinery* (Berkeley, 1931), 134–35.

17. Ibid., 128.

18. M. Denison, *Harvest Triumphant* (Toronto, 1948), 32.

19. W.T. Hutchinson, *Cyrus Hall McCormick*, vol. 2 (New York, 1935), 647.

20. Denison, *Harvest*, 50.

21. Ibid., 64.

22. Phillips, *The Agricultural Implement Industry*, 10, 40.

23. Hutchinson, *Cyrus Hall McCormick* 1: 311.

24. Ibid., 73.

25. Ibid., 365. Olmstead, "The Mechanization," 331–32, argues that "the useful life of a reaper or mower was typically closer to five years or less" before the 1870s. An increased value of d for 1850 and 1860 would increase the threshold farm size and reduce the estimated number of reapers in these years. It would not, however, alter the shape of the projected diffusion path, nor any of the other conclusions based on table 3.

26. Rogin, *The Introduction*, 95.

27. Hutchinson, *Cyrus Hall McCormick* 1: 337, 369.

28. H.A. Innis and A.R.M. Lower, *Select Documents in Canadian Economic History, 1783–1885* (Toronto, 1933), 809.

29. Denison, *Harvest*, 59.

30. As quoted in Denison, *Harvest*, 59.

31. Cf. Jones, *A History*, 96; and Phillips, *The Agricultural Implement Industry*, 40.

32. Jones, *A History*, 55n.

SECTION 2

ECONOMIC DEVELOPMENT IN THE SECOND HALF OF THE NINETEENTH CENTURY

ATLANTIC CANADA AND THE AGE OF SAIL REVISITED†

ERIC W. SAGER AND LEWIS R. FISCHER

The wooden ships that once sailed from the builders' yards of Atlantic Canada have little place in the collective mythology of a nation that has long since forsaken its role as a maritime power. As we developed our western frontier and determined to serve as the hinterland of a continental economy, our growth centres shifted from our eastern shores and the Canadian Confederation lost touch with the trade and culture of its thalassic peoples. Today the great ocean fleets of the nineteenth century are present only in the mythology and folklore of provinces eager to revive what few sources of dignity and pride remain from their past. In the 1920s Frederick William Wallace sought to awaken Maritimers' memories of their "past glories," and it is no accident that he wrote in a decade when the eastern economy entered a steep decline and Maritimers raged at the failure of Confederation.[1] Only in recent years have Wallace's valuable chronicles been superseded by the works of other popular historians and by a few serious attempts to assess the economic importance of the Canadian shipbuilding and shipping industries.[2] Many of the older myths surrounding the age of sail have disappeared in the process and a reassessment of that age is long overdue. The new realities which are emerging come from an empirical base and a methodology which Wallace would not have recognized; but he would have acknowledged that the "era of maritime effort and industry" remains a worthy source of pride, and a salutary reminder to an insular nation of the wider vision and the entrepreneurial acumen of our eastern Canadian forebears.

The traditional views of the history of shipping in the Maritimes, although never combined within a single interpretation, might be summarized as follows. We have been told that shipbuilding and shipping were both directly linked to the timber trade: timber was the major cargo for colonial-built vessels, and timber, together with the British demand for shipping tonnage, determined the pattern

†*Canadian Historical Review* LXIII, 2 (1982): 125–50. This paper is based on research undertaken by members of the Atlantic Canada Shipping Project at Memorial University of Newfoundland. The paper is therefore the result of a collective effort by many friends and colleagues. We are particularly indebted to David Alexander, Gerald Panting, Keith Matthews, and Rosemary Ommer. The Atlantic Canada Shipping Project is funded by the Social Sciences and Humanities Research Council of Canada and by Memorial University of Newfoundland.

of colonial shipbuilding. "Launched, rigged, and loaded with the ubiquitous and every-ready cargo of timber, the ship would be sent to Great Britain consigned to brokers who made a specialty of selling such vessels."[3] Colonial timber and British demand sustained the industry until some Canadian shipowners, encouraged by mid-century gold rushes and the Crimean War, entered into ship operation themselves. But this was still mainly a shipbuilding industry, since "net earnings by entrepreneurs came largely from taking the price risk involved in the marketing of wooden ships."[4] The collapse of British demand for wooden-hulled sailing vessels in the 1860s caused a crisis in the industry and left Maritimers with no option but to keep their vessels on registry in Canada and to run them for what profit they could. Thus there followed the "palmy days" of Canadian shipowning, when the vessels of the Maritimes sailed to all four corners of the world for cargoes of cotton, guano, and tea.[5]

Concerning the vessels themselves, we have been told that the colonial-built vessel was a floating coffin of execrable quality, and that wooden sailing vessels of this period were not susceptible of significant improvements in productivity.[6] There was in any case no great incentive to improve sailing times or labour productivity, since these "floating warehouses" were often valuable as much for their stowage as for their transportation functions. Despite the clumsiness of his vessel, however, the Bluenose skipper was "the terror of duffers and slackers" and the "reputation of the Bluenose mate is such that sailormen shudder at the mention of the name."[7] But inevitably the industry in which these "iron men" served was destroyed by a new technology. According to Harold Innis, "the competition of iron and steel destroyed a magnificent achievement, an integration of capital and labour, of lumbering, fishing and agriculture, on which rested a progressive community life."[8] From this assumption about the splendid "integration" of shipbuilding with local lumber and trade, Innis concluded that the decline of shipbuilding was the most serious single difficulty faced by the economy of the Maritimes in the half-century before 1930.

Such are the myths about eastern Canadian shipping. Almost everything in this chronicle must now be either qualified or rejected. Only one part of this account has ever been seriously questioned. In 1966 Peter McClelland sought to refute Innis's argument that shipbuilding had been the "linchpin" of the New Brunswick economy.[9] This was not a difficult task, but in the process McClelland left many questions unanswered and he might have created a few myths of his own had his work been more widely read. For McClelland argued that both shipbuilding and shipowning were "of negligible significance" in stimulating economic growth; that shipowning offered "a dubious earnings record after 1865"; and that shipowning meant "gambling" with an obsolete technology, a drain of entrepreneurial talent from manufacturing, and hence a "constraint" on the growth of local industries.[10] In different ways both Innis and McClelland overestimated the importance of the industries which they studied: for shipbuilding was never so critical in its contribution to the economy as Innis thought; and shipowning was never the wasteful gamble which McClelland thought it to be.

In revising these traditional portraits of the shipping industry we have begun by examining the patterns of vessel registration in the major ports of registry in Atlantic Canada.[11] It is clear that the pattern of investment in both shipbuilding and shipping is a complex phenomenon which cannot be explained merely by reference to the timber trade and to British demand for shipping. This was not a monolithic industry but two industries—shipbuilding and shipowning—and the incentive to invest in either industry varied from one port to another within the region. By far the largest fleet of vessels was registered in Saint John, New Brunswick. Here the timber trade does appear to have had a considerable influence upon both shipbuilding and ship operation in the early decades of the nineteenth century. A series of correlations between New Brunswick timber exports, tonnage clearing New Brunswick ports, and investment in new tonnage in Saint John suggests that the relationship may have been very close: correlating annual changes in these series yields correlation coefficients of between $+.61$ and $+.69$ for the period from 1820 to 1850. Since we know that a large proportion of vessels in this fleet were owned initially by timber merchants or shippers of timber and sawn lumber, it seems likely that returns from the shipping of timber were the most important single incentive toward investment in shipping.[12]

While timber provided the major stimulus to the growth of shipping in Saint John, this was not true of shipowning throughout the region. Large as it was, the fleet of Saint John accounted for less than a third of all shipping registered in the Atlantic region in the nineteenth century. And a significant proportion of new shipping in the region was coastal shipping, built for use in the fisheries, in coastal trading, or in runs to the West Indies. This was true even in the centres of ocean-going shipping. In the four largest ocean-going fleets — those registered in Saint John, Charlottetown, Yarmouth, and Halifax — vessels designed primarily for coastal trading accounted for 30 percent of all new tonnage between 1820 and 1860 (included among these vessels are schooners, which averaged fifty-six tons in these ports, and brigantines, which averaged 150 tons).[13] If all ports of registry were included coastal and fishing vessels likely would account for over 40 percent of the entire industry in the nineteenth century. The sixth largest fleet in the region, that of St. John's, Newfoundland, consisted almost entirely of coastal vessels; here the pattern of investment was determined by the demand for vessels as a factor of production in the cod and seal fisheries and by the need to supply outport communities and the Labrador summer fishery. In the fourth largest fleet, that of Halifax, vessels under 150 tons accounted for 45 percent of all investments in the nineteenth century, and in the first half of the century there was a close correlation between investment in shipping and patterns of West Indian trading. The timber trade was a major stimulus to the shipping industry in the Bay of Fundy and on the Saint John and Miramichi rivers in the early decades of the century. In eastern Nova Scotia and ports of the Gulf of St. Lawrence, timber was less important than the growing demand from coastal and West Indian trades and the fisheries; in Newfoundland the timber trade was of no significance at all.[14]

Impressed by the importance of shipbuilding for Quebec and New Brunswick, Richard Rice and others have proposed an even more direct link between shipbuilding and the timber trade. For many places in these provinces shipbuilding was a forward linkage from the timber industry, inspired not only by the need to carry timber but by the opportunity to sell the finished product in the British market. From this quite acceptable assumption stemmed others which, however true for some shipbuilding centres, were less valid for the Maritimes as a whole: it was assumed that the pattern of investment in shipbuilding was determined primarily by British demand and that the shipowning industry in eastern Canada was confined mainly to the 1860s and 1870s.[15] Of the importance of British North America as a supplier of vessels for Britain there can be no doubt. But those who argue the primacy of British demand for Maritime Canadian shipbuilding run the risk of underestimating the substantial local demand for coastal and fishing vessels, vessels which were least likely to be transferred to Britain. Even in the major shipbuilding centres the importance of British demand has been exaggerated. Of all tonnage built in Saint John and its immediate outports between 1820 and 1850, only half was transferred ultimately to Britain, and much of this transferred tonnage had first been retained for use by Saint John's shipowners.[16] The fleet of vessels retained on registry in Saint John grew particularly rapidly in the 1830s (an annual rate of 12.5 percent), and in the three decades after 1826 our estimates of the fleet actually on registry in Saint John show that this fleet grew almost as rapidly as did gross physical investment (4.4 percent compared with 4.7 percent per annum). This suggests that the sale of vessels to Britain did not limit the sustained long-term growth of the local shipowning industry.

The second largest fleet in the Atlantic region was registered in Charlottetown, the only port of registry on Prince Edward Island. Of all tonnage registered in P.E.I. between 1787 and 1914 (and this includes almost all vessels built on the island), 69.3 percent was transferred to ports elsewhere. Of these transfers 72 percent of the tonnage went to Britain. But in the peak decades of vessel construction in P.E.I., from 1840 to 1889, only 57 percent of all transferred tonnage went to Britain. British North America (and particularly Newfoundland) was always an important market for vessels built in P.E.I., as well as for vessels built around Miramichi and Pictou. And there was a substantial shipowning industry in P.E.I. itself. After the 1840s island shipowners retained their vessels on registry for longer periods of time: the mean registry life of all vessels rose from 2.2 to nine years between the 1840s and 1880s, and the mean life of transferred vessels rose from 1.9 years to four years over the same period. Our estimate of the size of the fleet on registry suggests an impressive long-term growth rate of 3.9 percent per annum between 1826 and 1875.[17] Clearly P.E.I. was more than a shipbuilding factory for Great Britain. Thus even in the major shipbuilding centres of New Brunswick and P.E.I. there was substantial capital accumulation in shipping. For the industry outside New Brunswick and P.E.I., and for the entire region after the 1840s, it is no longer possible to argue that "few of these [Canadian] vessels were operated under Canadian register" or that "net earnings by entrepreneurs came largely from taking the price risk involved in the marketing of wooden ships."[18]

The great boom in Canadian shipowning in the 1860s and 1870s was not a novel "gamble" forced upon shipbuilders and owners by the decline in British demand for wooden sailing ships. The scenario in which "the would-be short-term owner became a full-time shipowner by default" does not explain what happened in the 1860s and 1870s. The boom in Canadian shipping in these decades was merely the accelerated growth of an industry already well established in

TABLE 1

Annual Growth Rates of Gross Physical Investment and of Tonnage on Registry in Major Ports

Port	Years to Peak	Tonnage on Registry[a] (percent)	Gross Investment
Saint John	1826–77	+4.0	+2.1
Charlottetown	1826–75	+3.9	+2.9
Yarmouth	1843–79	+6.9	+4.4
Halifax[b]	1826–74	+2.3	+3.0
Windsor	1853–91	+5.8	+2.0
St. John's	1826–74	+2.1	+1.2
Pictou	1846–84	+1.9	+3.5
Miramichi	1833–64	+3.3	+4.1
Total[c] (8 ports)	1828–78	+4.3	+2.8
U.K. (all ships)	1828–78	+2.5	+3.6

a. All growth rates are calculated from regression equations of the form $\log Y = a + bt$. In our estimates of tonnage on registry, the date when the vessel actually went out of service was used, rather than the official date of registry closure. Where the date of actual disposal is unknown, the vessel was given an estimated service life based on the mean service life of vessels with known dates of disposal. The result is a much more accurate estimate of capital stock than that given in official figures.
b. Halifax growth rates are calculated for vessels with at least one owner resident in Halifax County, in order to reduce the impact of fluctuations caused by the opening of new ports of registry in Nova Scotia, particularly Yarmouth (1840), Pictou (1840), and Windosr (1849).
c. All vessels registered in Halifax are included here, since this was the major port of registry in Nova Scotia before the opening of Yarmouth, Pictou, and Windsor.
SOURCE: BT5 107/108 vessel registries; B.R. Mitchell and Phyllis Deane, *Abstract of British Historical Statistics* (Cambridge, 1962), Transport 1 and 2, 218–22.

the North Atlantic. Table 1 suggests that there was a sustained high growth in the fleets of the major ports from the 1830s to the 1870s. The industry grew more quickly than did the fleet of the United Kingdom in every decade before the 1880s. The pattern of investment in all ports (except St. John's, Newfoundland) was very closely correlated with the pattern of investment in shipping in Britain. This coincidence in trends results only in part from shipbuilders' responsiveness to British demand; of greater importance is the fact that British and Canadian shipowners were responding to the same demand for ocean shipping during a period of sustained growth in the volume of international trade.[19] No single model of growth will apply to the shipbuilding and shipping industries of Atlantic Canada. But it is clear that there was a gradual extension of trading activities from an early dependence on timber or coastal trades to a wider involvement in many North Atlantic trades by the 1850s, and from there to varying degrees of involvement in certain world trades.[20]

Virtually nothing has been known until very recently about the voyages of Canadian vessels. On the one hand Innis's argument about the "integration" of the industry with the local economy assumes that vessels on Canadian registry must have operated from Canadian ports. On the other hand Wallace leaves us with the impression that Canadian vessels never saw their home ports after launching but traded in every part of the world.[21] Our analysis of the "Agreements and Accounts of Crew" for our major fleets allows some greater precision about the deployment of ocean-going vessels, at least after 1863.[22] It is likely that a substantial proportion of voyages earlier in the century began from ports in Canada; by the 1860s this was no longer true. But it is no more true that Canadian vessels were operating extensively in all world trades. As figure 1 indicates, Canadian ocean-going vessels operated mainly in the North Atlantic after 1863. In spite of this concentration on North Atlantic trades, they operated infrequently from Canadian ports. The United Kingdom, United States, and Europe accounted for 63 percent of all entrances into port by Saint John vessels, 76 percent of all entrances by Yarmouth vessels, and 70 percent of all entrances by Halifax vessels. Vessels in the Saint John fleet traded more often outside the North Atlantic throughout the period, but in all ports there was a significant shift out of the North Atlantic after the 1870s. Nevertheless, it is clear that the growth and decline of total entrances were determined very largely by North Atlantic trades, and particularly by trades between the United States and Britain or northern Europe. The Yarmouth fleet, for instance, was particularly narrowly based. David Alexander has estimated each region's contribution to the net growth of world entrances by Yarmouth vessels: these estimates suggest that 98 percent of the growth of total entrances before 1879 was accounted for by ports in the United States, United Kingdom, and Europe.[23] In the 1880s the same regions contributed almost as much to the rapid decline in world entrances. Maritimers' vessels did not operate extensively in Canadian export trades; nor did they penetrate all world trades. Canadian shipowners had seized the opportunities afforded by a narrow range of staple exports from the United States. It is no surprise to find a high correlation between investment in ocean shipping in our major ports and freight rates for such American exports as grain, tobacco, petroleum, and cotton. We have constructed an index of freight rates for the major American bulk cargoes for the three decades after 1855. The high correlation between this index and investment in ocean shipping in our major ports tends to confirm that returns from such freights were of crucial importance for the growth and decline of Canadian shipping before and after the late 1870s.[24]

In retrospect the decision to deploy wooden sailing vessels in trades soon to be overwhelmed by iron and steam may seem a short-sighted gamble. But shipowners were businessmen, not economists or social engineers. They were not planning the economic future of the Maritimes within Confederation; they were making profits in a business which they understood thoroughly and in which most had worked for two decades. They continued to make profits, and they adjusted the supply of vessels to meet a dwindling demand. They did this not by disposing of vessels recently purchased, but by drastically reducing all new investment in response to the declining freight rates of the late 1870s and 1880s. At the same time they guaranteed the returns from vessel operation by wresting

FIGURE 1

Voyage Distribution of Vessels on Registry in Saint John, Yarmouth, Halifax, and Windsor

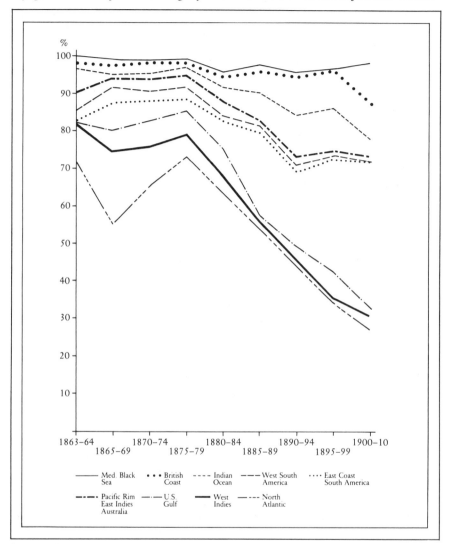

SOURCE: Crew Lists and Agreements for vessels registered in Saint John, Yarmouth, Halifax, and Windsor.

improvements in performance and productivity from the vessels which they retained. Although some historians have noted the improved reputation and rating of Canadian-built vessels by the middle decades of the century, none has suspected the remarkable improvements in performance which these vessels achieved between the 1860s and 1880s.[25]

We know, first of all, that eastern Canadian builders and owners were able to effect a remarkable change in the rate of depreciation of vessels in the nineteenth century. In the Halifax fleet vessel life expectancy increased by over 50 percent between the 1840s and 1870s, for instance (vessels above 250 tons built in the 1840s lasted 6.3 years on average; vessels built in the 1870s lasted 9.6 years). Similar changes in the life expectancy of ocean-going vessels happened in all ports. These changes occurred in spite of an apparent tendency to take greater risks at sea: in some fleets there was a substantial increase in the proportion of vessels involved in marine disasters after the 1850s (in Halifax marine disasters accounted for 12 percent of registry closures for vessels registered in the 1850s and 34 percent for vessels registered in the 1870s; the comparable figures for P.E.I. vessels are 13 percent and 25 percent).[26] Whatever the reason for registry closure, mean life expectancy increased. If all other factors remained constant (and in spite of short-term fluctuations average vessel prices remained quite flat or declined slightly between the 1850s and early 1870s), then increased longevity had increased by 50 percent the likelihood of amortizing the investment in an ocean-going vessel by the 1870s.

Improvements in vessel productivity must at the same time have increased total output in the fleet and even compensated for much of the decline in freight rates in the 1880s. In all fleets, first of all, there was a substantial increase in mean tonnage from one decade to the next, as owners sought to reap the advantages of greater carrying capacity. The average Saint John vessel operating in the growth period from 1863 to 1877 was 801 tons; there was a 36 percent increase (to 1093 tons) in the period from 1878 to 1890, and a 37 percent increase in the next period, from 1891 to 1912 (to 1497 tons).[27] Of equal importance was the fact that Canadian shipowners did not sacrifice speed to carrying capacity: the advantage of operating these vessels as "cheap warehouses" does not seem to apply. Data on passage times leads inescapably to the conclusions, not only that passage times were shortening, but also that actual sailing speeds were increasing over time. On westward passages from Liverpool to nine major ports, and on four eastward passages, passage times improved on eleven of thirteen routes between the 1863–77 period and the 1878–90 period (improvements ranged from 1.3 percent on the Liverpool–New Orleans route to 26.1 percent on the Liverpool-Philadelphia run; the mean percentage change was 5.3 percent).[28] A similar analysis was undertaken for passages by Halifax vessels from eastern American ports (between New York and Baltimore) to ports in the United Kingdom or northern European ports (between Amsterdam and Havre). These passages were chosen to allow a sufficient number of cases and to reduce the possibility that shorter distance might account for reduced passage times. Sailing eastwards, over six days were saved between the 1860s and 1880s, representing a 15 percent improvement; in the other direction eleven days were saved, which means that sailing times improved by 20 percent. At the same time significant improvements were recorded in turn-around times between the end of one voyage and the beginning of the next, and in port times during a voyage. In the Saint John fleet there was a 7 percent decrease in all turn-around times between the periods 1863–77 and 1878–90, with the biggest decreases recorded by the largest classes of vessel and by European and American ports. Port-of-call times declined by 10 percent between the same two periods. Taking into account the changes in sailing times and port times, the typical voyage from an eastern American port to the United Kingdom and back, with stops on both sides of the Atlantic, took fourteen fewer days between the periods 1863–77 and 1878–90. This represented a potential gain in gross output of over 10 percent between the two periods. These changes apply to sailing vessels only, since steamers were excluded. After 1890 all port times increased, and they increased most rapidly in British and American ports. These improvements suggest that great efforts were made to maintain the profitability of vessels by forcing masters to make more voyages within the same period of time.

Improvements in vessel productivity were accompanied by improvements in labour productivity. Labour productivity can be measured either by the ratio of labour to capital (the man-ton ratio), or in terms of output per unit of labour employed. In the fleets of Halifax and Yarmouth the man-ton ratio fell by over 2 percent a year between 1863 and 1899; in the large Saint John fleet there was a comparable saving in labour to 1890, and then a much steeper decline, at an annual rate of 5 percent between 1891 and 1912. A major reason for this improvement was that capital inputs increased faster than did labour inputs, even in this "traditional" industry. As vessel size increased there was not a proportionate increase in labour requirements, because in these fleets the number of masts and sails to be handled did not increase as hull size expanded. But increases in vessel size are not the only reason for declining man-ton ratios. It has been possible by various methods to hold tonnage constant and to observe changes in labour requirements owing to factors other than changes in tonnage. A significant proportion (probably about a third) of the decline in man-ton ratios was due to factors other than increasing vessel size. For instance, between the 1860s and the 1880s masters of 1000-ton vessels reduced their crews by 20 percent, and shipowners benefitted from a substantial saving in their wage bill.[29]

It is difficult to determine what caused these improvements in the performance of vessels and crew. There appears to have been no major change in the structure of vessels, apart from their increasing size, although students of naval architecture might well pursue the question further. So far no satisfactory explanation for increasing vessel life has emerged, although the desire of shipowners to extend the revenue-earning life of their assets was likely to be an important factor, particularly when freight rates were declining. The improved Lloyds rating of Canadian vessels after mid-century, and the prices received for Canadian vessels in Britain, suggests that improvements in construction had occurred.[30] Some technological innovations did help to save labour and improve performance: these included the use of double rather than single topsails, wire rigging, patented reefing gear, canvas windmill pumps, and donkey engines.[31] Masters and officers were also more experienced in handling larger crews as time passed and as vessel size increased, and as G.S. Graham noted long ago masters were becoming more familiar with prevailing winds and currents in this period.[32] It is likely that when freight rates declined after the mid-1870s shipowners pressured masters to cut costs and improve performance. If the correspondence published in the *Novascotiaman* is representative, shipowners scrupulously trimmed expenditures wherever they could. N.B. Lewis and B.F. Gullison repeat the credo of parsimony on almost every page: "Hold things up as cheaply as possible and make all you can of it."[33] It is also possible, as Robin Craig has suggested, that improvements in performance reflect the "different time horizon" of owners of short-lived softwood vessels: "Canadian shipowners did not sacrifice speed to carrying capacity because they were operating softwood vessels in which the capital had to be written down fairly rapidly."[34] Certainly Lewis preferred not to leave his vessel waiting for an uncertain advance in freights: "Were glad to get her fixed even at this low rate. Never found any money in waiting. Any advances is lost in time and expense with the best of softwood ships."[35]

There may also be some substance to the old image of the brutal Bluenose masters, "those crude bully-boys that bang their way around the world with belaying pins and pistols, taking pot-shots at people on the royal yards when they feel a little disturbed or unhappy."[36] Certainly Canadian shipowners preferred to hire local masters: in the fleets of Yarmouth, Windsor, and Halifax, Maritimers were a majority among masters and officers (in the Yarmouth fleet 81 percent of voyages were undertaken by Nova Scotian masters); and in the fleets of Halifax and Yarmouth the Nova Scotian master achieved more rapid savings in labour than did other masters (with other factors held constant), particularly when he was working for a Nova Scotian managing owner.[37] Captain B.F. Gullison of the *N.B. Lewis*, writing from New Orleans to his managing-owner in Yarmouth, suggests how far a master was prepared to go in order to secure a good first officer, preferably one "from home": "I telegraphed you on Saturday asking you to send me mate. I received yours today.' Can't find mate, will have to do best you can.' I am very sorry as I am in want of one very much, the fact is I cannot get along with the one I have and there is none here at present that I would take and no likelihood of being any very soon. I know the cost is considerable from home here but sometimes the dearest article is the least expensive in the end. . . ."[38]

There is also some evidence of preference for local sailors, and in large port cities masters were able to exercise some discretion in selecting their crews. The seafaring labour pool as a whole may have been a polyglot mixture (we shall soon be able to answer this question for British shipping in the late nineteenth century); but the labour force on Canadian ocean-going vessels was not, as Wallace believed, truly international or "composed of all nationalities."[39] A majority were English-speaking, coming particularly from Canada, the United States, and Britain. The proportion of Canadian sailors decreased over time, presumably because alternative opportunities for employment on land became more attractive in the last decades of the century. The proportion of European (particularly Scandinavian) sailors increased, until by the 1890s British and western European sailors were the overwhelming majority of the crew. There existed, however, a noticeable preference for local sailors: it is necessary to take into account the relative size of the national populations from which crew might be drawn. On a per capita basis Nova Scotians and New Brunswickers were conspicuously overrepresented in our fleets, even if masters and officers are excluded (in the Yarmouth fleet Nova Scotians had by far the highest participation rate on a per capita basis, at sixty-two per ten thousand population; the rate for New Brunswickers was thirty-three per ten thousand followed by Scandinavians at a mere nine per ten thousand).[40] Wherever possible masters exercised discretion in selecting their crew; furthermore there is no reason to believe that sailors were drawn from a depressed and relatively ill-educated lumpenproletariat.[41] These factors, and the greater experience of crews (their average age increased over time), help to explain improvements in labour productivity between the 1860s and 1890s. Labour costs were a major component in the costs of vessel operation, and savings in labour helped to sustain profit levels for the owners of sailing vessels in these decades. Since wages in the industry increased only slightly in the 1860s and thereafter fell slightly, and since other costs (capital cost of hulls, insurance, port charges, victualling) remained constant or declined slightly in these decades, the chances of amortizing the investment in a wooden sailing vessel remained favourable even as freight rates declined in the 1880s.

The continued investment in wooden sailing vessels in the 1860s and 1870s was not an unpropitious gamble but a finely judged attempt to seize expanding opportunities, and then to maintain rates of return as the demand for sailing ship services fell. The hypothesis that investment in wooden shipping was an unfortunate diversion of resources and a constraint on the growth of other industries can be accepted only if one could prove that better investment opportunities existed in the Canadian context in the 1860s and 1870s, and that these better opportunities were rejected in favour of investment in shipping. No such proof exists. It is not yet possible to compare rates of return in shipping with rates of return on landward investments. But we have been able to estimate the growth of output in shipping, and so to compare output in shipping with output in landward enterprises. These output growth rates allow a rough comparison between the expansion of market opportunities in landward and seaward sectors. The estimates of output in shipping also help to confirm that labour productivity improved in terms of output per unit of labour employed.

In estimating the growth of output in shipping we begin by measuring the annual rate of growth of physical output in terms of the relationship:

$$\overline{GO} = \overline{EN} + \overline{SV}$$

where $\overline{GO}$ is the rate of growth of gross output, $\overline{EN}$ is the rate of growth of the total number of entrances into port by all vessels operating in the fleet, and $\overline{SV}$ is the rate of growth of average vessel size. This relationship measures the growth in output in terms of both total entrances into port and cargo capacity entering port; this growth will be determined by available freights, sailing and turn-around times, time lost in repairs, total fleet size, and so on. This method of measuring output is feasible only because our sample of Crew Lists is so large.[42] The equations are then revised to take into account the inevitable increase in the ratio of ballast to cargo on North Atlantic routes. We think it reasonable to assume that vessels entering British or European ports carried cargo and that outward sailings to regions other than North America were mainly with cargo. But we know that an increasing number of sailings to North America were with ballast. We assume, very conservatively, that only 75 percent of North American entries in 1863 were fully laden, and that this proportion fell at a constant rate to only 10 percent in 1890. The trend in total entrances is then deflated to produce $\overline{REV}$, which estimates the growth in cargo-carrying entrances. The equation allows only an estimate of physical output, however. Estimates of revenue are introduced by adjusting for trends in freight rates. For Saint John and Yarmouth the Isserlis index was used; for Halifax our own index of sailing-ship freight rates for American bulk cargoes was used (the two indices follow very similar patterns, in fact). These freight rate indices have been deflated to take into account price changes in the Atlantic economy; since Canadian owners would be likely to assess their investments in terms of prices in the Canadian economy, a Canadian import price index has been used. Real gross output in each fleet is estimated by

$$\overline{GO} = \overline{REV} + \overline{SV} + \overline{FRW}$$

where $\overline{FRW}$ is the rate of growth of the weighted freight-rate index.[43]

The results (table 2) suggest that a very high growth in output occurred in all three ports well into the 1870s. Market opportunities allowed an expansion of output substantially higher than output growth in other sectors of the economy. It has been estimated, for instance, that Canadian GNP grew at 2.4 percent per annum in the 1870s and that gross output in manufacturing grew 2.9 percent in the same decade.[44] In Nova Scotia total industrial output in real terms grew at an annual rate of 5.7 percent in the 1870s; output in shipping grew at a similar rate in Halifax until 1876, and somewhat faster in the Yarmouth fleet until 1879. In New Brunswick industrial growth was much more sluggish in the 1870s (growing at an annual rate of 1.9 percent), and our estimate of output in the Saint John fleet suggests that market opportunities in shipping were growing three times as fast as were opportunities in landward industries.[45] It is difficult to argue that shipowners were collectively mistaken about potential returns in landward industries, since we know that shipowners were already involved in a range of businesses, including banking, insurance, retailing, mining, and occasionally manufacturing. If the census data on "capital invested" have any meaning, then the value of fixed and working capital in industry grew more quickly than did real output or value added in both Nova Scotia and New Brunswick in the 1870s, which suggests that returns on capital invested may have been disappointing (a unit increase in capital was not matched by a comparable increase in real output or value added).[46] On the other hand, in those counties where local resources or the arrival of a railway expanded market opportunities, and where the growth of output was faster than the growth of capital stock, the exodus from shipping occurred as early as the 1870s (this applies particularly to Halifax, and to Northumberland and Westmorland counties in New Brunswick, which were located on the Intercolonial Railway).[47] In the 1880s shipowning was even less a constraint upon investment in industry, since tonnage in service declined in all ports except Windsor, while industrial investment and output accelerated in both Nova Scotia and New Brunswick. Where other opportunities appeared favourable the movement of capital from shipping was smooth and rapid, and it is difficult to imagine how in these circumstances one industry acted as a constraint upon others.

TABLE 2

Estimated Gross Output in Shipping, 1869–90

	Gross Output		
	GO = REV + SV + FRW		
Saint John	1869–77 +6.8%	1878–90	−0.8%
Yarmouth	1869–79 +7.4%	1879–90	−1.6%
Halifax	1866–76 +5.4%	1877–90	−4.9%

SOURCE: Crew Lists and Agreements for vessels registered in Saint John, Yarmouth, and Halifax. In each case the two periods are centred on the peak year of investment in each port.

Although we cannot yet compare profits in shipping with profits in landward enterprises, it is likely that profits as well as total output were increasing rapidly in the 1860s and 1870s. The decline in freight rates in the late 1870s did not prevent an output growth rate of over 7 percent for the Yarmouth fleet in that decade. In the same period total man-months of labour grew by only 4.1 percent a year, and total wage costs for the fleet grew by 5.1 percent, which suggests that output per unit labour cost was growing by more than 2 percent a year. Even in the 1880s there were significant gains in labour productivity in the Yarmouth fleet, since estimated output fell by only 1.6 percent a year, whereas total man-months fell by 5.8 percent a year and the total wage bill fell by 4.6 percent a year. Since other costs were generally steady or falling, rates of return must have increased in the 1870s. In the 1880s rates of return likely remained positive for those vessels retained in service (otherwise the vessels would have been sold or abandoned), but returns were probably lower than in the 1870s, since freight rates (and hence gross earnings) were falling more quickly than were operating costs.

Rates of return may have improved in the 1860s and early 1870s, but it is possible that profits began at a low level and remained relatively poor, as McClelland argued. Freight rates and costs fluctuated steeply in this industry. In favourable circumstances the returns from a particular voyage could be enormous; but the overall earnings record in a fleet could still be poor. McClelland's evidence is based mainly on an analysis of net earnings by Moran family vessels between 1867 and 1878.[48] Earnings per ton and net earnings after depreciation were calculated for an average of eleven vessels a year from 1867 to 1878. If they do nothing else, the results lend further weight to our argument that output and revenues were growing rapidly at least until the mid-1870s. Between 1867 and 1874 gross earnings per ton increased by 4 percent a year, and the rate of return (net earnings as a percentage of the depreciated value of the fleet) increased by 7 percent a year.[49] But how large were those earnings? Certainly they were greater than McClelland believed: he underestimated the rate of return on these vessels because he overestimated the capital value of the vessels when newly built, and underestimated the rate at which the average wooden vessel in this period depreciated. If we recalculate the rate of return using an initial capital valuation of seven pounds per ton rather than ten pounds, the mean annual rate of return on these vessels was close to 20 percent before 1874, and it remained positive, although declining steeply, after 1874.[50] Such a rate of return is remarkably high; but analysis of returns for other ocean-going vessels, where detailed records exist, suggests that net earnings as a proportion of the depreciated value of a vessel were often as high as 20 percent, and for some vessels the rate could remain above 10 percent even in the 1880s. The *Magna Charta* of Saint John, for instance, earned gross revenues of $8300 a year between 1868 and 1883; deducting operating costs and depreciation, the annual average return was 15 percent of the depreciated value of the vessel.[51] The *N.B. Lewis* of Yarmouth earned over $3100 a year, net of operating costs and depreciation, between 1885 and 1892 (a rate of return of about 12 percent).[52] We have attempted to reconstruct the potential earnings of vessels carrying particular cargoes in the North Atlantic, using a standard formula and available data on freight rates, vessel tonnage, stowage factors, and operating costs (mainly wages, depreciation, insurance, victualling, port charges, and repairs). The results of this exercise (with grain as the standard cargo) tend to confirm that a rate of return of 20 percent was not unexpected in the early 1870s.[53]

It is risky to assume that entire fleets enjoyed precisely the same rates of returns as did particular cases. But it is no longer possible to argue that shipping experienced a "dubious earnings record after 1865." Capital stock in the industry in the Maritimes was growing by almost 4 percent a year in the 1860s and 1870s; it is difficult to believe that such a sustained growth would have occurred if profits had not been high. If rates of return were high, then shipping must have made a significant contribution to capital accumulation in Saint John, Yarmouth, Windsor, and even Halifax. It is unlikely that all such savings were lost to the community, since we know that shipowners were investing in many local enterprises in this period.[54] If the entire Saint John fleet experienced rates of return approaching 20 percent, then shipping would have accounted for a net flow of income of over a million dollars a year in the early 1870s, or a fifth of the declared value of New Brunswick exports in each year.

This does not confirm the argument that shipping and shipbuilding were the "linchpin" of the economy; nor does it refute McClelland's argument that these industries were poor contributors to economic development. The shipping industry probably contributed to the accumulation of savings in shipowning centres, and to the extent that shipowners channelled these savings into a variety of landward enterprises (as we know many did), there was an important contribution to industrial growth and diversification. But in other ways these industries were weak contributors to economic development: this was McClelland's argument in 1966, and it remains substantially unquestioned.[55] Since Maritimers' vessels operated largely outside Canadian trades, the linkages between shipping and the local economy were few (except with shipbuilding). In spite of the preference for local sailors, employment opportunities offered to Maritimers were not numerous. Shipbuilding itself employed little more than 2 percent of New Brunswick's labour force, and its demand for timber and metals was not a significant stimulus to either industry.[56] Although shipping was a capital-intensive service industry, it did not directly stimulate much local capital formation. The skills acquired in shipping and shipbuilding were highly specialized ones, and not readily transferable (except in the case of ship carpenters, who moved into construction). Even the entrepreneurial skills acquired in the shipping business were specialized, and not easily shifted into manufacturing industries serving Canadian markets. The evidence collected by Gerry Panting suggests that shipowners (although not ship-builders) tended to move their capital and energies into banking, transportation, and other service industries, rather than into manufacturing.[57] The shipping industry was no engine of economic growth; and it is worth noting that the 1870s was a decade of slow industrial growth in most of the region's shipowning centres and a decade of massive out-migration from the major shipping centre, Saint John.[58]

In one respect McClelland's argument about the direct economic benefits of shipping may be qualified. In Newfoundland and Nova Scotia particularly, coastal and fishing vessels were themselves a type of backward linkage from another marine industry, the fisheries. Shipping was the linchpin of a marine-based economy, such as that of Newfoundland, since the supplying of outport com-munities, the extension of the fishery to Labrador and the Grand Banks, and the very existence of the seal fishery depended upon capital inputs in the form of vessels of various types. It is no surprise to find a very high positive correlation between the growth of outport populations and the building of schooners. There is also a positive correlation between the gross value of fisheries output and investment in schooner tonnage.[59] Nevertheless, McClelland's argument about linkages from shipping itself remains intact: even if the owners of ocean-going shipping made respectable profits, they were investing in a service industry having limited linkage effects, particularly of the kind which might have stimulated the development of a more diversified manufacturing industry. Until this argument is refuted, it is not possible to claim that the decline of shipping and shipbuilding was a major cause of the relative economic weakness of the Maritimes in the decades which followed.

At the same time it remains difficult to accept McClelland's more extreme claim that shipping and shipbuilding acted as serious constraints upon the growth of other industries. Capital employed and revenues earned in the industry were highly mobile; when alternative investment opportunities appeared more tempt-ing, shipowners could shift their capital and run down their investment in ship-ping very quickly. It was all the more easy to do this since a majority of the major shipowners in the region were involved from the beginning of their careers in merchandising, banking, finance, and other landward activities. By the late 1870s and 1880s a declining portion of shipping revenues was being ploughed back into shipping; shipowners were probably contributing capital to the growing industrial and service sectors of the 1870s and 1880s.[60] Shipping was also an essential factor in many of the primary industries which continued to exist in the new industrial age. Coastal shipping was essential not only to the production and marketing of fish, but also to trade within the region and to trade with other parts of British North America and to the United States. As S.A. Saunders pointed out, coastal shipping in the Maritimes was briefly stimulated by railway con-struction, until branch lines and steamships reduced the demand for small wooden coasters.[61] The argument that traditional economic activities such as shipping and shipbuilding constrained the growth of manufacturing industry and a more diversified economic development has not been proved. It is more likely that the eager pursuit of new industries diverted capital and resources from traditional marine-related activities, and particularly from the fisheries. If these conclusions appear tentative it is because informed discussion of these issues has scarcely begun.

These conclusions have a direct bearing upon the most potent of all myths about the Canadian shipping industry. The decline of the industry has always been explained in terms of technological obsolescence: the Canadian industry was destroyed by the competition of iron and steam. The difficulty of making the transition to a new technology may help to explain the decline of the ship-building industry: it would have required an enormous effort and substantial subsidies to compete with British and European builders. But technological obsolescence merely begs the question: why did shipowners in Atlantic Canada not invest in iron and steam vessels? It appears that shipowners did not lack the capital to make such investments. Certainly they did not withdraw from the shipping industry because they were losing money: shipowners in Windsor appear to have been satisfied with returns in the North Atlantic even in the 1880s, and expanded their stock of vessels until 1891. There were still 110,000 tons of shipping on registry in Saint John by the mid-1890s (78 percent of these were deep-sea vessels of 250 tons or more); it is unlikely that businessmen would retain so large a fleet if they were not making some profits. Since it is not possible to compare rates of return in shipping with rates of return in landward enterprises, we cannot estimate precisely the opportunity costs of capital invested in shipping. There can be little doubt, however, that by the 1880s (and in some ports in the 1870s) various landward enterprises appeared to offer rates of return which, if less spectacular, were at least more stable than returns in shipping. In both Nova Scotia and New Brunswick market opportunities in landward sectors appeared to be expanding very rapidly in the 1880s: in Nova Scotia industrial output grew in real terms by 6.4 percent a year and value added grew by 7.2 percent; in New Brunswick industrial output grew by 3.6 percent a year and value added by 5.4 percent a year.[62] Growth rates were above the provincial average in the major shipowning counties of Yarmouth, Hants, Pictou, and Saint John (in Halifax they were already above average in the 1870s). By the 1880s there were sound reasons for not reinvesting in wooden sailing vessels: given the continuing decline in freight rates, a rapid amortization of the investment seemed less certain than before. There were even better reasons for not investing in iron steamers: the initial capital cost was high, amortization would require a long-term commitment, and the management of fleets of iron steamers probably required a different corporate structure from the old family firm which had dominated the wooden shipping business. Even if in some cases the returns from shipping remained high, this was an industry subject to great risk; the young Canadian Confederation, and its National Policy, appeared to be offering stable opportunities in a range of landward enterprises. Most shipowners were content to expand their existing assets in landward service industries, and to reap what they could from an expanding industrial economy.

The passing of the eastern Canadian shipping industry was not simply the result of businessmen's calculation of opportunity costs. The decline of this industry occurred in no textbook free market, but in a society where political decisions and national policy shaped the environment in which businessmen made their choices. The economic power of the Canadian state was used in this generation to stimulate western development and central Canadian manufacturing. There would be massive subsidies for railways but few for shipbuilding or ship operation; there would be no Canadian navigation acts. This is not to say that public investment in shipping would have been a better allocation of Canadian resources than was our public investment in railways. To prove such a contention would require a complicated (and probably inconclusive) exercise in counter-factual speculation. It is worth reminding ourselves, however, that a political decision was taken to subsidize certain sectors and not others; the choice necessarily involved costs and foregone opportunities. There were opportunities for profitable investment in Canadian carrying trades, both before and during the "wheat boom." The demand for carrying capacity in Canadian ports grew by 4.5 percent a year in the 1880s and by 3.1 percent a year in the 1890s; in the early 1900s tonnage clearing all Canadian ports grew by 4.2 percent a year.[63] Even if we take into account the decline in freight rates there remained an expansion of gross returns from Canadian carrying trades; in the 1910s opportunities mushroomed as freight rates soared.

It is not self-evident that our economic and political interests were best served by the collective failure to sustain a shipping industry to serve Canada's export trades. There were politicians, both local and national, who wanted the National Policy to include a shipping industry and Atlantic seaports as part of a truly national economic structure. But the vision of Canada as a maritime power soon faded, even in the Maritimes.[64] It is impossible to know how far a shipping industry might have contributed to prosperity in the Maritimes in the twentieth century. We are spared that knowledge by the decisions of the late nineteenth century, when Canadians pursued a landward development strategy and left the people of the Maritimes to dream of past glories and foregone opportunities.

Notes

1. Frederick William Wallace, *Wooden Ships and Iron Men* (London, 1924); *In the Wake of the Wind Ships* (Toronto, 1927); *Record of Canadian Shipping* (London, 1929).

2. See particularly Stanley T. Spicer, *Masters of Sail: The Era of Square-rigged Vessels in the Maritime Provinces* (Toronto, 1968); Charles A. Armour and Thomas Lackey, *Sailing Ships of the Maritimes* (Toronto, 1975); Richard Rice, "The Wrights of Saint John: A Study of Shipbuilding and Shipowning in the Maritimes, 1839–1855," in *Canadian Business History: Selected Studies, 1497–1971*, edited by David S. Macmillan (Toronto, 1972); David Alexander and Gerald Panting, "The Mercantile Fleet and its Owners: Yarmouth, Nova Scotia, 1840–1889," *Acadiensis* VII, 2 (1978): 3–28; Eric W. Sager and Lewis R. Fischer, "Patterns of Investment in the Shipping Industries of Atlantic Canada, 1820–1900," *Acadiensis* IX, 1 (1979): 19–43. The proceedings of the conferences of the Atlantic Canada Shipping Project are mentioned below. For a review of some recent literature on the subject see David Sutherland, "Wooden Ships and Iron Men Revisited," *Acadiensis* VIII, 1 (1978): 101–7.

3. Wallace, *Wooden Ships and Iron Men*, 35; see also J.G.B. Hutchins, *The American Maritime Industries and Public Policy, 1789–1914* (New York, 1941), 300–1, 412.

4. Peter D. McClelland, "The New Brunswick Economy in the Nineteenth Century" (Ph.D. thesis, Harvard University, 1966), 186.

5. Wallace, *Wooden Ships and Iron Men*, ix; J.P. Parker, *Sails of the Maritimes* (Halifax, 1960), 55.

6. Hutchins, *The American Maritime Industries*, 300–1.

7. Wallace, *Wooden Ships and Iron Men*, 165, 174.

8. C.R. Fay and Harold Innis, "The Maritime Provinces," *Cambridge History of the British Empire*, VI, *Canada and Newfoundland* (New York, 1930), 663.

9. McClelland, "The New Brunswick Economy"; "The New Brunswick Economy in the Nineteenth Century," *Journal of Political Economy* XXV, 4 (1965): 686–90.

10. McClelland, "The New Brunswick Economy", iii, 168–235.

11. Data on major fleets are taken from the Board of Trade (hereafter BT) series 107 and 108 vessel registries in the Public Record Office, Kew, supplemented where necessary by data from port copies of registries held by Canadian registrars of shipping or by the Public Archives of Canada. Registries have been analyzed (from 1820 or from date of registry opening) to 1914 for the following ports of registry: Saint John, Miramichi, Halifax, Yarmouth, Windsor, Pictou, Charlottetown, and St. John's.

12. On Saint John shipping see Esther Clark Wright, *Saint John Ships and Their Builders* (Wolfville, 1975); Lewis R. Fischer, "The Great Mudhole Fleet: The Voyages and Productivity of the Sailing Vessels of Saint John, 1863–1912," in *Volumes Not Values: Canadian Sailing Ships and World Trades*, edited by David Alexander and Rosemary Ommer (St. John's, 1979), 117–55.

13. By coastal vessels we mean those rigged as schooners, brigantines, sloops, shallops, and ketches. There was a high correlation between rig and tonnage, and almost all vessels having these types of rigging were under 150 tons.

14. On the Newfoundland fleet see Eric W. Sager, "The Merchants of Water Street and Capital Investment in Newfoundland's Traditional Economy," in *The Enterprising Canadians: Entrepreneurs and Economic Development in Eastern Canada, 1820–1914*, edited by Lewis R. Fischer and Eric W. Sager (St. John's, 1979), 75–95.

15. Richard Rice, "Measuring British Dominance of Shipbuilding in the Maritimes, 1787–1890," in *Ships and Shipbuilding in the North Atlantic Region*, edited by Keith Matthews and Gerald Panting (St. John's, 1977), 109–55.

16. BT 107/108 vessel registries.

17. Ibid. On P.E.I. shipping sees R.S. Craig, "British Shipping and British North American Shipbuilding in the Early Nineteenth Century, with special reference to Prince Edward Island," in *The Southwest and the Sea*, edited by H.E.S. Fisher (Exeter, 1968); Lewis R. Fischer, "The Port of Prince Edward Island, 1840–1889," in *Ships and Shipbuilding*, 41–70. In the 1840s 41.5 percent of all vessels transferred from the Pictou registry went to other ports in British North America; see Rosemary E. Ommer, "Anticipating the Trend: The Pictou Ship Register, 1840–1889," *Acadiensis* X, 1 (1980): 75–76.

18. Hutchins, *The American Maritime Industries*, 301; McClelland, "The New Brunswick Economy," 186.

19. There was a fairly close correlation between annual changes in new tonnage added to the registry in our ports and annual changes in sailing tonnage built and first registered in the United Kingdom, particularly in the early registration cycles (1820–30, 1830–43, 1843–53) and from 1858 to 1869; this applies not only to P.E.I. but also to the non-transfer-trade ports (Yarmouth and Halifax).

20. A non-computerized analysis of early Crew Agreements in the BT 98 series for vessels registered in Halifax and Saint John confirms that an overwhelming majority of voyages were in the North Atlantic in the 1840s and 1850s; see Lewis R. Fischer and Gerald Panting, "Harbour and Metropolis: The Shipping Industry of Saint John and the Urban Economy, 1820–1914," in *Merchant Shipping and Economic Development in Atlantic Canada*, edited by Lewis R. Fischer and Eric W. Sager (St. John's, 1982).

21. Wallace, *Wooden Ships and Iron Men*, 193.

22. Most of these "Crew Lists" for vessels registered in the British empire between 1863 and 1939 are contained in the archive of the Maritime History Group, Memorial University of Newfoundland. We have analyzed 4172 voyages for Yarmouth vessels, 8829 voyages for Saint John vessels, 3577 voyages for Windsor vessels, and 1844 voyages for Halifax vessels. The Crew List computer files for these four ports also contain entries for 170,000 seamen. See Lewis R. Fischer and Eric W. Sager, "An Approach to the Quantitative Analysis of British Shipping Records," *Business History* XXII, 2 (1980): 135–51.

23. David Alexander, "Output and Productivity in the Yarmouth Ocean Fleet, 1863–1901," in *Volumes Not Values*, 84–85.

24. Sager and Fischer, "Patterns of Investment," 41–42. Correlating annual changes in Keith Matthews' sailing-ship freight index and annual changes in newly registered ocean-going tonnage for four ports yielded $r^2 = +.61$ for 1869/70–1879/80 and $r^2 = +.67$ for 1879/80–1885/86. See Keith Matthews, "The Canadian Deep Sea Merchant Marine and the American Export Trade, 1850–1890," in *Volumes Not Values*, 195–243.

25. It is worth noting that Douglass North found no significant improvement in sailing speeds between 1820 and 1860, and doubted that the fall in real shipping costs in this period was influenced by increased speed. Our data suggest that, for Canadian vessels at least, there may have been some productivity improvements as a result of increased sailing speeds. North, "Sources of Productivity Change in Ocean Shipping, 1600–1850," *Journal of Political Economy* LXXVI, 5 (1968): 1953–70.

26. BT 107/108 vessel registries. For Yarmouth, however, marine disasters as a proportion of tonnage on registry did not increase significantly. Loss rates were never so high that they might have threatened the financial basis of the industry. Alexander and Panting, "The Mercantile Fleet and its Owners," 15–16.

27. There were disadvantages, however, to larger vessels: the range of ports was restricted, and so was the range of cargoes that could be carried profitably. See Robin Craig, "Conference Summary," in *Volumes Not Values*, 364.

28. The routes selected were Liverpool to New York, Boston, Philadelphia, New Orleans, Saint John, Callao, Quebec City, Havana, and Rio de Janeiro; New York to Liverpool, London, and Havana; and Saint John to Liverpool. Fischer, "The Great Mudhole Fleet," in *Volumes Not Values*, 136.

29. On man-ton ratios see David Williams, "Crew Size in Trans-Atlantic Trades in the Mid-Nineteenth Century," and Eric W. Sager, "Labour Productivity in the Shipping Fleets of Halifax and Yarmouth, Nova Scotia, 1863–1900," in *Working Men Who Got Wet*, edited by Rosemary Ommer and Gerald Panting (St. John's, 1980), 105–53, 155–84.

30. The firm prices for Canadian vessels are reflected in the papers of the shipbrokers Messrs. Kellock and Co. of Liverpool, contained in the National Maritime Museum, Greenwich; the improved Lloyds' rating is noted by R.S. Craig, "British Shipping and British North American Shipbuilding in the Early Nineteenth Century," in *The Southwest and the Sea*.

31. On the purchase of a windmill pump see Clement W. Crowell, *Novascotiaman* (Halifax, 1979), 123. We are indebted to Neils Jannasch for pointing out many of these improvements.

32. G.S. Graham, "The Ascendancy of the Sailing Ship, 1850–85," *Economic History Review* IX, 1 (1956–57): 75–81; R.O. Goss, "Economics and Canadian Atlantic Shipping," in *Merchant Shipping and Economic Development*.

33. Crowell, *Novascotiaman*, 153.

34. Craig, "Conference Summary," 364.

35. Crowell, *Novascotiaman*, 95.

36. Craig, "Conference Summary," 364. One of the best descriptions of a pistol-carrying Bluenose master appears in Samlet au Svein Molaug, *Sjofolk forteller; therdagshistorien fra seilskutiden* (Oslo, 1977), 15–16. We are indebted to Captain Lewis Parker for this reference.

37. In the Halifax fleet, for instance, the Nova Scotian master sailed with a smaller crew in every tonnage class under 1500 tons; his man-ton ratio was 5.3 percent lower than that for non-Nova Scotians, when time and tonnage class are held constant (calculated from the Crew Lists for Halifax vessels).

38. Crowell, *Novascotiaman*, 158.

39. The portrait of crews serving on British vessels will come from our current analysis of a 1 percent sample of the entire Crew List archive for British imperial shipping from 1863 to 1913.

40. These ratios are merely the total appearances from 1870 to 1889 by crew born in each region relative to the average of the total population of that region in two decennial censuses (usually 1871 and 1881). For a more refined analysis see Rosemary E. Ommer, " 'Composed of All Nationalities': The Crews of Windsor Vessels, 1862–1899," in *Working Men Who Got Wet*, 191–227.

41. Literacy rates suggest that sailors usually did not come from an illiterate substratum of the national populations from which they were drawn. In the late 1860s 69 percent of all crew were literate, and this proportion rose to 85 percent in the 1890s. See David Alexander, "Literacy Among Canadian and Foreign Seamen, 1863–1899," in *Working Men Who Got Wet*, 1–33.

42. The Yarmouth Crew List file probably contains data on two-thirds of all voyages ever undertaken by Yarmouth ocean-going vessels between 1863 and 1900.

43. It is possible that the use of vessel entrances as a basic component in this estimate may produce misleading results: as time passed more voyages were on long-distance routes having fewer entrances, even though vessels may have been profitably employed on those routes. A second estimate, replacing $\overline{REV}$ with $\overline{RVT}$, where $\overline{RVT}$ represents the growth of time spent on potential revenue-earning voyages, yielded the following annual growth rates for Saint John: 1863–77: +6.4 percent; 1878–90: −0.2 percent. See Fischer and Panting, "Harbour and Metropolis," *Merchant Shipping and Economic Development*.

44. O.J. Firestone, "Development of Canada's Economy, 1850–1900," National Bureau of Economic Research, *Trends in the American Economy in the Nineteenth Century* (Princeton, 1960), 222, 234.

45. Growth rates for Nova Scotia and New Brunswick are calculated from Canada, *Census*, 1871, 1891, and 1901. In order to approximate growth in landward industries ship construction was excluded from the totals. Values from which growth rates were calculated were constant 1935–39 dollars; census figures were deflated by the Canadian wholesale price index J34 in M.C. Urquhart and K.A.H. Buckley, *Historical Statistics of Canada* (Cambridge, 1965), 294.

46. Thus in New Brunswick fixed and working capital grew by 4.6 percent a year in real terms between 1870 and 1880, whereas gross value of industrial production grew by 1.9 percent a year and value added by 0.8 percent a year; the comparable figures for Nova Scotia in the 1870s are 6.5 percent, 5.7 percent, and 4.3 percent, respectively. Canada, *Census*, 1871, 1881.

47. In Northumberland industrial output grew by 10 percent a year in constant dollars in the 1870s; in Westmorland the growth rate was 9.8 percent a year, and in Halifax City it was 7.7 percent a year.

48. His calculations are from the Moran-Galloway Account Books, New Brunswick Museum.

49. We use "rate of return" in the same sense as McClelland did: it is net profit after depreciation as a percentage of capital employed. Loan capital and working capital are excluded from capital employed: there is little evidence that major shipowners borrowed extensively to acquire new vessels, and even if they did profits net of debt charges must still have been high; and large amounts of working capital were not required, since most operating costs were paid out of vessel earnings, often by a broker.

50. McClelland relied heavily upon data contained in the Moran-Galloway Account Books for his cost estimates, but this superb source has led to an overestimate of building costs because by the early 1870s the firm was buying most of its new tonnage from shipyards in Saint John City, where building costs were higher. Our time series on newly built tonnage has been compiled from a variety of sources, including the Peake Letterbooks (Public Archives of P.E.I.) and the Hilyard, Fisher, and Ward Papers (New Brunswick Museum). For a more complete description of sources see Lewis R. Fischer, *Enterprise in a Maritime Setting: The Shipping Industry of Prince Edward Island, 1787–1914* (St. John's, 1982), chap. 5. We have estimated depreciation, very conservatively, at 7 percent a year.

51. Calculated from Hilyard Papers, New Brunswick Museum. See also the examples in Spicer, *Masters of Sail*, 196–97.

52. Calculated from data contained in Crowell, *Novascotiaman*. We are indebted to Rosemary Ommer for compiling data from this source. Insurance expenditures of $800 a year are included among costs; the vessel (purchased in 1880 for $40,000) was depreciated at a rate of 7 percent a year.

53. The results appear in Lewis R. Fischer, Eric W. Sager, and Rosemary E. Ommer, "The Shipping Industry and Regional Economic Development in Atlantic Canada, 1871–1891: Saint John as a Case Study," in *Merchant Shipping and Economic Development*.

54. See, for instance, Gerald Panting, "Personnel and Investment in Canadian Shipping, 1820–1889," in *Working Men Who Got Wet*, 335–60; Panting, "Cradle of Enterprise: Yarmouth, Nova Scotia, 1840–1889," in *The Enterprising Canadians*, 253–71. Shipowners had always invested in a variety of landward enterprises; thus twenty-nine of T.W. Acheson's "Great Merchants" were among the largest shipowners in Saint John. Acheson, "The Great Merchant and Economic Development in St. John, 1820–1850," *Acadiensis* VIII, 2 (1979): 3–27.

55. McClelland, "The New Brunswick Economy"; see also Peter D. McClelland, "Commentary: On Demand and Supply in Shipping and Regional Economic Development," in *Merchant Shipping and Economic Development*.

56. McClelland, "The New Brunswick Economy," 181, 275.

57. Gerald Panting, "Shipping Investment in the Urban Centres of Nova Scotia," and Fischer and Panting, "Harbour and Metropolis," in *Merchant Shipping and Economic Development*.

58. In a recent study of population movement Thornton has discovered significant out-migration from both New Brunswick and Nova Scotia as early as the 1870s; Saint John lost over 20 percent of its population in the 1870s. Patricia Thornton, "Some Preliminary Comments on the Extent and Consequences of Out-Migration from the Atlantic Region, 1870–1920," in *Merchant Shipping and Economic Development*; see also T.W. Acheson, "The National Policy and the Industrialization of the Maritimes, 1880–1910," *Acadiensis* I, 2 (1972): 5–7.

59. Eric W. Sager, "The Port of St. John's Newfoundland, 1840–1889: A Preliminary Analysis," in *Ships and Shipbuilding in the North Atlantic Region*, 36. There is a consistently positive correlation between estimated returns to schooner tonnage (in terms of the dollar value of cod exports per ton in service) and new investment in schooner tonnage between 1880 and 1929. Each upward surge in revenues from the fishery and in average prices per quintal of cod was followed by a flurry of new investment in schooner tonnage, and also in such imported inputs as fishing gear, gasoline engines for boats, cordage, seines, and lines. This point is discussed in detail in Eric W. Sager, "Sailing Ships and the Traditional Economy of Newfoundland, 1850–1934" (paper presented to the Annual Meeting of the Canadian Historical Association, Halifax, 1981).

60. The size of investments in landward industries remains to be discovered, but the active participation of shipowners and former shipowners is known from the work of Gerald Panting, T.W. Acheson, and others. It is likely that some portion of shipping revenues were lost to the region; see J.D. Frost, "Principles of Interest: the Bank of Nova Scotia and the Industrialization of the Maritimes, 1880–1910" (M.A. thesis, Queen's University, 1979); Christopher Armstrong, "Making a Market; Selling Securities in Atlantic Canada before World War I," *Canadian Journal of Economics* XIII (1980): 438–54.

61. S.A. Saunders, *The Economic History of the Maritime Provinces* (Ottawa, 1939), 17–18.

62. Calculated from Canada, *Census*, 1881, 1891. See also Acheson, "The National Policy and the Industrialization of the Maritimers," 1880–1910, 4–5.

63. Calculated from Dominion Bureau of Statistics, *The Maritime Provinces Since Confederation* (Ottawa, 1927), 88.

64. There was, however, federal support for shipbuilding in Nova Scotia during the First World War; L.D. McCann, "The Mercantile-Industrial Transition in the Metal Towns of Pictou County, 1857–1931," *Acadiensis* X, 2 (1981): 57.

CANADIAN RAILWAYS AS MANUFACTURERS, 1850-1880†

PAUL CRAVEN AND TOM TRAVES

Most accounts of Canadian industrialization in the mid-nineteenth century attribute a dual role to the railways. First, by breaking down the old "tariff of bad roads" that protected small local markets for artisanal producers, they laid the groundwork for the concentration of industrial production in a handful of metropolitan centres. Second, it is often recognized that the railway companies were themselves important markets for a wide range of commodities, and so helped to create the opportunity structure for new investment in manufacturing. While the significance of the railways in the development of the market is indisputable, however, it is less frequently recognized that the railways were important industrial *producers* as well. Indeed the well-worn argument that railways represented commercial, as *opposed* to industrial, capital becomes quaintly irrelevant once it is realized that these companies owned and operated some of the largest and most sophisticated manufacturing plants in the Canadian economy from the early 1850s on.[1]

Railways were not just simple transportation companies. To understand their operations and management from their inception in the 1850s it is necessary first to appreciate the range of functions they performed in the daily course of business. In some respects they operated almost like states unto themselves; their company rules had the force of law, they employed their own police, and their executives, as the Grand Trunk's goods manager put it, were "as important as generals in an army or Ministers of State."[2] By 1860 the typical large railway, like the Grand Trunk or the Great Western, had the capacity to rebuild its line and repair its tracks, to manufacture its own cars and locomotives and even a good part of the machinery and equipment used in these manufacturing processes, to communicate telegraphically, to store and forward freight, to operate grain elevators and steamships, and to maintain large depots and complex administrative offices, all in support of its basic service as a common carrier. In short, the railways were Canada's first large-scale integrated industrial corporations.

†*Historical Papers/Communications historiques* (1983): 254–281. Research for this paper, and for the larger Canadian Railways Industrial Relations History Project of which it forms a part, has had the generous support of the Social Sciences and Humanities Research Council of Canada. The authors gratefully acknowledge the research assistance of David Sobel and Rose Hutchens.

This essay focusses on one aspect of integrated railway operations, the manufacturing activities of the railways' locomotive and car departments. By describing the nature and scope of these activities, and some features of the plant, organization and technology that sustained them, it is intended to contribute towards a reassessment of the railways' place in the history of Canadian industrialization.

The Scope of Manufacturing

The Grand Trunk and the Great Western, in common with some smaller roads, built extensive car shops as part of their original construction program in the early 1850s, but at the outset they leased these structures to private contractors who equipped them to supply larger orders for cars. Although they had to cope with eager competition from British and American car builders, and had to import such crucial parts as wheels and axles, independent Canadian car manufacturers were able to realize their considerable transportation cost advantage to dominate the local market. Dissatisfaction with the quality of the product, and even more pressing difficulties with financing large purchases, soon brought the railway companies to the view that it would be both cheaper and more efficient to build some of their cars themselves. In March 1855, the cash-poor Great Western attempted to cover its debts by foisting GWR bonds on its principal suppliers; shortly thereafter the company cancelled outstanding contracts and began building its own cars. "It is believed that a considerable saving, both in first cost and repairs, may be effected," its president explained, "by the company building cars in their own workshops, besides insuring the use of none but the best materials, which is the greatest safeguard against accidents. . . ."[3]

The Grand Trunk entered the car business for exactly the same reasons. After its major supplier refused to do any more work on credit, the GTR board accepted its chief engineer's proposal to operate the company's Point St. Charles workshops on its own account. By July 1857 the GTR car works were supplying half the road's requirements, and the board was so impressed with this success that it decided to construct an iron foundry, rolling mills and machinery to produce its own rails as well.[4]

The more complicated task of building locomotives was not undertaken until a little later. Independent Canadian suppliers certainly were active in this market as in cars, but at first the bulk of the orders went to large producers in Britain and the United States. While there was a certain bias in favour of the British engines, not only because they were heavier and more substantially built, but also because of the preponderance of British capital invested in the Canadian railways, American locomotive builders were able to capture a substantial share of the market because of shipping costs and the readier availability of spare parts. Still, there were complaints about quality from both sources and some British engines proved to be unsuitable for the sharp curves and rough roadbeds characteristic of the Canadian lines. Gradually such Canadian suppliers as Kinmond Brothers (Montreal), Daniel C. Gunn's works (Hamilton), William Hamilton's St. Lawrence Foundry (Toronto), Good's Foundry (Toronto), and the Canadian Locomotive Works (Kingston) began production. By 1857 the Grand Trunk was placing orders for eight engines from British manufacturers, seven from Americans, and thirty-two from Canadian builders.[5]

Both the Grand Trunk and the Great Western began to consider building locomotives in their own shops, not only for the familiar reason, that it would "doubtless effect a considerable saving in expense," but also because it could furnish slack-time employment for skilled shopworkers in whose recruitment and retention the railways had a large investment. Grand Trunk shops turned out the *Trevithick* in May 1859, and the Great Western's *George Stephenson* was put to work a few months later.[6]

Between January 1864 and December 1873, the Grand Trunk shops built forty-nine new locomotives, or five per year on average. In the same period, they produced 1224 new freight cars (122 per year) and rebuilt, thoroughly renovated or converted substantial proportions of their existing stock. Over the ten years, the Grand Trunk built 172 new passenger cars (seventeen per year). In 1880, when the pattern of shopwork characteristic of the early 1870s had been reestablished after the disruptions occasioned by the change of gauge, the Grand Trunk built eighteen locomotives, thirty-one new passenger cars and 550 new freight cars, as well as converting, rebuilding or thoroughly renovating fifty-two passenger and 1414 freight cars. The shops also manufactured or remanufactured substantial quantities of parts to be used in repair; in the early 1870s, for example, the GTR car shops were turning out approximately six hundred new and renewed trucks per year, as well as between a thousand and fifteen hundred additional new and renewed axles.[7]

Similarly, the Great Western's locomotive shop manufactured or rebuilt sixty-eight engines — four a year on average — between 1860 and 1876. Like the Grand Trunk's it also produced parts and components used in locomotive manufacture and repair. For example, in the year ending 31 January 1871 the GWR turned out five crank axles (four steel, one iron), eleven straight engine axles, eleven truck axles, twenty-two tender axles, sixty-four axle boxes, twenty-six pistons, eight eccentric pulleys, four eccentric straps, twenty-one crank pins, three cross heads, nine driving wheels (eight cast iron, one unspecified), 389 chilled wheels, forty-five engine springs, sixty tender springs, eleven engine bells, 118 steel tires, two tender trucks, one connecting rod, four valve spindles, two tender frames, and two flue-sheets (one copper, one steel), as well as completing three new boilers to be used in rebuilding locomotives and beginning work on three others. The Great Western's car shops were equally busy with new construction and rebuilding.[8]

Figures like these seriously underestimate the extent of manufacturing activity in the car and locomotive departments of the major railways, however. First, the published reports provide little or no systematic information about the production of all sorts of parts and components, although we know from various sources that a wide range of such things, such as iron bridge castings, locomotive boilers, springs, cast iron and wrought iron wheels, and lamps of various descriptions, were made in quantity by the shops, as well as such items of operating equipment as semaphore signals.[9]

Second, there is a dearth of systematic quantitative information about the manufacture of tools and machinery for use by the railway shops themselves.

Again, we know that they produced a wide range of such equipment, from the machinery for turntables and grain elevators to such sophisticated machine tools as the "powerful drilling machine with six drills . . . for drilling the iron skeletons for our new trucks, and a similar machine with fine drills . . . for boring the wood-work of the same trucks," which the Grand Trunk built in 1869; "by the use of these and other labour-saving machinery we are enabled to build trucks at a much lower cost than in former years."[10]

Third, and perhaps most important, it is necessary to consider the extent to which shopwork characterized as "repair" really amounted to manufacturing activity. On the Great Western, it was said that "a first-class car . . . only lasts nine years, or, in other words, at the close of a nine years' servitude, the repairs will have been so numerous and extensive that not one atom of the original car remains in use." The Grand Trunk's mechanical superintendent said that much of the "general repairs" consisted in "actual rebuilding of cars," and warned not to take the construction figures as a "measure of the actual work done towards maintenance inasmuch as a very large number of cars receive from one half to four fifths of new material into their construction, none of which are reckoned as new cars."[11]

The work of the railways' car and locomotive shops might be classified under five headings: maintenance, repair, renewal, replacement, and capital construction. Replacement and capital construction involved essentially the same sorts of activity — building cars or locomotives "from scratch" — but for the most part they were reported differently in the railways' accounts.[12] Great Western (subsequently Grand Trunk) locomotive superintendent Richard Eaton defined renewals as "that class of work which adds new and additional life to the Engine, beyond its average term of fifteen years. Consequently new fire boxes, Tubes, Tyres or Wheels, supplied to Engines under the ordinary heavy repairs cannot be considered as renewals, as these, and other articles, are necessary to the life of fifteen years alone."[13] At the other extreme maintenance might be distinguished from light repairs by limiting it to routine cleaning, lubricating, and so forth.

Expenditure on Manufacturing

In attempting to draw the line between manufacturing and other types of activity in the locomotive and car departments, there is a risk of making the distinctions unnecessarily fine. In contemporary discourse, we are prepared to consider simple parts-assembly operations to be manufacturing plants, and workers who sweep the floors and keep the tools to be production workers. It is difficult to see why any greater terminological precision should be required of nineteenth-century industry. The most sensible demarcation between manufacturing and nonmanufacturing activity in the locomotive and car departments is that between light repairs and maintenance. In practice, the distinction may be drawn (where the data permit) between "running repairs" or "front-shop" work, and "back-shop" work; in other words, between repair work done in the main car and locomotive shops, and repairs done in the engine houses and car sheds, or at minor running shops along the line. This is more or less the distinction embodied in the modern

Standard Industrial Classification, which views in-shop repair work as manufacturing activity, and maintenance and running repairs as a service incidental to transportation. It is a reasonable compromise between theoretical rigour and practical applicability.[14]

Unfortunately, it is not possible on the basis of the available data to separate maintenance from other mechanical department activities, or running repairs from work done in-shop, on any really satisfactory basis for the period of this paper. Mechanical superintendents on the larger railways reported in some detail the volume of repair and renewal activity of various sorts, but these reports almost always excluded running repairs; thus Eaton reported on "heavy," "medium," and "light" engine repairs on the Grand Trunk, but noted that his figures did not include "those repairs done in Steam sheds, or which only occupied a week or so in the repair shops." His successor Herbert Wallis used a similar three-fold distinction, "without taking into account the light or running repairs done at our *ten* outside Loco. Stations," but included engines which had been three days or more in the shops under "light repairs." In reporting on repairs in the car department, he listed "the more prominent items, leaving out of the record all Cars less than twenty-four hours under repair, and upon which a large staff are continually employed."[15]

Two data series are available. One, to be found for the most part in the mechanical superintendents' reports on the larger railways, provides information on the range of shopwork and some quantifiable material on the volume of certain activities. The other consists of mechanical department expenditures summarized in the railway company accounts. The first series does not report systematically on out-of-shop and maintenance activity, while the second does not systematically distinguish between manufacturing and maintenance expenditures. The first type of data has been drawn on extensively in the first part of this essay. Here we turn to the financial series in an attempt to estimate the value of manufacturing activity in the railway mechanical departments.

Manufacturing activity in locomotive and car departments appears in both the capital and revenue accounts. Railway accounting practices were inconsistent in this period (especially in the earlier years), and one suspects that the assignment of an item to one or the other frequently depended on a political assessment of the shareholders' collective frame of mind rather than on any theory of industrial finance. New equipment built in the railway shops was sometimes assigned to capital and sometimes to revenue. Renewals and replacements were frequently charged to revenue simply because they brought the department's stock up to numerical strength, without any regard to the substantial improvement of the stock that they often represented. Unfortunately, the schedules of additions to capital account reported by the major railways are very difficult to work with. The information they provide is incomplete, and items are sometimes accounted for years after the expenditure has been made. About all that can be said of the capital account data is that the railway shops evidently produced a substantial annual volume of rolling stock over and above the expenditure shown in the revenue accounts.

The locomotive and car repair schedules in the revenue accounts supply a more satisfactory basis for estimating the value of manufacturing activity in the

FIGURE 1

Great Western Rwy: Trends 1859–76

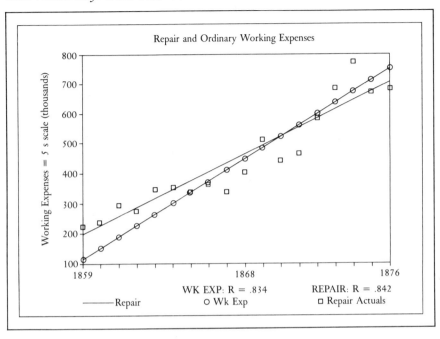

Repair and Ordinary Working Expenses

WK EXP: R = .834   REPAIR: R = .842

———— Repair   o Wk Exp   □ Repair Actuals

railway mechanical departments. Tables 1 and 2 summarize the locomotive and car repair schedules in these accounts for the Great Western (1858–76) and Grand Trunk (1861–80) respectively, while figures 1 and 2 illustrate the growth trends. "Repair" in these schedules included new construction (on account of renewals or otherwise charged to revenue), rebuilding, conversion, and so forth — in short, the whole range of shopwork as discussed above. Our tabulations incorporate a number of adjustments for the inclusion of nonmanufacturing items and the exclusion of costs that may properly be attributed to manufacturing.

The total expenditure on locomotive and car repair shown in the tables should be taken as a minimum estimate of expenditures on manufacturing in the mechanical departments. It ignores entirely expenditure on capital account (which fluctuated widely from year to year and which, as discussed above, cannot be systematically quantified), and it does not take into account other costs of manufacturing which are charged elsewhere. Among the latter are manufacturing-related expenditure in the storekeepers' departments, and possibly some transportation expenditures as well. In sum, it is a conservative claim that the Great Western mechanical departments expended a quarter of a million dollars on manufacturing activity in 1859, and over three-quarters of a million in 1874; or that the Grand Trunk spent over $600,000 a year on mechanical department manufacturing in the early 1860s and about $1.5 million annually in the later 1870s.

FIGURE 2

Grand Trunk Rwy: Trends 1862–80

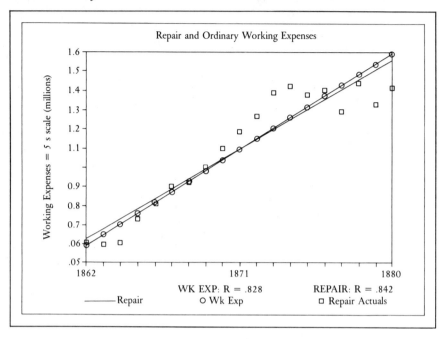

Manufacturing expenditure on revenue account grew steadily over the period as a proportion (approximately 20 percent) of total ordinary working expenses.[16]

It should be noted that these expenditure figures are not equivalent to census value-added statistics, in that they include no profit component and, so far as we can ascertain, no market price adjustment for materials and components manufactured by the railway companies themselves. But even on a straight comparison of mechanical department expenditures to census value-added figures for other manufacturers, it appears plain that the railways were among the largest manufacturing firms in Canada in the period, and quite possibly the largest bar none. Table 3 draws together returns from car factories, engine builders and railway shops in the 1871 manuscript census. It is clear that the central car and locomotive shops on the two largest railways—the Grand Trunk's at Brantford and Montreal, and the Great Western's at Hamilton — were as big as the largest independent establishments in those industries, and that as *integrated*, multiplant manufacturers the larger railways were bigger by far — in terms just of *manufacturing* employment, consumption of materials, and output—than any of the independent firms. The exclusion of the railway company facilities from the aggregate tables published in the 1871 census reports resulted in a grossly distorted picture of the scale and organization of the Canadian railway supply and heavy engineering industries.[17]

TABLE 1

Great Western Railway Mechanical Expenditures on Revenue Account 1858–1876

For Year Ending 31 July —	1859	1860	1861	1862	1863	1864	1865	1866	1867
Revenue Account ($) Ordinary Working Expenses	1056514	1093184	1150179	1185289	1289903	1296856	1276358	1407214	1670578
Locomotive Repair: Materials, fuel & light	63324	59491	80305	69437	77361	77351	73418	77648	75410
Wages	100497	106150	99041	98407	102688	101051	96301	93765	91918
Car Repair: Materials	24955	25215	55563	57998	91080	105135	90019	103756	102771
Wages and salaries	42451	47780	61844	48426	77320	73255	83021	92831	71568
Total Loco. & Car Repair	231227	238636	296753	274268	348449	356793	342759	368000	341666
Loco. & Car Repair as % of Working Expenses	21.89	21.83	25.80	23.14	27.01	27.51	26.85	26.15	20.45

	1868	1869	1870	1871	1872	1873	1874	1875	1876
Revenue Account ($) Ordinary Working Expenses	1928958	2132458	2389675	2591103	3116615	3864456	4161520	3626863	3440306
Locomotive Repair: Materials, fuel & light	81114	83235	71599	57584	113910	136078	178196	146525	139111
Wages	96348	107546	84963	98744	98410	97593	100868	91526	99193
Car Repair: Materials	131396	158090	168116	193830	238691	250913	293055	260581	322161
Wages and salaries	100243	167980	120675	119753	140364	200451	202445	171054	123399
Total Loco. & Car Repair	409100	516851	445353	469910	591375	685034	774564	669686	683864
Loco. & Car Repair as % of Working Expenses	21.21	24.24	18.64	18.14	18.97	17.73	18.61	18.46	19.88

TABLE 2

Grand Trunk Railway Mechanical Expenditures on Revenue Account 1861–1880

For Year Ending 30 June —	1862	1863	1864	1865	1866	1867	1868	1869	1870	1871
Revenue Account ($)										
Ordinary Working Expenses	3216588	3048838	2950474	3830136	3995466	4217006	4368914	4527229	4887459	5311995
Locomotive Dept.:										
Materials for repair	143824	103893	102804	129216	152364	175409	164223	172570	228051	235428
Wages for repair	124174	135461	146680	143178	168034	196168	197975	210555	208419	210160
Repairs to tools &c	23709	32640	37366	52821	63889	77639	74613	96416	81158	85086
Workshop fuel	18484	11608	9350	11350	13216	14999	19896	17909	17138	20041
Car Dept.:										
Materials for repair	148224	175113	160665	220460	238833	240378	258453	266191	315548	351471
Wages for repair	138689	136579	148101	178113	177629	191016	202248	233758	249138	284508
Repairs to tools &c	8523									
Total Loco. & Car Repair	605625	595293	604966	735138	813964	895608	917406	997399	1099450	1186694
Loco. & Car Repair as % of Working Expenses	18.83	19.53	20.50	19.19	20.37	21.24	21.00	22.03	22.50	22.34

	1872	1873	1874	1875	1876	1877	1878	1879	1880	1881*
Revenue Account ($)										
Ordinary Working Expenses	5769919	6429224	7399655	7959598	7761781	6905539	7182064	6715908	6940761	3919473
Locomotive Dept.:										
Materials for repair	209776	234646	223214	203710	219670	150559	213649	181678	237820	135126
Wages for repair	243216	263539	219490	213401	241849	259164	308569	303564	323949	172079
Repairs to tools &c	91586	101329	111358	110429	115588	111135	118350	106435	95953	55375
Workshop fuel	24160	29739	32116	36630	37549	32454	29721	26346	25046	12445
Car Dept.:										
Materials for repair	386651	425073	469196	438340	432614	384809	389330	345169	357795	184970
Wages for repair	311923	332654	366460	378264	348530	354279	381120	365284	367876	200119
Repairs to tools &c										
Total Loco. & Car Repair	1267313	1386979	1421834	1380774	1395799	1292399	1440739	1328475	1408439	760114
Loco. & Car repair as % of Working Expenses	21.96	21.57	19.21	17.35	17.98	18.72	20.06	19.78	20.29	19.39

*First half of fiscal year.

Table 3

Census of 1871: Car Factories, Engine Builders and Railway Shops (see text)

Establishment	Total Employees	Annual Wages	Motive Power	Value of Material	Value of Product
1. Independent Car Factories from Aggregate Census					
John McDougall & Co., Car Wheel Factory, Montreal (West)	60	36000	15 HP	85000	144000
James Crossen, Railroad Car Manufactory, Cobourg, Northumberland Co.	40	12000	N/A	22000	150000
Toronto Car Wheel Company	20	6000	20 HP	40000	54000
A. Holmes, Montreal Car Works, Hochelaga	20	2500	Manual	20000	120000
Wm Hamilton & Sons, St. Lawrence Foundry, Machine and Car Shop, Toronto (East)[a]	200	100000	60 HP	35000	150000
2. Independent Engine Makers from Aggregate Census[b]					
Hyslop & Ronald, Steam Engine Factory, Chatham, Kent Co.	42	18000	Shared: 50 HP	6000	50000
C. H. Waterous & Co., Manufactory of Steam Engines, Boilers, &c, Brantford, Brant Co.	118	40573	40 HP	19700	120000
F. G. Beckett & Co., Manufacturers of Locomotives, Steam Engines, Boilers &c., Hamilton	120	40000	50 HP	40000	100000
Charles Levey & Co., Steam Engine Factory, Toronto (West)	46	10000	30 HP	20500	70000
Hamilton & Martin, Engine Builders and Machinists, Toronto (East)	9	7000	8 HP	2400	25000
Canadian Engine & Machinery Co., Locomotive and Car Factory, Kingston	173	75000	20 HP	201058	306000
Davidson & Doran Machine Shop, Kingston[c]	47	11000	15 HP	12000	40000
George Brush, Eagle Foundry and Machine Shop, Montreal (West)	80	25000	20 HP	25000	80000

TABLE 3 (continued)

Census of 1871: Car Factories, Engine Builders and Railway Shops (see text)

Establishment	Total Employees	Annual Wages	Motive Power	Value of Material	Value of Product
E. E. Gilbert, Engine and Machinists Works, Montreal (West)	145	50000	40 HP	46500	120000
W. P. Bartley & Co., Engine Works and Foundry, Montreal (West)	222	49200	Water: 160 HP	36250	128175
3. Railway Shops from Manuscript Census					
Grand Trunk: Point St. Charles shops[d]	790	250000	185 HP	500000	750000
Grand Trunk: car and loco shops, Brantford	315	182000	30 HP	82000	326000
Great Western Locomotive Shop, London	34	12786	35 HP	2330	20000
Great Western: Hamilton return[c]	984	500000	N/A	N/A	N/A
Northern: Toronto (West) return[c]	561	215808	139 HP	34533	N/A

a. Hamilton's was not included under car shops in the aggregate census. Its return suggests that car building was its principal business at this date, however.

b. One shop in Co. de Quebec and one in Montreal (C), each employing 5 men, are excluded.

c. Not included in aggregate census: principal product seems to be steam engines.

d. "Running shed, Repairs to Engines, Pattern Shops, Brass Foundry, Fitting Shops, Car Shops, Saw & Planning Shops, Blacksmith & Carpenters Shops." The product was reported as "Engines, cars & repairs."

e. These returns seem to include other railway facilities besides the shops. On the Northern's return the enumerator noted that the quantities and value of products could not be ascertained, "as the Company are manufacturers or producers merely on their own Account."

The Principal Shops

In June 1853, the Great Western's chief engineer informed the company's shareholders that their car factory, blacksmith's shops, setting-up shop, paint shops and machine shop at Hamilton were well advanced towards completion, and that similar plans had been approved for London. Later that summer the *American Railroad Journal* reported that GWR machine shops, depots and warehouses were being built, "of a size calculated to astonish even those who had made the largest calculations as to Western progress." The car factory was "not only the largest workshop of the kind, but perhaps, the most extensive manufacturing establishment of any description in Western Canada," exhibiting "the most efficient specimens of labor saving machines that we have ever witnessed."[18]

By 1857, when a local journalist visited the plant, the locomotive shop had between twenty and thirty locomotives under repair daily. Twelve tracks, each capable of holding two engines, passed through the ground floor of the erecting shed.

> The first room we entered seemed to be the general hospital, in which the sick giants were disposed in long rows and supported at a considerable height, on wooden blocks and beams. Passing in we came to two rows of ponderous machines. There were drilling machines, boring holes of various sizes through any thickness of metal. There were planing machines which dealt with iron and brass as if they were soft wood, and rapidly reduced the blocks of metal to the necessary form—machines which cut iron as if it were paper, and punched holes through quarter inch plates as easily as you would punch a gun-wad from a piece of pasteboard. Lathes of all imaginable shapes and sizes, for doing all imaginable things, and in short, the complete furniture of a first class establishment.

The upper floor of the building held the carpentry shop, 165 feet long by 83 wide, where lathes, shapers, planers and drilling machines were used to build buffers and cow catchers. The machinery was run by a sixty-horsepower engine, built at Chippawa, and shared between the locomotive and car departments, which also shared the services of a brass foundry, a coppersmith's shop and a smithy in which cranks, wheels and rails were manufactured and repaired in the glow of twenty-five or twenty-six forges.[19]

The car shops built and repaired rolling stock, manufactured furniture for the stations, and cut timber for fences and bridges. In the machine shop cast-iron car wheels were made and repaired with the use of "machinery the most powerful, and at the same time the most delicate. . . . One engine cuts through, with ease, bars of cold iron, an inch thick and three inches broad, while others turn the edges of the wheels so accurately that they do not differ the thousandth part of an inch from a true circle." The car department built baggage racks in the brass foundry, and kept cabinet, upholstery, finishing and paint shops at work, along with shops for making water coolers, signal lamps, stationary signals, hand cars, and gas fittings for stations. There was also a huge body-building shop, 300 feet by 50, to assemble the cars.[20]

When Richard Eaton became locomotive superintendent in 1858, he took charge of a planned expansion in the shops' capacity. By midyear he was able to report that the greater part of the improvements had been made: "the steam hammer, tyre furnaces, stores and coppersmith's shop are complete; and the tanks, plates, and crane for fixing and blocking the tyres are also erected and but little remains to complete the blocking machinery. . . . The travelling steam crane for large lathes &c and the few remaining improvements are in a very forward state. . . ." A fifty-hundredweight Nasmyth steam hammer had been ordered from England, and Eaton had a blooming furnace for working up wrought iron scrap installed and in production by the end of the year. The hammer was used to beat the heated scrap into plates an inch thick. A drawing published in 1863 shows it towering four times the height of the men crowded around it, forging a 14-foot, 1600-pound shaft for the stationary engine. Next door was the boiler shop with its riveting machines, drills, and "a large punching and shearing machine which will clip you off a piece of boiler plate half an inch thick and ten inches wide in a shorter time and with less manual labour than is required to cut as much cheese."[21]

A year later, the shops boasted an elaborate heating apparatus, which distributed the waste steam from the stationary engine and steam hammer furnace through a mile of piping; the whole system was extended the following year so that more than two miles of heating pipes snaked their way through the Hamilton works. Eaton undertook an extensive rearrangement of the shop machinery, added a hoist for moving materials between floors, rebuilt some wooden buildings in masonry, and supplied new lathes, new forges for making wrought-iron wheels, and a steam riveting machine for iron-bridge construction.[22] A report from late November 1860 gives an impression of the nature and rhythm of shopwork in this period:

> The Plates for Boilers for next pair of Engines have also been ordered from England and will arrive here about the middle of January next, and the Wrought Iron Framing, Driving Wheels and remaining Iron Work, will be put in hand on 3rd December (next Monday) at which time the Blooming Furnace will be put to work in order to use up the scrap iron. The Blooming Furnace will be kept to work until we have provided all the heavy forgings required for new Engines and for general use during the ensuing 12 months. A considerable portion of the Castings required for next year's new Engines are already made and the best use will be made of all the men and machines we can spare from the regular repairs in order to forward the new Engines and other improvements that are being made in the Locomotive Stock.[23]

The plant and equipment were expanded further over the succeeding years. The flooring was relaid and lorries and tramways installed to expedite the movement of heavy materials and parts. New furnaces for brass moulding and heavy iron work were added. By 1869 the stationary engine required new boilers and pistons, which were built in the shops; when they were completed the engine was fully refitted. New machinery was built or purchased — a radial drill, a screw-cutting lathe, a car wheel boring machine, nut- and bolt-making machinery, an improved hydraulic car wheel press, and a hydrostatic locomotive wheel press. By 1870, when additional carshop facilities were badly needed, there was no room for expansion at Hamilton so work began on a new car facility at London. The following year it became clear that the existing overcrowding at Hamilton posed a serious fire risk, and the Great Western management began to discuss moving the entire car department to London. Two hundred and fifty GWR carshop workers moved from Hamilton to London in November 1874, when this transfer was made; the decision may have been hastened when fire broke out at Hamilton in September 1873, although it caused little damage. In the interim, the Hamilton shops were hard-pressed.[24]

The Great Western established a locomotive repair shop in London as part of its original plant in the 1850s, and for a time the outside locomotive department (locomotive running) was headquartered there. A journalist visiting the works in 1857 described the round-house with its metal-working lathes, drilling and bolt-making machines, and eight blacksmith's forges, whose draft was supplied by a steam rotary fan, "for making of that work which cannot be done by machinery." The whole was powered by a sixty-five-horsepower horizontal engine. This was evidently a running shop, although some heavy repairs may have been done there, and there was talk at the time of expanding its capacity by introducing steam hammers. Under Eaton's program of shop improvement, though, the heavy repair work was to be done in the Hamilton shops, and the stationary engine and machinery were removed to the newly consolidated Hamilton works in 1858. "This will make thirty or forty dwellings in the city vacant," complained a local newspaper, "and materially decrease the population, which has already been more than sufficiently thinned."[25]

The tables were turned some fifteen years later when London became the new locale for the Great Western's principal carshops. "The removal of this large population from Hamilton, while depressing matters a little in the ambitious city, has considerably enlivened the town of London East, where the demand for house room is just at present unusually brisk." The total cost of the shops, sidings and machinery amounted to about £50,000, or a quarter of a million dollars. About $150,000 of this was paid to a London contracting firm, Messrs. Christie & Green, while the remainder was accounted for in work done by the Great Western itself and in purchases of new machinery. There were six buildings,

> all of them of extraordinary size, and with the exception of that used for the storage of dry lumber, are built of brick with slated roofs. They cover an immense area of ground, though clustered as closely together as convenience would allow. There is the blacksmith shop, the machine shop, the iron repair shop, the wood-working department, the storehouses for iron, coal, and other necessaries, and the offices, all in close proximity. A huge transfer table is used to convey the work from one department to another, and the numerous rail tracks that are seen in each building show that the shops are intended to accommodate almost any amount of work.[26]

After the car department's move to London, the buildings it had vacated at Hamilton proved to be too small for the locomotive department there to use. In October 1874 two large shops were dismantled, placed on twenty-car trains, and reerected at Suspension Bridge to replace running repair sheds that had been destroyed by fire there. The Great Western's principal locomotive shops remained at Hamilton for some years after the company's absorption into the Grand Trunk system in 1882. In 1889 their machinery and staff were transferred to the enlarged Grand Trunk motive power shops in Stratford, and the Hamilton shops were closed.[27]

The first substantial railway shops in the Montreal area were those of the Champlain & St. Lawrence, at St. Lambert (South Montreal) across the river from the city. In 1852 the terminus included a machine shop 100 feet by 50, a boiler house 25 feet square, and a blacksmith's shop 50 feet square. Together with the station buildings, engine house and workingmen's cottages they occupied an area of about twenty acres, and promised to be the making of a "handsome compact railway town." In the same year, the St. Lawrence & Atlantic, a Grand Trunk constituent, was soliciting tenders to build a car repair shop at nearby

Longueuil. When the Grand Trunk commenced to build its own terminus and shop facilities, however, they were located on the island, at Point St. Charles.[28]

In 1854, when the line was taken over from the contractors, the Grand Trunk's chief engineer explained the works under way at Point St. Charles:

> It is intended to get in the foundations for the Station Buildings, at Montreal, throughout this season, these extend to an aggregate length of 3000 feet, in sundry buildings, varying from 40 to 90 feet in width, some of which are two stories in height, and consist principally of Passenger Stations, Goods Warehouses, Locomotive erecting shops, Engine Stables, Car erecting shops, Smiths, and Foundry shops. It is proposed to complete the Car and Smiths shops this season, so as to admit of commencing the construction of the car rolling stock, which is to be built upon the premises. The remaining buildings of this establishment being so far prepared this autumn, will be readily advanced to completion next year.[29]

By the beginning of 1855, the works were advertising for bolt-makers and coppersmiths, and car building (by contractors) had so far advanced by the spring of 1856 that a shopworkers' protest meeting was held to denounce the *Pilot* and other local newspapers for their disparaging remarks about the quality of the cars. The works had their own sawmill in 1856; by 1857, when the Grand Trunk was building cars on its own account, its locomotive superintendent could speak of the "ample and well appointed workshops" which "have no equal either in extent or in completeness of arrangement on this side of the Atlantic." Some idea of the scale of these works is suggested by a report that they were illuminated by seven hundred gas lights; by 1858 the company was considering spending $20,000 for the plant to make its own gas at a price 40 percent below that charged by the Montreal Gas Company.[30]

When W.S. Mackenzie succeeded Frederick Trevethick as locomotive superintendent in 1859, he predicted the need for substantial additions to and mechanization of the shops, including the introduction of steam hammers, which had come into use on the Great Western the previous year. There appears to be no record of whether he was successful in persuading his board to update the facilities, but when C.J. Brydges left the Great Western to become the Grand Trunk's general manager in 1862 it quickly became apparent that the company's shop arrangements were in terrible disarray. Brydges appointed Henry Yates and Richard Eaton to investigate the working of the mechanical and fuel departments, and they found room for considerable improvement. Repair facilities were scattered among numerous shops and running sheds along the line, several of them located very inefficiently; responsibility for the car stock was diffused; there was no effective renewals policy in force; the locomotive stock required to be standardized; and the stores department was in total disorder. Most importantly for this discussion, they recommended a thoroughgoing consolidation of repair shops, closing many of the smaller ones, converting others into running shops, and concentrating heavy repairs and car and locomotive building at Point St. Charles.[31]

Under Eaton's superintendency, the facilities and equipment at Point St. Charles were rapidly improved. In 1863 the shops built a 10-inch hydraulic power press and a very large mortising machine, and screwing and drilling machines were purchased. The machinery was rearranged and covered ways were built between the smiths, erecting and machine shops. More repairs were done to the shops the following year, and new lathes and machines were added. In 1865 work on the shops was "extraordinarily heavy," and Eaton reported that the company was deficient in shop room for more than fifty engines. Heavy expenditures on shop facilities and machinery continued throughout the 1860s, and by 1869 work was under way on a new paint shop, 270 feet by 40, and a saw and planing mill, 170 feet by 63, at Point St. Charles.[32]

New machinery was added in 1870, and in the same year a fireproof storage building for paints and varnishes was erected and a steam-heating system of the same sort introduced on the Great Western was put into operation. In 1872 new machinery was added, the existing machinery was rearranged, and the steam hammer was placed on new foundations. In 1873 the company bought an additional 40.6 *arpents* of land adjacent to the shops from the Grey Nunnery, in preparation for further expansion, and "extensive additions" were made during the year. In March 1875, the two principal car shops at Point St. Charles, with all their machinery, were destroyed by fire, but by the end of the year they had been replaced. Two years later the car shops were expanded, and additions were made to various of the locomotive shops as well. Over the course of the next several years, there were substantial additions to the stock of machinery. In 1880, "in consequence of the greatly increased work being done at Point St. Charles," the boiler shop was extended 95 feet, the smith's shop 44 feet, the passenger car shop 300 feet, and a new tube shop was erected.[33]

At Brantford, the old Buffalo, Brantford & Goderich company had agreed as one of the terms of its 1854 municipal bonus to erect a "large and commodious machine shop" in the town within fifteen months. A paint and finishing shop for cars, 150 feet by 40, collapsed while under construction in 1854. When the BB&G became the Buffalo & Lake Huron in 1856, Henry Yates was hired away from the Great Western to become its mechanical superintendent, and he brought some skilled shopworkers with him from Hamilton. By August of that year, the company's general manager was able to report that "the workshops are beginning to exhibit some signs of order and arrangement — we are obliged to create everything as we want it," and by November he expressed great satisfaction at the "interior economy" of the shops. The following year, the Brantford works began producing cars for the line, and in 1858 they began rebuilding some old BB&G engines.[34]

When the Grand Trunk absorbed the Buffalo & Lake Huron in 1868 it took over and operated the Brantford shops, leasing the old company's cars from the Brantford Car Company. The railway centralized its locomotive repair facilities at Toronto, transferring most of the engine shop mechanics from Brantford to the shops at Queen's Wharf and placing the former Brantford foreman, Thomas Patterson, in charge. The GTR's Toronto facilities had never been adequate, however; in 1862 Eaton and Yates had singled them out as being the most inconvenient in terms of location and arrangement of any on the line. In the general shops consolidation program of the early 1870s it became apparent that Toronto offered insufficient room for expansion, and Stratford, at the geographic centre of the district, was selected as the site for new locomotive repair shops.

Construction began in June 1870 on a 300 foot by 90 workshop building, a storehouse 100 feet by 40, and a roundhouse; all were of brick on cut stone foundations. The shops were illuminated with ten thousand panes of glass (most of which were to be broken in a hailstorm three years later), and a local firm got the glazing contract. Another won the contract to supply castings. When the Stratford shops were completed in 1871, the Queen's Wharf machinery and workforce were transferred there, again under Patterson's general foremanship.[35]

The same consolidation program saw Brantford chosen as the site for a new freight car factory, constructed by Henry Yates at a cost of $31,000. When it began operations in 1871 the Brantford works was the largest in Canada. Capable of admitting fifty cars at a time, it was "provided with every possible labour-saving convenience, the machinery from the old shops having been transferred to it, and arranged to the best advantage, in order to facilitate the preparation of material and to reduce the cost of repairs." Besides carrying out a substantial proportion of the GTR's car repairs, Brantford was to be the company's chief freight car building facility. The "monster workshop" was 336 feet by 144, and 21 feet high. It had five sets of track running along its length and one across its width, with turntables at every intersection. The outside tracks were for repairing Pullman cars, and the three inside ones for freight car building and repair. It was built of brick on stone foundations, and with an iron-truss roof containing seventeen skylights of about 150 square feet each; additional illumination was provided by fifty-four windows. A 30 foot by 20 foot engine room, complete with "monster smoke stack, such as one has never before seen in Brant City," was connected at one side. On the same site stood the old engine house, now converted for car repairs, and a number of specialized workshops, stores buildings and machine rooms.[36]

Shop Practice

It remains to consider briefly some features of organization and practice that characterized the railway shops in the years before 1880. A substantial amount of technological innovation took place in the shops, not only in the form of "tinkering," but also in terms of systematic experimentation. Alongside this must be placed a dual concern with standardization, first with regard to the economy of interchangeable parts, and second to the standards which were imposed by necessity where several companies shared traffic and equipment. These industry standards sometimes restricted innovation. Finally, shop practice was informed throughout by an anxious interest in cost-saving. This found expression not only in the extensive recycling of old equipment and materials and the introduction of labour-saving machinery, but also in the evolution of relatively sophisticated cost-accounting methods and the development of renewals policies.

Most of the mechanical superintendents and at least some of the foremen developed and often patented technological innovations, many of which found their way into the everyday practice of the shops. To take only a few examples among many, Richard Eaton patented a steel locomotive boiler and heater, Henry Yates an improved firebox, and Samuel Sharpe a lateral motion truck and a ventilating apparatus for passenger cars. W.A. Robinson invented a rear-view mirror for engine cabs, Great Western engine shop foreman Joseph Marks had several patents to his credit, including a spark-arresting smokestack that was widely advertised in the industry press, and a Grand Trunk locomotive shop foreman (subsequently foreman of the Kingston Locomotive Works) named Nuttall invented a car lifting and truck transfer device which was indispensable to the company's operations during the transitional years of the gauge change.[37]

Innovation was accompanied by rigorous experimental testing of certain kinds of equipment. The best example is likely wheels, for the debate over the relative merits of cast iron and wrought iron wheels, and of steel tires, continued over the whole period. To some degree the technical questions were tangled up with the rival claims of British suppliers and North American practice, for wrought iron had become so firmly established as the British standard that the Canadian railways' British proprietors were susceptible to enthusiastic lobbying by English and Scottish manufacturers. In 1856 the Great Western's directors decided to replace cast iron driving wheels with English wrought iron wheels, "which, it is expected, will have a very beneficial result, both in respect to safety and ultimate cost for repairs." But three years later Robert Gill, chairman of the railway's English board, told the shareholders that "it was a very extraordinary fact that these wheels, which were cast in America, with charcoal, were found to be more durable and less liable to accident than wrought iron wheels. . . . It was a long time before the Board would give in, but at length they were obliged to let the fact of the small percentage of breakage of these [cast iron] tyres prevail over their own prejudices."[38]

This hardly ended the affair, however, for the wheels question was placed on the agenda of practically every shareholders' enquiry into the workings of the Canadian railways. The mechanical departments responded by manufacturing their own wheels in both cast and wrought iron, ordering test quantities from various manufacturers (including, in 1869, the Intercolonial Iron and Steel Company of Londonderry, Nova Scotia), and conducting exhaustive tests. The battle was still raging when, in 1873, the Grand Trunk's president invited the proprietor of an English railway car company to visit Canada and report on the GTR's rolling stock. He reported in favour of his own brand of wheels and tires, saying "it is almost impossible to estimate the evil effects of the use of Cast Iron Wheels upon your permanent Way. . . . I have no doubt that it would be found that the use of Cast Iron Wheels has been the cause of thousands of rails breaking. . . . I consider it would be an act of barbarism to destroy that road by perpetuating the use of your Cast Iron Wheels."[39]

The GTR management accordingly ordered another test of the English wheels, and two years later mechanical superintendent Wallis supplied an exhaustive accounting of every wrought iron wheel removed from service in January 1875, showing the nature of the defect and the number of miles run, and comparing the experience of wrought and cast iron wheels. This was only the opening salvo in an exchange of information and opinion that lasted for most of the year and resulted in general agreement among the company's officers in Canada that the existing types of English wheels were impracticable. In September the Grand Trunk managers awarded contracts to Canadian firms for the supply of cast iron engine, truck and car wheels, but agreed to try a further test of twelve English wheels with steel tires, made to the mechanical superintendent's new specifications. These were evidently a success, for at the end of 1877 the locomotive superintendent reported that "with regard to our Passenger Cars, we have, after two years' trial, adopted the standard English steel tyred car wheel of 43 inches diameter, in place of the cast iron chilled wheel of 33 inches, and so far as introduced these wheels have given satisfaction, having produced a marked general economy and improvement."[40]

The technological sophistication of the locomotive and car departments and their interest in mechanical invention and improvement seems to run contrary to T.C. Cochran's judgment that innovation was a talent not much looked for in American railway managers because of the difficulty of gaining competitive advantages in an industry that placed such a premium on co-operation. But in Canada, at any rate, the relationship between innovation and interindustry co-operation was fairly complex. Over the period, it was indeed increasingly true that the need to accommodate "foreign" traffic, and to have the company's rolling stock operate on "foreign" lines, precluded certain unilateral changes. On the other hand, technological superiority occasionally led to interindustry co-operation, as when the Grand Trunk agreed to let the Great Western run over its line to Portland for a year, in exchange for having the GWR mechanical department build it a terminal elevator at Toronto. And the need to conform to industry-wide standards could sometimes be a positive spur to innovation, as for example with the variety of appliances developed on both the Grand Trunk and the Great Western to cope first with breaks of gauge with connecting lines, and subsequently with breaks of gauge on their own main lines once the project of changing to the standard North American gauge was begun.[41]

Most significantly, though, technological developments were crucial to the railways' continuing efforts to reduce their costs. Certainly the attention of those in charge of the mechanical departments was constantly drawn to the need for reducing costs; indeed, it was the perception that in-house production could lead to substantial economies that accounted for the railways' role as large-scale manufacturers in the first place. But a sophisticated mechanical superintendent realized, and considered it part of his job to persuade his general manager and board of directors, that true economies could not be secured through simple cost-cutting. "No exertions or expense has been spared, in order to increase the efficiency and durability of the Engines," Eaton reported, "because such is the only way to effect real economy, and advantage to the Company. Our general reductions in expenses are due to the prevention of waste, and not to any false economy in repairs."[42]

Achieving "real economy" was an extremely complex task. Among its components were the establishment of standards permitting mechanization and interchangeability of parts, rational shop arrangement, the reduction of waste through heroic efforts at recycling used materials, experimentation with new materials and techniques, and effective accounting for expenditures and depreciation. Taking all these elements together, advanced railway shop practice in the three decades before 1880 bore a striking resemblance to several of the important "discoveries" of the new industrial management theorists of the early twentieth century.[43]

Standardization of equipment and parts was an important aspect of workshop economy. "Nothing tends so much to increase the working expenses of the Locomotive Department in this Country than by the adopting or ordering more than two or at most three classes of Engines," reported Eaton and Yates in 1862. "However great a number may be required they should be of one build and design, for apart from the comparatively smaller expenditure required for Patterns, Castings, Spare Gear, &c necessary to be kept always on hand, the advantages and saving arising from the use that could be made of parts of Engines under repairs during the Winter to meet emergencies could be of the greatest possible benefit to the Company."[44]

They estimated that standardization would reduce the proportion of engines under repair by at least 20 percent, and would mean extensive savings in labour and materials costs. They noted that the Grand Trunk locomotives were of a "great variety of Patterns and build which have been supplied from no less than fourteen different establishments, the varieties of Engines being still further increased from the fact of several of the same firms having furnished several lots of Engines of different kinds, from designs of their own, some of which have been found quite unsuitable for the road and Traffic, until important alterations and additions had been made by the Company," a fact which of course further varied the stock. Indeed, the more different kinds of engines a railway possessed, the more engines it needed to do the work because it could not achieve speed and efficiency in upkeep and repair.

Eaton and Yates recommended that a uniform standard for all leading dimensions be established and adhered to in altering the present stock and supplying new engines, so that in the course of time "a tolerable near approach to uniformity" might be achieved. Both the Grand Trunk and the Great Western adopted such standards for building new engines in their own shops, and they supplied specifications to the Kingston Locomotive Works as well. By 1868 the Great Western had five of these built at Kingston: "they are similar in all essential parts to the new standard freight engines built in our own works, with which their parts are interchangeable." The shops seem to have managed a judicious balance of standards and innovation. "I am using every means to secure a powerful Engine having only a moderate weight," wrote Eaton in 1867. "For obtaining this desirable object we are making the Boiler and other available parts of Steel, and substituting wrought- for cast-iron wherever it is possible to do so. I may also state that although differing in some details all the essential parts — such as wheels, axles and Machinery — will be strictly uniform with the Grand Trunk standard."[45]

Rational shop arrangement and recycling waste also produced efficiencies and economies. As we saw in the earlier discussion of the development of the railways' physical plant, the mechanical superintendents often rearranged their heavy machinery, sometimes in concert with the development of new equipment, and introduced hoists, tramways, overhead cranes and other appliances for the easy movement of heavy machines and materials. The kind of savings such integration involved is suggested by Eaton's account of the new furnace installed to heat scrap to be worked by the Great Western's steam hammer in 1858:

> The objects aimed at were, to get the fullest possible benefit from the enormous amount of waste heat evolved from the furnace, and we shall be able not only to raise steam for working the Steam Hammer, but there will be an overplus to assist the Stationary Engine, instead of taking from it as before, and from the same waste heat we shall be able to do all the Spring Makers Work and to re-heat for forging the same quantity of iron which is done by one of our largest Smiths Hearths, consequently saving the amount of Coal used by that hearth.[46]

Along with shop rearrangement went the shops consolidation programs undertaken by both the Great Western and the Grand Trunk. The effects of these have already been described; their purpose was stated succinctly by Eaton and Yates when they recommended that car renewals and repairs be concentrated at Point St. Charles, "where under a well regulated System with every appliance in the way of tools and machinery, the work can be done at a much less cost than by workmen employed at out of the way stations and under no regular supervision."[47]

Efficiencies and economies were also accomplished by recycling waste. The steam heating system installed at Point St. Charles was fuelled exclusively by sawdust and small cuttings from the woodworking shops. Eaton reported of the first engine constructed by the Great Western that "the Framing has been made by ourselves from our own scrap iron, the inside and outside connecting rods and the valve motion &c are made from worn out Lowmoor Tyres, the Piston Rods and Slide Bars we have made from old broken springs, and the greater part of the Cylinders consist of old Car Wheels, there being no better metal in the world for that purpose." Two years later he was proposing to use the machinery from one or two old locomotives to drive the company's proposed rolling mills. In 1874 the Grand Trunk's mechanical superintendent proposed to convert sufficient broad gauge car trucks to the standard gauge to be used for about one thousand new cars; some of the new car bodies would be built in the GTR shops and others would be contracted for. The same year, the Grand Trunk's storekeeper noted that "it will not be necessary to contract for Washers as they can be more economically made in the Company's shops out of the old sheet Iron on hand by the breaking up of the old broad guage [sic] tenders."[48]

Railway shop accounting is really a subset of the much larger topic of railway accounts and statistics generally, a subject too broad to be considered fully here. Concern about the keeping of adequate workshop accounts began with the inception of railway operations; in December 1854, some months before the Great Western's board decided on a policy of tendering for expenditures over £1000, it instructed the managing director and secretary to report "as early as possible upon the system of accounts to be kept in the Mechanical Department." Shop bookkeeping seems to have involved establishing a separate account for every piece of rolling stock (adjusted from time to time by a census of cars), along with additional accounts for major pieces of machinery, for tools and for general shop maintenance. Wages and the cost of materials for repairing the stock would be charged to the appropriate account, so that it was possible, however tediously, to establish the costs of repair (and of running) for each item or class of equipment, compile comparative statistics such as those already discussed for wrought iron versus cast iron wheels, and to prepare, as a matter of course, half-yearly tabulations of costs of various kinds per mile run in the various types of service. By 1875 at the latest, shopworkers' daily work records were organized so as to show the allocation of working hours to each item of equipment. In principle, this might have enabled long-term efficiency checks on individual workers, or the tracing of faults in workmanship back to the individual responsible, although there is no evidence that such use was in fact made of these records. In any event, the detailed record-keeping systems in use in the railway shops and, with a complex system of cross-accounting, in other branches of the railway service, amounted to real cost-accounting, far removed from the simple double-entry bookkeeping systems that characterized most other industry in the period. This accounting system was the backbone of shop practice, for without it the superintendents' claims to be achieving real economies through judicious expenditure could hardly have been justified.[49]

Summary and Conclusions

While the railways have long been a favourite topic of Canadian economic historians, little attention has been paid to aspects of their activities other than finance and construction. For the most part, they have been viewed as transportation companies pure and simple. But this distorts the reality: the major railways were transportation companies, to be sure, but they were very large, vertically and horizontally integrated transportation companies, whose activities covered a much broader range of economic endeavour. In the period before the National Policy (and perhaps for many years later as well) the major railways were, *inter alia*, among the biggest manufacturing firms in the economy.

From the beginning, the railway companies erected the plant to build their own cars, leasing it to independent contractors. They took over these car works and operated them themselves for three principal reasons. First, they considered (with good reason given that they already owned the physical plant and had a substantial workforce engaged in repairs) that they could build cars more cheaply than the contractors. Second, they were unhappy with the quality of the contractors' product. Finally, manufacturing activity of this sort offered alternative employment for shopworkers in periods of slack traffic, thereby protecting the railways' substantial investment in labour recruitment. From manufacturing cars it was a short step to manufacturing locomotives and other railway equipment as well, wherever it was cost-effective, in the broadest sense, to do so.

With the growth of the system, the scope of shopwork expanded. Parts and components that had formerly been purchased from outside suppliers as a matter of course, and had often to be imported at great expense and with some uncertainty, were now frequently made in the railways' own works. Heavy investments in new shop capacity were made, and existing facilities were consolidated and modernized. Operating under an imperative to keep costs low, both in shopwork and in the train running that it supported, the works invested heavily in machinery, some of it made in the shops, attempted to improve the efficiency of equipment through innovation, experiment and exhaustive testing, and instituted sophisticated systems of cost control. As a result, the railway shops were not only among the largest manufacturing establishments in the Canadian economy, but were among the most advanced technologically and managerially as well.

If this is accepted, then it appears evident that traditional views of the railways' place in Canadian industrialization require some revision. The distinction between "commercial" railways and "industrial" factories is plainly absurd, and should be abolished. The view that the railways' contribution to industrialization consisted of expanding the effective market for domestic industry is no longer adequate. It must be supplemented by enquiries about the interaction between the railways' manufacturing activities and the rest of the industrial economy. In particular, the broader industrializing effects of the railways' shop location decisions, in terms of the local labour force, sources of supply (including the surplus materials and equipment that the railways placed on the market), and the independent railway supply industry deserve examination. It may be that in the final analysis one of the critical questions to be asked about the development of Canadian manufacturing is why other producers in the economy took so long to follow the railways' lead.

Notes

1. In December 1862, the Great Western's Inside Locomotive Department (i.e., shops as distinct from running trades) employed 255 men at Hamilton, and the Car Department 265; see Hamilton Public Library, GWR Mechanical Dept. Paysheets. In early 1860 the company held a dinner for six hundred men to celebrate the completion of the first locomotive built entirely in its shops; see Hamilton *Spectator*, 10 Feb. 1860. The Grand Trunk published a breakdown of employment and wages in its locomotive department in its *Report* for the half-year ending 31 June 1859, showing 684 men employed in its locomotive shops alone.

2. Myles Pennington, *Railways and Other Ways* (Toronto, 1894), 119.

3. Public Archives of Canada (hereafter PAC), RG 30, Canadian National Railways Papers (henceforth *CNR*), vol. 1, 24 Aug. 1855, Report of G.L. Reid, Chief Engineer to the Shareholders; ibid., 4 June 1853; *CNR* 1000, 11 Dec. 1856; PAC, John Young Papers, 20 Apr. 1852; *CNR* 2, 2 Sept. 1853; 2 Feb. 1855; 2 Mar. 1855; 30 Mar. 1855; Hamilton *Spectator*, 15 Sept. 1855.

4. *CNR* 1000, 11 Dec. 1856; Montreal *Pilot*, 1 Aug. 1857.

5. Toronto *Globe*, 28 Apr. 1853; W.M. Spriggs, "Great Western Railway of Canada," *Bulletin of the Railway and Locomotive Historical Society*: 51; John Loye, "Locomotives of the Grand Trunk Railway," ibid.: 25. The rivalry of British and American locomotive builders was regularly vented in industry periodicals on both sides of the Atlantic. For a contemporary comparison of costs and labour content see *American Railway Review* 5 (1862): 230, copying *The Engineer* (London), 22 Nov. 1861. Independent Canadian producers were extremely vulnerable to recession, and only the Kingston works survived as a locomotive builder to the end of the century. See W.G. Richardson, "The Canadian Locomotive Company in the Nineteenth Century" (paper presented to Canadian Historical Association, Annual Meeting, Kingston, 1973). Hamilton *Spectator*, 9 Aug. 1856, 28 Feb. 1857, 3 Sept. 1857 and 4 Jan. 1858; Toronto *Globe*, 28 Apr. 1853; Toronto *Leader*, 6 Feb. and 24 Mar. 1854; *CNR* 2, no. 1148, 16 Jan. 1857; *Railways and Other Ways*, 86; *Dictionary of Canadian Biography*, X (Toronto, 1972), 330f. [William Hamilton]; Bryan D. Palmer, *A Culture in Conflict* (Montreal, 1979), 14; Montreal *Pilot*, 1 Aug. 1857; Montreal *Gazette*, 30 Apr. 1852; *CNR* 2, no. 709, 8 June 1855. Hamilton's abandoned the locomotive and general machine business to specialize in producing railway cars and railway iron; see Toronto *Mail*, 18 Apr. 1872.

6. Hamilton *Spectator*, 25 Jan. 1861. See Paul Craven and Tom Traves, "Dimensions of Paternalism: Discipline and Culture in Canadian Railway Operations in the 1850s," in C. Heron and R. Storey, eds., *On the Job* (Kingston, 1986), 47–74. Hamilton *Spectator*, 10 Feb. 1860; Hamilton *Times*, 12 May 1859; Toronto *Globe*, 17 May 1859.

7. The data in this paragraph are calculated from mechanical (or locomotive) superintendents' reports and associated tables published in the Grand Trunk's half-yearly *Reports* (varying titles) for the appropriate dates. We have so far been unable to compile a wholly unbroken run of these reports from mid-1854 (when the first one appeared) to mid-1863. The December 1873 cut-off date is used here because the Grand Trunk's change of gauge substantially altered the pattern of shopwork in the years immediately following.

8. For details on locomotive components and construction see, for example, Matthias N. Forney, *Catechism of the Locomotive* (New York, 1883). The figures in this paragraph are calculated from the Great Western's *Reports* for the appropriate dates.

9. *CNR* 7, no. 1597, 27 Aug. 1861; no. 1643, 15 Jan. 1862; GTR *Report*, half-year ending 30 June 1869, p. 11; GWR *Report*, half-year ending 31 Jan. 1861, p. 27; Hamilton *Spectator*, 9 Aug. 1860; *CNR* 1042, 28 Nov. 1879; *CNR* 6, no. 1649, 26 Feb. 1864.

10. *CNR* 7, no. 1380, 20 May 1859; ibid., nos. 1651–2, 11 Mar. 1862; GTR *Report*, half-year ending 30 June 1869, 11.

11. Hamilton *Spectator*, 4 Mar. 1857; GTR *Report* for half-year to 30 June 1864; ibid., half-year to 30 June 1865. "Maintenance" here meant keeping the car stock up to numerical strength.

12. It was not until well into the 1860s that the larger railway companies worked out even a moderately consistent accounting response to the problem of depreciation; previously, new equipment had frequently been charged to revenue account, and renewals to capital.

13. *CNR*, no. 1643, 15 Jan. 1862.

14. Dominion Bureau of Statistics/Statistics Canada, *Standard Industrial Classification Manual* (Ottawa, 1948); ibid (Ottawa, 1960); ibid (Ottawa, 1970); ibid (Ottawa, 1980). The latest revision is somewhat opaque in its criteria as compared to earlier versions.

15. Canadian National Railways Library, Richard Eaton, ms. half-yearly report of mechanical superintendent, GTR, for 31 Dec. 1864; GTR *Report* for half-year ending 30 June 1878, 12; ibid., half-year ending 31 Dec. 1879, 14; ibid, half-year ending 30 June 1878, 13.

16. Car and locomotive renewal funds have been included in the tables whether or not they were reported separately in the original accounts. On both railways, mechanical department expenditures increased rapidly during the change of gauge due to new construction and (especially) the herculean task of conversions. In the years immediately following the change, repair and renewal expenditures dropped sharply since so much of the stock was new or had recently undergone extensive rebuilding. These factors account for the larger departures from trend in the Figures.

17. "Engine builders" included manufacturers of all manner of steam engines, not merely locomotives. A detailed systematic examination of the industrial schedules for locations other than those surveyed here might well turn up other misclassified and/or omitted establishments. The published report should be used with the greatest caution: Canada, *Census (1870–1)* (Ottawa, 1875), vol. 3.

18. *CNR* 1, p. 17: Report of John T. Clark, 4 June 1853; *American Railroad Journal*, 27 Aug. 1853.

19. Hamilton *Spectator*, 28 Feb. 1857.

20. Ibid., 4 Mar. 1857.

21. Ibid., 7 Oct. 1857; *CNR* 6, 31 July 1858; *CNR* 7, no. 1308, 17 Dec. 1858, ibid., no. 1319, 31 Dec. 1858; *Canadian Illustrated News*, 14 Feb. 1863.

22. *CNR* 7, no. 1441, 18 Nov. 1859; GWR *Report* for half-year to 31 Jan. 1860; GWR *Reports*, half-years to 31 Jan. 1860 and 31 July 1860; *CNR* 7, no. 1474, 10 Feb. 1860; *CNR* 6, no. 1142, 28 Nov. 1860.

23. *CNR* 6, no. 1142, 28 Nov. 1860.

24. GWR *Reports*, half-years to 31 July 1862, 31 July 1865, 31 July 1869, 31 Jan. 1870, 31 July 1870, 31 Jan. 1871, 31 Jan. 1872 and 31 Jan. 1873; *CNR* 4, no 3335, 23 June 1871; ibid., no. 3341, 29 June 1871; GWR *Report* for half-year to 31 Jan. 1875; London *Advertiser*, 10 and 25 Nov. 1874; London *Free Press*, 11 Nov. 1874; *CNR* 4, no. 4096, 18 Sept. 1873; GWR *Reports*, half-years to 31 July 1873 and 31 Jan. 1874; *CNR* 8, 5 Nov. 1873.

25. Hamilton *Spectator*, 12 Mar. 1857, copying London *Prototype*; Toronto *Leader*, 7 Apr. 1858, copying London *Journal*.

26. London *Advertiser*, 10 and 21 Nov. 1874; GWR *Reports*, half-years to 31 July 1870, 31 July 1873, 31 Jan. 1874, 31 July 1874, 31 Jan. 1875 and 31 July 1875; *CNR* 4, no. 4112, 9 Oct. 1873.

27. *CNR* 4, no. 3965, 10 Apr. 1873; London *Advertiser*, 16 Oct. 1874; Canadian National Railways Library, Montreal, H. Spencer, "An Historical Review of the Canadian National Railways Motive Power Shops, at Stratford, Ont., from its Inception in 1870 to August 1951," unpublished typescript.

28. Montreal *Gazette*, 2 and 18 Feb. 1852, 10 Aug. and 30 Nov. 1853; Montreal *Gazette*, 17 Sept. 1852. In the United States, the Grand Trunk had substantial engine shops at Gorham, New Hampshire and at Island Pond, Vermont, and a major car shop at Portland, Maine. These American facilities are not discussed further in this paper. Montreal *Gazette*, 15 and 16 Feb. 1855; Montreal *Transcript*, 25 Sept. 1857; GTR *Report*, 1855.

29. GTR *Report*, 1854.

30. Montreal *Gazette*, 15 Jan. and 2 Oct. 1855, 10 May and 22 July 1856; GTR *Report* for half-year to 30 June 1857; *Journal of the Franklin Institute of the State of Pennsylvania*, 3rd ser., 36 (July 1858).

31. GTR *Report* for half-year to 30 June 1859. For an engraving of the Grand Trunk workshops in 1860, see C.P. DeVolpi and P.S. Winkworth, eds., *Montréal: Recueil Iconographique* (Montreal, 1963), vol. 1, 137. The Eaton-Yates report was predicated on the contemplated merger of the Grand Trunk and Great Western, so they proposed to make Montreal the focal point for repairs and renewals on the Portland to Toronto section, and Hamilton for the western section. When the merger plans fell through, their major recommendations were adapted for the Grand Trunk alone. *CNR* 1001, 9 June 1862; *CNR* 10190, fo. 77.

32. Canadian National Railways Library, GTR, ms. Locomotive Superintendent's Reports, half-years to 31 Dec. 1863, 30 June 1864, 30 June 1865 and 30 June 1868; GTR *Reports*, half-years to 31 Dec. 1868 and 30 June and 31 Dec. 1869.

33. GTR *Reports*, half-years to 30 June 1870, 31 Dec. 1870, 30 June 1872 and 31 Dec. 1872; 92 *CNR* 1039, 6 Dec. 1873; GTR *Reports*, half-years to 31 Dec. 1873, 30 June 1875, 31 Dec. 1875 and 31 Dec 1877; *CNR* 1042, 20 May 1880; GTR *Reports*, half-years to 30 June 1880 and 31 Dec. 1880.

34. Brantford *Expositor*, 14 Mar. 1854 and 15 July 1870; University of Western Ontario, Regional History Collection, published evidence in *Whitehead v. Buffalo*, II: 36 (Barlow to Heseltine and Powell, 5 July 1856); II, p. 44 (Barlow to Heseltine and Powell, 16 Aug. 1856); II, p. 55 (Barlow to Powell, 15 Nov. 1856); I, p. 111 (Barlow to proprietors, 16 Feb. 1857); III (*Report* for half-year to 31 July 1857); I, p. 122 (Powell to proprietors, 21 Sept. 1857); III (*Report* for half-year to 31 July 1858).

35. *CNR* 10190, fo. 77. See generally, H. Spencer, "Canadian National Railways Motive Power Shops," 113; Stratford *Beacon*, 12 Aug. 1870, 4 Nov. 1870, 11 Nov. 1870, 11 Apr. 1873, 16 May 1873, 13 June 1873 and 18 July 1873, Stratford *Herald*, 15 June 1870 and 10 and 24 May 1871.

36. *CNR* 1038, 6 May 1871; Brantford *Expositor*, 7 Oct. 1870, 2 June 1871, 14 July 1871 and 28 July 1871; GTR *Report* for half-year to 31 Dec. 1871.

37. *The Engineer* (London), 9 Mar. 1860, 155; *Whitehead v. Buffalo*, III, *Report* for half-year to 31 Jan. 1858; Montreal *Transcript*, 6 Nov. 1857; Hamilton *Spectator*, 28 Aug. 1860 and 27 Apr. 1863; *Canadian Illustrated News*, 6 Dec. 1862; *Canadian National Railways Magazine*, Aug. 1934; *American Railway Review* 5 (1862): 210; Stratford *Beacon*, 1 Aug. 1873, and see Montreal *Transcript*, 8 Oct. 1857; *CNR* 1039, 3 June 1873.

38. *CNR* 1, Report of R.W. Harris, 12 Mar. 1856; ibid., Car Superintendent's Report, 18 Feb. 1859; Hamilton *Times*, 26 Apr. 1859. Discussions of the inadequacies of wrought iron wheels and the superiority of cast iron occur regularly in the mechanical superintendents' half-yearly reports; the most common problem with the English wheels was their high rate of winter breakage.

39. University of Western Ontario, Regional History Collection, Thomas Swinyard Papers, v. 1430, Swinyard to Livesey, 28 Dec. 1869; *CNR* 1039, 22 Oct. 1873; London *Advertiser*, 19 Mar. 1874.

40. Canadian National Railways Library, Wallis to Hickson, ms. report on steel wheels, 2 and 3 Mar. 1875; ibid., ms. bundle, "Correspondence and Reports on English Steel Tyred Wheels," Hannaford to Hickson, 26 Aug. 1875; *CNR* 1040, 21 Sept. 1875; GTR *Report* for half-year ending 31 Dec. 1877.

41. Thomas C. Cochran, *Railroad Leaders, 1843–1899* (Cambridge, Mass., 1953), 147ff.; GTR *Report* for half-year to 31 Dec. 1877. The argument that interdependence of firms prohibited unilateral innovation was advanced by several railway managers to excuse their failure to introduce certain safety appliances that might

reduce the frequency of accidents to brakemen; see Ontario, Select Committee on Railway Accidents, *Report*, 1880, passim; *CNR* 7, #1617, 18 Oct. 1861.

42. GWR *Report* for half-year to 31 Jan. 1862; Canadian National Railways Library, GTR, ms. Locomotive Superintendent's Report for half-year to 30 June 1864.

43. A very important difference, however, arose from the fact that "scientific management" assumed a fully formed labour market, while the railway managers had to incorporate the retention of skilled workers into their economy project. But by the late 1870s this was beginning to change, and the railway shops found it possible for the first time (with some minor exceptions in the crisis of the late 1850s) to reduce the size of their workforces, where earlier they had only reluctantly reduced the length of the working day. In terms of *labour* management, then, it would strain the argument to say that the railways of the 1860s and 1870s anticipated scientific management, but in terms of industrial organization and cost-control methods of other kinds, they were in the vanguard of managerial innovation.

44. *CNR* 10190, fo. 77, 31 May 1862.

45. Canadian National Railways Library, GTR, ms. Locomotive Superintendent's Reports, half-years to 31 Dec. 1864 and 30 June 1867; GWR *Report* for half-year to 31 July 1868.

46. *CNR* 7, no. 1319, Locomotive Superintendent's Report for half-year to 31 Dec. 1858. One of the fullest discussions available of railway workshop layout was published by the Grand Trunk's Master Mechanic at Stratford in 1889; see J. Davis Barnett, "Work Shops, Their Design and Construction," Engineering Institute of Canada, *Transactions* 3 (1889): 1.

47. *CNR* 10190, fo. 77, 31 May 1862.

48. GTR *Report* for half-year to 31 Dec. 1870; *CNR* 7, no. 1467, 27 Jan. 1860; no. 1643, 15 Jan. 1862; ibid., no. 1039, 2 Oct. 1874 and 23 Sept. 1874.

49. *CNR* 2, no. 501, 5 Dec. 1854; the tendering policy was adopted in May 1855 (ibid, no. 662); GTR *Report* for half-year to 30 June 1859; Hamilton Public Library, GWR, ms. locomotive shop work records, 1875; on accounting practices in contemporary industry, see A.D. Chandler, *The Visible Hand* (Cambridge, Mass., 1977), 69ff.

RATES OF RETURN IN RAILWAY INVESTMENT AND IMPLICATIONS FOR GOVERNMENT SUBSIDIZATION OF THE CANADIAN PACIFIC RAILWAY: SOME PRELIMINARY RESULTS†

PETER J. GEORGE

I

This paper is concerned with determining the economic profitability of the Canadian Pacific Railway as an investment project and with ascertaining the amount and necessity of subsidies awarded to the Canadian Pacific Railway Company by the government of Canada.

The economic profitability of the transcontinental railway project was determined by estimating the rate of return on investment in the CPR. The private rate of return is defined, after R.W. Fogel, on an annual basis, as the ratio of net operating profits (gross earnings less working expenses) in a given year to the cost of investment up to and including that year.[1] The private rate of return on the book value of investment in the railway has been calculated by the CPR company[2] but this measure was improved by the calculation of the private rate of return on the actual cost of the investment, that is, the cash cost of construction of the railway.[3] Annual private rates of return were calculated for the ten-year time period 1886 to 1895.

The second problem concerned the subsidy given by the Canadian government to the company in order to assist in the construction of the mainline. By 1870, the Pacific railway was acknowledged to be both politically indispensable and

†*Canadian Journal of Economics/Revue canadienne d'Economique* I, 4 (Nov. 1968): 740–62. This paper is based upon the author's unpublished Ph.D. thesis, "A Benefit-Cost Analysis of the Canadian Pacific Railway" (University of Toronto, 1967). The guidance and helpful comments of Professor John H. Dales and constructive suggestions by Professors A.W. Currie, I.M. Drummond, W. Walsh, M.H. Watkins, and D.M. Winch are gratefully acknowledged. Earlier versions of this paper were presented to the Workshop in Economic History at the University of Toronto in April 1967 and to the joint meeting of the Canadian Political Science Association and the Canadian Historical Association in June 1967.

economically desirable. From the inception of the project, the government was concerned that a private company be organized to build the railway, a decision which depended solely on economic considerations, not on a state of political urgency. If potential investors had believed that the railway would be profitable, then they would have built it without subsidy. In fact, private enterprise never seriously considered building the CPR without the financial assistance of the government. Anticipated profits were too small in view of the considerable risks attached to the project. In Fogel's terminology, the CPR represented "premature" enterprise.[4] An extremely large amount of capital was required for construction costs, especially through the largely unsurveyed and difficult terrain in British Columbia and north and west of Lake Superior; in addition, earnings were likely to be small for several years after the completion of the railway since the development of freight traffic was predicted largely on the future settlement of the west, and there would be a time lag of indeterminate duration before traffic was sufficient to yield profits. Moreover, long stretches of track through the Canadian Shield and the Rocky Mountains were unlikely ever to be productive of earnings, and this greatly increased the overhead costs to be borne by areas which were.

Although the railway was not thought profitable by private investors, it was considered to be necessary politically and "profitable" in the sense that it would promote the general economic progress of the country. For construction to proceed, government intervention was necessary and, consequently, it was decided that the railway should be constructed by a private company and subsidized by the Canadian government: "The Railway . . . should be constructed and worked by private enterprize [sic], and not by the Dominion Government; and . . . the public aid to be given to secure that undertaking, should consist of such liberal grants of land, and such subsidy in money, or other aid, not increasing the present rate of taxation, as the Parliament of Canada shall hereafter determine."[5]

The railway was "an essential adjunct of nationhood for the new Dominion" which "had to be built for political reasons, whatever the subsidy involved. . . ."[6] Although this might have to be considerable, "sensible economic policy required only that the subsidy be kept as low as possible."[7]

The rate-of-return calculations were employed to test the validity of the assumption that a subsidy was necessary to induce construction by a private company. If the private rate of return on investment in the CPR was in fact high relative to rates of return in other investments, then there is *prima facie* evidence for concluding that the railway ought to have been built by a private company without subsidy, for if investors had correctly foreseen the profitability of the investment they would have invested their capital in it without the inducement of a subsidy. If, on the other hand, the private rate of return was low, then some amount of subsidy was necessary. The necessary subsidy *ex post* would be that portion of the total cash cost of construction required to be paid to the company in order to raise the private rate of return on the contribution of private investors to at least the normal rate of return in alternative investments. Assuming that the Pacific railway was politically necessary,[8] it was possible to estimate, *ex post*, the "required" subsidy to the company, and to compare the "required" subsidy with the value of subsidies actually paid by government to the company.

II

The first calculation of the private rate of return is based on the book value of investment in road and equipment as reported by the company. The rate of return on investment for a given year is equal to railway net earnings for that year taken as a percentage of the book value of investment in that year.

For the decade 1886 to 1895 the private rate of return was found to vary from a low of 1.9 percent in 1887 and 1888 to a high of 3.5 percent in 1891 and 1892. The average rate of return for the period was 3.0 percent (as shown in table 1). However, to estimate the profitability of an investment the calculated rate of return must be compared with the normal or market rate of return to contemporary investors, that is, the best approximation to the opportunity cost of the capital invested in the project.[9] The calculation of the private rate of return on book value of investment fails to support the impression that the CPR was a remarkably successful economic venture, given that the normal rate of return to investors from alternative investment projects was likely between 6 and 10 percent.

The rate of return on book value of total assets, however, does not accurately portray the economic profitability of the railway project, because the book value of road and equipment presented in the company's financial statements cannot be regarded as an accurate representation of the actual cost of the property: " 'Cost of road and equipment,' as set up on the books of a company, frequently represents not the actual cash outlay but the par value of the bonds and shares which have been issued to obtain cash or property. 'Cost of road and equipment' may therefore include . . . discounts on securities sold, and other items not strictly construction cost. And it may include sums to offset the par value of securities which have been issued for other than a cash consideration."[10] In fact, in the *Commercial and Financial Chronicle* dated 26 April 1884, it was reported that $55 million par value of CPR common stock had netted the company only $25,236,828 cash to be applied against construction costs.[11]

The use of book value in the rate-of-return calculations thus imparts a downward bias to an estimate of the profitability of the investment. In order to avoid this bias, it was decided to estimate the actual cash expenditure, by both the company and the government of Canada, on the construction of the railway, and to recalculate the private rate of return on this base.

III

The calculation of the private rate of return on a base of the cash cost of construction is undertaken below. An estimate of construction costs of the CPR is reported. Expenditures on construction are divided into two parts: expenditures, excluding payments of the cash subsidy, by the government of Canada; and expenditures by the CPR company.

Government Expenditures

Government expenditures on construction of the CPR began in March 1871. The initial expenditures in 1871 and 1872 were concentrated on surveying the

TABLE 1

The Rate of Return on the Book Value of the Canadian Pacific Railway[a]

Year Ended December 31	Book Value of the Road[b] ($)	Net Earnings[c] ($)	Rate of Return[d] (%)
1886	174,746,879	3,703,487	2.1
1887	188,000,988	3,504,118	1.9
1888	200,331,512	3,870,775	1.9
1889	206,469,363	6,006,059	2.9
1890	220,916,661	6,299,701	2.9
1891	228,731,997	8,009,660	3.5
1892	239,343,284	8,420,348	3.5
1893	247,584,365	7,741,416	3.1
1894	250,492,561	6,423,309	2.6
1895	252,931,701	7,480,951	3.0

a. Average rate of return on book value for the ten-year period 1886-85 is 3.0 percent.
b. The column entitled "Book value of the road" represents the book value of investment in owned and leased railway properties.
c. "Net earnings" was used by the CPR to mean net operating profits, that is, gross earnings less working expenses. Working expenses included payment of railway taxes but not fixed charges on bonded debt. Taken in this context, "net earnings" is the relevant concept of returns to capital for calculating the private rate of return.
d. The average rate of return is found by dividing the sum of the "net earnings" column by the sum of the "book value of the road" column.

SOURCE: Canadian Pacific Railway Company, "Submission of Canadian Pacific Railway Company to the Royal Commission on Transportation," 27.

probable route of the mainline from east to west, while the government awaited the formation of a private company to undertake construction.[12]

With the Pacific Scandal and the lapsing of the Canada Pacific's contract in early 1874, the government of Alexander Mackenzie committed itself to a start of construction on parts of the route strategically located for settlement.[13] Surveying operations were continued and expanded, especially in British Columbia; the improvement of the Dawson route from Lake Superior to Red River was undertaken; and provision was made for the extension of the Canada Central Railway to Georgian Bay along the Georgian Bay Branch, for construction of the Pembina Branch from Red River to the United States boundary, and the laying of track westward from Red River. Throughout the remainder of the 1870s, both the Mackenzie and Macdonald administrations again tried to interest private enterprise in undertaking the project.[14]

The contract between the government and the CPR company was finally signed on 21 October 1880.[15] As part of the subsidy offered to the company, the government was to complete, at its own expense, the construction of two sections of the line, between Thunder Bay and Selkirk, and from Port Moody to Kamloops in British Columbia. The mainline of the CPR was completed on 7 November 1885. Government expenditures on construction and improvements of the mainline continued to be reported throughout the period 1886 to 1895.

Government construction costs were straightforward and uncomplicated, comprising expenditures on surveying, excavation, track-laying, timber and rails, etc. The reported expenditures by the government of Canada on surveys and construction from 1871 to 1895 have been presented in summary form.[16] These figures require adjustment before incorporation into the estimated cash cost of construction. The actual expenditures by the government during the period through 1880 were not necessarily equal to the amount that might have been spent by the CPR to perform the same operations; the company would undoubtedly have built those same lines at a lower cost. Consequently, the reported expenditures by the government on the railway require adjustment downwards. There are at least two pieces of evidence that can be adduced to support this view.

First, the royal commission appointed to inquire into the progress of the CPR came to the conclusion that "the construction of the Canadian Pacific Railway was carried on as a Public Work at a sacrifice of money, time and efficiency."[17] The commissioners commented at length on many improprieties during the period of government construction — viz., the inefficiency of the surveying system employed by Sandford Fleming, instances of patronage in the hiring of employees, and the system of letting contracts — that served to inflate the cost of the government-built lines. Secondly, some portion of government expenditure was aimed, not at completing the transcontinental railway, but directly at rendering the all-rail route unnecessary, at least in the short run. The emphasis of the Mackenzie administration during 1874 to 1877 on the Dawson route and the Georgian Bay Branch was intended to permit postponement of the rail connection north of Lake Superior by employing a combined water-rail route from Lake Nipissing (and the Canada Central Railway extension) to Red River. This waterway section of the transcontinental route was to be replaced by railway as soon as was practicable. Expenditures by government on surveys and construction of these portions of the Dawson and water-rail routes were really superfluous from the point of view of transcontinental railroad construction.[18] Thus, the cost of the government lines handed over to the CPR company is inflated over the probable cost of construction by the private company itself. The excessive cost can be expressed in quantitative form, thereby allowing a calculation of *adjusted* governmental expenditures for use in determining the rate of return on cost of construction.

Government expenditures on the construction of the CPR to June 1880 could have been reduced by a total of $2,964,808[19] if there had been a rationalization of surveys, early selection of the western terminus at Burrard Inlet in British Columbia, no expenditure on the Dawson route or on the Georgian Bay Branch, and improvements in the procedure whereby contracts were awarded (in particular, more detailed information being made available to tenderers). This estimate of adjusted government expenditures is still likely to overstate the probable construction costs which would have been incurred by a private company in performing the same operations because of the incidence of non-quantifiable sources of upward bias on reported government expenditures.

No adjustment of reported government expenditures on construction from 1881 through 1895 was attempted. Adjusted government expenditures, on a calendar year basis, for the period from 1871 to 1895 are presented in table 2.

TABLE 2

Total Annual Capital Expenditures on Construction and Equipment of the Canadian Pacific Railway, by the Government of Canada and the Canadian Pacific Railway Company, 1871–95

Year	Adjusted Government Expenditures[a] ($)	Company Expenditures[b] ($)	Estimated Value of Leased Lines ($)	Total Annual Expenditures ($)
1871	236,840	—	—	236,840
1872	335,067	—	—	335,067
1873	347,291	—	—	347,291
1874	713,515	—	—	713,515
1875	1,531,982	—	—	1,531,982
1876	1,809,673	—	—	1,809,673
1877	1,347,522	—	—	1,347,522
1878	2,184,790	—	—	2,184,790
1879	2,995,012	—	—	2,995,012
1880	4,506,513	—	—	4,506,513
1881	3,673,790	10,167,380	—	13,841,169
1882	3,544,900	21,970,922	—	25,515,822
1883	4,324,619	21,963,342	—	26,287,960
1884	3,488,297	21,222,886	17,620,680	42,331,863
1885	1,910,119	21,159,403	3,940,000	27,009,522
1886	618,564	10,023,884	2,706,120	13,348,568
1887	253,535	5,482,890	—	5,736,425
1888	69,407	5,641,297	1,468,000	7,178,705
1889	63,848	2,953,176	3,240,000	6,257,024
1890	39,174	5,233,554	6,500,000	11,772,728
1891	51,789	5,450,455	—	5,502,244
1892	240,024	5,109,421	—	5,349,445
1893	280,188	5,018,789	—	5,298,977
1894	97,875	1,995,753	—	2,093,628
1895	57,440	908,373	—	965,813

a. Government expenditures are presented in source materials for the fiscal year ending 30 June. Fiscal-year data have been converted to the calendar year ending 31 December. Estimates of excessive or unnecessary expenditures by government have been deducted from calendar-year expenditures for the year in which the unnecessary expenditures were incurred.

b. Where company expenditures were reported to the government of Canada on a fiscal-year basis from 1881 through 30 June 1886, they have been converted to the calendar year ending 31 December. Expenditures were presented in the *Annual Reports* of the company on a calendar-year basis. Columns may not add due to rounding.

SOURCES: *Sessional Papers* XVI (1883), no. 27: 161; ibid., XVII (1884), no. 31f: 46; ibid., XVIII (1885), no. 25a: 175; ibid., XIX (1886), no. 35a: 227; ibid., XX (1887), no. 34b: 138; ibid., XXXI (1897), no. 10, Part II: 39; Canadian Pacific Railway Company, *Annual Reports for the Years 1886 to 1895*; for rentals on which the estimated values of the leased lines are based, see *Annual Report for the Year 1885*: 9; ibid. (1886): 19; ibid. (1888): 16, 46-7; ibid. (1890): 32; and P. George, "A Benefit-Cost Analysis," chaps. 3 and 4.

Company Expenditures

There remains the question of the actual expenditures on construction by the CPR itself.[20] However, we here meet a complication that was not encountered in the estimation of government expenditures, namely, the difficulty of valuing certain branch and leased lines, where these values were not accurately represented in the summary financial statements of the company.

Development of the estimates of company expenditure on construction is divided into: expenditures on construction of the mainline, defined as the line from Montreal to Vancouver, and expenditures on branch lines, up to 31 December 1885; estimates of the capital value of leased lines acquired by the company before 1896; and, expenditures on the mainline, branches, and improvement of leased lines during 1886 to 1895.

Company Expenditures on Construction, 1881 to 1885

The CPR company returned statements concerning its actual expenditures on construction of the mainline and branches of the railway to the government of Canada.[21] These depict cumulative expenditures on engineering, construction, and rolling stock, based on the fiscal year ending 30 June. These data represent a starting point for the calculation of the company's expenditures on construction up to 31 December 1885; they are approximations to the real cash outlay on construction by the company, since they are exclusive of any discount on securities sold by the company at less than par. In fact, the reports to the government state explicitly that the data represent actual cash expenditure on construction.[22]

Two items contained in these summary reports require some further comment. First, the reports as presented in the *Sessional Papers* included an item "Costs in connection with the administration of the Land Grant in aid, if any." However, since this item is of no direct relevance to the estimation of construction costs, I have subtracted it from reported expenditures. Secondly, the item "Lines and branches acquired in Eastern Canada" reported in fiscal year 1882 pertains to the extension of the mainline from Callander to Montreal, specifically to the acquisition by the company of the Canada Central Railway and the western section of the Quebec, Montreal, Ottawa and Occidental Railway. The valuation of these lines at $8,710,000 could be inferred from the report of the company to the government for fiscal year 1882.[23] However, this figure appeared unreliable as a proxy for the capital value of the Canada Central Railway and the western section of the Quebec, Montreal, Ottawa and Occidental Railway. The difficulty lay essentially in the subsequent alteration of entries concerning the value of these lines after fiscal year 1882. In other words, the values assigned to the Canada Central Railway and the western section of the Quebec, Montreal, Ottawa and Occidental Railway varied in the reports of the company from fiscal year 1882 to fiscal year 1886. This reporting procedure can be explained in the light of the title assigned to the relevant "item" in fiscal year 1883 — viz., "Unpaid balance of cost of the Canada Central Railway and the Quebec, Montreal, Ottawa and Occidental Railway."[24] Since the entries actually represented the balance owed by the CPR on the acquisition of the two railway systems, it was necessary to construct a more appropriate estimate of the value of capital represented by the lines extending the mainline from Callander to Montreal.

This was determined by adding an estimate of the unpaid balance of costs of acquisition owing on the two rail systems to costs of acquisition already met as of 31 December 1883. Accumulated expenditure on the purchase of the two railways was reported by the company in a memorandum dated 15 January 1884, as $3,203,050[25] and was complemented by estimating, as of 31 December 1883, the unpaid balance owing on the purchase of the rail systems. This latter estimate was found by averaging the appropriate entries in the company's returns for fiscal years 1883 and 1884 submitted to the government, and was equal to $7,710,854.[26] The resulting sum of paid and estimated unpaid costs of acquisition of the Canada Central Railway and the Quebec, Montreal, Ottawa and Occidental Railway was $10,913,904, and this value was employed as a proxy for the capital value of the lines at their acquisition during fiscal year 1881–82.

The items included in expenditures during 1881 to 1885 were restricted to costs of land and land damages, costs of grading, masonry and bridging, station building, engineering, etc., cost of rolling stock, and costs associated with extending the mainline from Callander to Montreal via the Canada Central Railway and the western section of the Quebec, Montreal, Ottawa and Occidental Railway — the cost of acquisition of the former being incorporated during calendar year 1881, and that of the latter during 1882.[27]

Estimated Value of Railways Leased by the Company to 1895

The second major component in estimated company expenditure on construction involves accurate representation of the capital values of leased lines. The lines of importance are the Ontario and Quebec Railway system, the St. Lawrence and Ottawa Railway, the Manitoba and South-West Colonization Railway, and the North Shore Railway — all acquired before completion of the mainline at year-end 1885 — and the Atlantic and North-West Railway, and the New Brunswick Railways acquired after 1886.[28]

There appeared to be two alternative methods of approximating the value of plant and equipment of the leased lines. In the first place, the *Annual Reports* of the Minister of Railways and Canals (reprinted in the *Sessional Papers*) contain a summary statement of capital invested in railway and canal properties in Canada. In this statistical summary, an estimate of the total cost of railway and rolling stock for several of the lines leased by the CPR company was presented. The capital value of railway and rolling stock was depicted by the par value of securities issued by the railway company in question. Thus, these estimates are likely to overstate the real value of capital invested in construction and equipment of the railways leased by the CPR.

In fact, the difficulty of estimating the amount of capital represented by the leased lines of the CPR system was solved by capitalizing the annual rentals of those lines from the date of acquisition. The company did not identify separately the capital value of its leased properties in the financial statements contained in its annual *Reports*. However, it did estimate the value of the leased lines in the

…t of the *Reports* on occasion, by capitalizing the rentals of those leased lines at
percent. Consequently, the annual rentals of the leased lines were capitalized at
5 percent in order to obtain a value for each line approximating its construction
or replacement cost. The imputed value of each leased line was incorporated
into the estimate of total expenditures on construction by the CPR company in
the year in which that line was leased by the company.

Annual Company Expenditures on Construction, 1886 to 1895

The third major field of company expenditures comprised construction and
improvements on the mainline, branch lines, and leased lines during the period
1886 to 1895 inclusive. In fact, these expenditures were reported on a calendar-
year basis in the financial statements presented in the annual *Reports* of the company.
These expenditures were allocated into three categories: expenditures on additions and improvements, mainline and branch lines; expenditures on additions
to and improvement of leased lines; and expenditures on rolling stock, shops and
machinery, equipment, construction plant and outfit.

Conclusion

To the company's expenditures can be added *adjusted* government expenditures
on construction of the Pacific railway from 1871 to 1895 inclusive. The resulting
estimate of total annual expenditures on the construction of the CPR is presented in
table 2.

The Private Rate of Return on Cost of Construction

Given the annual net earnings reported by the CPR and the estimates of
construction expenditures by both the government of Canada and the company
to 1895, it is now possible to calculate the private rate of return on the cash cost
of construction of the railway.

The annual private rate of return on investment has been defined above as the
ratio of railway net earnings in a given year to the cost of investment up to and
including that year. However, there are two factors which might affect the reliability
of this calculation: first, the matter of depreciation; secondly, the possibility of
bias in the rate-of-return calculations when net earnings and cumulative expenditures are measured in current dollars.

Professor Fogel in his study was faced with the difficult problem of adjusting
net earnings of the Union Pacific Railroad company for depreciation since the
company did not deduct depreciation charges from net earnings.[29] However, the
estimation of annual depreciation charges neglected by the CPR was not felt to
be of great significance to the rate-of-return calculations. It appears[30] that the
company carefully maintained its equipment during the period of the rate-of-
return study.[31] Moreover, it is not clear to what extent the failure to subtract out
depreciation charges from company net earnings biases the calculation of the
private rate of return. Under depreciation accounting, company net earnings

would require downward adjustment for annual depreciation charges; furthermore, the capital stock would have to be corrected for replacement of retired capital goods since annual investment by the company would be comprised of both replacements and net additions to capital stock. The company did not practise depreciation accounting: both the numerator and denominator in the rate-of-return calculations are "too large," the former being gross of annual depreciation charges and the latter gross of replacements.[32] In any case, careful maintenance would tend to prolong the useful life of a capital good and, to some extent, offset the effect of neglecting depreciation.

Furthermore, it was not likely that the failure of the CPR company to take depreciation into account was of great significance to contemporary investors since this procedure was not standard for railroads.[33] An investor wishing to compare the financial performance of the CPR with other railways necessarily would have based his comparison on rates of return gross of depreciation. On the other hand, the fact that the CPR was relatively well maintained was probably readily appreciated by potential investors and of some importance to their decision to invest.

The second difficulty involves the possibility of bias in the rate-of-return calculations if net earnings and cumulative expenditures on construction are presented in current dollars. Current-dollar comparisons of net earnings and construction costs would be somewhat less suspect if the acts of investment and generation of net earnings occurred together throughout the time period. In the case of the CPR two factors recommend the conversion of current-dollar figures to their constant-dollar equivalents: (i) the investment of capital in the construction of the CPR was already achieved in large part at the beginning of the time period over which the private rate of return is calculated (additional investment from 1886 to 1895 was small compared with the capital stock existing in 1886); (ii) there were fluctuations in relative price levels in Canada over the period from 1871 to 1895, with the trend of prices being generally downwards throughout the period. Thus, the private rate of return, estimated from comparison of net earnings and cumulative expenditures expressed in current dollars, would tend to understate the *real* private rate of return on investment in the railway, given that the bulk of the capital in construction was invested during the years of relatively high prices before 1886. The current-dollar figures for annual expenditures on construction and for net earnings were therefore converted into constant dollars of 1885.[34]

Two different estimates of the private rate of return on the cash cost of construction of the CPR, over the decade 1886 to 1895, are presented in table 3. The private rate of return is first calculated with data in current dollars, and then calculated after conversion of dollar values for net earnings and cumulative expenditures into constant dollars of 1885 by the Dominion Bureau of Statistics general price index. The private rate of return in current dollars varied from a low of 2.1 percent in 1887 to a high of 4.1 percent in 1892, averaging 3.2 percent over the decade. When the current-dollar estimates were deflated by the above-mentioned price index, the rate of return varied from a low of 2.2 percent in 1887 and 1888 to a high of 4.4 percent in 1892, and the ten-year average was 3.4 percent.[35]

TABLE 3

Private Rate of Return on the Cost of Construction of the Canadian Pacific Railway, 1886–95

	Cumulative Expenditures		Net Earnings		Private Rate of Return	
Year	Current $	Constant $ of 1885 (DBS index)	Current $	Constant $ of 1885 (DBS index)	% (Current $)	% Constant $ of 1885 (DBS index)
1886	164,343,111	152,568,172	3,703,487	3,763,706	2.3	2.5
1887	170,079,535	158,270,383	3,504,118	3,483,219	2.1	2.2
1888	177,258,240	165,133,390	3,870,775	3,700,550	2.2	2.2
1889	183,515,264	171,126,708	6,006,059	5,752,930	3.3	3.4
1890	195,287,992	182,233,055	6,299,701	5,943,114	3.2	3.3
1891	200,790,236	187,423,851	8,009,660	7,556,283	4.0	4.0
1892	206,139,681	192,860,279	8,420,348	8,557,264	4.1	4.4
1893	211,438,658	198,169,876	7,741,416	7,756,930	3.7	3.9
1894	213,532,286	200,411,447	6,423,309	6,877,205	3.0	3.4
1895	214,498,099	201,466,980	7,480,951	8,175,903	3.5	4.1
Average private rate of return, 1886-95, is					3.2	3.4

NOTE: The average private rate of return is found by dividing the sum of a "Net Earnings" column by the sum of the appropriate "Cumulative Expenditures" column.

IV

The calculated private rates of return on CPR construction expenditures have implications for the private profitability of the investment project. The private profitability of an investment is determined by comparing the private rate of return on that investment with the normal rate of return available to investors in alternative investments. In the decade from 1886 to 1895, the normal rate of return on investment (or, the opportunity cost of capital) is assumed to have been in the neighbourhood of 6 to 10 percent. If so, it was likely that the investment of capital by private investors in the construction of the CPR would not have occurred, unless government financial assistance also was directed towards completion of the railway. Undoubtedly, some amount of government subsidy was necessary for construction and operation of the CPR by a private company. It is possible to employ the above estimates of the private rate of return on CPR investment to determine *ex post* the appropriate level of subsidization of the project by the Dominion government. Moreover, the amount of estimated "required subsidy" can be compared with the calculated value in 1885 of subsidies actually awarded to the company by the government.

Value of Government Subsidies to the Company

The government of Canada[36] agreed to give to the company the completed sections of railway from Thunder Bay to Selkirk, and from Kamloops to Port Moody, a cash grant of $25 million and a grant of 25 million acres of land "fairly fit for settlement." There were also tax concessions to the company: material for the construction of the railway could be imported free of duty, the capital stock and equipment of the company were to be free of taxation in perpetuity, and the land grant was to be exempt from taxation for twenty years after its location. Moreover, the company received right-of-way and road-bed concessions, as well as permission to take construction materials from Crown lands. Finally, the construction of any railway south of the CPR mainline in the west within fifteen miles of the American border was prohibited for twenty years, and the authority of the government to regulate railway rates was restricted. In addition to subsidies awarded by the Dominion government, provincial and municipal governments also presented the company with grants in money and land.

Estimated expenditures on surveys and construction of sections of the mainline by the government of Canada were summarized in table 2. Data on cash subsidies were contained in the *Sessional Papers*. The estimation of the value as subsidy in 1885 of these two components of aid to the company was straightforward.[37] However, there were difficulties associated with determining the value to the company of the land grant, tax exemptions, and the remission of import duties.

A satisfactory estimate of the value of the land grant was derived from data on net proceeds from land sales.[38] These data were netted for sales and colonization expenses, and irrigation costs. However, the company did not report net proceeds from land sales from 1881 to 1888 or after 1930. Net proceeds from land sales during the earlier period were estimated from available data on gross receipts from land sales and the ratio of net to gross receipts during the decade 1889 to 1898, and implicit prices per acre in agreements for large-scale land transfers from the company to the Canada North-West Land Company in 1882–83, and to the government of Canada in 1886. Secondly, a company estimate of the value of remaining lands was incorporated into net proceeds in 1930 as a proxy for the value of lands as yet unsold by the company. Finally, the estimated value of the land grant to the company in 1885 was found by summing the present value of net proceeds from land sales over the period from 1886 to 1930, and the compound values of net proceeds from 1881 to 1884.

Some element of downward bias is imparted here by employing company net proceeds from land sales. The CPR did not attempt to maximize profits from land sales but from overall railway operations, particularly from the carrying of freight. Settlement of government homesteads and railway lands was emphasized in order to increase the volume of freight available for the railway. The company sold its land at prices lower on average than the Hudson's Bay Company, for example, in spite of the fact that the CPR's lands were undoubtedly of better average quality, and presumably able to bear higher prices.[39] Further, the land grant, when compared with other items of subsidy, may have had a singular impact on investor confidence in purchasing CPR securities; that is, it is possible that the land subsidy, if it was regarded by investors as a particularly promising component of total subsidies, reduced the cost of financing the CPR, and thus conferred a valuable indirect benefit on the company. On the other hand, the likelihood of an unreliable estimate of the value of the land subsidy in 1885 was increased because of the possibility of distortion, given the length of the time period, with an inappropriate assumption concerning the interest rate at which compounding and present value calculations were undertaken.

A second difficulty involved estimating the value of tax exemptions to the company. Although railways were customarily subject to taxation in the United States at the time, the CPR was to benefit from a clause relieving it from taxation — a clause vigorously debated during the passage of the railway's charter through the House of Commons.[40] Two estimates of the value to the CPR company of exemption from taxation of its capital stock and property have been developed,[41] based on the assumption of two different tax bases: first, a tax per mile of railway in operation; secondly, a tax on railway gross earnings.

Several alternative rates of tax per mile were suggested by contemporary United States experience in railroad taxation.[42] It was decided to perform the calculations with the tax rate assumed initially to be $75 per mile in 1885, since the analogy between the CPR and the Northern Pacific Railroad was most direct. (Subsequently, tax rates of $150 and $225 per mile were incorporated into the results.) Annual taxes were estimated as the product of the tax rate and average mileage of railway operated by the CPR from 1885 to 1965, determined from the company's *Annual Reports*.

The alternative basis employed for estimating the value of tax exemptions to the CPR was the percentage tax on annual railway gross earnings. The practice of taxing railway companies a percentage of annual gross earnings was already well developed in the United States in the 1880s.[43] By 1890, the tax on gross earnings was used exclusively in several states — Maine, Maryland, Michigan, Minnesota, Vermont, and Wisconsin — and in conjunction with property and other taxes in some states — Alabama, Illinois, New York, Pennsylvania, and Texas.[44] The rates of tax on gross earnings (when that system of taxation was used exclusively) ranged from 2 to 7 percent. The most common practice among state governments seems to have been to tax gross earnings at 3 percent.[45] Consequently, in the second estimate of the value in 1885 of the tax exemption to the company, annual taxes were estimated as 3 percent of company gross earnings over the period from 1885 to 1965.

These estimates provide an approximation, given the assumed rates of railway taxation, to the value of the tax exemption to the CPR in 1885. These results are biased downwards since the estimation of annual taxes due on company operations was terminated at 1965 and biased upward to the extent that taxes actually paid by the company to various levels of government in Canada have not been subtracted from estimates of annual taxes due. In both cases bias would appear to be relatively small since taxes were only paid by the company after 1900. Finally, given the length of the time period over which the present value calculations were performed, the possibility of some distortion in the estimates because of the selection of an inappropriate rate of interest was increased.

The fifth component of subsidies paid by the Canadian government to be quantified was the remission of import duties on materials imported by the CPR for the construction of the railway. The contract for the construction of the railway permitted the company to import, free of duty, "all steel rails, fish plates and other fastenings, spikes, bolts and nuts, wire, timber and all material for bridges to be used in the original construction of the railway, and of a telegraph line in connexion [sic] therewith, and all telegraphic apparatus for the first equipment of such telegraph line."[46]

The estimation of the value of remitted import duties was based on data[47] concerning the value of construction materials imported by the company, and the specified rates of duty pertaining to those items imported by the company for construction. The value of duties remitted for each item was estimated by calculating the amount of duty which would have been paid by the company on the value of materials imported, if the company had been required to pay duty. The company was assumed to have perfectly inelastic demand for the items over the range of pre-duty and post-duty prices; that is, it would have paid for the same quantity of imported construction materials a higher price determined by the value of materials imported, as reported in the annual *Tables*, plus the estimated value of duties remitted. The estimated value of duties remitted was rather small primarily because steel rails could be imported duty free by all railway companies;[48] consequently, there was no foundation for considering as subsidy the estimated value to the company of duties remitted on steel rails, since the subsidy was not peculiar to the CPR.

Finally, several aspects of the subsidy awarded to the company were not quantifiable. The CPR received subsidy in the form of lands for its rights of way, in addition to the land grant *per se*, both for the mainline and any branch lines that it might construct.[49] Secondly, the company was authorized to take construction materials from Crown lands; unfortunately, the value of this component of subsidy was not quantifiable because of lack of data on exact quantities of construction materials. Thirdly, the company was awarded a monopoly privilege in Manitoba, the North-West Territories, and British Columbia for a twenty-year period. The monopoly clause was a source of considerable friction between the government of Manitoba and the company and the Dominion government, until the clause was finally rescinded in 1888 in return for a government guarantee of interest on a company bond issue of $15 million.[50] However, the value of the monopoly clause to the CPR company was not quantifiable, since the value to the company of the government guarantee of bond interest could not be determined. Finally, the company received from the government of Canada a guarantee that the profitability of its operations would not be unduly restricted by government regulation of its railway rate policy.[51] Again, the value of this component of subsidy to the company was not calculable, although it was unlikely to be of great significance, given the nature of the general stipulations concerning government rate regulation in the Consolidated Railway Act.

The estimates of the total value in 1885 of all quantifiable components of subsidy paid to the CPR company are summarized in table 4. Measured in constant dollars of 1885 (Dominion Bureau of Statistics general price index), the total value of subsidies in 1885, in which the tax exemption was defined as 3 percent of company gross earnings from 1885 to 1965, varied from $120,232,677 at an interest rate of 6 percent, to $110,327,522 at 8 percent, and $107,578,448 when the rate of interest was assumed to be 10 percent. The non-quantifiable components of total subsidy awarded to the CPR company could not be incorporated into the estimate of the value of subsidies. However, their existence

TABLE 4

Total Value in 1885 of Components of Subsidy to the Canadian Pacific Railway Company: Government-Built Railway, Government Cash Subsidies, Land Subsidy, Tax Exemption, and Remission of Import Duties on Construction Materials

Item	Units	Assumed Rate of Interest		
		6%	8%	10%
(1) Value in 1885 as subsidy of government built railway	(1) Current dollars	45,552,735	50,186,680	55,448,027
	(2) Constant dollars of 1885 (DBS index)	40,267,133	44,168,939	48,583,085
(2) Value in 1885 of government cash subsidies	(1) Current dollars	27,816,250	28,558,085	29,327,798
	(2) Constant dollars of 1885 (DBS index)	25,939,283	26,596,277	27,278,496
(3) Value in 1885 of the land subsidy	(1) Current dollars	39,978,222	30,190,366	24,762,415
	(2) Constant dollars of 1885 (DBS index)	32,790,777	26,119,855	22,336,755
(4) Value in 1885 of the tax exemption (3% of gross earnings)	(1) Current dollars	31,873,256	17,537,992	11,258,163
	(2) Constant dollars of 1885 (DBS index)	20,865,027	13,063,378	8,991,320
(5) Value in 1885 of remission of duties on materials imported for the construction of the railway	(1) Current dollars	395,796	405,926	416,353
	(2) Constant dollars of 1885 (DBS index)	370,457	379,073	388,792
(6) Total value of all components of subsidy	(1) Current dollars	145,616,259	126,879,049	121,212,756
	(2) Constant dollars of 1885 (DBS index)	120,232,677	110,327,522	107,578,448

SOURCES: *Sessional Papers* XXXI (1897), no. 10, Part II: 39; *Annual Reports of the Minister of Railways and Canals, Railway Statistics of Canada*, 1881–96; Canadian Pacific Railway Company, *Annual Reports*, 1881–1965; *Tables of the Trade and Navigation of the Dominion of Canada*, 1881–88. The sources of data and derivation of the estimates are discussed in detail in George, "A Benefit-Cost Analysis."

provides considerable support for the opinion that the estimates of the value of subsidies are likely to understate the actual value of subsidies paid to the company rather than exaggerate their amount.

Estimation of "Required" Subsidy

To estimate the subsidy "required" by the CPR company to undertake construction of the transcontinental railway, suppose that construction costs of the CPR are comprised of two parts, privately contributed funds and government of Canada funds. The amount of the former was determined by investors' expectations that their investment would yield at least the normal rate of return on investment. Government investment was based on the assumption of the political necessity of the investment. Given the estimated cost of construction of the CPR and the actual level of net earnings reported by the company over the decade 1886 to 1895, it is possible to estimate *ex post* the portions of construction expenditure which ought to have been contributed by private enterprise and by government respectively. The estimate of the amount of construction costs payable by the government of Canada is termed "required" subsidy.

The "required" subsidy was defined as that capital grant, payable by the government in 1885, sufficient in amount to allow company net earnings to yield the normal rate of return on privately contributed capital.[52] The following general formula was employed:

$$(1) \quad \sum_{t=1}^{10} L_t = \sum_{t=1}^{10} \left(K_t - \frac{R_t}{r} \right).$$

Here, K_t is the present value in 1885 of the capital base—the cumulative cost of construction and equipment—in year t; R_t is the present value in 1885 of company net earnings in year t; r is the assumed normal rate of return; and L_t is the estimated present value in 1885 of the "required" capital grant in year t which would allow reported company net earnings to yield the normal rate of return on privately contributed capital in year t. Estimates of "required" capital grant by the government to the company were calculated with this formula from data on company net earnings and railway construction costs. The results of these calculations are presented in table 5.

These estimates would appear to be biased upward and, consequently, to represent an upper limit on the amount of ex-post "required" subsidy. The estimated amount of the capital subsidy in 1885 depends upon the level of company net earnings during the period 1886 to 1895, and the rate of return earned by company investment during that period. The average rate of return over the first ten years of operation of the CPR was lower than for any succeeding period; there is a downward bias in the estimate of the average rate of return earned by the company over this period as compared with a longer period. Since the private rate of return employed in the estimation of "required" subsidy tends to be downward biased with respect to the normal rate of return, the estimates of "required" subsidy are biased upwards.

Moreover, under this system of subsidy, the capital grant to the company would have been left intact at the end of the decade; that is, the capital grant scheme represents the case of a perpetual subsidy. Since company net earnings begin to increase relative to the capital base after 1895, the earned rate of return on CPR investment began to increase as well. However, the "required" subsidy developed in this estimate on the basis of the period from 1886 to 1895 would still be in effect in the post-1895 period. Since the retention of the subsidy after 1895 by the company is allowed for, some type of repayment provision might logically have been attached to the initial capital subsidy. The company could have been constrained in the original subsidization agreement to return the initial capital grant to the government if it expected to earn the normal rate of return on its investment after the first ten years of railway operation. On the other hand, if expectations as to the profitability of future company operations were less optimistic, the subsidy could have been retained by the company after 1895. In sum, this estimate probably overestimates the ex-post "required" subsidy since the company's earnings record did improve considerably, relative to its capital stock, after the period from 1886 to 1895.

TABLE 5

"Required" Subsidy in 1885, Under a Government Capital Grant to the Canadian Pacific Railway Company

	Assumed Rate of Return, Rate of Interest		
Units	6%	8%	10%
(1) Current dollars	68,319,860	78,830,936	81,054,792
(2) Constant dollars of 1885 (DBS index)	59,227,541	70,575,840	73,515,915

NOTES: The amount of "required" subsidy in 1885 was estimated for each assumed normal rate of return by calculation of the mean L_t, mean K_t, and mean R_t, where T refers to the number of time periods:

$$1/T \cdot \Sigma^{10}_{t=1} L_t = 1/T \cdot \Sigma^{10}_{t=1} (K_t - R_t/r)$$

$$= \Sigma^{10}_{t=1} K_t/T - 1/r(\Sigma^{10}_{t=1} R_t)/T;$$

$$\bar{L} = \bar{K} - 1/r \cdot \bar{R}.$$

The amount of benefit accruing to the company from the capital subsidy is the difference between the initial capital subsidy in 1885, and the amount of that subsidy at compound interest in 1895. With the estimates of "required" subsidy derived from constant-dollar data, the company would have benefited from the subsidy to the amount of $46,840,101 over the decade at an interest rate of 6 percent, $81,791,752 at 8 percent, and $117,165,254 at 10 percent, the original capital subsidy remaining intact at the end of the period.

The Question of "Excessive" Subsidy

The value of subsidies paid to the CPR company is compared with the estimate of *ex-post* "required" subsidy in table 6. Subsidies actually paid to the company exceed *ex-post* "required" subsidy by amounts ranging from $61,005,136 to $39,751,682, and $34,062,533 in constant dollars of 1885, when the rate of interest incorporated into the comparison was assumed to be 6 percent, 8 percent, and 10 percent respectively.

These estimates are undoubtedly underestimates rather than exaggerations of *ex-post* "excessive" subsidy. The estimate of the value of subsidies paid to the company was biased downward, and the estimated *ex-post* "required" subsidy was biased upward. The direction of the biases in the estimates of both the value of subsidies paid and "required" subsidy implies that the residuals in table 6, the derived estimates of *ex-post* "excessive" subsidy, are downward biased; that is, the estimates presented in table 6 represent minimal amounts of, or lower bounds on, "excessive" subsidy.

V

In this paper, it has been demonstrated that, *ex post*, the CPR company was awarded "excessive" subsidies by the government of Canada. This conclusion is reinforced when account is taken of the direction of biases in the estimates of the

TABLE 6

Comparison of Value in 1885 of Subsidies Paid to the Canadian Pacific Railway Company with Estimate of "Required" Subsidy in 1885

Item	Units	Assumed Rate of Return, Rate of Interest		
		6%	8%	10%
(1) Value in 1885 of subsidies paid to the company	(1) Current dollars	145,616,259	126,879,049	121,212,756
	(2) Constant dollars of 1885 (DBS index)	120,232,677	110,327,522	107,578,448
(2) "Required" subsidy in 1885	(1) Current dollars	68,319,860	78,830,936	81,054,792
	(2) Constant dollars of 1885 (DBS index)	59,227,541	70,575,840	73,515,915
(3) Residual: (2) minus (1)	(1) Current dollars	−77,296,399	−48,048,113	−40,157,963
	(2) Constant dollars of 1885 (DBS index)	−61,005,136	−39,751,682	−34,062,534

value of subsidies actually paid to the company and of biases in the estimates of *ex-post* "required" subsidy.

The estimates of "excessive" subsidy have at least two implications of particular interest. First, the potential long-run significance of possible initial excess in subsidies paid to the company calls attention to the government's failure to attach some provision for repayment, either partial or complete, of the principal of the subsidy once the profitability of the investment became apparent. Secondly, we might regard the land grant and the tax exemption as those particular components of total subsidies paid to the company which best represent calculated "excessive" subsidy. The alienation of Dominion lands to the CPR company and the exemption of these lands and company property and equipment from taxation has been especially burdensome to the provincial governments of Manitoba, Saskatchewan, and Alberta, where the social costs of these particular aspects of the subsidy have undoubtedly been concentrated.[53] Indeed, these features of the subsidy with their peculiar impact on the prairie provinces would appear to be an excellent example of the relative inefficiency of subsidies in property and privilege as compared with outright cash grants.

Of course, a complete answer to the question whether the CPR was excessively subsidized would require examination of the *ex-ante* situation governing the bargain made between the company and the government in the autumn of 1880.[54] Such an examination, however, does not appear feasible on the basis of available information and data.

Notes

1. *The Union Pacific Railroad: A Case in Premature Enterprise* (Baltimore, 1960), 94–97.

2. "Submission of Canadian Pacific Railway Company to the Royal Commission on Transportation," Appendix to Part I (Montreal, Oct. 1949), 27.

3. As there were external economies produced by railway investment and operation, the social rate of

return on investment is conceptually distinguishable from the private rate of return. Calculation of the social rate of return is, however, not necessary for estimation of the required subsidy undertaken in this paper.

4. "Premature, that is, when the measuring rod of its maturity and practicability was the willingness of unaided private enterprise, guided solely by the search for profits, to undertake the project." *The Union Pacific Railroad*, 18.

5. *Journals of the House of Commons* IV (1871): 266. The relations between government and private enterprise were specified in An Act Respecting the Canadian Pacific Railway, 35 Vic., c. 71, assented to on 14 June 1872. The railway was finally completed in 1885 under the charter granted to the CPR company in An Act Respecting the Canadian Pacific Railway, 44 Vic., c. 1, ratified on 15 Feb. 1881.

6. J.H. Dales, "Some Historical and Theoretical Comment on Canada's National Policies," *Queen's Quarterly* LXXI (1964): 304.

7. Ibid.

8. Whereas the political basis of the government's decision to subsidize the CPR may be accepted without hesitation, the relevance of the economic grounds for that decision remains to be established. Any subsidy paid by the government to secure construction of the railway could be justified economically only on the expectation that the social rate of return on investment in the railway was likely to be higher than the private rate of return, and higher than or at least equal to the normal or market rate of return.

9. The actual normal rate of return has not been calculated. It is assumed in this paper to have been between 6 and 10 percent over the decade 1886 to 1895. This range is identical with that employed by Fogel to assess the profitability of investment in the Union Pacific Railroad. See *The Union Pacific Railroad*, 94–95.

10. *Report of the Royal Commission to Inquire into Railways and Transportation in Canada* (Ottawa, 1917), xiii.

11. New York, *Commercial and Financial Chronicle* XXXVIII (Jan. to June 1884): 508.

12. The first CPR company, and the Interoceanic Railway Company were both incorporated by statute early in 1872, and amalgamated later in the same year, under the presidency of Hugh Allan, as the Canada Pacific Railway Company. See H.A. Innis, *A History of the Canadian Pacific Railway* (Toronto, 1923), 78–81.

13. An Act to Provide for the Construction of the Canadian Pacific Railway, 37 Vic., c. 14. This Act provided that the railway could be built either by a private company with subsidy of up to $12,000 and 20,000 acres of land per mile, or by the government itself, the work to be let out by contracts offered for public competition. In fact, both procedures were adopted. For example, a subsidy was granted to the Canada Central Railway company for an extension from Pembroke to the proposed eastern terminus of the Pacific Railway on Lake Nipissing in November 1874. However, no private company came forward with an offer to build the entire line, so that the government was forced to proceed with construction.

14. For example, in 1877, the government called for tenders for construction and operation of the whole line or sections of the line. In fact, Sandford Fleming actively solicited potential tenderers in England. His failure to interest British contractors in the project was at least partly due to the hostility of Grand Trunk interests. H.A. Innis, *A History*, 95.

15. For details of the contract and subsidy, see *Sessional Papers* XV (1882), no. 48e: 16–33.

16. Ibid., XXXI (1897), no. 10, Part II: 39.

17. *Report of the Canadian Pacific Railway Royal Commission*, III, Conclusions (Ottawa, 1882), 495.

18. The calculated excessive expenditures by the government on the Dawson route and the Georgian Bay Branch may greatly underestimate the "social" costs of the diversion of funds from rapid construction of the all-rail route. In fact, C.M. Studness has suggested that early completion of the railway from Winnipeg to Fort William in the 1870s might have significantly reduced the preference of migrants for the American western agricultural frontier over the Canadian alternative, and accelerated the development of the wheat economy. See C.M. Studness, "Economic Opportunity and the Westward Migration of Canadians during the Late Nineteenth Century," *Canadian Journal of Economics and Political Science* XXX (1964): 584.

19. Sources of potential savings included:

a. Rationalization of surveys, and early selection of Western terminus in British Columbia — $1,092,423
b. No expenditure on Dawson route — 391,321
c. No expenditure on Georgian Bay Branch — 101,431
d. Improvement of procedure of letting contracts, and provision of detailed information to tenderers — 1,379,633

Total, potential savings — $2,964,808

The procedure whereby potential savings were estimated has not been reproduced here because of space limitations. For a detailed description of the derivation of the estimates, see P. George, "A Benefit-Cost Analysis," chap. 3.

20. I have assumed that the company was concerned with efficiency in construction; that is, concerned to minimize its financial outlay on construction, given the standard of construction to which it was obliged to adhere (the Union Pacific Railroad standard). This assumption is analogous to the use of a hypothetical private enterprise alternative in the section on government expenditures (above) as the basis for downward adjustment of reported government expenditures.

21. These returns were required of the company by a Standing Order of the House of Commons, dated 20 February 1882. Under the terms of this Order, a report was to be presented by the company to the House of Commons within fifteen days from the opening of the session outlining the progress of the railway to that date. As well, details of the financial aspects of the construction program, in particular capital and revenue accounts, were required by the Consolidated Railway Act, and contained within the report to the House. These reports were subsequently published in the *Sessional Papers* annually from 1883 to 1887.

22. See, for example, the report for the fiscal year ending 30 June 1882: "The above total [expenditure] to show the *real cash cost* of construction and rolling stock." (Italics mine.) Also, for the fiscal year ending June 30, 1886: "This cost [total expenditure] *does not include discount on securities or stocks sold*." (Italics mine.) *Sessional Papers* XVI (1883), no. 27: 161; ibid., XX (1887), no. 34b: 138.

23. Ibid., XVI (1883), no. 27: 161.

24. Ibid., XVII (1884), no. 31f: 46.

25. Ibid., no. 31c: 6.

26. Ibid., no. 31f: 46; ibid., XVIII (1885), no. 25a: 175.

27. The price of the western section of the Quebec, Montreal, Ottawa and Occidental Railway to the CPR company was set by the government of Quebec at $4 million. This amount was taken as an estimate of the capital value of plant and equipment for the line, and charged as expenditures during 1882. The remaining $6,913,904 was taken as indicative of the capital value of the Canada Central Railway and charged to the company during 1881. (The relative size of these amounts is only roughly proportional to the number of miles of track in each of the two rail systems; with these estimates, the per-mile value of the Canada Central Railway is $24,605, and is $27,875 for the western section of the Quebec, Montreal, Ottawa and Occidental Railway.)

28. Three other major lines were leased by the company: the Southeastern Railway in 1883; the Qu'Appelle, Long Lake, and Saskatchewan Railway in 1889; and the Calgary and Edmonton Railway, also in 1889. However, the operation of these lines had no readily calculable bearing on the net earnings of the CPR which paid no rental for these lines; nor were the expenses of operation and maintenance or earnings of these lines included in the accounts of the company. (See Canadian Pacific Railway Company, *Annual Report for the Year 1891*: 8; also ibid. (1892): 7–8). Consequently, I have excluded estimates of the capital value of these lines from the estimated costs of construction.

29. *The Union Pacific Railroad*, 96–97.

30. See, for example, the statement by President W.C. Van Horne in Canadian Pacific Railway Company, *Report* (1888): 14.

The validity of Van Horne's statement was corroborated by comparing maintenance charges as a percentage of working expenses during 1886 to 1895 with the period after 1900. However, a complication arose in the calculation of maintenance charges from 1886 to 1903, since only a portion of the item "motive power" was devoted to the maintenance of locomotives. The company's accounting procedure was altered in 1904 to do away with "motive power" as a separate element in working expenses; the company's *Report* for 1904 allocated 25.5 percent of expenditures on "motive power" in 1903 to "maintenance of equipment" and the remainder to "conducting transportation." Ibid., (1904): 26. It was assumed that 25.5 percent of expenses entered under "motive power" from 1886 to 1903 could be regarded as estimated expenditures on the maintenance of locomotives.

The percentage of maintenance charges to working expenses was calculated over 5-year periods and averaged 37.3 percent from 1886 to 1890, 36.5 percent from 1891 to 1895, 36.9 percent from 1896 to 1900, 41.2 percent from 1901 to 1905, 41.2 percent from 1906 to 1910, and 38.2 percent from 1911 to 1915. The 5-year average has tended to be about 41 percent since 1915. The fact that the ratio of maintenance charges to working expenses from 1886 to 1895 was lower on average than in the period after 1900 is consistent with Van Horne's opinion that the railway was "well maintained," given the relative newness in the earlier period of the bulk of CPR equipment and structures.

31. There were six major technological innovations in the railway industry in the last half of the nineteenth century: the use of the telegraph to control railway traffic, block signalling, steel rails, the automatic coupler, the air brake, and increased equipment capacity. The telegraph and block signalling were both introduced relatively early, in 1851 and 1863 respectively. Albert Fishlow has argued that the automatic coupler and the air brake were of small economic value compared with steel rails and improved equipment, and were adopted slowly by the industry. A. Fishlow, "Productivity and Technological Change in the Railroad Sector, 1840–1910," in NBER, *Output, Employment, and Productivity in the United States after 1800*, Studies in Income and Wealth 30 (New York, 1966), 635–38. Steel rails were employed in the initial construction of the CPR. Increased equipment capacity was incorporated into the CPR's capital stock with net additions to the capital stock, and with replacements (although these latter were relatively small during this period). It appears that the rate of technological obsolescence of CPR equipment was quite low, and that physical wear and tear accounted for the bulk of replacements.

32. The company's failure to account for depreciation probably imparts an upward bias to the private rate of return. Suppose we assume, as Professor Fogel did, a life span of 10 years for rails and ties, 20 years for rolling stock, and 50 years for structures (*The Union Pacific Railroad*, 96–97). Some company property, taken over from the Canadian government and existing private railway companies, was built and equipped in the 1860s and 1870s; a portion of this capital would have exhausted its useful life during the period from 1886 to 1895 and required replacement. To the extent this was the case, the capital base in the rate-of-return calculations overstates the real value of capital invested in the railway. On the other hand, most of the company's equipment would still have been relatively new during the period of the rate-of-return study, and would not likely have been retired before 1896; however, net earnings would have been overstated to the extent that annual depreciation charges were neglected. Since the proportion of "new" to "old" capital in the total capital stock of the company was undoubtedly large during 1886 to 1895, the failure to account for depreciation is likely on balance to bias the calculated private rate of return upwards. However, the longer the time period under consideration, the greater the impact of neglecting to subtract replacements from the capital base, and the greater the likelihood of developing a downward bias on the calculated rate of return.

33. Neglect of depreciation was not confined to the railroad sector. For example, C.A.S. Hall has written of the electric utilities industries in Ontario before 1914 that "the accounting practices of the day did not call for a clearly defined item of depreciation in the presentation of financial statements; and, at least for the electrical utilities under investigation, there seems to have been greater importance attached to maintenance as contrasted to depreciation accounting." C.A.S. Hall, "Electric Utilities in Ontario under Private Ownership, 1890–1914" (Ph.D. thesis, University of Toronto, 1968), 128.

34. Two price indexes were used in the deflating procedure: the Dominion Bureau of Statistics general price index (excluding gold), 1935–39 = 100; and the Michell wholesale price index, 1900 = 100. Both indexes were converted from their original base years to time reference base 1885 = 100. Only the results obtained with the Dominion Bureau of Statistics general price index are presented in the paper.

35. The Michell index yielded a private rate of return averaging 3.5 percent over the decade, with a low of 2.2 percent in 1887 and a high of 4.6 percent in 1892. Similar calculations of the annual private rate of return were attempted with cumulative expenditures on construction measured up to but *not including* the year for which the private rate of return was being calculated. This alternative definition of the capital base raised the average rate of return during 1886 to 1895 for each of the series of estimates by 0.1 percent.

36. For complete details of the subsidy, see An Act Respecting the Canadian Pacific Railway, 44 Vic., c. 1, reprinted in *Sessional Papers* XV (1882), no. 48e: 16–33. The procedure whereby the value of the several components of subsidy to the company was estimated has not been discussed fully because of space limitations. For a detailed description of the sources of data and derivation of the estimates, see George, "A Benefit-Cost Analysis," chap. 5.

37. Of course, the mere addition of reported government expenditures and cash grants does not represent the value of these items as subsidy to the company. In fact, the valuation in 1885 of all items of subsidy necessitates the compounding, at the appropriate interest rate, of expenditures occurring before the base year 1885, and the calculation of the present value in 1885 of expenditures occurring after 1885. The rates of interest employed in these calculations were identical with those assumed to represent the range of the normal rate of return, 6 to 10 percent.

38. Data published in the company's *Annual Report* from 1889 to 1930. This estimate involved a larger land grant than 25 million acres since the CPR company earned additional lands with the construction of the Souris Branch in 1890–91, and the Pipestone Extension in 1894, and through the acquisition of subsidiary

companies which previously had been awarded land grants, including the Alberta Railway and Coal Company, the Manitoba and North-Western Railway, the Manitoba and Southwestern Colonization Railway, the Great Northwest Central Railway, the Calgary and Edmonton Railway, and the Saskatchewan and Western Railway. The total acreage received by the company and its subsidiaries, including the portion of the grant allowed to revert to the Dominion government, was 31,857,477 acres. See C. Martin, " 'Dominion Lands' Policy," in *Canadian Frontiers of Settlement* II, edited by W.A. Mackintosh and W.L.G. Joerg (Toronto, 1938), 280, 302–3.

An alternative estimate of the value of the land subsidy was based upon opinions of contemporary political observers of land values in the Canadian west at the negotiation and passing through Parliament of the CPR contract in 1880–81. In this estimate, the land grant was valued at $1.00 per acre in 1880–81, giving the land subsidy an apparent present value to the company of $25,000,000 at the time when the contract was under discussion. See George, "A Benefit-Cost Analysis," 102–6.

39.   From 1893 to 1930, the average sales price of Hudson's Bay Company land was $12.10 per acre. Moreover, in Manitoba, Saskatchewan and Alberta, school lands were sold at average prices of $9.79, $16.85, and $14.40, respectively up to March 1928. CPR Company lands were sold, during the same period, at an average price of $7.63 per acre, excluding irrigated lands, and $8.55 per acre with irrigated lands included. C. Martin, *"Dominion Lands" Policy*, 309, 341–43.

40.   For example, Mr. Charlton referred to several kinds of railway taxation practised in the United States, including the tax on gross earnings and the tax per mile of railway operated. Moreover, he referred explicitly to tax revenues yielded by the Union Pacific Railroad, and attempted, with this information, to estimate the value of tax concessions to the company by capitalizing his estimate of annual taxes foregone at 4 percent. His upper estimate of the value of tax concessions in 1881 was $27,900,000. See *Debates of the House of Commons* (1880–81), I, 742.

41.   The value of tax exemptions on the land grant was not estimated since the levying of taxes on lands held by the company might be thought of as merely reducing the value of the land subsidy.

42.   For example, total miles of railway operated in the United States in 1888 were 149,902, and total railway taxes were $25,435,229; the average tax paid per mile of railway in operation was $169.68. Again, a sample comprised of thirty-two railway companies, each of which operated more than one thousand miles of railway, was selected from the railway data. The total mileage of railways in the sample was 63,881, and taxes paid by the sample railways averaged $198.92 per mile. Finally, the two railway companies most directly comparable to the CPR were the Union Pacific Railroad and the Northern Pacific Railroad. In 1887–88, the Union Pacific Railroad operated 1,824 miles of track, and paid taxes of $312.56 per mile. The complete Union Pacific Railroad system was 6,019 miles; total taxes of $1,266,834 were paid by the entire system, an average of $210.47 per mile. The Northern Pacific Railroad operated 3,317 miles of track, and paid taxes of $241,288, or $72.74 per mile. The average tax paid by the Northern Pacific Railroad and the Union Pacific Railroad system together was $161.54 per mile. See United States, *First Annual Report on the Statistics of Railways in the United States to the Interstate Commerce Commission for the Year Ending June 30, 1888* (Washington, 1889), 28–103, 262–309, 338–39.

43.   Charlton's comments, for example, attest to the existence of the tax on railway gross earnings in the United States in early 1881. *Debates* (1880–81), I: 741–42.

44.   United States, *Railways in the United States in 1902. Part V. State Taxation of Railways and Other Transportation Agencies* (Washington, 1903), 17–18.

45.   Charlton stated that the rate of tax on gross earnings in Michigan was 2 percent of gross earnings to a certain level of earnings, and 3 percent after that level was reached, and that the rate was 3 percent in Minnesota. See *Debates* (1880–81), I, 741. The rate of tax was still 3 percent of gross earnings in Minnesota in 1888. See *Report of the Royal Commission on Railways* (Ottawa, 1888), 25. In fact, the tax on gross earnings was subsequently recommended by the Ontario Royal Commission on Railway Taxation in 1905 as the most appropriate base for railway taxation, and 3 percent was selected as the most appropriate percentage at which to tax gross earnings. See *Report of the Ontario Commission on Railway Taxation 1905* (Toronto, 1905), 23, 30.

46.   *Sessional Papers* XV (1882), no. 48e, 20.

47.   See the annual *Tables of Trade and Navigation of the Dominion of Canada*, presented by the Minister of Customs, 1881 to 1888.

48.   Ibid.; see also a statement concerning this general feature of the Canadian tariff on materials imported by railway companies by Sir Charles Tupper in *Debates* (1880–81), I: 73.

49. When calculated, the value of the right of way to the company did not appear to be significant enough to warrant inclusion in the estimates of the value of subsidies to the company. If we assume a right of way of 100 feet for the length of the CPR system in operation in 1885, the area of the right of way was only 48,457 acres. Valued at the values per acre of company lands derived in the estimate of the value of the land grant above, the value of the right of way concessions was quite small, ranging from $48,911 to $33,920 in constant dollars of 1885. The value of station ground would probably have been quite low as well.

50. Concerned about local complaints of alleged high freight rates on the CPR, the government of Manitoba issued charters to several railway companies in the province between 1881 and 1887, in spite of the intent of the monopoly clause. The Manitoba government chartered the Winnipeg South-Eastern Railway, the Manitoba Tramway Company, and the Emerson and North-Western Railway Company in 1881. The Canadian government disallowed these charters in 1882 and 1883. Again, in 1887, the government of Manitoba undertook to incorporate the Manitoba Central Railway, the Winnipeg and Southern Railway, and the Red River Valley Company, and once again the Dominion government intervened to disallow the charters. H.A. Innis, A History, 174–83, concisely summarizes the dispute.

51. The authority of the government to effect a reduction in railway rates was provided for in the Consolidated Railway Act of 1879. In the case of the CPR, the government was limited in its exercise of this power: the company was assured that Parliamentary intervention in its rate structure would not occur until the annual rate of return on capital invested in railway construction was 10 percent, and actual net income exceeded 10 percent of construction costs. In fact, this concession to the company was not of particular advantage to it, since the Consolidated Railway Act offered analogous "guarantees" at the 15 percent level to other railways. The reasons for the lowering of the percentage in the case of the CPR lay in its strategic national position and the alleged peculiar vulnerability of the west to monopolistic rate practices.

52. A second estimate was developed in which "required" subsidy was defined as a stream of annual payments by the government to the company which would raise railway net earnings to yield the normal rate of return over the decade 1886 to 1895. This procedure underestimated ex-post "required" subsidy because of the selection of the ten-year time period. The assumption that the company and the government both expected the company to earn the normal rate of return after its initial decade of operations underlay the calculations. In fact, if the company's anticipated period of shortfall in net earnings were longer than ten years, then "required" subsidy in 1885 would be larger by the present value in 1885 of annual payments in subsidy necessary after 1895. Some element of upward bias is also contained in this estimate since the normal rate of return ought to be adjusted downwards from those employed in the calculations to reflect the absence of risk to the company. As R.W. Fogel points out in his discussion of alternative methods of financing the construction of the Union Pacific Railroad, government subsidization by means of a guaranteed rate of return scheme would shift all of the risk of railway investment ex ante to the government. Then, the company could expect minimum earnings on its investment equal to the rate of return on risk-free investment. On the other hand, a government subsidy by means of a capital grant would force the company to bear all the risk of railway investment. Fogel, The Union Pacific Railroad, 108. See George, "A Benefit-Cost Analysis," 143–49.

53. The Dominion government has levied income taxes on the CPR company since 1917, and various agreements for payment of taxes by the company to provincial governments have been concluded. Even so, H.A. Innis writes that "the burden of taxation on the earnings of the company has been slight because of charter provisions" and that "attempts of the prairie provinces to tax [company] lands for school and municipal purposes have been unsuccessful." A History, 239, 263. In fact, as H.E. Dougall has written, "this provision has substantially decreased the income from railway taxation of all the provinces, particularly those in the west, because of the predominance of [the] Company's lines," in "Taxation of Railways in Canada: Development and Present Status," Journal of Land and Public Utility Economics V (1929): 266.

54. Given an assumption of perfect foresight on the part of investors in the CPR, we can conclude unequivocally that the subsidy was "excessive" ex-ante as well as in the ex-post sense. That is, if investors in the company could accurately have foreseen in 1880 the annual rates of return actually to be earned by the railway in the decade 1886 to 1895, the subsidy paid to the company was ex ante too large. Without a crude assumption of this sort, however, a tentative conclusion concerning the likelihood that the subsidy was "excessive" from the ex-ante point of view is not possible. Perhaps, investors in the railway expected smaller annual company net earnings during 1886 to 1895 than the company was actually to earn. Subsidies paid might have been "excessive" in the ex-ante sense; ex post, subsidies paid by the government to the CPR were "excessive."

SECTION 3

ECONOMIC GROWTH AND CHANGE, 1870–1926

THE RATE OF SETTLEMENT OF THE CANADIAN PRAIRIES, 1870–1911†

K.H. NORRIE

An issue of continuing interest in Canadian economic history is the lag between the formulation of policies directed toward settling the prairies and the appearance of any significant agricultural population. Proposals to develop the region preceded the union of the British North American colonies in 1867. By 1872 the first Homestead Act had been passed and a commitment made to construct a transcontinental railway linking the western provinces to Central Canada. Yet except for a brief speculative boom in the early 1880s, occasioned by the CPR reaching Winnipeg, the rate of settlement remained well below expectations. Homestead entries averaged under 3,000 from 1874 to 1896, and in many years there were nearly as many cancellations as new entries. In the same period adjacent American lands were filling up, in large part with emigrant Canadians. Settlement of the Dakotas, beginning in 1870 but depressed from 1873 to 1878, boomed from 1879 to 1886. Over the thirty years from 1870 to 1900 an estimated 120,000 Canadians chose the American prairies over the Canadian.[1]

The situation, however, was reversed after 1896. Homestead entries began to rise in 1897, falling in only two of the next fifteen years. They jumped from 1,857 in 1896 to 7,426 in 1900 and 44,479 in 1911.[2] The increase in homesteads was matched by a jump in land sales by private companies. By the end of the decade most of the potential agricultural area of the prairies was at least thinly settled[3] and the region was rapidly becoming one of the world's leading wheat producers. The emigration of Canadians was replaced by a large migration of American farmers to the Canadian prairies. Thirty years of frustration were rewarded by one of the largest booms in Canadian history.

This lag between plan and performance has been as puzzling to later writers as it was to politicians and entrepreneurs of the time. It is commonplace in histories of the period to cite the "favorable conjuncture" of events appearing in the

†*Journal of Economic History* XXXV, 2 (June 1975): 410–27. Earlier versions of this paper were presented to the Sixth Conference on Quantitative Methods in Canadian History at Saskatoon in October 1973, and at the Canadian Economics Association Meetings in Toronto and Simon Fraser University in June 1974. The author wishes to acknowledge numerous useful comments made by participants on these occasions, by Professor Sylvester Damus of the University of Winnipeg, by several of my colleagues at the University of Alberta, and the ubiquitous "anonymous referee." Support was received from the University of Alberta General Research Fund.

mid-1890s that finally made prairie settlement feasible on a large scale. The list invariably includes a rise in wheat prices as a result of industrialization in Europe and the United States; falling transport costs on wheat exports; the end of the American land frontier; the resumption of international capital flows and labor migration; technical breakthroughs in the production, transportation and further processing of wheat; and, occasionally, the basis laid by the federal government development policies.[4]

Merely listing the factors in this manner leaves the impression that all were equally important and that all constraints to settlement were removed simultaneously. But this view is not supported by a more detailed examination of the available literature. World wheat prices were generally higher in the 1870s and early 1880s than they were in the first decade of the twentieth century.[5] The importance of the development of earlier-ripening varieties of wheat such as Marquis has apparently been dismissed, as have federal government development policies such as the Homestead Act.[6] Studies of capital flows and labor migration in the first decade of the twentieth century find them responding to economic opportunity rather than initiating it. Penelope Hartland argues that the most important determinant of expansion after 1900 was technical improvements in methods of wheat production.[7] But dry-farming techniques were understood as early as 1860 in Utah and California and were being used at Indian Head, Saskatchewan by 1886,[8] so there is a problem in suggesting that more extensive use of these innovations would have hastened settlement. Their limited diffusion before 1900, coupled with the rapid use thereafter, needs explanation.

The thesis that settlement in Canada had to wait the filling up of the superior American wheat lands has received extensive support.[9] But this overlooks the fact that the disposal of the public domain via homesteading in the United States took place at a greater rate after 1896 than before. Between 1881 and 1890 there were 497,083 homestead entries on 69,773,000 acres of land. In the 1890s these figures dropped to 456,943 and 62,857,000 respectively. But from 1901 to 1910 homestead entries rose dramatically to 832,140 and the acreage potential nearly doubled to 130,647,000. In addition, as Hartland notes, the expansion of Australian and Argentinian wheat production and exports in the 1880s and 1890s suggests that the world market for food was expanding rapidly enough to absorb supplies in excess of the American output.[10]

C.M. Studness goes even further and argues that American lands were not even productively superior to the Canadian ones. He estimates revenues and costs for representative wheat producing areas in Manitoba and North Dakota and finds that net revenue per acre in Canada was from $0.75 to $1.25 higher than in North Dakota—a result of higher yields and wheat prices and in spite of higher operating costs.[11] This leads him to suggest that the impediment to settlement prior to the 1890s was not the productive inferiority of prairie farms but the lack of available free homestead land relative to North Dakota. If the Canadian government had located Canadian Pacific Railway lands in more remote areas,[12] and had encouraged more extensive railroad construction through cost subsidies ". . . there is little reason to believe that development before the turn of the century could not have been more extensive."[13]

Stabler approaches the question of the settlement lag more generally, and attempts a more rigorous statistical corroboration. He divides the period of stagnation into two, arguing that technical problems associated with the production and delivery of grain were the primary constraints to the mid-1880s only. Thereafter there were no structural impediments to settlement. The further lag to 1896 and the boom thereafter can be explained mainly by trends in the price of the region's staple.[14] The first claim is supported by the literature on the relevant technical developments. The second part of the argument is based on a regression equation that shows a significant positive correlation between changes in homestead entries and changes in wheat prices over the period 1880–1898.

The regression equation, however, is not an adequate test of the hypothesis. Stabler's argument, in effect, says that the homesteading process in the period before 1885 or 1886 was structurally different from that in the years thereafter. A single regression equation run over part of this period tests nothing of this sort, significant correlation or not. In fact, an equation covering 1880 to 1898 even contradicts the hypothesis, since Stabler himself has argued that the first five or six years do not belong in the same regression as the subsequent ones. What is needed instead is any of the standard significance tests for the stability of regression coefficients over sub-periods. In the absence of such a procedure the hypothesis remains unsubstantiated.

In sum, the famous "conjuncture of events" explanation, as usually presented, fails to provide us with an adequate explanation of the timing of the wheat boom. Some of the supposed causes of the upturn are actually consequences of it, and there is considerable doubt about the validity of other claims. Clearly a reexamination of the period is in order. The present article first develops and estimates a model of homestead response which can identify the existence and nature of structural changes. These results are then used to support a reinterpretation of prairie settlement over the period 1870 to 1911. A final section contains some concluding comments.

II

The model used here has homestead entries in any year t as a function of wheat prices in Winnipeg in year $t - 1$. A necessary refinement is the introduction of a lag structure. For any given level of expected net returns there was some potentially identifiable feasible area of homesteading. But the reaction to a change in the independent variable was not instantaneous. There were delays in migrating, even if only from Ontario to the prairies. But more importantly there was always some degree of ignorance about the exact extent of the feasible area of settlement. As expected net returns rose, some settlers were immediately induced to venture into new areas. If the new area were indeed feasible, and those initial homesteads proved successful, others followed. Thus any extension of settlement beyond initial areas was spread over several years.

The formal model is:

$$FH_t^* = a + bG_{t-1} \qquad (1)$$

with the adjustment function written as:

$$FH_t - FH_{t-1} = \beta(FH_t^* - FH_{t-1}) \qquad (2)$$

where FH_t is free homestead entries in year t, G is Winnipeg wheat prices and β is the proportion of the adjustment to a change in prices that is accomplished in the first year.

The estimating equation implied by this model can be used to isolate any significant structural changes over the period of settlement, and to identify the nature of these changes.[15] The period chosen is 1879 to 1911. Since a railroad was an obvious prerequisite to any significant agricultural settlement, there is no point in including the years prior to 1879. Nineteen eleven was the end of the first wave of settlement.[16] It is late enough to include several years of boom conditions, yet early enough to be able to disregard the effects of the War. The three sub-periods to be tested for stability are 1879 to 1886, 1887 to 1896, and 1897 to 1911. Eighteen eighty-six is the specific date chosen to test Stabler's hypothesis, since it was the year the CPR was completed and an all-Canadian rail route established to the export points. Eighteen ninety-six is traditionally taken as the last year of the period of stagnation.

The test for structural breaks among these periods is made utilizing dummy variables, with both intercepts and slope coefficients allowing to vary over all periods. The estimating equation contains a lagged dependent variable so the regression was corrected for serial correlation of the error term.[17] The results,[18] with all variables in logarithmic form, are:

$$QFH_t = -7.81 + 5.86DA + 7.42DB + 0.20QFH_{t-1} + 0.37DFA$$
$$(-1.81) \quad (1.01) \quad (1.51) \quad (0.81) \quad (0.87)$$

$$+0.60DFB + 3.04QG_{t-1} - 1.81DGA - 2.48DGB$$
$$(2.32) \quad (3.16) \quad (-1.58) \quad (-2.15)$$

$$R^2 = 0.937 \qquad (3)$$

Figures in brackets are t statistics. DA and DB are the dummy intercepts for the first two sub-periods, DFA and DFB are the dummies for the lagged dependent variable, and DGA and DGB the same for the price variable. The value of δ is -0.30 and its t-statistic is significant at the ninety-five percent level.

The results of equation (3) indicate rejection of the hypothesis that 1886 was a statistically significant breaking point. None of the dummies for this period is significant.[19] Any fundamental structural factors of the type Stabler mentions as being constraining prior to the mid-1880's but not thereafter should have affected the functional relationship between homestead entries and prices over the two periods. But statistically the two periods can be treated as one.

One cannot reject the traditional hypothesis that 1896 was a significant turning point. The intercept terms are common in the three periods but both slope coefficients are significantly different after 1896. Equation (3) was rerun imposing a common intercept over all three periods and common slope coefficients on the first two, while still allowing those for the third to vary.

$$QFH_t = 1.05 + 0.26QFH_{t-1} + 0.54DFB + 1.10QG_{t-1} - 0.84DGB$$
$$(0.58) \quad (1.30) \quad (2.30) \quad (2.84) \quad (-1.89)$$

$$R^2 = 0.913 \quad dw = 1.998 \qquad (4)$$

TABLE 1

Implied Parameter Values

	a	$b\beta$	b	β
1879–1896	1.42	1.10	1.49	0.74
1897–1911	5.25	0.26	1.30	0.20

SOURCE: Equation (4).

Equation (4) reports the values for ordinary least squares, since the serial correlation proved insignificant. The parameter values implied by equation (4) are reported in table 1. The second column ($b\beta$) is the short-run price response while the values for b are the long-run elasticities.

The essential differences in pre- and post-1896 settlement decisions are the higher intercept value and the much slower speed of reaction in the latter period. The long-run price elasticities on the other hand are virtually identical. An increase of one percent in the wheat price gave rise to an ultimate response of 1.5 percent in homestead entries prior to 1896 and 1.3 percent thereafter. But this reaction was completed in just over one time period in the first instance but took nearly four times as long in the second. In the boom years it was apparently some time before the actual number of homesteaders approached that number made feasible by the prevailing price level. By contrast, in the period preceding the boom, settlement was very quick to move into new areas. The higher intercept value after 1896 indicates that for any given level of wheat prices there was a greatly expanded number of feasible new homestead entries.

In summary, the results of these statistical tests suggest rejection of the Stabler hypothesis, but not of the more traditional view that the boom period differed fundamentally from the years preceding it. But these purely statistical results still need an economic explanation. The following section provides an explanation of the nature and timing of settlement of the Canadian prairies.

III

An answer to these questions lies in the fact that agricultural settlement in both Canada and the United States from 1870 to the 1890s was largely an extension of traditional methods of wheat cultivation, while after the mid-1890s it was largely dry-land farming. It is the intention of this section to show that this hypothesis is sufficient to explain the existence, and nature, of the break in the homestead response function after 1896, the similarity of this response over the period 1879 to 1896, and the relative timing of the Canadian and American booms and the pattern of migration they induced.

Dry farming is defined as "agriculture without irrigation in regions of scanty precipitation."[20] Semi-arid[21] areas normally do not receive sufficient rainfall during the growing season to support continuous cropping. Grains sown on land cropped the previous year will do well if the year has ample precipitation. But if rainfall is poor the result will be partial or total failure. Dry farming involves selecting plant types that require the least amount of moisture and practising methods of cultivation which conserve whatever precipitation is available. Normally, part of the land is left fallow or is devoted to a use which requires relatively little moisture and which permits continuous surface cultivation and weed control. Not all of the rainfall of that year is used and the periodic working of the soil prevents evaporation over the hot dry summer. The result is a "reservoir" of moisture available to crops sown on the land the following spring. Even if rainfall is deficient, crops have a chance of success. Continuous cropping under the same drought conditions would be much more likely to fail.

To fully appreciate the nature of farming semi-arid as opposed to more humid land it is useful to employ the concept of expected value. One can conceive of a distribution of yields possible from sowing land to wheat, ranging from a bumper crop in a year of abundant rainfall to total crop failure in a drought year. To each possible outcome is attached a subjective probability of its occurrence. The expected yield is then the sum of potential yields multiplied by their respective probabilities.

Once the issue is framed in these terms three important economic implications follow. The first is that with a much higher probability of significant crop failure on semi-arid land the expected yield will normally be less than that for areas comparable in other respects but with more certain rainfall. For given product prices and costs, then, one would expect the more humid areas to be settled first. If the normal assumption of risk aversion on the part of potential homesteaders is made, the argument is even stronger. A risk averse individual would only be indifferent to settling on semi-arid versus sub-humid land if the expected yield of the former were actually higher than the latter. Thus, even if the long-run expected values were equal, there would still be a general preference for land in the more certain climatic zones. Only as the supply of such land became depleted would there be an incentive to move into the riskier lands.

The second implication is that appropriate dry-farming techniques can increase the expected return to cultivating semi-arid land. Proper cultivation methods secure at least some crop even in bad years, and increase the yield in years of marginal rainfall. The expected return to the land is thus increased by reducing the risk of a zero or very low yield on that portion of the acreage cropped and in spite of the fact that the remainder of the land remains idle.[22] In addition, the reduction in variance makes the land more attractive to risk averse individuals independently of the augmentation in expected yield. These factors suggest that the homestead response to given levels of input and output prices will be significantly greater once the use of dry-farming techniques becomes general.

The final observation is that even if the gains from applying this technology were fully recognized theoretically, one still would not expect much settlement in these areas while there was a supply of more humid land available. In the first place, the theory of dry farming is standard, but specific techniques vary greatly from region to region. Practices successful in one area could not automatically be applied to others, even in such apparently similar areas as the American and Canadian prairies.[23] Particular methods will depend on soil types, the nature of subsurface soils, the distribution of precipitation over the year, topography, length of growing seasons, and so on. Thus successful establishment initially required some years of experimentation locally.

Even after the methods are understood locally, however, there are reasons for delaying their diffusion. Dry farming involves costs beyond those incurred in farming more humid areas. There are additional capital and labor expenses occasioned by the more extensive cultivation. If land is left fallow there is the potential diminution of organic matter in the soil plus the increased probability of erosion. But most obviously there is an opportunity cost to taking land out of its most profitable use. In some areas of the United States, corn, potatoes or sorghum can be rotated with wheat, having the same beneficial effect as fallow and providing some possible cash income. But shorter growing seasons and limited markets prevented even this in the Canadian prairies.[24]

Settlement in both Canada and the United States prior to 1896 conforms to the expected pattern. In the United States the line dividing the sub-humid from the semi-arid lands, the Prairie Plains from the High Plains,[25] is usually approximated by either the 98th or the 100th meridian.[26] West of this zone rainfall does not normally exceed twenty inches, meaning dry-farming techniques are indispensable. Plains areas east of this receive from twenty to thirty inches of rainfall and have only a limited dependence on such methods. Before 1900 the bulk of settlement in the American Plains had either remained east of this transition zone or, in those areas where significant ventures further west had been made in response to abnormal rainfall conditions, attempts to farm using traditional techniques had proved disastrous once more normal precipitation patterns returned.

Settlement during the Dakota Boom from 1879 to 1886 was generally confined to the sub-humid areas where crop conditions were more certain. Of the 27,611 farms in North Dakota in 1890, for example, 24,171 or 87.5 percent lay east of the 100th meridian. These units contained 90.3 percent of the 7,660,330 acres in farms and 94.7 percent of the 4,658,015 acres of improved land. The figures for the area east of the 98th meridian are 76.0 percent, 78.5 percent and 87.5 percent respectively. Between 1890 and 1920, however, there was substantial movement onto the semi-arid lands. Of the 77,690 farms in existence in 1920 only 51.6 percent lay east of the 100th meridian. They accounted for less than half (48.9 percent) of the total farm acreage of 36,214,751 and 58.6 percent of the 24,563,178 improved acres.[27]

The Central Plains area[28] comprising the western sections of Kansas and Nebraska and eastern Colorado are a good example of the consequences of attempting to cultivate semi-arid lands in the same manner as the more humid eastern zones. Settlers began pouring across the transitional zone in Kansas and Nebraska in 1878 and 1879. Poor crops in 1879 and 1880 then discouraged much further immigration for a few years. Unusually favorable rainfall conditions from 1883 to 1888 occasioned the filling of the last portions of these two states and the eastern section of Colorado. But severe droughts in 1889 and 1890 and again after 1892 created great distress in the region and prompted the exodus of thousands of people after 1889. Traditional agricultural practices were feasible as long as rainfall was abnormally high, and under these conditions the frontier of settlement spread from sub-humid to semi-arid land quite readily. But once the more typical precipitation patterns returned, the extra-marginal nature of the region was clearly demonstrated.

In Canada prior to 1896 there were encroachments of settlement onto prairie land in the Souris and Qu'Appelle valleys and thin strips of settlement along the mainline of the CPR and along the northern branch lines to Saskatoon-Prince Albert and Edmonton, but the concentration was in the Red River Valley. This latter region is the one area of the Canadian prairies where neither drought nor frost was a major problem to early settlers. Its average annual rainfall is among the highest of any sub-region, and its growing season is exceeded only by southern Alberta.[29] Due west of this region lay the prairie plains and northwest was the Park Belt. Economically, these regions were the margin of feasible settlement in 1895.

The risk of drought was the main drawback to the semi-arid prairies. Because of the opportunity cost involved in leaving land fallow, its incidence across the prairies after the techniques had been generally diffused should be a good indication of the distribution of expectations about the adequacy of rainfall. This distribution can in turn be used to represent the range of expected returns to farming semi-arid land without the appropriate technology. In 1920 the ratio of fallow land to field crop acreage in central Manitoba (counties 2, 6 and 9) was 23.3 percent, 27.4 percent and 25.9 percent respectively.[30] In the most southwestern counties of Manitoba, the beginning of the prairies and the margin of settlement in the mid-1890s, these ratios are (for counties 4, 8 and 11) 37.2 percent, 36.1 percent and 33.5 percent. Further west, into southwestern Saskatchewan, they became 39.4 percent, 37.8 percent, 44.1 percent and 45.7 percent for counties 1, 5, 2 and 6, respectively. In the northwest sweep of the dark brown prairie soils between the Park Belt and the Pallisers Triangle area of southwestern Saskatchewan the figures are 35.4 percent, 36.8 percent and 38.5 percent for counties 11, 12 and 13. With traditional techniques of cultivation, the more humid areas of central Manitoba would have had a greater expected yield. In Canada, as in the United States, the ventures onto the more arid western lands were marginal ones under this technology. They generally followed years of unusually favorable moisture conditions, and were the first areas to be abandoned or avoided when more normal conditions returned.

Frost rather than drought was the chief problem of the northern Park Belt regions of Saskatchewan and Alberta. A map of the wheat-growing areas in 1910 shows production limited to the southeastern end of the range.[31] Extensions onto the Park Belt in the more northerly regions are beyond the line showing the southern limits of areas where earlier-ripening varieties of wheat were judged "especially desirable" in the 1930s. From this one can assume that the danger of frost damage in these areas before the advent of earlier-ripening wheats was great, and therefore that the expected return would be low compared to areas with longer growing seasons. Since Marquis, the first of the new varieties, was not available before 1910, it is easy to understand why this region was not competitive with the more southerly sub-humid areas of Canada and the United States in the period under review.[32]

The above discussion suggests that Canada in this period be viewed not in isolation but as the northern frontier of the phase of continental agricultural expansion after 1870. The more humid areas of both Canada and the United

States were naturally settled first. Given the existing state of agricultural technology, expected yields and hence expected returns from farming these areas were higher than for semi-arid lands farther west. Thus settlement in the years to the mid-1880s is naturally concentrated in the Red River Valley in Canada and, except for an overextension in the Central Plains region occasioned by unusually propitious rainfall for a few years,[33] east of the 98th to 100th meridian transitional zone in the United States.

By the mid-1880s, however, the supply of sub-humid land in both countries was virtually exhausted. This, plus the demonstration of the precariousness of the extreme western settlements in the drought years after 1888, provided an incentive to develop ways to more effectively farm the semi-arid prairies. It is thus no accident that the apparently independent efforts of Angus Mackay at Indian Head, Saskatchewan and H.W. Campbell in South Dakota in developing and popularizing appropriate dry-farming techniques date from the late 1880s.

Up to 1890 the Canadian experiments with dry farming were restricted to the Indian Head experimental farm. The practice spread throughout the Qu'Appelle Valley after that date, but a more extensive diffusion was discouraged by the depressed wheat prices after 1888. With a low net return in effect until the eventual upturn of grain prices after 1895 the expected return to patenting a homestead in the semi-arid region was not adequate to induce settlement, even with the new technology. The development of appropriate local dry-farming experiments had been delayed until the mid-1880s by the availability of readily accessible sub-humid land. But even after the viability of the techniques had been clearly established after 1890 their widespread adoption had to await the end of the depression in world wheat prices.

When viewed in this manner the nature and structural similarity of the homestead response equation over the period 1879 to 1896 is easily interpreted. Identical technology was employed in Canada as in the United States, meaning the innovations that made settlement in the Dakotas feasible after 1873 were adopted in Canada as production conditions warranted. It is obviously erroneous, then, to suggest that inadequate technology in such areas as farm machinery and supplies, railway equipment and milling techniques was a serious obstacle to settlement in Canada after the mid-1870s.

In addition, access to rail services was adequate throughout the period, meaning that singling out the completion of the CPR transcontinental line as an important structural change is also misleading. A connection to American export points was available by 1879. The CPR was chartered in 1880 and began construction immediately, linking Winnipeg with the Lakehead in 1882 and stretching across the prairies at the same time. Branch lines, CPR or other, stretched northwest and southwest by the early 1880s. As settlement spread into new areas the railroads were quick to follow. By 1890, "of the area west of the Red River and within 110 miles of the international boundary, only the southwestern corner of the province contained significant acreage that was not within ten miles of a railway."[34] The relative lack of railroads in the more arid part of the province is significant, for it indicates that branch lines in this period reflected the pattern of settlement rather than explained it.

Finally, the limited diffusion of dry-farming techniques before the upturn in wheat prices means that the nature of the homestead response to prices from 1887 to 1896 was more similar to that prevailing prior to 1887 than that after 1897 when expansion onto the semi-arid prairies became widespread. The adjustments to changing wheat prices made after 1887 were still largely based on an understanding of economic relationships derived from farming sub-humid land. Since the limits of feasible settlement in this area were fairly well understood, the high value obtained in the regression equation for the speed-of-adjustment coefficient is not surprising.

This interpretation also resolves Studness' apparent paradox, and gives a more satisfactory explanation of the large emigration of Canadians before 1896. The basic problem with his argument is a misinterpretation of the yield comparisons presented. By taking a long-term average for 1924–60 he is implicitly incorporating the effects of using appropriate dry-farming techniques in semi-arid areas. But it is clearly inappropriate to extrapolate these yields back to a time before such methods were practised. Adjusting actual data to conform to a pre-summer-fallowing technology involves more than a simple deflation of the long-run average yield. By increasing the probability of total or significant crop failure the expected yields of these semi-arid areas would be substantially lower. Yield comparisons based on a long-run average are not a valid measure of the prospects facing homesteaders in the nineteenth century.

Settlement to 1886 or 1887 was concentrated in the more humid areas, and since there was a greater supply of such land in the United States than Manitoba it was inevitable that the American boom would dwarf the Canadian one. The appropriate lands in Manitoba were filled up over the period, along with those in Dakota. But the relative lack of this type of land drove many Canadian settlers to the United States where the land was more abundant. Their choice was not restricted by the lack of free homestead land adjacent to rail lines as Studness suggests. There was plenty of free land along rail lines in southwestern Manitoba and into the Territories. And the railroads had shown a willingness to extend new lines into areas of settlement. The choice, rather, was to venture onto these semi-arid lands with their low expected yields, or take up land with more certain yields east of the 100th meridian in the Dakotas. Once the comparisons are made in this manner the migration pattern is more readily understood.

The rise in net returns after 1896 initiated the subsequent expansion. But now the feasible area of cultivation was greatly extended. With appropriate cultivation methods, the potential long-term yield of the semi-arid prairie land was higher. Thus for any given level of wheat prices and costs, a much greater homestead response was possible. The homestead response curve had shifted upwards.

This structural change was not immediately evident. It was only after some initial homesteaders had ventured onto the prairie, employed the new techniques and been successful, that the true potential of the region became apparent. Thus the total response to the change in net returns was lagged over several years. The structural change separating 1879–96 from the later boom years was the opening of new areas of settlement following the development and diffusion of dry-farming techniques. With the limits of the feasible area shifted out dramatically in this manner the "appropriate" number of homestead entries for any given net returns had to be re-established. The slower speed-of-adjustment coefficient obtained for the boom period is picking up this structural change.

The reversal of net migration flows after 1896 is easily understood now. Here Studness' calculations are valid. They represent the relative expected yields and net returns facing farmers entering the semi-arid prairies employing appropriate dry-farming techniques. The Canadian averages are seen to be higher and the net flow of migrants, not unexpectedly, is northward. As settlement proceeded into new areas branch rail lines followed, and sales of land by the various land agencies boomed along with homestead entries. The lack of branch lines in the Territories prior to 1900 was a symptom rather than a cause of the retardation of settlement, and the lagging land sales in the same period reflected not so much a policy of withholding land from sale as an inability to dispose of it even at low prices. In the second phase of prairie settlement, as in the first, the homesteader ignored boundaries in seeking out areas with the highest expected net returns.

IV

The timing of settlement in the Canadian prairies emerges more clearly now. Before 1879 development was constrained by the lack of rail connections to export points. The line to the U.S. border in that year, immediately followed by the CPR, removed that barrier, but this obviously was not sufficient. High wheat prices in the early 1880s induced some settlement in Canada, but touched off the Dakota Boom in the United States. It is in this period that the thesis that Canada had to await the settlement of superior U.S. lands is valid. Agricultural expansion in these years moved onto the last remaining frost-free, sub-humid areas of North America. The supply of such lands east of the 98th or 100th meridian in the United States was greater than in the Red River Valley of Manitoba. Successful cultivation of the remaining Canadian lands would require the local adoption of imperfectly understood and more expensive dry-farming techniques, and on an earlier ripening wheat variety. As such, they could not be competitive with U.S. lands of the type settled during the Dakota Boom.

The Mackay and Campbell dry-farming experiments increased the expected long-term yield of semi-arid lands, and prepared the way for their eventual exploitation. But extensive use of their innovations had to await the end of the depression in world wheat prices which lasted until 1895. The increase in net returns after that date induced a new flow of homesteaders. But now conditions were propitious for Canada. With a basic transportation trunk line in place, the end of the American frontier of sub-humid land and the appropriate dry-farming technology understood, the rise in wheat prices after 1896 was sufficient to set off the long-awaited wheat boom.

Notes

1. See H.E. Briggs, *Frontiers of the Northwest* (New York: Appleton-Century Co., 1940) and C.M. Studness, "Economic Opportunity and the Westward Migration of Canadians During the Late Nineteenth Century," *Canadian Journal of Economics and Political Science* (Nov. 1964).

2. W.A. Mackintosh, *Economic Problems of the Prairie Provinces* (Toronto: Macmillan of Canada, 1935), 282.

3. See W.A. Mackintosh, *Prairie Settlement: The Geographical Setting* (Toronto: Macmillan of Canada, 1934), 62–68, figures 43–49. Agricultural expansion after 1911 consisted largely of filling in areas already thinly settled. The only new regions opened up were the northern fringes of the Park Belt and the Peace River Country.

4. See W.T. Easterbrook and H.G.J. Aitken, *Canadian Economic History* (Toronto: Macmillan of Canada, 1965); W.A. Mackintosh, *The Economic Background of Dominion Provincial Relations* (appendix III of the Royal Commission on Dominion Provincial Relations, Ottawa, 1939); J.B. Hedges, *Building the Canadian West* (New York: Macmillan, 1939).

5. The price of "Good Red Foreign Wheat" at Liverpool averaged $1.54 in the decade 1871–80, $1.15 in the 1880s, $0.90 in the 1890s and $1.00 in the period 1901–10. Mackintosh, *Economic Problems*, 283, table IV.

6. V.C. Fowke, *Canadian Agricultural Policy* (Toronto: University of Toronto Press, 1946); J.H. Dales, *The Protective Tariff in Canada's Development* (Toronto: University of Toronto Press, 1965).

7. For capital flows see G. Meier, "Economic Development and the Transfer Mechanism: Canada, 1895–1913," *Canadian Journal of Economics and Political Science* (Feb. 1953). For labor migration see D.C. Corbett, "Immigration and Economic Development," *Canadian Journal of Economics and Political Science* (Feb. 1953). See also P. Hartland, "Factors in Economic Growth in Canada," *Journal of Economic History* XV (Mar. 1955).

8. J. Bracken, *Dry Farming in Western Canada* (Winnipeg: Grain Growers' Guide, 1921), 4–8.

9. K.A.H. Buckley, *Capital Formation in Canada* (Toronto: University of Toronto Press, 1955), 15.

10. *Historical Statistics of the U.S., Colonial Times to 1957* (Washington: U.S.G.P.O., 1960), 237; Hartland, "Factors."

11. Studness, "Economic Opportunity." For a critical evaluation of his calculations, see K.H. Norrie, "Economic Opportunity and the Westward Migration of Canadians During the Late Nineteenth Century: A Comment," *Canadian Journal of Economics* (Feb. 1974).

12. The contract with the CPR in 1881 gave the company, among other things, 25 million acres of land. The grant was to be taken in alternate sections on each side of the main line. A novel provision was that the land had to be "fairly fit for settlement." If the company did not consider land along the trunk line to be suitable it could be replaced by a similar grant elsewhere. By careful selection then the railway early on controlled considerable acreage in southwestern Manitoba and southeastern Saskatchewan which was just at the margin of settlement. Studness is arguing that ownership of the even-numbered sections of every township in this prime area deterred settlement since ". . . it appears that Canadian settlers occupied the good homestead land that was within a reasonable distance of railroads, and then turned to homestead land in northern North Dakota rather than purchase the more productive Canadian land from the CPR or Hudson's Bay Company." Studness, "Economic Opportunity," 582. The latter institution, in surrendering its exclusive claims to the area granted by royal charter in 1670, received land grants totaling one-twentieth of the fertile belt.

13. Studness, "Economic Opportunity," 583, 21ff.

14. The introduction to the paper summarizes the results as follows:
(1) The problems of overcoming the physical environment had definitely been solved by the mid-1880s;
(2) . . . the principal reason for lack of settlement after the mid-1880s was a demand for the region's major potential export which was insufficient to ensure its profitable exploitation; and
(3) that development after 1897 was primarily due to an increase in the profitability of producing that export. . . .
See J.C. Stabler, "Factors Affecting the Development of a New Region: The Canadian Great Plains, 1870–1897," *Annals of Regional Science* (June 1973): 75–76.

15. J. Johnston, *Econometric Methods* (New York: McGraw-Hill, 1972), 301.

16. Easterbrook and Aitken, *Canadian Economic History*, 282–86.

17. The normal assumption of a first-order auto-regressive scheme was made. Thus $U_t = QU_{t-1} + h_t$ where h_t is not autocorrelated. See, for example, F. Fisher and P. Temin, "Regional Specialization and the Supply of Wheat in the United States, 1867–1914," *Review of Economics and Statistics* (1970): 140–41.

18. The data are from Mackintosh, *Economic Problems*, tables III and IV, 282–83. The series for wheat prices is not consistent since the figures to 1889 are for No. 2 White Wheat at Toronto while those after 1889 are for No. 1 Northern at Winnipeg. The direction of bias is not clear since the Toronto price will exceed the Winnipeg price by an amount equal to the transportation charges between the two points, but No. 1 Northern Wheat will bear a premium over No. 2 White. If a statistically significant break had been found for the period 1879 to 1896 there would have been the problem of deciding whether to ascribe it to this defect in the time series for wheat prices or to more fundamental economic reasons. But since the regression equation over the period did not pick up a structural change, the biases must be largely offsetting.

19. For twenty-four degrees of freedom the required value of t for significance at the 95 percent level is 1.711.

20. M.W.M. Hargreaves, *Dry Farming in the Northern Great Plains, 1900-1925* (Cambridge: Harvard University Press, 1957), 3. Other useful historical references to dry farming are J. Bracken, *Dry Farming in Western Canada*, and J.A. Widtsoe, *Dry Farming* (New York: Macmillan, 1913).

21. Employing Widtsoe's classification, areas receiving less than ten inches of precipitation are arid; those receiving between ten and twenty inches are semi-arid; those receiving between twenty and thirty inches are sub-humid; and those with over thirty inches are humid. In semi-arid areas dry farming is "indispensable."

22. The expected yield of semi-arid land farmed in the conventional manner can be written as:

$$E[u(X)] = \sum_X u(x)f(x)$$

where yield, u, is a function of rainfall, X, and f(x) is the probability density function of rainfall. The expected yield of the same piece of semi-arid land under summer-fallowing is:

$$E[v(X)] = p[\sum_X v(x)f(x)]$$

where $v(x)$ is the new functional relationship between yields and rainfall and p $(0 \leq p \leq 1)$ is the proportion of the land cropped. The latter term enters since the portion of the land left fallow $(1 - p)$ will have a zero yield. The contention is that the gains to be made in higher yields from planting on land left fallow the previous crop year more than compensates for the necessity of leaving a portion of the land unproductive. The universal use of summerfallowing in the semi-arid Canadian Prairies after 1900 would seem to confirm this. Obviously p becomes a choice variable reflecting the trade-off between foregone production and more certain yields. The more arid the region or the more uncertain the rainfall, meaning the greater the probability of a poor crop sown on stubble, the higher will be the value of p for given wheat prices.

23. The differences are illustrated by the diversities of opinion among area experts reported in Bracken, *Dry Farming in Western Canada*, chap. 16.

24. If the expected yield of sub-humid land is written as:

$$E[w(X)] = \sum_X w(x)f(x)$$

and that for the same average of semi-arid land under summerfallowing as in note 22:

$$E[v(X)] = p[\sum_X v(x)f(x)]$$

then it is being argued that for contiguous areas such as then under discussion there would be no significant difference in $v(x)$ versus w(x) or, even if there were, it would generally be insufficient to offset the foregone production in the latter case.

25. The terms are from W.P. Webb, *The Great Plains* (Boston: Ginn and Company, 1931), 3–9.

26. Ibid., 3. Webb puts the eastern boundary at the 98th meridian, while G.C. Fite places it at the 100th. See G.C. Fite, *The Farmer's Frontier, 1865-1900* (New York: Holt, Rinehart & Winston, 1966), 3.

27. See United States Bureau of the Census, *Census of the United States, 1890*, vol. I and *Census of the United States, 1920*, vol. VI, part I.

28. This paragraph is based on Fite, *Frontier*, chap. 7.

29. Mackintosh, *Prairie Settlement*, 48–49, figures 32–34. Ibid., 86–89.

30. Calculated from Canada Bureau of Statistics, *Census of Canada, 1921*, vol. V.

31. Mackintosh, *Prairie Settlement*, 90.

32. Vernon Fowke, *Canadian Agricultural Policy*, 236–37, has argued that an earlier discovery of Marquis would have hastened western settlement "only slightly." The analysis here suggests modifying this negative viewpoint somewhat. More adequate rainfall and a slower evaporation rate meant that the more northern Park Belt regions were nearly comparable in moisture conditions to the Red River Valley area. Thus if Marquis had been available in the 1870s it is possible these northern areas would have been settled in the period after 1879 along with southern Manitoba and the eastern Dakotas. The extension onto the semi-arid prairies, and thus the bulk of Canadian settlement, would still have had to await the end of the sub-humid lands, but the relative sizes of settlement would not have been so skewed in favor of the U.S.

33. In contrast the Canadian semi-arid lands did not receive this stretch of favorable rainfall. In the period from 1883 to 1890 only 1888 was very favorable moisture-wise, with 1887 being "fairly good." See A.S. Morton and C. Martin, *History of Prairie Settlement and Dominion Lands Policy* (Toronto: Macmillan of Canada, 1938), 65–95. Thus the Canadian settlement phase from 1879 to 1886 or 1887 lacked this large-scale premature expansion onto semi-arid land, accounting in part for its relatively much smaller scale.

34. Studness, "Economic Opportunity," 580–81.

New Estimates of Output Growth in Canada: Measurement and Interpretation†

A.G. GREEN AND M.C. URQUHART

This paper utilizes estimates of gross national product and of various related gross national expenditure components for Canada for the years 1870 to 1926 for a new look at Canadian economic development for the period. It is composed of two parts: first, the new data and some related material relevant to their interpretation are presented; second, some of the implications of the new data for Canadian economic development are examined. We look only at the most evident implications that can be derived from the new data and also only at developments in the large. Consequently, we do not present much of the detail contained in the new estimates nor use it in our discussion of economic developments. The detail has been presented elsewhere and its analysis must come later. In addition, the consumer price index we use, while based on a considerable amount of hitherto unused material, may be subject to change if someone does a major study of this price index. In the latter event, our estimates would not be the definitive constant-dollar estimates of gross national product. Having made these reservations, we add that we believe our material sufficiently good to support the conclusions about Canadian economic development that we draw.

The Background Data

The occasion for this paper lies in the new estimates of gross national product for 1870 to 1926. These estimates are the culmination of a major project of approximately ten years duration, involving many persons. They will appear in the NBER Conference on Research in Income and Wealth.[1]

The new annual estimates of gross national product, in three measures, are given in table 1. The data for gross national product, at market prices, are based upon[2] estimates of gross value added — in a comprehensively large number of sectors such as agriculture, mining, manufacturing (seventeen sub-groups), transportation, finance, government and other service sectors, to which was added

†This article has not been previously published. It was presented at the Social Science History Association meetings, Toronto, October 1984.

TABLE 1

Gross National Product in Current and Constant Dollars and Real Gross National Product Per Capita, 1870 to 1926

Year	Gross National Product in Current Market Prices ($M)	Gross National Product in Constant (1900) Prices ($M)	Implicit Price Index (1900 = 100)	Population (thousands of persons)	Real GNP per Capita (in 1900 $)
1870	382.6	369.5	104	3,625	102
1871	412.7	385.9	107	3,689	105
1872	447.3	382.8	117	3,754	102
1873	487.8	419.3	116	3,826	110
1874	485.5	427.8	113	3,895	110
1875	452.5	417.1	108	3,954	105
1876	421.7	391.1	108	4,009	98
1877	434.7	416.5	104	4,064	102
1878	409.6	402.6	102	4,120	98
1879	445.1	441.8	101	4,185	106
1880	482.0	462.1	104	4,255	109
1881	568.7	527.0	108	4,325	122
1882	618.9	547.2	113	4,375	125
1883	611.5	545.7	112	4,430	123
1884	585.2	592.0	99	4,487	132
1885	554.5	556.3	100	4,537	123
1886	560.7	559.4	100	4,580	122
1887	611.1	579.0	106	4,626	125
1888	630.3	616.1	102	4,678	132
1889	655.8	620.9	106	4,729	131
1890	685.4	652.4	104	4,779	138
1891	703.5	679.9	104	4,833	138
1892	700.3	676.2	104	4,883	138
1893	682.4	666.9	102	4,931	135
1894	651.5	700.7	93	4,979	141
1895	633.4	698.7	91	5,026	139
1896	640.8	680.7	94	5,074	134
1897	717.0	757.2	95	5,122	148
1898	769.4	786.5	98	5,175	152
1899	826.0	857.8	96	5,235	164
1900	907.4	907.8	100	5,301	171
1901	990.7	984.1	101	5,371	183
1902	1,119.6	1,073.6	104	5,494	195
1903	1,178.2	1,115.1	106	5,651	197
1904	1,205.8	1,131.4	107	5,827	194
1905	1,361.5	1,248.2	109	6,002	208
1906	1,525.9	1,380.6	111	6,097	226
1907	1,728.4	1,456.0	119	6,411	227
1908	1,653.8	1,383.3	120	6,625	209
1909	1,838.3	1,520.4	121	6,800	224
1910	2,022.8	1,655.4	122	6,988	237
1911	2,233.2	1,770.7	126	7,207	246
1912	2,493.9	1,905.4	131	7,389	258

TABLE 1 (continued)

Gross National Product in Current and Constant Dollars and Real Gross National Product Per Capita, 1870 to 1926

Year	Gross National Product in Current Market Prices ($M)	Gross National Product in Constant (1900) Prices ($M)	Implicit Price Index (1900 = 100)	Population (thousands of persons)	Real GNP per Capita (in 1900 $)
1913	2,651.5	1,979.8	134	7,632	259
1914	2,448.6	1,835.6	133	7,879	233
1915	2,688.6	1,964.4	137	7,981	246
1916	3,242.7	2,182.5	149	8,001	273
1917	3,991.9	2,273.2	176	8,060	282
1918	4,261.5	2,141.4	199	8,148	263
1919	4,367.4	1,994.9	218	8,311	240
1920	5,060.9	1,992.0	254	8,556	233
1921	4,073.8	1,800.3	226	8,788	205
1922	4,233.9	2,060.9	203	8,919	231
1923	4,555.3	2,194.0	208	9,010	244
1924	4,501.5	2,210.1	203	9,143	242
1925	4,995.7	2,450.3	204	9,294	264
1926	5,345.3	2,611.8	205	9,451	276

SOURCE: M.C. Urquhart, "New Estimates of Gross National Product, Canada, 1870 to 1926: Some Implications for Canadian Development" (data on file in the Institute for Economic Research, Queen's University, and forthcoming in the NBER Conference on Research in Income and Wealth, vol. 51).

indirect taxes less subsidies and an adjustment for net international income flows. Gross national product in constant dollars was obtained by deflating the current-dollar estimates of gross national expenditure (which is equal, of course, to GNP) according to two components: gross fixed capital formation, including that of governments, was deflated by a price index of capital goods obtained, in the main, from a Statistics Canada publication; all the rest of gross national expenditure was deflated by a consumer price index of our own making. This consumer price index was constructed by splicing together the official cost-of-living index (Dominion Bureau of Statistics) for 1913 to 1926, a cost-of-living index derived from a study by R.H. Coats, for 1900 to 1913, as amended by Bertram and Percy,[3] and a cost-of-living index for Kingston, Ontario, based upon data from an M.A. thesis at Queen's University and supplemented by an index of rents prepared by Marion Steele for 1870 to 1900. The implicit price index is, as usual, the quotient of the gross national product in current dollars divided by the constant-dollar estimates. The population figures are the standard ones, which include the population of Prince Edward Island, British Columbia, Manitoba, and the Territories from 1870 onward. The fact that the population data include Prince Edward Island and British Columbia before their entry into Confederation may bias the per capita income estimates of column 5 slightly downward in the 1870s since some of the income of these provinces may not have been recorded in our gross national product estimates.[4]

TABLE 2

Comparative Annual Growth Rates of Population, Total and Per Capita Real Gross National Product, Canada and the United States **

| | Canada
Annual Growth Rates | | | United States
Annual Growth Rates | | |
	Population (1)	Real GNP (2)	Real GNP per Capita (3)	Population (4)	Real GNP (5)	Real GNP per Capita (6)
1871–1880	1.6	2.6	1.0	2.3	5.7	3.3
1880–1890	1.2	3.2	2.0	2.3	3.5	1.2
1890–1900	1.0	3.5	2.4	1.9	3.6	1.7
1900–1910	2.8	6.0	3.2	2.0	4.3	2.3
1910–1920	2.0	1.6	−0.4	1.4	1.4	0.0
1920–1926	1.7	4.7	2.9	1.7	5.2	3.5
1871–1890	1.4	2.9	1.5	2.3	4.5	2.2

*Growth rates of GNP and per capita GNP are compound rates percent per annum between averages for three years centred on the beginning and ending year for each period.
SOURCES: Col. 1: Population from *Historical Statistics of Canada*, 1st ed., Series A.1.
   Col. 2: Derived from table 1.
   Col. 3: Derived from table 1.
   Col. 4: Population from *The Statistical History of the United States to 1976*, Series A7.
   Col. 5: GNP and GNP per capita in constant prices: for 1900 to 1926, from *The Statistical History of the United States to 1870*, Series F1-5; for 1870–1900, rates kindly provided by Robert Gallman, University of North Carolina, Chapel Hill.

To give these figures meaning, we compare rates of growth of population and incomes in Canada with similar rates of growth in the United States. The data of table 2 present such comparative growth rates for the nine-year period from 1871 to 1880, the decadal periods from 1880 to 1920, and the period 1920 to 1926. Annual growth rates of population are based on the changes in population between the single years at the beginning and end of each period. The growth rates of real gross national product and of per capita gross product are based on the changes in averages for three years centred on the beginning and averages for three years centred at the end of such period on the stub.

The choice of the time periods used in table 2 has been in part related to the nature of the data — for instance, decennial censuses are taken at decade ends or beginnings — and in part to convention. As we shall note later, the use of other time periods may, on occasion, be more illuminating.

The data on comparative growth rates have their limitations but they are probably sufficiently good for us to draw some useful inferences about comparative growth rates. It is quite clear that in the period from 1870 to 1900, and especially in the 1880s, population growth rates in Canada were much lower than in the United States; conversely Canadian population growth rates were higher than the American from 1900 to 1920 and especially in 1900 to 1910; from 1920 to 1926 they are about identical. The differences in growth rates are principally the result of differences in rates of net immigration.

The pattern of growth rates of real per capita income is different. The most striking difference in the rates between the two countries occurs in the 1870s when the excess of the American growth rate over the Canadian was very large. No doubt a part of the high growth rate in the United States was accounted for by recovery from the Civil War; the other part undoubtedly reflected a high basic rate of growth whilst that in Canada was relatively low. Canadian rates of growth were higher in the 1880s and 1890s. Of course, measures for single decades are always subject to the vagaries of measurement of the statistics. If one looks at longer periods, the Canadian per capita growth rates for the whole nineteen-year period from 1871 to 1890 were less than those of the United States, but for the twenty-nine-year period from 1871 to 1900 roughly matched that of the latter. From 1900 to 1910, the Canadian per capita income growth rate appears to clearly exceed that of the United States, and from 1910 to 1920 it seems to have fallen short.

For some purposes, the growth rates of aggregate real gross national product are significant. Compounded as they are of population growth and per capita income growth, the United States rates were clearly above those of Canada for 1871 to 1900 and clearly below those of Canada for 1900 to 1920, even allowing for its possibly greater growth rates in the wartime decade.

For analytical use in the second part of our paper, some ratios of critical economic quantities to gross national product, derivable from the new data, are given in table 3. The numerators of the ratios are: gross fixed domestic capital formation; net inflow of capital from other countries; implied gross domestic savings; and commodity exports. We will make substantial use of these ratios when we deal with the implications of our data for the interpretation of Canadian economic development: our comments now are limited to a factual description of the data.

The presentation of overall ratios of gross fixed capital formation to gross national product submerges the detail in the movements of components of capital formation. Some of these submerged features of the data are the following. The ratio of gross fixed capital to GNP includes government as well as private capital expenditures. All government expenditure, excluding public school building, has typically amounted to less than ten percent of total fixed capital formation, with few exceptions until the First World War. Public school capital formation typically accounted for between one and two percent of total gross capital formation until 1913; for two to three percent in the wartime years; and from three to four percent from 1920 onward. It follows, of course, that movements in total gross capital formation were dominated by the private-sector components as we have defined them. However, the rise in the ratio of fixed capital formation to GNP in 1872 to 1876 was accounted for by the building of the Intercolonial Railway, which was really a public project though not treated as such in our data. Similarly, the increase in the early to mid-1880s was caused by the building of the Canadian Pacific Railway, which had considerable public support. On the other hand, the relatively high levels of the late 1880s were based on private residential construction in cities, especially in Montreal. The rise in the ratio of gross capital formation to GNP from the late 1890s onward, and especially from 1900 to 1913, was based on a growth of all types of private capital spending.

TABLE 3

Ratios of Gross Fixed Capital Formation, of Capital Inflow and of Exports of Goods to Gross National Product at Market Prices

Year	Ratio, Gross Fixed Capital Formation to GNP (1)	Ratio, Inflow of Capital to GNP (current account balance to GNP) (2)	Implied Private Savings Ratio Col. (1)–Col. (2) (3)	Ratio, Commodity Exports to GNP (4)
1870	.157	.062	.095	.174
1871	.152	.083	.068	.177
1872	.174	.092	.082	.183
1873	.173	.093	.080	.176
1874	.191	.104	.087	.166
1875	.188	.080	.106	.170
1876	.166	.062	.103	.181
1877	.141	.058	.082	.175
1878	.135	.057	.076	.181
1879	.126	.036	.090	.174
1880	.137	.034	.103	.188
1881	.136	.048	.088	.174
1882	.173	.063	.110	.160
1883	.198	.074	.124	.151
1884	.222	.068	.154	.149
1885	.157	.069	.088	.154
1886	.152	.077	.075	.154
1887	.163	.077	.086	.146
1888	.168	.084	.084	.140
1889	.170	.083	.087	.137
1890	.144	.088	.056	.138
1891	.150	.069	.081	.147
1892	.139	.070	.069	.160
1893	.135	.062	.073	.167
1894	.115	.056	.059	.171
1895	.123	.051	.072	.175
1896	.115	.045	.070	.191
1897	.126	.021	.105	.199
1898	.154	.027	.127	.199
1899	.153	.036	.117	.186
1900	.155	.028	.127	.186
1901	.182	.033	.149	.181
1902	.186	.036	.150	.177
1903	.217	.057	.160	.169
1904	.230	.075	.155	.156
1905	.229	.068	.161	.154
1906	.236	.078	.158	.157
1907	.259	.095	.164	.145
1908	.265	.094	.171	.152
1909	.259	.085	.174	.153

TABLE 3 (continued)

Ratios of Gross Fixed Capital Formation, of Capital Inflow and of Exports of Goods to Gross National Product at Market Prices

Year	Ratio, Gross Fixed Capital Formation to GNP (1)	Ratio, Inflow of Capital to GNP (current account balance to GNP) (2)	Implied Private Savings Ratio Col. (1)–Col. (2) (3)	Ratio, Commodity Exports to GNP (4)
1910	.295	.121	.174	.141
1911	.311	.160	.151	.132
1912	.341	.177	.164	.140
1913	.328	.159	.169	.159
1914	.245	.114	.131	.199
1915	.175	.025	.150	.252
1916	.154	.008	.146	.321
1917	.148	−.034	.182	.366
1918	.129	.006	.123	.314
1919	.151	.003	.148	.298
1920	.166	.031	.135	.250
1921	.179	.041	.138	.220
1922	.158	.030	.128	.217
1923	.189	−.012	.201	.229
1924	.169	−.017	.186	.239
1925	.154	−.039	.193	.254
1926	.151	−.040	.191	.242

SOURCE: M.C. Urquhart, "New Estimates of Gross National Product, Canada, 1870 to 1926," op. cit., table 10.

Capital inflow from abroad, which financed much of Canada's gross fixed capital formation until 1914, is given in column 2 of table 3. This net borrowing from other countries can be measured in two ways. First, it can be measured by the current account balance, the difference between the receipts from sale of goods and services abroad and expenditures on purchases of goods and services from abroad. To the extent that the latter exceeds the former, then debt to residents of other countries grows. Second, it can be measured by the net sales of securities abroad and by direct measures of other forms of financial lending and borrowing. If the data were complete, these two measures of international borrowing would be identical, but the data are never complete and very often the two measures differ substantially one from the other. Such was true of our data, just as it has been true of the data of other advanced countries, especially before 1900. Typically, the measured deficit on current account, characteristic of the early period, exceeded the directly measured capital flow. In common with the practice of researchers in other countries, we used the current account deficit as the measure of capital inflow. It is believed to be based on more accurate data than those of the direct measures of capital inflows.

Implications

In an earlier work[5] on the patterns of economic growth, Simon Kuznets suggested that the best way to proceed in expanding our knowledge in this area is through the study of ordered evidence. By this one presumes he means the systematic collection and study of the basic facts of economic growth. It is in this spirit that we have brought together our new estimates of gross national product plus other evidence, which we believe bear on the strategic factors of long-term Canadian development.

What, then, do the facts outlined in the first section say about the course of Canadian economic growth between 1870 and 1926? This half-century has often been seen as the seminal period in the development of Canada, at least by economic historians. These years embrace the emergence of this country as an independent nation-state as well as the emergence of basic development strategies concerning transportation, immigration, land, tariff policies, and the like. They saw the completion of the Intercolonial Railway, which linked the Maritime provinces to Central Canada in the 1870s, and the spanning of the continent by the Canadian Pacific Railway in the early and mid-1880s. They saw the settlement of the Canadian Prairies in the years before the First World War and, at the same time, the development of an urban-industrial sector of considerable stature. It is for these reasons that so much attention has been directed toward the economic development of this period.

Despite this concentration of interest, a consensus about the actual determinants of observed economic change has not emerged. Part of the reason for a lack of consensus lies in the limited amount of systematic or ordered evidence on the actual progress of the country during this period. Of course, a considerable amount of material, both quantitative and non-quantitative, and including early national accounts[6] estimates, has been assembled on the period. However, these earlier national accounts estimates were prepared on a fairly aggregate basis, and for census years. These data then, although they brought into question some traditional patterns of growth, especially concerning the three-decade period of stagnation that supposedly followed Confederation, often opened more areas of controversy than they resolved. Part of the reason for this was the lack of detail in the data series, either in terms of the number of yearly observations (decennially) or in sector detail. The new estimates presented here, based as they are on annual figures, and broken down into industry elements, should narrow the areas of disagreement — at least that is our hope.

The "Vent-for-Surplus" Model of Economic Growth

The staple model provides us with an effective framework within which to analyse Canadian economic development. This model relates export expansion directly to total (aggregate) economic growth and indirectly to the advancement of welfare (i.e., the growth in real output per head of the population). Recently, a debate has emerged over the extent of the link between export growth and the rise in average income. The question of how much of the observed change in per capita income could be explained by larger export sales was raised by Chambers and Gordon.[7] Their conclusion was that, in the case of the Canadian wheat boom period (defined by these authors to be between 1900 and 1910), very little of the growth in real per capita income could be accounted for by settlement of the Canadian West, which was based on the production of wheat for sale abroad. Hence, they challenged the validity of the staple model. This conclusion drew a substantial response.[8] We will not pursue this controversy but rather adopt the vent-for-surplus model developed by Richard Caves.[9] This latter approach, we believe, provides a balanced interpretation of the relationship between exports and economic growth for a country like Canada.

Caves hypothesized that the timing of *accelerated* expansion in a country of recent settlement depended on the discovery of an exportable resource. In Canada's case, it was the discovery that Prairie wheat could be grown and marketed profitably. The pace of total income growth that followed this discovery was set by the rate of factor migration and absorption.[10] This process of discovery and movement Caves sees as superimposed on an underlying pattern of neo-classical growth. The latter occurs as a result of the growth in population, capital stock (from domestic savings), and the general advance in labour efficiency that accompanies improvements in technology. Neo-classical growth is generally seen as more stable than export-related growth over time. Export-based growth then explains *variations* in aggregate expansion (i.e., deviations around the long-term trend in the growth of total real output). Using a neo-classical growth model to determine the long-term rate of growth has the additional advantage of offering an explanation for growth in efficiency in the absence of new resource discoveries.

We proceed now to see how the Caves model may be applied to Canada. The matters to be explained are the following. From 1870 to 1900, the rates of growth of population and of aggregate real gross national product were clearly higher in the United States than in Canada; the rate of growth of real income per capita was much higher in the United States than in Canada in the first part of the period, although for the entire three decades only slightly above the Canadian rates. Between 1900 and 1920, for the period as a whole, the Canadian growth rates for population and aggregate GNP were substantially higher than those of the United States; growth rates of income per capita were also higher for Canada from 1900 to the war but, for the period as a whole, were approximately the same as for the United States. All three rates of growth were about the same in Canada and the United States from 1920 to 1926. The question to be answered, then, is how Canada moved from being a laggard in growth vis-à-vis the United States before 1900 to being a leader following 1900.

Before we look at our data in detail, we present in encapsulated form our view of the driving forces of the time. Canadian stagnation in the 1870 to 1900 (or better, 1896) period was a relative rather than an absolute matter. Population did grow, aggregate real gross national product did grow, and real output per capita did grow. But, especially the first and second of these series grew much less than the comparable series not only in the United States but also in Australia and Argentina.

The difference between Canada and these other countries in this period lay in the absence of a particular economic opportunity that matched those elsewhere.

The United States, in exploiting its great interior, was expanding both foreign and domestic markets for products, was encouraging and was encouraged by the rapid expansion of railways and the growth of urban centres and of manufacturing and mining industries. It was of a size to permit realization of economies of scale internally but also benefitted from growth of particular external markets. Argentinian and Australian growth was especially based on the growth, or anticipated growth, of the external markets of Europe for particular agricultural products in which they had a strong advantage in production. At this particular time, Canada was not especially favoured in any of these matters. Its internal market was not of a size to encourage activities in which scale was important. Canada was losing rather than gaining external markets for grain products until the later years of the period. Its foreign markets for lumber and timber were relatively flat. Only the market for animal products, especially dairy products, showed some buoyancy. Despite these handicaps, real product per capita rose throughout the period, though at a considerably lower rate than in the United States in the early years of the period. While population grew, there was nevertheless a net outflow of persons from Canada in contrast to the large net inflows of immigrants to the United States, Argentina, and Australia. As a consequence, real aggregate gross national product rose much less in Canada than in these other countries. Some relief from this rather lacklustre picture was provided by the building of the Intercolonial Railway in the early to mid-1870s and the building of the Canadian Pacific Railway to the west coast in the early 1880s, the former being entirely publicly financed and the latter receiving much public assistance in the form of cash and land grants. But there was not what might be called a really buoyant economy at any time through these years. Domestic saving rates were low and much of the investment of these decades was supported by borrowing (capital inflow) from abroad.

All this changed at the turn of the century (or, in Canada's case, 1896). A number of developments accounted for the change, but first among them appears to have been the developments that made the production of wheat on the Canadian prairies a viable economic operation, both in fact and in prospect. Fundamental, at the beginning of the period, was the availability of the Canadian Pacific Railway and the Great Lakes transportation systems: their availability and improvements therein led to substantial reductions in transportation costs of wheat. In addition, the development of new strains of wheat and the use of dry-farming methods made possible the production on the prairies of high-grade wheat at a price fully competitive on the international market. (As the period progressed, the development of the pulp and paper industry and the non-ferrous mining industry provided additional exportable products, but wheat took first place.) The consequence was a great net migration of people to Canada, who went both to the Prairies and the eastern cities, and an internal migration of Canadians to the Prairies. These large movements of people, and the prospects of large movements of grain, led to an enormous investment expenditure on railways, on housing, on industrial plants and equipment and, of course, in agriculture.

It was the enormous investment expenditure of the time that was the real driving force of the expansion from 1900 (or 1896) to 1913. It provided a large direct market for many construction materials and industrial products, and it provided a great deal of employment and income for Canadian workers. Indirectly, through the incomes generated in capital goods production, it contributed strongly to a great growth in the market for consumer goods. At this time, while the prospects for the sale of Canadian wheat abroad were the strong motivating factor in land settlement, immigration, internal migration, and the like, the actual production and sale of wheat was only in the emerging stages; the gains to be derived from trading wheat abroad in abundance for other products Canadians wished were still largely in the future, although the quite near future.

There are several consequences of the developments of the 1900–13 period that are worthy of note. First, it was at this time that the development of the more advanced sectors of the Canadian manufacturing industry took place. In particular, the development of an up-to-date and quite large iron and steel industry took place only after 1895. Second, while there was still much capital import to finance the extraordinarily large capital expenditure, saving increased from the anemic levels of 1870 to 1895 to levels that were characteristic of advanced economies. Third, in contrast to what happened between 1910 and 1926, the share of agriculture in gross national product fell between 1900 and 1910, not because growth in agriculture, which was seminal in the period's development, was small, but because the great investment expenditure caused the non-agricultural sectors to grow even faster than agriculture — the direct impact of agricultural developments was to be felt more fully in the immediately following years. Finally, and of great importance, the production and sale of western grain was on a scale that permitted the development of a highly efficient grain-handling system. The system of country and terminal elevators, of rail and water transport, and of grading all commercially handled wheat (and other grains) provided the facilities for efficient transferral of grain over long distances. In addition, the institution of dependable grading of grain and the availability of the financial and market facilities of a branch banking system and a grain exchange were other elements in an effective marketing system.

The year 1914 marked the end of the period of the great investment boom. Among the changed features beyond the decline in investment of the period, three stand out. First, the level of exports relative to GNP became much higher than it had been in all of the prior years within our period. The settlers of the West who in earlier years had been motivated in large part by prospects of wheat sales — it took considerable time, even on prairie lands, to establish a new farm as a full-blown ongoing concern — now found their hopes realized. A very large part of the country, the Prairies, was supported in the main by one single exportable crop. Parenthetically, we should note that the difficult transition that the country went through from 1914 onward was strongly eased by the emergence of the war and the existence of wartime demand. Second, the large inflow of capital that had been an ongoing feature of the Canadian economy since 1870 ceased. This change meant that imports were balanced by exports, as they had not been before, thus throwing considerable levels of demand on the Canadian market. At the same time, Canadian domestic saving ratios remained about where they had been in the previous boom, or became slightly higher. Third, and relatedly, the share of gross domestic product accounted for by agriculture remained relatively unchanged at about the level of 1910, in strong contrast to what was happening in the United States. The establishment of one big export-based agricultural sector had offset the tendency of agriculture's share in a developing economy to decline, a tendency that had been present in Canada's earlier experience between 1870 and 1910.

The Evidence

To test Caves' vent-for-surplus model of the staple theory for Canada, we divided our period into three parts: 1870–1896, 1896–1914, and 1914–1926. The first (1870–1896) is a period when our export performance was languishing. The second (1896–1914) covers the boom years of western settlement; and the third (1914–1926) includes World War I and the period of the maturing of the Canadian economy. Table 4 presents additional explanatory variables to test the Caves model.

TABLE 4

Selected Explanatory Series

Year	Railroads (miles of first main track), Miles in Operation (1)	Net Immigration (thousands of persons) (2)	Net Exports of Wheat and Flour Crop Year Ending in Year Given (millions of bushels) (3)	Terms of Trade Export Prices as Percent of Import Prices 1900 = 100 (4)
1870	2,617	3	−0.6	68.1
1871	2,695	4	−2.9	65.6
1872	2,899	9	−0.9	71.7
1873	3,613	4	−0.6	76.1
1874	3,832	−2	−0.7	78.2
1875	4,331	−10	−1.5	82.1
1876	4,804	−12	0.4	82.3
1877	5,218	−7	−3.5	88.9
1878	5,782	−7	−0.6	87.8
1879	6,226	−3	3.6	85.7
1880	6,858	4	7.0	86.1
1881	7,194	—	3.5	91.3
1882	7,331	−6	4.9	93.1
1883	8,697	−9	6.9	91.7
1884	9,577	−7	−1.1	92.5
1885	10,273	−9	0.1	94.7
1886	10,773	−15	4.2	98.6
1887	11,793	−9	7.2	106.0
1888	12,184	−7	3.4	99.2
1889	12,585	−12	−0.1	101.1
1890	13,151	−2	0.0	99.8
1891	13,838	−11	3.0	105.3
1892	14,564	−5	10.2	104.6
1893	15,005	−9	10.9	107.8
1894	15,627	−10	11.0	113.1

TABLE 4 (continued)

Selected Explanatory Series

Year	Railroads (miles of first main track), Miles in Operation (1)	Net Immigration (thousands of persons) (2)	Net Exports of Wheat and Flour Crop Year Ending in Year Given (millions of bushels) (3)	Terms of Trade Export Prices as Percent of Import Prices 1900 = 100 (4)
1895	15,977	−13	9.1	105.9
1896	16,270	−20	10.5	108.5
1897	16,550	−9	9.6	109.2
1898	16,870	−13	24.4	106.5
1899	17,250	5	13.6	100.0
1900	17,657	12	20.0	101.5
1901	18,140	−6	14.5	106.4
1902	18,714	43	30.6	106.8
1903	18,988	64	38.6	105.3
1904	19,431	69	23.7	102.5
1905	20,487	119	20.4	105.3
1906	21,353	118	47.1	104.1
1907	22,446	147	46.3	106.2
1908	22,967	72	47.3	113.7
1909	24,104	63	56.5	114.2
1910	24,730	83	67.6	111.9
1911	25,400	75	62.0	112.6
1912	26,840	80	97.2	111.4
1913	29,304	100	114.8	103.5
1914	30,795	10	135.2	115.4
1915	34,882	−102	84.6	124.2
1916	36,985	−98	268.9	133.7
1917	38,369	−58	174.3	128.7
1918	38,252	26	168.9	121.8
1919	38,329	93	96.7	118.0
1920	38,805	99	92.3	108.0
1921	39,191	18	166.7	106.2
1922	39,358	−44	185.4	105.4
1923	39,654	−21	279.0	95.9
1924	40,059	−2	346.1	101.9
1925	40,350	8	192.1	112.8
1926	40,350	49	324.2	115.9

a. Net exports = gross exports minus gross imports.

SOURCES: Col. 1: *Historical Statistics of Canada*, 1st ed., Series S28 and S78 (data until 1919 are for the year ended 30 June; data from 1920 are for calendar years).

Col. 2: O.J. Firestone, *Canada's Economic Development, 1867–1956* (London: Bowes & Bowes, 1958), 240.

Col. 3: Same as col. 1, Series L142 and L143.

Col. 4: Same as col. 1, Series F359.

1870–1896

According to the Caves hypothesis, this is a period when neo-classical factors should predominate (i.e., years in which there is an absence of new resource 'discoveries'). During such a period, aggregate growth should be close to its long-run average, and population and savings should grow at their natural rates.

Between 1870 and 1896 Canadian population growth was positive but slow. Canada actually lost population by migration. This experience was in sharp contrast to the United States, which had high rates of net immigration and consequently high rates of population growth. Per capita income grew at lower rates than the U.S. in earlier years but higher in the later years. The consequence is that, compared to the United States, real aggregate income growth in Canada was desultory through much of the period. The per capita figures would support the view that Canada was closing the productivity gap between the United States and itself in later years. The reasons for this performance were twofold: our export industries, including agriculture and forest products, were languishing; and the rates of capital formation relative to GNP (table 3) were not all that robust, even in terms of neo-classical growth, except for the periods of railway building (i.e., from 1872 to 1876 during the building of the Intercolonial Railway and from 1882 to 1884 during the building of the Canadian Pacific Railway). However, they appear to have been sufficient to provide for a substantial increase in per capita output.

All of these factors fit well with the neo-classical view of the determinants of growth. The part that does not fit the Caves hypothesis is the source of savings. Table 3 shows quite high rates of capital inflow relative to GNP over this period, that is, in the six to eight percent range. This suggests that Canada did not have the internal driving force to provide its own dynamics. Without this capital inflow, there would undoubtedly not have been as much growth. At the same time, we should note that part of the investment we did have was diverted into international demand since our imports exceeded our exports through the normal balance-of-payments adjustment to this capital inflow.

1896–1914

This period covers the years of the great boom and, as such, corresponds to Caves' period of export-led growth. The basic external stimulus lay in the prospect of profitable sales of wheat from the Prairies. Population growth rates were high owing to large net immigration: output per capita increased at higher rates than at any other time; consequently aggregate real growth rates were very high in terms of the Canadian and U.S. rates shown in table 2. The emergence of the great wheat industry was explained, first, by the improvement in the country's terms of trade (column 4, table 4) and, second, by reduction in costs of delivering Prairie grain to the seaboard, facilitated by reduction in land and water transportation costs and supported by improvements in the wheat and by productivity increase in the prairie farms due to new wheat strains and the use of dry-farming techniques. These developments are reflected in the increase in net wheat and flour exports (column 3, table 4) that began in the early 1890s.

The great role played by capital formation is evident from the very high ratios of capital formation relative to GNP (column 1, table 3), reaching very high levels by 1910. A large part of this demand for capital is clear from the growth in railway mileage (column 1, table 4). Two points in connection with this rise in capital formation are worth noting. First, that although a large share of this investment was met by importing capital (column 2, table 3), levels of domestic savings were of clearly higher order than earlier (column 3, table 3). Second, it is worth noting that, with the sharp increase in the rate of growth of total GNP, due to higher capital formation levels, the ratio of exports to GNP actually fell (i.e., from levels of seventeen to nineteen percent, to thirteen to fourteen percent) during the first decade of the twentieth century. This change took place because the whole economy grew so rapidly in response to the high levels of capital formation. Exports also actually grew substantially, despite the fall in the export ratio.

1914–1926

This last period has similarities to and differences from the first period. It corresponds more closely to the neo-classical than to the export-led phase as defined by Caves, although the dynamics are quite different from the pre-1900 decades. Its features are:

1. Capital formation ratios declined sharply after 1914, although they continued to run at levels higher than during the period 1870 to 1900, except of course for the years when the Intercolonial and the Canadian Pacific railways were being built.
2. Capital imports disappeared. In fact, by the early 1920s Canada had become a net capital exporter (column 2, table 3). Domestic savings were now sufficient to meet the lower levels of capital formation. With commodity exports exceeding commodity imports, the external trade sector added aggregate demand to the Canadian economy in contrast to the years before 1900.
3. War expenditures increased the level of economic activity and exports during the wartime period. These higher export ratios, which continued on into the postwar period (column 4, table 4), were of a distinctly higher magnitude than the pre-1900 levels. The high productivity export sector had become a major factor in the determination of real income growth. A feature of this export industry permitted a realization of economies of scale for a large sector of the economy. The specialized transportation, grain handling, and marketing facilities permitted a most efficient grain delivery system. Although the period before 1900 and the years after 1914 can be characterized as ones dominated by neo-classical growth factors, the dynamics are very different and the consequences for growth are different. We can see this in the near equality in the growth of real per capita income between Canada and the United States during these years (table 2).

Structural Change

The structural change in output that accompanied this trade and growth experience is shown in table 5. It is important to observe these shifts since part of the observed

TABLE 5, PART A

Distribution of Gross Domestic Product at Factor Cost among Major Sectors, for Three-Year Periods Centred on Census Years and for 1925 and 1926 (proportions)

	Agriculture (1)	Mining (2)	Manufacturing (3)	Other (4)
1870	.371	.013	.224	.392
1880	.362	.011	.219	.408
1890	.278	.019	.253	.450
1900	.248	.050	.222	.480
1910	.216	.029	.226	.529
1920	.210	.030	.253	.507
1926	.200	.030	.211	.559

PART B

Shares of Agricultural and Manufacturing Output as a Percent of the Total of these Two Sectors (current prices)

	1870	1880	1890	1900	1910	1920	1926
(1) Agriculture	65.1	60.6	51.8	50.9	47.1	44.9	46.6
(2) Manufacturing	34.9	39.4	48.2	49.1	52.9	55.1	53.4
Total (1) + (2)	100.0	100.0	100.0	100.0	100.0	100.0	100.0

SOURCE: Urquhart, "New Estimates of Gross National Product," op. cit., table 12.

growth in productivity comes from redistribution of labour from relatively low (agricultural) productivity sectors to relatively high productivity sectors (manufacturing). In this connection, two interesting trends can be observed. First, the share of output in agriculture, after remaining relatively stable in the 1870s, dropped sharply in the 1880s and continued to decline slightly in the 1890s. Although we have no definite explanation for this sharp drop in the 1880s (wheat exports almost disappeared and were replaced largely by animal products), it is worth noting that it follows the years immediately after the introduction of higher tariff schedules introduced in 1879. The extent of the rise in manufacturing share is seen even more clearly in panel B of table 5 where agricultural and manufacturing sectors are shown separately. Second, during the extended period of the wheat boom (i.e., 1890 to 1920) the shares of agriculture and manufacturing remain relatively constant. Thus, the huge expansion in agricultural production that accompanied the opening of the West apparently was accompanied by significant growth in manufacturing activity. Agriculture, therefore, did *not* expand at the expense of manufacturing output. Canada, it seems, witnessed a long period of balanced economic growth. This is an important finding and one that deserves more detailed investigation than can be given in this paper.

The re-allocation of output (and labour) between agriculture and manufacturing over the whole period also points to the particular characteristics of sectoral development in an open economy. Since agricultural demand is virtually perfectly price elastic under such conditions, growth in income was not met by declining prices, as under a closed economy case where farm producers must face a price and income elasticity of demand of less than one. Furthermore, in our case, the terms of trade shifted in favour of resource producers, especially after 1915. This shift slowed the drop in agriculture's share in total output. In fact, in the early 1920s its share actually *rose* relative to manufacturing, (see table 5, panel B).

Conclusions

What do these new estimates of output tell us about the course of Canadian economic development between 1870 and 1926? First, a major break in relative growth rates between Canada and the United States occurred between the late nineteenth and early twentieth centuries. Second, this shift was accompanied by a massive investment boom that was apparently triggered by the possibilities of permanent settlement on the Prairies. The latter became evident in the 1890s as it was found that wheat from Manitoba could be successfully grown and sold on world markets. Third, this discovery was accompanied by a strong shift in the terms of trade towards agriculture and a substantial reduction in transportation and handling costs. Fourth, the subsequent expansion of agricultural production was accompanied by an equal expansion in the level of manufacturing activity (i.e., the country experienced a long period of balanced economic growth). Fifth, it was during the period of the First World War and after that international markets rose to great importance in the course of Canadian development. By that time, commodity exports per dollar of gross national product had climbed to between twenty-five and thirty percent.

It seems to us that the evidence gives strong support to the vent-for-surplus interpretation of the staple hypothesis. The absence of a strong export thrust in the late nineteenth century did not stop productivity growth, although it meant that real growth was less than that observed in the United States during this period. Finally, the acceleration in growth that came after 1900 seems to us to be strongly attached to the period of resource expansion that accompanied western settlement.

Notes

1. *Long-Term Factors in American Economic Growth*, vol. 51 (forthcoming).

2. The genesis of the project lay in the dissatisfaction of the authors with the information available for a course on Canadian development, viewed in an international setting, that they taught at Queen's University and, more specifically, for a paper, "Factor and Commodity Flows in the International Economy, 1870 to 1914: A Multi-Country View" published in the *Journal of Economic History* (March 1976): 217–52. On the basis of this dissatisfaction the venture was launched.

3. *Canadian Journal of Economics* (1979), 299.

4. Actually agriculture for P.E.I. is included in the 1870 estimates of gross national product, but *only* agriculture. The omissions are really quite small.

5. Simon Kuznets, *Six Lectures on Economic Growth* (Free Press, 1959), 117 ff.

6. O.J. Firestone, *Canada's Economic Development, 1867–1956* (London: Bowes and Bowes, 1958).

7. E.J. Chambers and D.F. Gordon, "Primary Products and Economic Growth: An Empirical Measurement," *Journal of Political Economy* 74 (Aug. 1965): 315–32, and reprinted in this volume.

8. The following are the responses to the Chambers and Gordon article: J. Dales, J. McManus, and M. Watkins, "Primary Products Growth: A Comment," *Journal of Political Economy* 75 (Dec. 1967): 876–80; R. Caves, "Export-Led Growth and the New Economic History," in *Trade, Balance of Payments and Growth*, edited by Bhagwati, Jones, Mundell, and Vanek (Amsterdam, North Holland, 1971), 403–42; Gordon Bertram, "The Relevance of the Wheat Boom in Canadian Economic Growth," *Canadian Journal of Economics* 6 (Nov. 1973): 545–56 and reprinted in this volume, and Frank Lewis, "The Canadian Wheat Boom and Per Capita Income: New Estimates," *Journal of Political Economy* 83 (Dec. 1975): 1249–57.

9. Richard E. Caves, " 'Vent for Surplus' Models of Trade and Growth," in Robert E. Baldwin et al., *Trade, Growth and the Balance of Payments: Essays in Honour of Gottfried Haberler* (Chicago: Rand McNally, 1965).

10. Ibid., 102.

SECTION 4

THE SIGNIFICANCE OF THE WHEAT BOOM

PRIMARY PRODUCTS AND ECONOMIC GROWTH: AN EMPIRICAL MEASUREMENT†

EDWARD J. CHAMBERS AND DONALD F. GORDON

One of the major issues in development economics is whether dependence on the export of one or a few primary products — a characteristic of less developed economies — tends to promote or retard the economic development of these countries.[1] It is alleged on the one hand that through various multipliers, linkages, demonstration, and leakage effects, such primary-product exports act positively; and it is argued, on the contrary, that through instabilities associated with fluctuations in primary-product prices and because, perhaps, of some inherent inferiority allegedly associated with primary production, concentration on such production retards development. The predominant attitude in the less developed countries, judging by the economic policies they pursue, is one of distrust of dependence on primary production. This skeptical view is supported by reference to such examples as rice in the case of Burma and tin in the case of Bolivia. On the other hand, a number of economists have stressed the importance of primary-product exports such as wool in the case of Australia, beef in the case of Argentina, cotton and grain in the case of the United States, and wheat in the case of Canada, in stimulating rapid general economic growth in the countries concerned during critical periods of their histories.

Canadian economists and economic historians, in particular, have long held that their country's experience is strong evidence of the positive effects of "staple" exports — as primary-product exports have been termed in the Canadian context — on economic development. While it is true that the staple theory of Canadian development is somewhat ambiguous, inasmuch as earlier Canadian writers on the staple theory did not distinguish mere population growth regardless of per capita income changes from growth in the sense of increases in per capita income, it is reasonable to think that they believed that successful staple exports

†The Journal of Political Economy LXXIV, 4 (Aug. 1966): 315–32. The authors wish to express their thanks for financial support received from a grant by the Ford Foundation to the Institute for Economic Research at the University of Washington. Earlier versions of this paper were discussed at conferences on quantitative research in economic history at Purdue University and the University of Toronto. We are indebted to the participants at those conferences and to our colleagues at the University of Washington for many helpful comments. Harry G. Johnson contributed improvements in presentation and clarity.

were crucial to growth in both senses.[2] More recently some writers have explicitly mentioned the effects of staples on per capita income.[3]

Despite the popularity of the staple theory in Canada, and the importance of the Canadian case in the debate over the effects of primary production for export on the presently less developed countries, there has been, so far as we are aware, no serious attempt to quantify the contribution of staple exports to Canadian economic growth. In this paper we set up a model indicating a possible method of measuring the effects of staple production upon per capita income, and apply that model to make the indicated measurements for a classic staple period, that of the wheat boom on the Canadian prairies between 1901 and 1911.[4] Our finding is that, even under the most generous interpretation of "wheat boom" and the most favorable assumptions about the magnitude of its effect, that effect could have amounted to no more than 8.40 percent of the total increase in per capita income during the period; under a less favorable, but more reasonable, set of assumptions the effect was only some 5.20 percent of the rise in per capita income.

If our findings are even reasonably correct, they have two important implications for development economics. In the first place the findings suggest that policymakers for presently underdeveloped countries have no good reason from this case to expect much in the way of rising per capita income from an expansion of primary-product production of the order of magnitude in this Canadian example. In the Canadian case the expansion in one industry alone amounted in a decade to over a fifth of the GNP at the beginning. This yielded under our "reasonable" assumptions an increase of per capita income of less than 1.5 percent of the original figure. In the second place they suggest that the wide apparent divergences among various countries in the effects of primary exports upon per capita income, on which the debate referred to above is based, may be illusory, and that in those cases where per capita incomes rose appreciably, the explanation may lie elsewhere than in exports — despite their concurrent expansion.

The Simplest Model

Although the period 1901–11 in Canada is referred to as one of wheat export boom, we measure the contribution to the growth in per capita income of the increase in *all* prairie agricultural *output*. First, despite the fact that the export market was by far the most important, there is, of course, no magic that assigns a greater social significance to a dollar's increase in exports than to a dollar's increase in domestic output. Second, wheat was produced in substitution with other field crops and livestock and the net effect of the "wheat boom" is therefore more reliably measured by its effect on total output than on wheat output alone. Third, only about two-fifths of the gross proceeds from farm production on the prairies in 1911 was accounted for by all wheat production, and it is impossible to separate the contribution of wheat from that of other farm production without introducing quite arbitrary assumptions in the allocation of costs.

To measure the effect of the wheat boom we must pose a counter-factual alternative. Let us imagine, for example, what would have happened if all the land that was brought under cultivation between 1901 and 1911 had been impenetrable rock. The labor and capital that developed the prairies would have been somewhere else. If they had been in Canada they presumably would have been working in other industries. Their physical and value productivities would depend upon the production and demand functions in those industries. And if their value productivities had been less, they would have demanded a smaller quantity of goods and services from other industries or from abroad. Moreover, whether these factors of production would have been located in Canada at all, or located in some other countries, could only be determined by reference to knowledge of the supply functions of these factors to Canada. Little can be said about the effects of staples without at least a crude general equilibrium model and without implying something about the nature of the relevant functions. In this paper we use such models, albeit very crude ones. Nevertheless, we believe they enable us to arrive at rough estimates of the effects of the wheat boom which, though not precise, still give a more accurate picture than is suggested in traditional writings.[5]

Consider the simplest model of the results of a boom in staple production. Let the Canadian economy circa 1900 be represented by two competitive industries: a "wheat" industry which is a staple export; and a domestic manufacturing industry producing, say, gadgets. The two production functions are:

$$w = w(L_w), \tag{1}$$
$$g = g(L_g), \tag{2}$$

where w, g, L_w, and L_g are wheat, gadgets, and labor in wheat and gadgets, respectively. For the moment we will abstract from capital and other factors.

We will suppose that the prices of both products, p_w and p_g, are exogenously determined, $p_w = \bar{p}_w$, the world price of wheat, and $p_g = \bar{p}_g$, the world price of gadgets plus transportation cost and the Canadian tariff.[6] For both products Canada is presumed to supply too little to affect the world price. The maximizing conditions in the two industries will be

$$p_L = \bar{p}_w w'(L_w), \tag{3}$$
$$p_L = \bar{p}_g g'(L_g), \tag{4}$$

where $w'(L_w)$ and $g'(L_g)$ are marginal physical products.

The supply conditions in the labor market will be

$$L = f(p_L), \tag{5}$$
$$L = L_g + L_w, \tag{6}$$

where p_L is the wage and L is the total supply of labor. Thus our model consists of the four equations $(3) - (6)$ which determine the equilibrium values of the four variables p_L, L, L_w and L_g.

The slope of the marginal physical product in wheat, w'', will be considered negative, indicating diminishing returns to the factor land, unspecified in equation (1). Since only a small fraction of the ultimately settled acreage was under cultivation in 1901, one might well ask: Why would diminishing returns prevail?

Following Ricardo we can envisage a wide and continuous variation in quality of all prairie land. With the technology in use in 1900 only a limited upper range would be settled, and within this range the variation in quality would account for diminishing marginal physical productivity.[7] On the other hand $g(L_g)$ will be considered to specify fully the gadget production function, that is, there is no (or a negligible amount of) land or any other scarce factor required; $g(L_g)$ will be linear and homogeneous, and g' equals average product, a constant.[8]

Now let technological change (Red Fife Wheat, the chilled steel plow, etc.) shift the production function for wheat such that marginal physical product rises by a constant amount for each quantity of labor. The resulting equilibrium in the labor market is simple enough to be illustrated diagrammatically in figure 1. Figure 1a depicts the supply curve of labor, S (or $f^{-1}(L)$). By adopting the convention of measuring wheat and gadgets in units such that each has a price of unity, the ordinates in figure 1b and 1c measure simultaneously goods and money. In figure 1b, d_w is the original marginal product of labor in wheat in both physical and value terms, and in figure 1c, s_g is the original supply of labor to gadgets. This supply curve is the horizontal distance for each possible wage level between the total supply of labor in 1a and the demand for labor ($=$ the value of the marginal physical product) in the wheat industry.

The demand curve for labor in gadgets (the value of the marginal product) is infinitely elastic at OM in the original equilibrium. This follows from the infinite elasticity of gadget demand ($p_g = \bar{p}_g$) and the constant marginal product (see eq. (4)).

When technological changes shift the demand for labor in the wheat industry from d_w to d'_w, the supply curve of labor in the gadget industry moves an equal horizontal distance, from s_g to s_g'. Labor transfers from gadgets to wheat ($PJ = XT$), new settlement occurs, and cultivation is extended until rent at the margin is again zero. However, there is no increased supply of labor to the country or increase in real or money wages, so long as any labor remains in the gadget industry at wage OM. The increase in total income is the increased rent of wheat land, $ABCD$, and presuming population and labor force are equal, the increase in per capita income is $ABCD/Y$.

But history does not perform controlled experiments. During the period in which we wish to measure the effects of the wheat boom other exogenous parameters were also shifting. Suppose, for example, there was an independent increase in productivity in the manufacture of gadgets which raised the constant value of marginal product in that industry from OM to ON. In that case the new equilibrium wage would rise by a similar amount. Rent in the wheat industry would amount to AHF in 1911 rather than ARD and the increase in rent would now be AHF-BRC rather than $ABCD$ as before. But if we are interested in isolating the effects of the wheat boom, we should not measure the increase in rent from 1901 to 1911 but rather the difference between the rent as it was in 1911 and as it would have been in 1911 had the wheat boom not occurred. If there was no wheat expansion, rent would have been *reduced* in the wheat industry to BHE by reason of the higher wages. Thus a true estimate of the increase in income due to the wheat boom can be found by subtracting from actual rent of land in 1911, not the observed rent in 1901, but a hypothetical 1911 rent. This latter is the observed

FIGURE 1

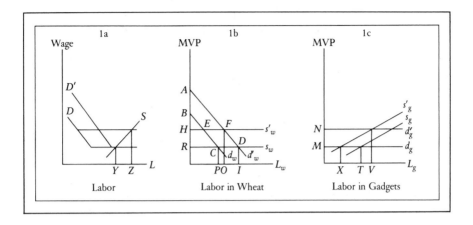

rent of 1901 (*BRC*) adjusted to allow for the higher wage level of 1911, that is, adjusted to *BHE*. Subtracting BHE from the actual 1911 rent, *AHF*, leaves the area *ABEF* as the increase in income due to the wheat boom.

Under the above assumptions the population would increase by *YZ* (= *PQ* + *TV*). But this growth is due solely to the autonomous shift in productivity in the gadget industry which, given the world price of the two commodities, establishes the real wage for the whole economy. The population would have been at *Z* in 1911 whether or not the wheat boom had occurred. Thus the increase in per capita income due to the wheat boom is *ABEF*/*Z*. (However, we later introduce changes in the model to allow for institutional forces that permit population growth to depend upon the agricultural expansion.)

We have estimated the area *ABEF* for the period 1901–11 at $40.4 million. The censuses for 1901 and 1911 list by province the average rental paid per acre on all farms under lease.[9] Leased acreage amounted to 11 percent and to 8 percent of total occupied acreage for the years 1911 and 1901, respectively, and we assumed these rents to be representative for their respective provinces. We thus multiplied these average rents by the total acreage in each province and summed over all three prairie provinces for each year. This resulted in total rent figures of $9.2 million for 1901 (*BRC* in figure 1b) and $45.8 million for 1911 (*AHF*). We made the adjustment to the 1901 rent (*HRCE* in figure 1b) by assuming (1) that wage costs were the same proportion of total farm output in 1901 as they were in 1911 (46 percent) and (2) that wage rates increased 2 percent per year in agriculture over the decade, as they did in the economy as a whole. This reduces the observed 1901 rent of $9.2 million to the hypothetical 1911 rent of $5.4 million which, subtracted from the actual 1911 rent of $45.8 million, leaves $40.4 million as the estimate of *ABEF*.[10]

This figure is 1.94 percent of national income for 1911.[11] Using this model, therefore, we conclude that in the absence of the "wheat boom" over the previous decade, per capita income would have been in 1911 some $5.61 below its actual figure of $288.75. Since per capita output grew at the rate of 2.1 percent per annum over the period 1901–11 or 23 percent for the decade, our figure is just under one-twelfth or 8.40 percent of the total growth. This contrasts sharply with the conclusions of Canadian staple theorists insofar as they argue that staples are responsible for rising per capita income. If our results are roughly accurate, the importance of staple expansion to the growth in per capita income must be questioned, and the contrast apparent to policy-makers in underdeveloped areas between successful and unsuccessful export economies may be a false one. "Successful" export economies may be successful, as was Canada, for reasons independent of their primary-product export expansion. It is of considerable interest, therefore, to inquire if any peculiarity of this highly simplified model accounts for these results.

The More Complicated Model

Capital

So far we have abstracted from capital (and other factors). The introduction of capital in the most general way complicates the model considerably by requiring a supply curve of capital and a consideration of elasticities of substitution of labor for capital in both industries and for land in wheat production. The number of equations becomes larger and the results more complicated, although not essentially different.

However, in a plausible special case the results can be seen intuitively. Since capital is highly mobile and Canada a relatively small country in the world economy, it seems reasonable to assume that the supply of capital to Canada is perfectly elastic. In this case the demand for labor in gadgets is still perfectly elastic. This follows from the fixed prices of the co-operating factor and the final product, and the constancy of returns to scale. So long as the demand curve for labor in gadgets is perfectly elastic, the effects of the wheat boom will merely be to transfer labor without any rise in wages or population, and the effects upon national income can be measured by $ABEF$ as before.

The same results would follow if we expand our model to include any other factors, such as fuel or raw materials, used by either industry, provided these factors are available to the two industries (from Canada or from abroad) at fixed world prices, or at prices fixed by the world market plus transportation and/or tariff.[12]

Other Industries

We now wish to consider whether the introduction of industries with different demand and production conditions into our simple two-industry model would affect the accuracy of our measure of the gain in per capita income attributed to the wheat boom. In the following we will imagine that the only shift in productivity occurs in the wheat industry; that is, the wage level in gadgets remains at OM and the gain is measured by $ABCD$. First let us suppose that we have a third industry which is wholly domestic. It is characterized by constant returns to its one factor, labor, and is protected from foreign competition by prohibitive tariffs and/or transport charges. Let it be "haircuts." In these circumstances the additional rental income will produce an increased demand for haircuts. The price of haircuts and wages in the industry will tend to rise. But this tendency will be prevented by a transfer of labor from the gadget industry, where the demand for labor is completely elastic. Thus so long as any labor is left in the gadget industry in the new equilibrium, wages will not rise in the economy as a whole, and population will therefore not expand. The contribution to aggregate and per capita income of the expansion of staples will be measured by the increased rent in wheat.

Next suppose we have a fourth industry (cheese), domestic or export, which experiences diminishing returns from the application of labor to "land." Like wheat and gadgets it has a world price which Canadian demand and supply cannot affect, but unlike wheat it experiences no shift in its production function. Given the constant real wage in the economy, there will be therefore no change in output or earnings in this industry. Our previous measures of the effect of the wheat boom will remain valid in this, now four-industry, model.

Our more complicated model can be illustrated in figure 2, where the supply of labor to the country and the demands and supplies for labor in each of our four industries are shown. Because of the shift in the production function for wheat, employment of labor expands in wheat and haircuts, contracts by an equal amount in gadgets and remains constant in cheese. Since wages remain constant, area I = II + III. Money income expands by the increased rent IV, and since all prices are constant, measured real income expands proportionately. The area above the demand curve for labor in haircuts is not income since, unlike the similar areas in wheat and cheese, there is no co-operating factor that receives income in this industry. Area V therefore is not an increase in money or in real income. In this expanded model, productivity in gadgets and fixed world prices no longer determine both money and real wages, but only the former. Real wages can also be affected by the prices of the domestic goods which can move independently of world prices through productivity improvements.[13]

Population Effects

For one basic reason the conclusion so far reached — that the expansion of prairie agriculture contributed only 8.40 percent to the total growth in per capita income — unquestionably exaggerates the effects of the staple. This is because the model produces no growth in population due to the wheat boom, and this in turn is due, among other things, to the assumption that population only migrates for wages. No part of the increase in rent would go to new immigrants, but would be captured in its entirety by individuals previously resident in Canada.

Suppose, however, that homestead legislation disposes of the newly valuable lands, not at the market price, which would be the expected long-run capital value, but at a reduced price; and simultaneously restricts the participation in this expected windfall to those who migrate to the region. Migrants may come from both Canada and abroad. Consider a unit of labor in, say, the United States, to

FIGURE 2

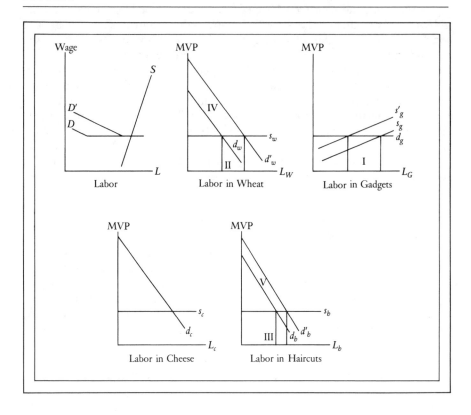

the right, in figure 1a, of the intersection of the supply function *S*, with the real wage. He would not ordinarily migrate. But he may perceive that the sum of his wages plus rents will be greater on the prairies than his supply price of labor alone at home. To the extent that foreign immigrants take up the homestead land before Canadians, the effective supply curve will have shifted to the right. (The additional labor in the country will not lower the real wage which is set independently, as demonstrated above.)

We have roughly estimated the number of people who might be supposed to have migrated for this reason at 200,000. Our procedure is (1) to estimate the total increase in numbers on newly settled farms at 370,000;[14] (2) to subtract one-third for those who come from Canada itself;[15] (3) to subtract another 10 percent for those who, having once acquired clear title to homestead, are in a position to enjoy its future income stream by sale (or lease) and return to their previously higher wage in, say, the United States;[16] and (4) to subtract a further 10 percent for those who, considering the huge migrant wave leaving Europe for North and South America and Oceania during this decade, would perhaps have migrated without the opportunity to capture any rent. This latter represents an exogenous shift in the supply curve *S* in figures 1 and 2.

If we now suppose (1) that the labor force participation rate of this 200,000 is the same as that existing in the prairie population as a whole (41.4 percent), and (2) that their wage earnings are equivalent to the estimated average annual earnings in Canadian manufacturing of males sixteen and over ($504 in 1911),[17] then the increased population would contribute some $42 million to the income stream in the form of wages, quite apart from the increased rent of $40.4 million already calculated. The addition of $82,400,000 income and 200,000 population to a country which in their absence totaled 7,007,000 population and $1,999 million in income, increases per capita output by 1.20 percent as compared with our original estimate of 1.94 percent. Its contribution to the decade's growth would be 5.20 instead of 8.40 percent.[18] The fundamental reason for these results is that in the revised model the additional population has no effect upon the real wage, while the same increase in rental income is distributed over a larger number of people.

A Note on Gadgets

A peculiarity of the above models which makes the area *ABEF* in figure 1 a "true" measure of the change in income attributable to the change in staple production is the existence of a gadget industry with a completely elastic demand curve for labor. This elastic demand curve for labor is a consequence of (1) the fact that the price of gadgets is fixed in world markets, (2) that the supply of other inputs is perfectly elastic to the industry (that is, there are no external pecuniary economies or diseconomies in the purchase of these inputs), and (3) that its production function is linear and homogeneous which implies no external technological economies or diseconomies.[19]

To fulfil the first condition in the Canadian case, the gadget industry will normally be producing for the domestic market subject to substantial foreign competition.[20] Appendix C contains a set of industries meeting this latter condition. It was constructed by reconciling industry classifications from the 1911 Census of Manufactures with commodity classifications from the foreign trade returns for the 1910–11 fiscal year. According to the census, wage and salary employment in Canada for these industries exceeded 125,000 in 1911, or 23 percent of the labor force in manufacturing.

With respect to our second condition, the supply of non-labor inputs to gadgets would not be perfectly elastic (1) if gadgets used a significant portion of a particular type of (scarce) land in Canada, or (2) if an intermediate product to gadgets uses a significant portion of a particular type of land in Canada, and if the price of the intermediate product is not fixed in world markets. While we cannot test the proposition that all inputs other than labor were available at a fixed price to our set of gadget industries, it is possible to speculate about the existence of a subset of industries from those in appendix C. Take cotton textiles as an example. Raw material and capital must be obtained at the world price leaving labor as an input with domestic origin. In the case of woolen textiles, while some producers used wool grown in Canada, the supply to the industry must have been close to perfectly elastic. Or, take the very large iron and steel products group (including foundries) in which we may plausibly say that the supply of iron ore, coal, and other material inputs approached perfect elasticity. We believe ourselves justified in concluding that within the set of industries found in appendix C there exists a subset whose input prices, apart from labor, were fixed and which account for well over half the total employment in the group.

This brings us to our third condition, the existence of external technological economies or diseconomies. Since so many of the ablest economists have labored so long to produce so little in the way of satisfactory concrete examples of these phenomena, it seems safe to conclude that such economies or diseconomies would not sensibly affect even a small fraction of the industries meeting our first two criteria.[21] Strictly all that we require for our argument is that some of them escape these influences. (It should also be noted that so far as external economies, either pecuniary or technological, are concerned, their existence is incompatible with equilibrium and a perfectly elastic demand curve for the industry.)

Some Qualifications

Like all theoretical models, what we have presented represents a gross simplification of reality. We wish now to consider briefly some possibly significant qualifications.

Gross Domestic Versus Gross National Product

One qualification to the model turns on the difference between national and domestic product. Our model assumed that the increased rental value of prairie land accrued solely to Canadian residents, that is, to gross national as well as to gross domestic product. The possibility mentioned above, that settlers, having acquired title through homesteading, could leave and enjoy their rents (or their equivalent) from abroad, shows that this may not be so. Moreover, railway and other land company sales of non-homestead land to settlers would further diminish the increment to Canadians if rents thereby capitalized and captured accrued to some foreign equity interest in these companies. To the extent that these factors were operative, our previous estimate of the contribution of wheat to per capita income is exaggerated.

The Effect of Decreasing and Increasing Cost Industries

At least one writer has suggested that, by increasing income and population initially, exports may increase demand so that a secondary improvement in productivity results from economies of scale.[22] On the other hand it is in principle also necessary to consider diseconomies of scale resulting from increased income and population.

Consider first economies of scale. In our model all industries other than gadgets or haircuts are by hypothesis industries of diminishing physical returns. We have already considered the question of increasing returns in gadgets. It is in haircut-type industries — insulated from world markets — where economies of scale, internal or external, may operate. Suppose, to take a fairly generous estimate, the average and marginal propensities to consume haircuts are both one-half. Then total income in haircuts is approximately $1 billion in 1911 (with no wheat boom), while the increase in expenditures on haircuts from the initial increase in wheat income of $82,400,000 is approximately $42,000,000 or some 4 percent of this. Suppose, second, that we tentatively use Denison's estimate that the coefficient of economies of scale is 10 percent, i.e., a 1 percent increase in input results in a 1.1 percent increase in output.[23] In this case the increase in productivity due to the transfer of factors from the gadget industry to the decreasing-cost haircut industry is about 0.4 percent in haircuts, and for the economy as a whole about 0.2 percent. This is spread over 10 years. It is fairly clear that an estimate rather than the above hypothetical arithmetic would be unlikely to change the order of magnitude of this result, and we shall therefore ignore it.[24]

Moreover the existence of increasing-cost haircut-type industries will work in the opposite direction. This will be the case if one such industry (say, lumber) uses a specific factor of production. When demand increases, the price of lumber and rents to landlords in lumber will both rise. The increase in rents to landlords represents only a transfer of income on the previous level of output from consumers to the producers of lumber. However, since the increment of output is obtained only at higher real cost, the increase in the price paid by consumers is not entirely offset by larger landowner income.[25]

The Method of Comparative Statics

Like so many attempts to measure economic forces we have employed the method of comparative statics, which presumes that we are observing points of equilibrium. In taking 1901 as the beginning of our period we may have a happy coincidence of empirical data and a reasonable approximation to an equilibrium. A question may be raised by some concerning the choice of 1911 as a terminal date for a comparative static analysis. Thus the shift in labor required by the parametric shift in the wheat industry may not have been approximated by 1911. If this were the case, the wage level in western agriculture would be abnormally high due to the short-run scarcity of labor. It would follow that rents would be abnormally low, and the true gain to the economy would be properly measured not by land rents alone but by land rents plus the quasi-rent to labor.

But, in fact, there is no convincing evidence that wages were abnormally high on the prairies. Annual farm wages in Saskatchewan, for example, were $402.50 in 1910, while the Coates Commission reports hourly wages for unskilled labor in Toronto in 1911 at a level such that a casual laborer working only 39 weeks a year (at 54 hours per week) could have earned $468 annually.[26] Considering the very real hardships of the plains winters, and the scarcity of social amenities, this suggests a depressed imputed wage due to overoptimistic expectations of yields and prices. Of course, it is also suggestive of the normal discrepancy between agricultural and urban money incomes. On balance we find no particular reason to adjust our estimate.

Sketch of an Alternative

We conclude therefore that, if the staple theory of economic growth is interpreted as explaining a rising per capita income, then it fails for a period which has been considered an example, par excellence, of its operation. A natural question arises: If not wheat, what did produce the reasonably satisfactory growth rate of the wheat era? We shall not here attempt a theoretical explanation of the differences in the wealth of nations over time and space, but we will sketch an alternative way of looking at growth in small economies.

First, whatever the original importance of natural resources, casual observation of per capita incomes the world over suggests that resource endowment has very little connection with income levels — serving to confirm our closer look at a particular Canadian period. (There are, of course, exceptions such as Kuwait.) Next, while domestic capital formation has been stressed in the literature on underdevelopment as a crucial variable, more recent empirical analyses in advanced countries have severely depreciated the quantitative importance of net capital formation as a cause of growth.[27] Moreover, for relatively small economies (that is, most of the world's economies) the supply of capital from abroad is presumably highly elastic. And the experience of certain countries such as Germany and Japan in the postwar world suggests that, if sufficiently high returns are available, domestic capital formation is fairly responsive.

If natural resources and capital are not important, then is technology a significant factor? Clearly for the world as a whole technological advance has been a necessary condition for much of whatever economic growth has taken place. But when we attempt to account for differences among countries at a point of time, technology, almost tautologically, is of little use. The state of the arts can be considered virtually identical for all countries. Barring a few fairly trivial royalty payments for patents, all countries have access to the same accumulated store of knowledge; it is the use of this technology which varies.

The causes of variation in the application of technology can perhaps be usefully classified in two categories. On the one hand, there are the potentially broad institutional, cultural, psychological, or sociological factors; on the other, there are the more narrow skills, economically productive education, or human capital. Given a certain institutional and cultural environment, the success of a small economy may be closely related to the level of technical training, encompassing all of its aspects, that permits it to use the wide spectrum of "free" technological advances occurring elsewhere. While no small country is likely to contribute a large proportion of the world's technical advances, its rate of growth, nevertheless, may vary significantly with its ability to apply them.[28] Application, in turn, may be highly dependent upon its human capital, or economically relevant education in the broadest sense, covering everything from the techniques of electron microscopy to the layout of supermarkets. We therefore tentatively suggest (with Schultz[29] and others) that these may be the fundamental forces that have produced economic growth in Canada and other "successful" economies, and that they can be more confidently expected to produce growth in presently underdeveloped societies. One elementary point should be kept in mind. In the absence of peculiar changes in production functions, ordinary theory would predict that economic growth would produce export booms; but an observed *ex post* correlation does not necessarily imply that exports were the causal factor.

Concluding Summary

As a conclusion let us summarize the argument:

1. We have constructed a model in which the increase in income to the economy by the expansion in primary-product exports can be measured by the rents paid to specialized natural resources critical for those exports.

2. We have argued that this model is applicable to the Canadian economy in the first decade of this century when per capita real income rose by 23 percent.

3. On the basis of this model we have calculated that the spectacular expansion of all prairie agriculture contributed at the most only 8.40 percent and, more realistically, 5.20 percent of this increase. Put otherwise, per capita income was at the most 1.94 percent and, more plausibly, 1.20 percent higher at the end of the decade than it would otherwise have been.

4. These conclusions are not substantially altered in one direction or another either by reasonable qualifications to the model or by possible erorrs in the data.

5. We suggest that, when successful exporting economies simultaneously experience a rise in per capita income, most of the latter may, as in the instance we have measured, be attributable to other factors.

On the other hand, to avoid a possible misunderstanding, we would emphasize certain things that we have not said. We have said nothing about the theory of international trade and in particular about the proposition that free trade will "normally" raise per capita income subject to the well-known theoretical qualifications. There is nothing in this paper that would constitute a new argument for protection. And further, we have not said anything about the contribution of international trade in general to per capita income, which for a small economy might be very great. Rather we have measured the contribution to per capita income of an export-oriented primary-product sector whose expansion amounted to one-fifth of the initial GNP. In its absence an alternative use of resources would have occurred and other exports would have been available.

Appendix A

Some Sources of Bias in the Estimate of the Increased Income

Despite the fact that our calculations suggest that only 5.20 percent of the increase in per capita income over the decade was attributable to the changes in prairie agriculture, there are various detailed reasons for supposing that this is in fact an overestimate:

1. We ignored as insignificant the portion of the rent per acre figure that represents the use of buildings on rented land, even though the buildings represented some 12.5 percent of the total value of both and despite the fact that yearly payments

for buildings should be a larger proportion of these assets as their payments represent depreciation as well as net earnings.

2. We have assumed the same level of market prices for agricultural products in 1911 as in 1901, which overestimates the contribution of the wheat boom. Actually hypothetical 1911 rents on 1901 acreage would have been higher and therefore the true gain was less than our estimates, because (1) the price of wheat rose in this period, and (2) presumably it would have risen more had the increase in Canadian wheat production (in 1911 some 5 percent of world output) not occurred. Similar corrections would have to be carried out on other agricultural products.

3. In applying rent per acre figures from an 11 percent sample (1911) to all occupied land, there is some reason to believe that we are overstating imputed rents. Britnell[30] thinks that for 1911–21 the tenancy rate was highest on the choicest land of well-established districts.

4. By 1911 some evidence on the "permanent" yield in the sense of the long-run average yield per acre was available, so that year-to-year changes in rent per acre would presumably be a function of expected crop prices. If rental agreements for 1911–12 were negotiated on the basis of projection of prices of the recent crop years as typical, the estimated rent figure will have an upward bias. The average farm price of wheat in the prairie provinces declined from $0.79, $0.82, and $0.78, respectively, in the 1908–9, 1909–10, and 1910–11 crop years to $0.61 in 1911–12. The price did not rise above $0.65 until the 1914–15 crop year.

5. In moving from the observed 1901 rent to the hypothetical 1911 rent by allowing for exogenous wage increases, we have assumed no substitution of other factors for labor. This exaggerates the increases in costs, hence minimizes the hypothetical 1911 rent, and in turn overestimates the difference between the actual and hypothetical 1911 rents.

Appendix B

Some readers may prefer a slightly more formal presentation of the argument that in our model the expansion of the wheat industry does not raise the wage of labor, even where production functions are presumed to use capital and/or other factors. Clearly it will not raise the wage if the demand for labor in the gadget industry is perfectly elastic, and the gadget industry is still in existence after the expanion.

To show that the demand for labor in gadgets is perfectly elastic, consider an expanded linear and homogeneous production function for gadgets, $G(L,K)$. If, as our model presumes, the price of gadgets and the price of capital are fixed in world markets, $\bar{p}_g$ and $\bar{p}_K$, the demand and supply conditions for labor in the gadget industry can be represented by

$$\bar{p}_K = \bar{p}_g G_K(L_g, K_g),$$
$$\bar{p}_L = \bar{p}_g G_L(L_g, K_g),$$
$$L_g = \phi(\bar{p}_L) + a.$$

The first two equations are the familiar marginal productivity conditions while the third is the supply of labor, derived from the total supply of labor, $f(p_L)$, minus the demand for labor in the wheat industry. Here a is a shift parameter. Differentiating all equations with respect to a, solving for $\delta p_L/\delta a$, and using the fact that the Hessian vanishes, yields $dp_L/da = 0$, that is, a shift in the supply curve of labor produces no changes in its price, or alternatively, the demand is perfectly elastic. An exactly parallel argument can be developed if we use a more general but still linear and homogeneous production function $G(K_1 \ldots K_n, L)$ where $K_2 \ldots K_n$ are all inputs, other than capital and labor, available at a fixed price.

Appendix C

"Gadget"-Type Industries: Gross Value of Domestic Production and Value of Imports Entered for Consumption, 1910

Decennial Census Classification of Industry	No. of Salary and Wage Employees	GVP 1911 Census of Mfg. ($000)[a]	Values Entered[b] for Consumption ($000)	Product Description of Imported Articles
Liquors, malt	3,062	12,648	695	Ale, beer, and porter
Boots and shoes	17,227	33,987	2,095	Boots and shoes of leather
Brooms and brushes	937	1,732	483	Brooms and brushes
Buttons	457	407	638	Buttons
Carpets	1,070	1,972	1,722	Wool manufactures — carpets (including $101,000 in non-wool mats)
Mats and rugs	88	113	530	Mats and rugs (30 sq. ft. or less) of wool
Carriages and wagons	5,523	11,767	1,338	Carriages, ex. automobiles and parts
Bicycles	53	72	147	Bicycles and tricycles
Cement, Portland	2,150	5,683	494	Portland cement
Combs	175	187	218	Combs
Cordage, rope, and twine	1,055	3,624	5,529	Cordage and twine and manufactures of
Corsets and supplies	1,138	1,572	416	Corsets and supplies
Cottons, textiles, dyeing and finishing	13,136	24,901	14,388	Imports of cotton manufactures ex. raw cotton, yarn and thread, socks and stockings, bags, shirts, clothing nop, blouses, lace, shawls
Thread	456	1,096	1,947	Yarn and thread of cotton
Woolen yarn	329	792	3,826	Woolen yarns
Hosiery and knit goods, woolen goods	12,876	19,133	18,278	Stockings, cotton and wool; blankets; cassimeres; cloths and doeskins; coatings and overcoatings; tweeds; felt cloth nop; flannels, plain; knitted goods, nop; shawls; bed comforters; wool fabrics; all fabrics composed wholly or partly of wool nop

"Gadget"-Type Industries: Gross Value of Domestic Production and Value of Imports Entered for Consumption, 1910

Decennial Census Classification of Industry	No. of Salary and Wage Employees	GVP 1911 Census of Mfg. ($000)[a]	Values Entered[b] for Consumption ($000)	Product Description of Imported Articles
Automobiles	2,438	6,252	4,757	Automobiles and motor vehicles of all kinds and parts thereof
Paints and varnishes	1,198	8,041	1,756	Total paints and colors, and varnishes
Electrical apparatus and supplies	6,345	15,022	5,130	Total electrical apparatus
Fertilizers	227	644	422	Fertilizers compounded or manufactured
Glass incl. mirrors and plate	2,586	3,167	3,447	Glass ex. ornamental glass
Gloves and mittens	1,651	2,995	2,099	Gloves and mitts of all kinds
Glue	264	585	263	Glue, glue stock and mucilage
Explosives	482	2,168	1,217	Total gunpowder and explosives
Rubber and elastic goods	1,315	5,849	2,210	Total gutta-percha and India rubber ex. raw and scrap rubber imports
Hairwork	297	487	238	Manufactures of hair
Hats, caps, and furs	4,639	11,155	3,509	Total hats, caps, and bonnets ex. manufacturers' suppliers
Liquors, distilled	844	12,064	3,396	Total spirits
Liquors, vinous	86	363	1,142	Total wines, sparkling and non-sparkling
Agricultural implements	9,560	20,723	4,516	Total agricultural implements
Boilers and engines	5,864	11,874	1,423	Engines including boilers
Cream separators	252	640	784	Cream separators
Brass castings	1,300	3,093	1,923	Total brass and manufactures of, ex. brass bars and scrap brass
Saws	486	879	113	Saws
Scales	260	506	113	Scales
Safes and vaults	449	460	194	Safes and vaults
Sewing machines	769	974	504	Sewing machines and parts and attachments
Umbrellas	256	610	117	Umbrellas, parasols, etc.
Shoddy	185	785	330	Shoddy
Soap	917	5,221	882	Soap
Wire and wire fencing	1,560	5,491	3,767	Wire and fencing
Foundry and machine shop products	26,835	45,611	26,606	Iron and steel pipe, chains, fittings for iron pipe, machinery, ex. sewing machines, stoves

APPENDIX C (continued)

"Gadget"-Type Industries: Gross Value of Domestic Production and Value of Imports Entered for Consumption, 1910

Decennial Census Classification of Industry	No. of Salary and Wage Employees	GVP 1911 Census of Mfg. ($000)[a]	Values Entered[b] for Consumption ($000)	Product Description of Imported Articles
Iron and steel products	11,286	34,614	40,679	Bar iron or rolled steel nop, forgings, frogs and railway switches, hoops, billets, ingots, nuts and bolts, rolling mill products, nails, railway brass, screws, skates, bearings, sheet steel, tubing, ware, miscellaneous steel manufactures
Drugs including chemicals	1,336	3,634	12,178	Drugs, dyes, and chemicals

a. 1911–1912 *Sessional Paper*, No. 10a.
b. 1911 *Census of manufactures*.

Notes

1. Cf. R.E. Baldwin, "Patterns of Development in Newly Settled Regions," *Manchester School of Economic and Social Studies* (May 1956): 161–79; Baldwin, "Export Technology and Development from a Subsistence Level," *Economic Journal* (Mar. 1963): 80–92; R.E. Caves and R.H. Holton, *The Canadian Economy* (Cambridge, Mass., 1959), 41–47 and chap. IV; Dudley Seers, "An Approach to the Short-Period Analysis of Primary-Producing Economies," *Oxford Economic Papers* (Feb. 1959): 6–9; J.V. Levin, *The Export Economies* (Cambridge, Mass., 1960); D.C. North, *The Economic Growth of the United States, 1790–1860* (Englewood Cliffs, N.J., 1961), esp. chap. 1; B.C. Swerling, "Some Interrelationships Between Agricultural Trade and Economic Development," *Kyklos* XIV, 3 (1961): 377–79; A.K. Cairncross, *Factors in Economic Development* (London, 1962), 214–28; M.H. Watkins, "A Staple Theory of Economic Growth," *Canadian Journal of Economics and Political Science* (May 1963): 141–58.

2. Cf. W.A. Mackintosh, *The Economic Background of Dominion-Provincial Relations* (Ottawa, 1939), 102, who mentions the effects of exports on "rates of economic and population growth." Since population growth is explicitly mentioned, then presumably "economic" refers to the growth in per capita income.

3. Cf. Watkins, "Staple Theory," and Caves and Holton, *Canadian Economy*. G.W. Bertram, "Economic Growth in Canadian Industry, 1870–1915: The Staple Model and the Take-Off Hypothesis," *Canadian Journal of Economics and Political Science* (May 1963): 159–84, by linking the staple theory to general theories of economic growth, implies something about the effects of staples on per capita income.

4. The period 1900–15 is impressed upon every Canadian student as a golden age in the economic growth of Canada, inextricably linked with wheat exports from the prairies. We use the period 1901–11 because of the availability of census data for those years.

5. The confusion that can arise through a failure to pose counter factual questions is well illustrated by Caves and Holton, *Canadian Economy*, chap. 4. They develop a short-run econometric model of the Canadian economy based on annual observations and find exports to be a reliable predictor of changes in

aggregate income lagged one year. This is in accord with the widely held belief that, if an autonomous sector of aggregate demand changes, then an induced sector of aggregate demand will move in the same direction. Given the long-run allocation of resources to staple production, such a model may be a test of the short-run sensitivity of income to changes in export demand. It is not, however, a test of the staple theory of economic development for it gives no clue as to how much higher per capita income is as a result of this allocation rather than the next best alternative. Without careful interpretation, such a test will exaggerate the economy's dependence on a single export for its real income.

6. To avoid complications introduced by exchange rates, gold flows, and the like, we can imagine a universal world paper currency.

7. Of course on the intramarginal land diminishing marginal productivity would also obtain.

8. We find it convenient to follow the convention that all production functions are linear and homogeneous if all factors are specified and all are divisible. When in fact a production function exhibits increasing or decreasing returns, it will be because of some indivisibility or because some factor is not included. This is a matter of classification only; the empirical substance is discussed later.

Here and elsewhere we are assuming that entrepreneurship, not specific to any industry, comes with each laborer in fixed proportions, so that it may be ignored in the analysis. Each laborer may be considered to be his own entrepreneur, or more plausbily, for every n laborers there is one entrepreneur. It is not necessary that the entrepreneurs be of uniform quality, but if not, then the number in existence of the highest quality, though not the number in use, must be large enough to reduce their return as entrepreneurs to zero. See M. Friedman, *Price Theory* (Chicago, 1962), 140.

9. Cf. *1911 Census* IV, lviii, xiv, and 422, "Instructions Relating to Schedule No. 7."

10. Further details of this calculation are given in appendix A together with sources of potential bias.

11. Our estimate of current-dollar national income for 1911, of $2,081 million is obtained by (1) calculating 1910 national income in current dollars by subtracting indirect taxes and capital consumption allowances from Firestone's adjusted gross national product, see O.J. Firestone, *Canada's Economic Development* (London, 1958), 65, 74; (2) applying the aggregate increase in real output between 1910 and 1911 to our 1910 national income estimate, see Firestone, *Economic Development*, 276; and (3) applying to the resulting figure the increase in prices between 1910 and 1911 as reported in *Report of the Board of Inquiry into the Cost of Living* (Ottawa, 1915), II: 240.

12. See mathematical note in appendix B. If we introduce any other factor such as capital the meaning of the two demand curves in figures 1b and 1c changes. Instead of representing the marginal physical products given the *quantity* of other factors, they become demand curves for labor given the *price* of the other factor. Of course at each price of labor the marginal physical product equals that price, but it is a marginal physical product for a quantity of labor combined with a varying amount of capital.

The ability of export staples to attract capital and thereby improve productivity has been a recurring theme in Canadian writings on the staple. There is no doubt that the production of primary products has this capacity, but the same is true of any economically worthwhile production. We must guard against the double counting that is involved in estimating the contribution of an export to an economy not alone in the value of the export but also in the attraction of the capital that contributed to its production. In fact it must be remembered that had it been possible to produce the wheat with *less* capital the gain in per capita income to the economy would have been obviously greater and not less. The same is true for labor. Despite some loose talk about the contribution of backward linkage to growth, it should be noted that, if the inputs to the primary product industry from backwardly linked industries were *not* required, then the rent, and therefore the gain, from the export industry would have been larger.

13. While some development theorists (and certainly Canadian economic historians) have stressed the role of exports, it is of some interest to note that, as we would expect, it makes no difference to the effect upon per capita income whether an increase in productivity occurs in a domestic or export industry. Thus a shift in productivity in the cheese industry would have the same effect as the shift in wheat. Given the emphasis placed on exports in much of Canadian economic history we were surprised to find (1911 census) that during the decade, agricultural production in Ontario increased absolutely as much as in Saskatchewan, while Quebec and Ontario increases were together fully 79 percent of that in the entire prairie region.

The reader will note that in our expanded model we have not considered the possibilities of increasing or decreasing returns in industries like haircuts that are domestic. This will be done below.

14. This is calculated from the 147,881 newly occupied farms for the decade 1901–11 (*1911 Census of Agriculture*, xii) and the approximate number of persons per homestead, 2.5 (Annual Reports of the Department of the Interior, 1902–1912, as reprinted in the *Dominion Sessional Papers*).

15. This is a rough average of the 37.3 percent which is the proportion of Canadians listed in the "general farmer" occupational group in the 1911 *Census of Occupations*, and 30 percent, which is the approximate proportion of Canadians and aliens "previously resident in Canada" taking up homesteads year by year for this decade (Annual Reports of the Department of the Interior). We are also assuming the family size of Canadian settlers is equal to that of non-Canadian settlers.

16. The homesteader obtained patent on his 160 acres and could pre-empt an additional 160 acres at the nominal price of $3 per acre after meeting residence requirements (six months on the land for each of three years; building a habitable house; breaking thirty acres and having two-thirds of this in crop). See C. Martin, *"Dominion Land" Policy* (Toronto, 1938), esp. chap. 12, 495–545.

17. The figure of $504 is derived as follows: average earnings of male persons in manufacturing in 1910 = $489 (*1911 Census of Manufactures*, vi) plus an adjustment of 2.9 percent for the increase in average weekly earnings 1910–11 = $15. See Canada, *Report of Board*, II: 558.

18. Some critics have suggested that a more plausible assumption about population would have been a completely elastic supply curve of labor. Originally we did in fact approach the problem this way but abandoned it when we realized that it was incompatible with a gadget-type industry and stability (a horizontal supply curve and a horizontal demand curve for labor). For reasons outlined below in the text we feel that some sizable fraction of Canadian industry possessed the gadget properties in 1911. However, if we do reject the gadget industry and adapt the horizontal supply curve of labor, the estimated increase in per capita income would be more limited and conceivably could be negative. This would be the case if the ratio of previous rental and other property income accruing to Canadians to previous wage income was higher than the incremental ratio of property income to wage income. The higher the marginal propensity to spend on domestic industries and hence the higher the population multiplier through immigration (given the wheat rent), the more likely is the negative result.

19. We can exclude internal economies and diseconomies, both technological and pecuniary. If pecuniary economies (diseconomies) are nonexistent for the industry, they are likewise for the firm. Net technological economies cannot exist for the competitive firm in equilibrium, while technological diseconomies, though they exist for the firm, do not affect the industry because of expansion or contraction in the number of firms.

20. More generally the gadget industry could be either export or import. Of course, if it were an export industry, then cheese and/or wheat must be import-competing in order to balance foreign trade. In general there is nothing in the logic of the model which dictates that any one of the three industries — wheat, cheese or gadgets — be either an export- or an import-competing industry. Indeed, since the gadget "industry" is a group of industries, they may be simultaneously net import-competing and net exporting; for example the agricultural implements industry in 1911 was in the latter category. Some readers may see a similarity between our gadget industry and the largely self-sufficient subsistence sector in Lewis' well-known theory of growth (see W.A. Lewis, *The Theory of Economic Growth* (London, 1955)), in that in both models the particular industry provides a completely elastic supply curve of labor to other industries. There are, however, important differences. In our model the gadget industry is in no sense "backward" as opposed to "progressive" other industries. In Lewis' subsistence sector real incomes appear to depend on productivity within that sector. Since, however, the gadget industry is not self-sufficient, real wages depend not only upon productivity in gadgets but also upon world prices and productivity in the insulated domestic industry with its resulting price effect. Finally Lewis' subsistence sector is not an exporting industry while, as just noted, gadgets could be so in principle although they were generally not in the period under consideration.

21. T. Scitovsky, "Two Concepts of External Economies," *Journal of Political Economy* (Apr. 1954): 145; J. Meade, "External Economies and Diseconomies in a Competitive Situation," *Economic Journal* (Mar. 1952): 54–67.

22. North, *Economic Growth of the United States*, 1–14.

23. E.F. Denison, *The Sources of Economic Growth in the United States and the Alternatives before Us* (New York, 1962), 175. Denison divides external economies into national and local. If the expansion on the prairies had the effect of reducing the size of the typical Canadian community, or slowing its increase, the external effects would be negative on the local level.

24. Of course while 0.2 percent is an insignificant fraction of the 23 percent increase in per capita income for the decade, it is one-sixth or a not insignificant fraction of the 1.20 percent that we have found to be the result of a decade of wheat expansion alone. It changes our 5.20 percent to 6.05.

25. If increasing- or decreasing-cost haircut-type industries are not offsetting, there may be a further effect upon per capita income through population changes. Owners of labor and other factors may immigrate (or fail to emigrate), for example, in response to net economies of scale since with given money earnings their real incomes will be raised by the lower average price of haircut-type products. (The former equivalence between real and money wages would be relaxed and the labor supply function in figures 1 and 2 would shift to the right.) The opposite would be true if net diseconomies prevail. However, in either case, if these net migrants possess a factor stock equal to the average already in the country, this further effect on per capita income will be zero.

26. Dominion of Canada, *Canada Yearbook* (Ottawa, 1914), 203, and *Report of the Board of Inquiry into the Cost of Living* (Ottawa, 1915), 653.

27. B. Massel, "Capital Formation and Technological Change in U.S. Manufacturing," *Review of Economics and Statistics* (May 1960): 182–88; R.M. Solow, "Technical Progress, Capital Formation and Economic Growth," *American Economic Review* (May 1962): 76–86.

28. Staple theorists have stressed the dependence of Canada upon foreign technology but, given their preoccupation with primary-product exports, have emphasized only those which shift production functions in those industries. Surely in a simple arithmetic sense per capita output will grow more if, for a given rate of technical advance, these advances occur in those industries which make up most of the national product, regardless of whether they are primary product or otherwise.

29. T.W. Schultz, *The Economics of Education* (New York, 1963).

30. G.E. Britnell, *The Wheat Economy* (Toronto, 1914), 45–46.

THE RELEVANCE OF THE WHEAT BOOM IN CANADIAN ECONOMIC GROWTH†

GORDON W. BERTRAM

Introduction

The relevance of the staple theory as an explanatory device in Canadian economic history has, quite appropriately, come under severe criticism in recent years. A staple-theory interpretation of the last decades of Canadian experience in the nineteenth century appears to be quite inadequate, while the wheat boom episode, regarded in the past as one of the most convincing demonstrations of the explanatory value of the staple approach, has been shown to have lacked empirical verification. Economists who are interested in long-run growth analysis have been responsible for widening the theoretical growth models available so that staple theory appears to be just one of the relevant analytical tools available to the Canadian economic historian.

The commonplace that each generation writes its own history raises a problem for the relevance of past work in the literature of economic history. What views and interpretations of the wheat boom episode should be revised is the subject of this paper. In 1966 Chambers and Gordon[1] published their well-known attack on certain received interpretations regarding the influence of the prairie wheat boom on the Canadian economy in the period 1901–11. This was followed by "A Comment" by Dales, McManus, and Watkins[2] with a "Rejoinder" by Chambers and Gordon.[3] The controversy was reopened recently by Richard Caves[4]. The purpose of this paper will be to show that the Chambers and Gordon article, while an extremely important milestone in the literature of Canadian economic history, is, in its present form, both theoretically and empirically inadequate. The main inadequacy of their model is that it permits only certain influences of the western agricultural expansion to be measured while the contribution they consider most important — agricultural rent — is measured incorrectly, resulting in a pronounced underestimate.[5]

†*Canadian Journal of Economics/Revue Canadienne d'Economique* VI, 4 (Nov. 1973): 545–66. The author wishes to express his thanks to Mr. Michael Percy, honours and graduate student, University of Victoria, for his able research assistance. This article is a version of a paper given at the Fifth Conference on Quantitative Methods in Canadian Economic History, Laval University, Quebec, March 1972. Financial support from Canada Council is gratefully acknowledged.

The Chambers-Gordon Model

In their "simplest model," Chambers and Gordon assume that 1901 and 1911 represent equilibrium years and that the Canadian economy can be represented by two sectors, agriculture and gadgets (manufacturing) and two factors of production, labour and land. They also assume constant costs in gadgets and increasing costs in agriculture. As specified, the model serves to determine money and real wages so that the authors are able to focus on agricultural rents as an unambiguous measure of the contribution of the 1901–11 wheat boom to the virtual exclusion of other additional income or efficiency changes that might be measured. As knowledgeable theorists, they employ a counterfactual technique which (though apparently startling to some) poses a relevant, but very broad question: what would have been the difference in Canadian per capita income growth if there had been no prairie wheat boom, compared to the observed fact of the wheat boom experience? There was no implication in their discussion that the wheat boom was not an important source of extensive economic growth. Rather, the issue being examined was the extent to which the wheat boom contributed to intensive economic growth.

A counterfactual question in economic history, such as that employed by Chambers and Gordon to isolate the net contribution of the wheat boom, has led some commentators to regard certain tasks of economic historians as formidable indeed. It would appear, however, that Chambers and Gordon were attempting to construct a type of model which Robert Fogel later described in his discussion of the search for an "efficient model."[6] When the Chambers and Gordon findings on agricultural rent are amended by the new and quite opposite empirical findings presented here, the emphasis of their model on rent as the main magnitude to be considered appears to be a useful, though incomplete, beginning in assessing the contribution of the early-period wheat boom to per capita income growth. As we shall show in part 2, their model is not "efficient" since the underlying assumptions represent too wide a departure from reality.

In the present paper the main discussion is allocated to the new empirical estimates of rent contained in part 1. Part 2 considers some difficulties apparent in the theoretical construction of the Chambers-Gordon model. More briefly, part 3 contains an analysis of the Chambers and Gordon supporting data, a further recent estimate of wheat boom contribution magnitudes, and certain additional factors to be considered.

1. The Empiricism of "Primary Products"

In this section our first main point is to show that even accepting the Chambers-Gordon model and time period of 1901–11, their empirical estimate of rent for 1911 is far too low. It turns out that it is the absolute size of the 1911 estimate of agricultural rent which is the most critical number in the Chambers and Gordon empirical work. Their introduction of a counterfactual question — if the wheat expansion had not occurred after 1901 — required computation of a 1911 hypothetical rent which is actually a small statistical magnitude. Only a relatively minor change is therefore made in their downward correction of the absolute size of their estimated 1911 rent. Their necessary introduction of 1911 hypothetical rent may have diverted some readers from an analysis of the size of the 1911 rent that they estimated.

Our interest, then, is to examine the reliability of prairie agricultural rent data on which the Chambers and Gordon estimates are based, to formulate an alternative method of estimating rents, and to extend the time periods studied to cover 1901–20/21 and 1901–21. We initially employ the Chambers and Gordon procedures and sources for calculating agricultural rents in the prairie provinces and their share in national income. National and per capita income estimates used by Chambers and Gordon from O.J. Firestone[7] are also employed in this paper, although in part 3 a brief exploration is made of the validity of the Firestone data. The same sources and methods for estimating total prairie rents (decennial census records) are used for one of the longer periods analysed, i.e., 1901–20/21. These simple exercises seem a modest and mandatory requirement when assessing the validity of Chambers and Gordon's controversial findings.

The arithmetic of the Chambers-Gordon 1901 and 1911 rent calculations is provided in table 1 and is shown mainly because it was omitted by them. Their method of calculation was the very simple one of finding from the census for 1901 and 1911 the average cash rent per acre of rented prairie farm land. This "cash proxy rent" per acre for 1901 and 1911 was multiplied by the entire occupied acreage in each prairie province for the same respective years, with the result that their estimate of agricultural rents for 1901 was $9.2 million and for 1911, $45.8 million. The rent per acre was given in the census of 1911 for that year and for 1901 and was enumerated by asking the tenant to provide the value per acre on a cash basis for rented land. The critical sum of the value of rents represented by both share tenancy and cash rents is omitted from the Chambers and Gordon rent estimate. As we will show below, rents represented by share tenancy must have been very significant in 1911. Since no consideration, as far as can be determined, was given either in the 1901 or 1911 census to per acre rent on a share basis, or the number of acres that may have been rented on a share basis,[8] an alternative method of estimating rent was required for 1901 and 1911.

Table 2 represents an alternative estimate of agricultural rent for 1901 and 1911 derived from census land values which do not contain the share tenancy rent deficiency noted for the censuses of 1901 and 1911. This alternative method used by Fogel and Mercer[9] — estimating agricultural rents by decapitalizing land values through multiplying by a mortgage rate of interest reflecting the opportunity costs of borrowing — yields an estimate of $9.6 million in 1901 and $98.6 million in 1911 — a marked change for 1911 from the Chambers and Gordon estimates of $45 million. Table 2 provides the necessary notes for this calculation.

We may assume that the value of land recorded by the *Census of Agriculture* in 1901 and 1911 represents the capitalized value of the flow of rents of agricultural land over some period of time. Differential agricultural land rents arose from differences in the fertility of the soil and differences in access to markets. The boundaries of feasible commercial prairie agriculture would be determined primarily by access to the railroad lines.[10] Prices received at the farm would fall the greater the distance from the railroad and the market, and without railroads,

TABLE 1

Estimate of Prairie Agricultural Rents, 1901–11

Province	Rent per Acre on a Cash Basis, 1901 ($)	Occupied Land, 1901 (thousands of acres)	Estimate of 1901 Agricultural Rent ($000)	Rent per Acre on a Cash basis, 1911 ($)	Occupied Land, 1911 (thousands of acres)	Estimate of 1911 Agricultural Rent ($000)
Alberta	0.15	2,736	410	0.57	17,752	10,119
Saskatchewan	0.74	3,833	2,837	0.83	28,643	23,774
Manitoba	0.67	8,843	5,925	0.97	12,228	11,861
Total prairies		15,412	9,172		58,623	45,754

SOURCE: Chambers and Gordon, "Primary Products," 320. Census and Statistics Office, *Census of Canada*, vol. IV (1911): xiv, lviii, and "Instructions Relating to Schedule No. 7," 422. Rents are inclusive of both land and buildings.

the high cost of alternative methods of transportation would have severely limited the extent of feasible commercial agriculture. Under these circumstances, land values would vary directly with the change in prices at the farm as transportation costs varied. We can assume that, aside from the speculative possibilities in holding land pending further transportation improvements, land values beyond the feasible region of commercial agriculture would fall to zero.

The approximate equality of the 1901 Chambers and Gordon rent estimate and our new estimate could be the result of coincidence but, more likely, the decapitalization method provides an estimate of rent for 1901 which was very similar to the Chambers and Gordon "cash proxy rent" method. It is concluded here that their method of using only cash rentals as a rent proxy in 1901 did not greatly underestimate observed rents. The amount of land taken up in 1901 was very small in relation to the supply and it is plausible that settlers would find little reason to adopt a significant share system.

The large difference between the Chambers and Gordon rent estimate of $45.8 million for 1911 and our new estimate of $98.6 million requires an evaluation of what the possible relative magnitude and trend of total prairie agricultural rent to the value of agricultural output actually might have been in the years 1901–11. One problem in examining the trend with the Chambers and Gordon cash proxy rent estimate is that 1910 was a poor crop year in the prairies according to the records of the period but, unfortunately, the value of prairie agricultural products in the 1911 census refer to this poor 1910 crop year.[11] Consequently the share of rent in the census value of total prairie agricultural output in 1900 and 1910 cannot be consistently compared without first estimating the "normal" production and value for 1910 field crops. We estimate that the "normal" value of prairie agricultural output in 1910 was $290,973,162 rather than the actual 1910 census value of $222,307,761.[12]

The proportion of agricultural rent to the value of total prairie farm production in the Chambers and Gordon estimate falls from 24.3 percent in 1901 to 20.5 percent in 1911. With our corrected output figure, the Chambers and Gordon

TABLE 2

Estimate of Prairie Provinces Agricultural Rents, Decapitalization Method, 1901 and 1911

Province	Value of Land, 1901[a] ($000)	Average Provincial Rate of Interest for 1st Mortgage on Farm Property[b] 1901	Estimated Yearly Value of Farm Rents[c] 1901 ($000)	Value of Land, 1911[a] ($000)	Average Provincial Rate of Interest for 1st Mortgage on Farm Property[b] 1911	Estimated Yearly Value of Farm Rents[b] 1911 ($000)
Manitoba	93,234	7.25	6,759	309,960	7.82	24,239
Saskatchewan	22,880	8.08	1,849	583,401	7.95	46,380
Alberta	13,157	7.91	1,041	344,760	8.11	27,960
Prairie provinces	129,271		9,649	1,238,121		98,579

a. Census and Statistics Office, *Census of Canada*, vol. IV (1911), xviii–lc. Land values represent a report of farmers to census enumerators of the value of land only.

b. Mortgage interest rates from Board of Inquiry into the Cost of Living, *Report*, vol. II (Ottawa, 1915), 730–33. The table provided, for 1901 and 1911, "the rate of interest on farm property, at which money could be borrowed from company on first mortgage." The interest rates noted represent, for 1901, a simple average provincially of the borrowing rate taken from 11 interest observations in Manitoba, and 6 interest observations each for Saskatchewan and Alberta. Similarly, for 1911, 16 interest observations were available for each of Manitoba and Saskatchewan and 13 observations for Alberta. Between 1901 and 1911, the composition of interest rate data sample may have changed, with the result that some unknown bias may be introduced in the above averages.

c. Estimated values of farm rents for 1901 and 1911 were obtained by multiplying farm values by the given rate of interest. The method used assumes perpetual yields. The calculated rental yields per annum would not be greatly reduced by assuming a yield life of say 50 years, or even a shorter period, since as well known, the longer the time period of yields, the smaller the impact on the present value of an annuity. The formula $V = N/i$ was used in the above rather than $A_n = R[1 - (1 + i)^{-n}]/n$. Fogel and Mercer make no adjustment for shorter time periods in their computations, no doubt for similar reasons.

estimate of rent taken as a proportion of output falls to 15.7 percent, while the new decapitalization estimate for 1911 shows that the proportion of rents rises from 24.3 percent in 1901 to 33.9 percent in 1911. This contrary evidence on the magnitude and trend of the share of rent in agricultural output is further explored below.

Importance of Share Tenancy in Prairie Agriculture

Table 3 indicates that in 1921 the share-of-crop basis of arranging farm rents accounted for about 74 percent of the total acreage rented by tenants and part owners–part tenants. Share tenancy was obviously the preponderant prairie practice in 1921 for the 19 percent of occupied land that was rented. The importance of prairie share tenancy in a period nearer to 1911 is provided by the *Census of Prairie Provinces* which shows that in 1916 there were some 10,000 share tenants on the prairie, compared to some 6,000 cash tenants. When this census data is converted into mean acreage for size of farms by province, it was found that 69.9 percent of prairie tenant farm acreage in 1916 was operated by share tenants, while 30.1 percent was operated by cash tenants.[13]

Some initial understanding of what was omitted by Chambers and Gordon in selecting only a cash rental proxy for prairie farm rent is gained by calculations of what the possible value of rent per acre might have been historically using a very conservative one-quarter share system — the lowest share proportion shown in the 1921 census enumerator schedule. It was found in these calculations, not shown here, that for 1908 (the earliest year available) through 1911, the value per acre of a quarter share of the weighted value per acre of four main prairie field crops ranged from $2.50 to $3.80.[14] These calculated per acre values are not meant to be directly compared with the 1911 census-derived rent per acre used by Chambers and Gordon of $0.57 to $0.97 (table 1), since they represent gross values per acre in a specific arrangement of share tenancy without any allowance for other inputs which may have been supplied by either party. However, the inference is that, as a result of the omission of share tenancy rent, the 1911 census data on fixed cash rents provide too low an estimate — a finding consistent with our 1911 decapitalization estimate.

A variety of evidence indicates that share tenancy not only was an important tradition in Ontario,[15] which supplied a large proportion of migrants to prairie farming, but was also the predominant practice among farm tenants in the states of the Middle West in 1900.[16] The latter states were also a significant source of agricultural immigrants to the Canadian Prairies after 1900 and, like many other of their practices, they probably brought share tenancy farm management methods with them. Further evidence appears to confirm the significance of share tenancy in prairie agriculture.[17]

We can conclude from the above discussions that the omission of share arrangements in the Chambers and Gordon computation for 1911 of the average value of rents per acre result in a serious downward bias in their average rent value per acre.

TABLE 3

Prairie Farm Rentals on a Cash Basis and Share Basis, 1921
(thousands of acres)

Type of Tenancy	Acres on Cash Basis	Acres on Share Basis	Totals
Tenants	1,880	8,231	
Part owners–part tenants	2,502	4,118	
Total cash and total share acreage	4,382	12,349	
Total acreage rented by tenants and part owners–part tenants			16,731[a]
Percentage	26.2%	73.8%	100.0%
Total acres of prairie occuped land			87,932
Percent of all acreage rented			19.0%-

a. The figure 16,731,000 represents the sum of the prairie cash and share acreage given in the table. The total prairie rental acreage shown in the census of 1921 included the category of cash *and* share tenants — a very small amount of acreage (32,367) which could not be allocated in the above manner and was therefore excluded from the total.
SOURCE: Dominion Bureau of Statistics, *Census of Canada*, vol. V (1921), 33, xiv–xv.

Estimates of Agricultural Rent, 1921 and 1920/21

In part 2 of this paper we reject the Chambers and Gordon assumption that 1911 was an equilibrium year. In this section further empirical estimates are made of the value of agricultural rent in 1920 and 1920/21 when the process of prairie agricultural activity had proceeded much further than in 1911. We consider that the term "wheat boom" could appropriately be applied to the whole of the period 1901–21. Extension of the period studied also offers an opportunity to test the magnitude of the 1911 rent estimate derived from the decapitalization method by comparing the 1921 results of this method with the 1921 census data on share and cash rent for 1920/21. Extension of the time period also permits an analysis of the long-run behaviour of the share of rent in the value of prairie agricultural output.

Table 4 provides two estimates of the value of agricultural rent for the prairie provinces in 1921. The estimates were based on a decapitalization of the value of prairie agricultural land enumerated in the 1921 census, using the two estimated rates of interest for farm mortgage loans of 9 and 9.5 percent in 1921. Footnote b of table 4 provides a rationale for the use of these rates. According to this table, agricultural rents in 1921 were between $185.9 million and $196.2 million.

Table 5 provides an estimate for 1920/21 of prairie agricultural rent of $211.3 million, following the same type of procedure used by Chambers and Gordon for their 1911 estimate. The census of 1921 provided a calculation of prairie agricultural rent per acre, based on a combination of the value of rents paid on a

TABLE 4

Estimate of Prairie Agricultural Rents, Decapitalization Method, 1921

Province	Value of Farm Land 1921[a] (millions of $)	First Estimate of Prairie Rate of Interest for 1st Mortgage on Farm Property 1921[b] (%)	Second Estimate of Prairie Rate of Interest for 1st Mortgage on Farm Property 1921[b] (%)	First Estimate of Yearly Value of Rents 1921 (millions of $)	Second Estimate of Yearly Value of Rents 1921 (millions of $)
Manitoba	394	9.0	9.5	35.5	37.4
Saskatchewan	1061	9.0	9.5	95.5	100.8
Alberta	611	9.0	9.5	54.9	58.0
Totals	2066			185.9	196.2
Average rent/acre[c]				$2.11	$2.23

a. Dominion Bureau of Statistics, *Census of Canada*, vol. V (1921), 5–6.
b. Rates of interest on a provincial or federal level for first mortgages on farm property in 1921 were not available. The attempt to estimate 1921 provincial farm property mortgage rates involved taking the interest difference between the yield on Canada 3 percent bonds in 1911 of 3.27 percent (regarded as virtually a riskless rate) and average provincial rates of interest on first mortgages for farm property (given in table 2). This difference, added to the 1921 average coupon rate of Direct and Guaranteed Bonds, Dominion of Canada at 5.07 percent (see *Royal Commission on Dominion Provincial Relations*, Book III (Ottawa, 1940), 123) gave estimates of rates for Manitoba of 9.62 percent, Saskatchewan 9.75 percent and Alberta 9.91 percent. For purposes of this exercise, 9.0 percent and 9.5 percent interest rates were employed. These rates do not appear unrealistic since the chartered bank prime loan rate in the years 1900–35 was between 6 and 6.5 percent.
c. Obtained by dividing estimates of 1921 rents by 87,932, the total acres of prairie occupied land, from 1921 census. See table 3.

cash basis in 1921 and the value of rents paid on a share basis, which the census computed from the value of 1920 prairie farm output per acre.

We conclude that our estimates of rent shown by the decapitalization method for 1921, shown in table 4, and the census rent data for 1920/21, shown in table 5, yield fairly similar magnitudes. The fact that the census estimate exceeded our decapitalization estimate by 7.6 percent is not unexpected since the land values recorded by the census were taken as at June 1921, when the 1920/21 business cycle was near its trough.[18]

Finally, the objection could be raised that the World War I experience invalidates the whole exercise of computing agricultural rents as of 1920/21. In a broader perspective, the events of World War I imposed exogenous disturbances on the prairie economy. It would appear quite inconsistent to employ exogenous variables such as international prices but to put aside other such events. The further prairie expansion resulting from the disturbance of World War I simply happened and was an irreversible part of Canadian economic history.

Table 5

Estimate of Prairie Agricultural Rent from Census Cash and Share Data, 1920–21

Province	Rent per Acre on Cash Basis and Share Basis ($)[a]	Occupied Land in 1921 (thousands of acres)	Total Rent 1920/21 ($000)
Manitoba	3.11	14,616	45,455
Saskatchewan	2.43	4,023	106,976
Alberta	2.01	29,293	58,879
Total and average rent per acre	2.40	87,932	211,310

a. Combined census computation of rent on a cash basis reported as of 1 June 1921, and rent on a share basis calculated in the value of the 1920 crop.
SOURCE: Dominion Bureau of Statistics, *Census of Canada*, vol. V (1921), xiv–xv, xxxv.

Long-Run Trend of Share of Rent in Agricultural Output, 1901–20/21

Table 6 summarizes the various prairie agricultural rent estimates made in this paper. Since our findings indicate that the share of rent in the value of total farm products runs from 25.4 to 33.9 to 34.0 percent in the period 1901, 1911, and 1920/21, while the Chambers and Gordon rent estimates imply a decline from 24.3 in 1901 to 15.7 percent in 1911, the following question arises. As prairie frontiers expanded,[19] would the share of rent decline, 1901–11, as the Chambers and Gordon estimates imply?

In the face of rising field crop prices and falling transportation costs for wheat over the period 1901–11[20] it is difficult to accept the Chambers and Gordon inference regarding a declining rent proportion. The rise in Fort William prices and the fall in Regina–Fort William freight costs would both increase field crop prices at the farm and contribute to a rise in prairie land rent. As prairie agriculture developed, there was an increasing specialization in field crops. The last column of table 6 indicates that the value of prairie field crops, as a proportion of the total value of prairie farm products, was rising over the whole period 1900–20 from 63.2 to 79.8 percent, and rose in the shorter period 1900–10 from 63.2 to 72.6 percent. Decisions to locate appear to have been based on considerations of transport costs, land fertility and the price of farm products. Since settlement was proceeding, the settler was likely motivated by desire to maximize returns and this involved capturing rents.

Calculations of the Contribution of Prairie Wheat Boom Rent to Growth in Real Per Capita GNP

Table 7 takes the various agricultural rent estimates discussed so far and shows them as a proportion of the same set of Firestone national income estimates used by Chambers and Gordon. This fraction is then employed as the numerator in

TABLE 6

Summary of Agricultural Rent Estimates, Chambers-Gordon and New Estimates

Case	Year	Estimated Rent (millions of $)	Method	Total Value of Prairie Farm Products (millions of $)	Rent as Percentage of Value of Total Prairie Farm Products	Value of Field Crop as Percentage of Value of Total Farm Products
C–G	1901	9.2	Census, cash basis	37.8 (1900)	24.3 (1900)	63.2 (1900)
New	1901	9.6	Census, decapitalization	37.8 (1900)	25.4 (1900)	63.2 (1900)
C–G	1911	45.8	Census, cash basis	222.3 (1910)	20.5 (1910)	64.1 (1910)
C–G	1911	45.8	Census, cash basis	291.0 (1910)[a]	15.7 (1910)	72.6 (1910)[a]
New	1911[a]	98.6	Census, decapitalization	291.0 (1910)[a]	33.9 (1910)	72.6 (1910)[a]
New	1920–21	211.3	Census, cash and share basis	621.2 (1920)	34.0 (1920)	79.8 (1920)
New	1921	196.2	Census, decapitalization	621.2 (1920)	31.6 (1920)	79.8 (1920)

a. Estimate of 1910 "normal" value of prairie agricultural products given earlier in this section.
SOURCES: Tables 1–3, 5; *Census of Canada* (1911), table 88, xcii; *Census of Canada* (1921), tables 7, 8.

the computation of the proportion of estimated growth in real per capita GNP attributable to the wheat boom.

In their "simplest model" — after subtracting hypothetical 1911 rent and expressing the remaining rent as a percent (1.94) of 1911 national income — Chambers and Gordon concluded that this percent, taken as a proportion of the growth of per capita real output, indicated that the early period wheat boom rent represented 8.4 percent of total growth, 1901–11.[21] A recalculation of the Chambers and Gordon estimate, using our new 1911 rent estimate, yields the conclusion that prairie agricultural rent contributed just under 20 percent of total growth.[22] In a similar manner, for the period 1901–20/21 with the new share and cash basis rent estimate, the longer wheat boom period contributed 23.5 percent of the total per capita growth.[23]

2. The Theoretical Model of "Primary Products"

As we have shown in part 1, the new empirical estimates give the Chambers and Gordon model certain useful explanatory power with respect to the importance of agricultural rent in the wheat boom. In determining what is to be measured, however, their model prevents an exploration of the influence of other factors which the wheat episode may have contributed to per capita income growth. A central theoretical problem is that Chambers and Gordon have chosen an equilibrium model to explain a disequilibrium situation. This section briefly examines a set of interrelated difficulties in the Chambers and Gordon model

TABLE 7

Summary of Calculations of the Contributions of Prairie Wheat Boom Rent to Growth in Real Per Capita GNP, 1901–11 and 1901–20/21

Period	Source of Estimate	Estimated Hypothetical Rent ($ millions)	Estimated Observed Rent ($ millions)	Estimated Wheat Boom Rent ($ millions)	National Income ($ millions)	Percentage of Rent to National Income (%)	Real Per Capita Growth in GNP (%)	Contribution of Wheat Boom Rent to Growth in Real Per Capita GNP (%)
1901–11	Chambers-Gordon (simplest model)	5.4	45.8	40.4	2081 (1911)	1.94	23	8.4
1901–11	New (decapitalization method)	5.4	98.6	93.2	2081 (1911)	4.48	23	19.5
1901–20/21	New (share and cash basis)	0.0	211.3	211.3	4866 (1920)	4.34	18.5	23.5
1901–21	New (decapitalization method)	0.0	196.2	196.2	4866 (1920)	4.03	18.5	21.8

SOURCE: Tables 1–3, 5, 6, and Firestone, *Canada's Economic Development*, 74.

discussed under the headings of the counterfactual alternative, the assumption of equilibrium, and the likely mis-specification of the model.

Counterfactual Alternative

A more complete empirical effort would involve other aspects of the Chambers and Gordon counterfactual question than its relatively small adjustment for rents, since the nature of the entire economy without the West — its implicit assumption — requires further analysis. While the rate of manufacturing growth in central Canada in the period 1870–90 might have continued at its satisfactory rate in 1900–10, if there had been no West, even a cursory investigation suggests that additional per capita income growth from manufacturing might have been missing in the absence of the wheat boom. There is an assumption in Chambers and Gordon that the next best alternative use of resources after wheat would have yielded only a slightly lower rate of return, but it is equally probable that, after wheat, alternative rates of return might have fallen sharply.

Certain other aspects of the counterfactual question concerning the magnitude of the wheat boom are explored in a recent essay by Richard Caves, where he argues "that significant influences of immigration and extensive growth on intensive growth may have been omitted . . . ."[24] We will consider Caves' computations in part 3.

Assumption of Equilibrium

Some major problems were resolved by the Chambers and Gordon assumption that they were observing two points of equilibrium in 1901 and 1911, since equilibrium in the model, along with their substantiating assumptions, implies that their measure of rents is ". . . a 'true' measure of a change in income attributable to the change in staple production. . . ."[25] In addition, as we shall note below, the equilibrium assumption for 1911 prevents any analysis of external economies. The Chambers and Gordon decision to use the 1901–11 period was determined by the availability of census data. However, there is unequivocal evidence that the appropriate period of the wheat boom was considerably longer. Selecting 1911 as an equilibrium period implies that at the margin, resources had moved to equate their marginal value products in every direction. But relative to the Canadian economy, factor movements were substantial, with occupation of land and employment of labour and capital proceeding throughout the period 1901–21.[26]

Evidence that this period did in fact represent points of equilibrium was not investigated by Chambers and Gordon except for a single examination when the existence of quasi-rents to labour was briefly considered, and rejected after incorrectly comparing urban annual wages for unskilled labour in Ontario with rural annual farm wages in Saskatchewan.[27] An examination of their data source[28] reveals a wide, and in some years an increasing, hourly wage differential over most of the period 1901–11 in favour of Winnipeg urban unskilled labourers relative to Toronto unskilled labour. The differential rose in the early part of the period to 23.3 percent, fell to reach parity in 1906, and then rose to a differential of 12.6 percent in 1910 and 1911. Unskilled labour in both cities was recorded as having 54-hour work weeks throughout 1901–11.

Shifting the comparison to rural wage changes, the average weekly wage income of rural farm labourers including board, among the provinces of Canada as reported by the 1911 census, shows that Saskatchewan (which can be taken to represent the prairies) relative to Ontario in 1900 and 1910, had an absolute wage differential in both years, rising from a 19 percent differential in 1900 to a 47 percent differential in 1910.[29] What is indicative of the possibility of quasi-rents in wages is the rise in differentials over the relevant time period. The wage data presented here introduce a highly speculative view of the Chambers and Gordon observations on quasi-rents.[30] We conclude from the above discussion of the counterfactual question and the assumption of equilibrium involving the existence of quasi-rents, that there is a strong probability that on these points alone, Chambers and Gordon underestimate the contribution of the wheat boom to per capita income growth.

Mis-specification of the Model

The operation of the Chambers and Gordon model as a device to determine the appropriate variables to be measured depends upon a basic set of assumptions contained in their specification of the gadget industry production function, $g = gf(L_g)$. "On the other hand $g(L_g)$ will be considered to specify fully the gadget production function, that is, there is no (or a negligible amount of) land or any other scarce factor required; $g(L_g)$ will be linear and homogeneous. . . ."[31] This assumption of constant returns to scale in the one-factor gadget industry is partly based on a constant marginal product of labour and given international prices. Other possible inputs for the gadget industry raise no problem in their model which specifies a homogeneous production function of degree one, since they also assume that intermediate and non-labour inputs to the gadget industry are in perfectly elastic supply. In their model the result is that the gadget industry sets money and real wage rates, while permitting the transfer of labour from gadgets to wheat without any rise in wages. Further, their specification of the production function means that external economies or diseconomies can be disregarded. Rent therefore emerges as "a 'true' measure" for their model.

All this, however, presents certain problems. Since Chambers and Gordon are unable to isolate wheat, they use the total value of agricultural output as representative of the wheat boom. Since their wheat production function is therefore an agricultural production function, revised production functions would then require, for the manufacturing sector, the inclusion of inputs of agricultural products while the agricultural sector would require inclusion of certain inputs of the manufacturing sector. The new production functions would now read

$$w = w(L_w, g) \text{ and } g = g(L_g, w),[32]$$

where w is understood to refer to agriculture.

Just as Peter Temin provided no justification (according to Fogel) for the assumption that agricultural commodities were used only for consumption,[33] so the

Chambers and Gordon model fails to take account of the importance of agricultural inputs in manufacturing. Actually, manufacturing firms employed in processing the products of land (agricultural-extractive) accounted in the Canadian case for some 30–40 percent[34] of the value added by the manufacturing sector in 1911. One implication of the revised production function is that the gadget industry would no longer have a negligible amount of land or any other scarce factor required, as Chambers and Gordon indicated.[35]

In an expanded model, the perfectly elastic demand for labour inputs for the gadget industry would be complicated by a less than perfectly elastic supply of intermediate inputs for the gadget industry. Chambers and Gordon state that "We believe ourselves justified in concluding that within the set of industries found in appendix C there exists a subset whose input prices, apart from labour, were fixed and which account for well over half the total employment in the group."[36] An inspection of the Chambers-Gordon appendix C indicates that industries with a possible perfectly elastic supply of intermediate inputs seem to be a rather small proportion—something more than 14 percent—of total manufacturing output.[37]

If there are any scarce factors, such as the products of land or other intermediate inputs for manufacturing, a shift in the demand for wheat would no longer result in an unchanged wage rate in the gadget industry, as Chambers and Gordon have demonstrated in their diagram. A downward sloping demand curve for labour in the gadget industry rather than a perfectly elastic demand curve would, with a shift in the supply curve to the left, cause a rise in wage rates. The equilibrium assumed in their model as of 1911 would no longer occur with the gadget industry setting unchanging wage rates as the supply curve of labour shifted to the left in response to an expanding wheat sector.[38]

The assumption of a perfectly elastic demand curve for the gadget industry also involves the nonexistence of external economies. As Chambers and Gordon state, ". . . so far as external economies, either pecuniary or technological, are concerned, their existence is incompatible with equilibrium and a perfectly elastic demand curve for the industry."[39]

If equilibrium is not assumed in 1911 and mis-specification does exist in the Chambers-Gordon model, it becomes necessary to investigate the possibility of external economies occurring between equilibrium periods. Tibor Scitovsky noted that "It seems that external economies are invoked whenever the profits of one producer are affected by the actions of other producers."[40] Unit costs and profitability of one firm depend not only on its own output and factor inputs but also on the output and factor inputs of other firms. Despite the tenuous nature of external economies in the literature, an undynamic model which does not permit an investigation of such firm interreaction could underestimate the impact of the wheat boom on the Canadian economy.

Since external economies experienced by some firms may turn out to be dependent on internal economies experienced by other sets of firms, an economies-of-scale estimate is interwoven with the question of the existence, in certain industries and locations, of external economies. In confining their estimate of economies of scale to the domestic and protected sector "haircut" industry (assumed to cover apparently about one-half of the total economy), they almost seem to imply that the infant industry claims made by earlier protectionists were in fact justified. Economies of scale could also have occurred in that portion of the manufacturing sector which was chiefly involved in resource and extractive processing with their main sales in international trade.

A good argument could be made for the case that economies of scale in the Canadian economy in an earlier period would be much higher than Chambers and Gordon estimate taken from U.S. experience after 1929.[41] A reduction of average variable cost could be attributed to some combination of scale factors and pecuniary external economies. Of course if a competitive equilibrium is assumed, such an inquiry is irrelevant. We may suppose, however, that the tendencies towards localization and specialization of industry noted for the earlier period 1870–90 would continue on perhaps even an expanded basis during the time period 1901–11.[42] An extension of this study for the later period might reveal the magnitude of the scale factors involved.

This brief exploration of the Chambers-Gordon model leads to the conclusion that there is a presumption of underestimate by the limitations imposed on the counterfactual question and by the lack of estimation for the existence of quasi-rents. Our exploration also indicates mis-specification in the model where it has been shown that an upward and downward bias in the final estimate has been introduced. Given the likelihood of additional economies of scale and the possibility of certain economies, there is a further presumption of underestimate. Some further research undertaken by Caves, noted below, provides an estimate of the magnitude involved for economies of scale.

3. Other Considerations in the Wheat Boom Estimate

Chambers and Gordon uncritically employ the pioneering national accounts estimates of Firestone for the wheat boom, although it has been well understood for some time that revisions were required.[43] Even a small change in the level of national income in 1911 and in the rate of per capita income growth, 1901–11, will significantly alter their measure of the contribution of the wheat boom. Kenneth Buckley's annual money and real GNP estimates, which were generally known to have existed in the early 1960s, sharply lower the growth rate of per capita real GNP for 1901–11 from the 23 percent estimated by Firestone to 13 percent. For the longer period, 1901–20, Buckley's estimates show a growth rate of 20.7 percent compared to Firestone's 18.5 percent. On the basis of Buckley's GNP data, the Chambers and Gordon estimate of the contribution of the wheat boom becomes 14.9 instead of 8.4 percent, while for our 1911 estimate of rent, the contribution of the wheat boom becomes 34.5 instead of 19.5 percent.[44] While we are unable as yet to accept the Buckley estimates as established numbers, there are reasonable grounds, based on movements of real wages, for considering the Firestone 1910 bench mark too high and his 1920 estimate too low. From this, the implication follows that if the Chambers and Gordon 1911 national income figure is biased upward, then their (and our) 1901–11 wheat boom contribution estimate based on rent is biased downward on this basis alone.[45]

Estimates by Richard Caves

A recent essay by Richard Caves contains the new net estimate, adjusted for population changes, that the Canadian wheat boom contributed $193.6 million or 21.4 percent to the total increase in per capita income that took place in the decade 1901–11.[46] His total estimate is built up as follows: acceptance of the Chambers and Gordon rent estimate and tariff revenue estimate, $53.4 million or 27.6 percent; his major new estimate of extra immigrant wages foregone in the absence of the wheat boom, $118.5 million or 61.2 percent; and his new estimates of $4.2 million interest on capital brought by immigrants, scale economies of $9.9 million on both the haircut and gadget industries, and $7.6 million interest on additional domestic saving — a sum of $21.7 million or 11.2 percent.

While an accounting of the inducement effect of the wheat boom on immigration and the labour force is correct in principle, the Caves estimates appear (at least to this author) to suffer from the old complaint about staple theory that certain linkages or multipliers are assumed, rather than demonstrated empirically.[47] In this paper we postpone an estimate of the magnitude of immigration pending further research. This means that we have not made estimates of the per capita income effects of the wheat boom which are adjusted for changes in population from net migration. The remaining 11.2 percent for the other factors considered by Caves, which would increase per capita income due to the wheat boom, appear to be very useful new measurements and will be considered in our summary of total estimates.

Conclusion

The new estimates of the contribution of the wheat boom to per capita real income growth, computed for agricultural rent only, indicate that, both for the shorter period 1901–11 and the longer period 1901 through 1921, the more traditional, albeit untested, view of the impact of the wheat boom was much closer to reality than the Chambers and Gordon view. The exercise of alternative estimates and alternative time periods reveals that the single and very low estimate of Chambers and Gordon for 1901–11 was based on inadequate empirical efforts. In fact, the empirical portion of their paper is disappointing in its limitations, compared to their theoretical constructs — a contrast which imparts the feeling that the authors were convinced of the outcome from the beginning and proceeded to employ, without forethought, some Procrustean techniques. Of course, when faced with a received doctrine which had not been subjected to adequate verification, it is always more interesting to dismantle a tradition, particularly when some of its advocates, at times, depended upon unanalysed assumptions.

A portion of the Caves estimates and the further possible avenues of investigation noted in this paper would, if added to the new agricultural rent estimates, appear to move the contribution of the Canadian wheat boom to real per capita income to within a range between 24 percent and a conservative 30 percent for both the shorter and the longer periods studied. Such a demonstration implies only that in particular periods of Canadian economic history, the staple theory is a useful explanatory device.

Appendix A

TABLE 8

Revisions of Gross National Product Estimates by Kenneth Buckley, 1900–1927 (millions of current and constant dollars)

Year	Current $	Constant 1949 $	Year	Current $	Constant 1949 $
1900	983	3174	1914	2394	5379
1901	1073	3447	1915	2540	5637
1902	1152	3561	1916	2973	6121
1903	1204	3758	1917	3608	6311
1904	1322	4015	1918	4050	6273
1905	1439	4235	1919	4704	6659
1906	1618	4485	1920	5394	6644
1907	1510	3871	1921	4101	5652
1908	1609	4235	1922	4266	6349
1909	1886	4879	1923	4549	6750
1910	1976	4924	1924	4328	6523
1911	2159	5227	1925	4915	7349
1912	2319	5326	1926	5152	7576
1913	2493	5644	1927	5549	8270

SOURCE: K.A.H. Buckley, "Worksheets of Professor Kenneth Buckley, June 1963," Kenneth Buckley Archives, University of Saskatchewan, Saskatoon, courtesy Professor Isabel Anderson, University of Saskatchewan. The identical constant-dollar column also appears in Buckley's work sheets provided for the Economic Council of Canada, Ottawa, circa 1965 and were the basis of the five-year moving averages of constant-dollar per capita income in Canada, 1902–26 in G. W. Bertram, *The Contribution of Education to Economic Growth*, Staff Study no. 12, Economic Council of Canada (Ottawa, 1966), appendix table A-1, 67.

Appendix B

Calculation of Richard Caves on Induced Immigrant Wages

In his article "Export-Led Growth and the New Economic History," Caves argued that significant influences of immigration may have been omitted in the Chambers and Gordon wheat boom estimate. After some experimentation with Caves' figures, data were located which appear to be the basis for his conclusion that the extra immigrant wage bill was $118.5 million for 1901–11. The guide for these computations is Caves' statement that:

> Employment growth in agriculture was 55% of a total including other primary sectors, one-half of construction, one-fourth of manufacturing, and one-third of unallocated labourers. Applying this agriculture percentage to Keyfitz' estimates of net immigration indicates total immigration as a result of the wheat boom of 392,000 which implicitly includes the 200,000 estimated by Chambers and Gordon as the direct increase.[48]

The data which underly Caves' computation appear to be as shown in table 9.

TABLE 9

Employment Growth in Canada, 1901–11		Amount or Fraction of Employment Given by Caves and Counted in Total	
All occupations	940,802		
Other primary	68,293	Δ1 Primary	68,293
Agriculture	216,875	Δ1 Agriculture	216,875
Manufacturing	72,699	Δ¼ Manufacturing	18,175
Construction	61,402	Δ½ Construction	30,701
Labourers	189,377	Δ⅓ Labourers	63,126
		Total Δ	397,170

Agricultural growth as a percentage of computed change in employment = 216,875/397,170 = 54.61 = 55 percent.

SOURCE: Dominion Bureau of Statistics, *Occupational Trends 1891–1931* (Ottawa, 1939), 6.

Applying the ratio of 55 percent to Keyfitz's estimate of net immigration, 1901–11 of 715,000[49] gives 393,250. Using the figure 392,000, Caves derives the labour force as 235,200 from a labour force participation rate of 60 percent which, multiplied by the Chambers and Gordon annual earnings of $504, yields of wage income of $118.5 million which would not have occurred in the absence of the wheat boom.

The above computation rests on Caves' assumptions concerning the fraction of employment growth occurring in the various sectors of primary products, construction, manufacturing, and unallocated labour. Any change in these fractions, which appear to be assumed rather than known, alter the estimate of the extra immigrants' wages which would be forgone in the absence of the wheat boom. Further empirical work is still required to determine with more precision what the relationship was between changes in employment in agriculture and changes in employment in related industries.

Notes

1. E.J. Chambers and D.S. Gordon, "Primary Products and Economic Growth: An Empirical Measurement," *Journal of Political Economy* (hereafter *JPE*) LXXIV, 4 (Aug. 1966): 315–32.

2. J.H. Dales, J.C. McManus, and M.H. Watkins, "Primary Products and Economic Growth: A Comment," *JPE*, LXXV, 6 (Dec. 1967): 876–80.

3. Chambers and Gordon, "Primary Products and Economic Growth: Rejoinder," *JPE* LXXV, 6 (Dec. 1967): 881–85.

4. R.E. Caves, "Export-Led Growth and the New Economic History," in *Trade, Balance of Payments, and Growth*, edited by J.N. Bhagwati, R.W. Jones, R.A. Mundell, and J. Banek (Amsterdam, 1971), 403–42.

5. For example, one of the central criticisms of the Chambers-Gordon model made in the "Comment" by Dales, McManus, and Watkins, was that staple theorists claimed that the wheat boom significantly affected many sectors of the Canadian economy other than prairie agriculture. "Chambers and Gordon have made

no attempt to test this claim. It could not in fact be tested, even roughly, without the use of a multi-equation model of the whole Canadian economy in 1911. What the authors have done is to turn a complex econometric problem into an over-simplified exercise in supply and demand curves" (see Dales et al., "A Comment," 878). There appears to be an inappropriate insistence in the first part of their "Comment" that the staple theory and economic history is somehow unconcerned with changes in per capita income, but the latter part provides a number of important criticisms of the Chambers and Gordon article.

6. See R.W. Fogel, "The Specification Problems," *Journal of Economic History* (hereafter *JEH*) XXVII, 3 (Sept. 1967): 297–98. The Chambers-Gordon article employed some of the analytical and quantitative methods associated with the "New Economic History." Much of what is distinctive in the "New Economic History" is simply the explicit use of economics. ". . . the application of standard economic reasoning in posing and answering of historical questions." (G. Wright, "Econometric Studies in History," in *Frontiers of Quantitative History*, edited by M.D. Intriligator (London, 1971), 416).

7. O.J. Firestone, *Canada's Economic Development 1867–1953* (London, 1958).

8. In the 1911 census, neither the instructions to enumerators for farm and urban values in Schedule 7 nor the actual Schedule 7 made any mention or provision for rents paid on a share basis. The 1901 census states that "Records of leased lands were given by tenants and the entries in the schedules of areas and rent values were made for such lands only." See vol. II, xlv.

9. See R.W. Fogel, *Railroads and American Economic Growth: Essays in Econometric History* (Baltimore, 1964), 55, 78–80. Fogel's innovation in this connection was to use rent theory to estimate social saving by finding the rental value of agricultural land which occurred through extending the feasible boundary of agriculture by railroads, relative to waterways. See also L.J. Mercer, "Rates of Return for Land-Grant Railroads: the Central Pacific System," *JEH* XXX, 3 (Sept. 1970): 607, 616–18. It is of interest to note that, while the Chambers-Gordon article was significantly influenced by the pioneering work done by Fogel, they failed to note this alternative technique of measuring agricultural rents. We can speculate that, while they read Fogel's "A Quantitative Approach to the Study of Railroads in American Economic Growth: A Report on Some Preliminary Findings," *JEH*, XXII, 2 (June 1962): 163–97, they apparently did not examine his book, which was published two years before the appearance of the Chambers-Gordon article.

10. There was an estimated 4051 miles of track in operation in the prairie provinces in 1901, while the *Census of Canada*, vol. IV (1911), table CXL, 345, gives 8081 miles in the prairie provinces for 1911. The 1901 estimate is based on Department of Agriculture figures (*Statistical Yearbook* (Ottawa, 1901), 374) where railway mileage for Manitoba and the Northwest Territories is given as 4141 in 1901. Subtracting 90 miles of track operated by the British Yukon Co. gives the estimate of 4051 miles for 1901.

11. Census and Statistics Office, *Canada Yearbook* (1911), 421, instructed the enumerators to provide information ". . . relative to field crops harvested in the year 1910." Dominion Bureau of Statistics, *Handbook of Agricultural Statistics*. Part 1. *Field Crops, 1908–1958* (Ottawa, 1959), lists in the tables a crop record that always covers two years, but the crop year refers to the first year (i.e., the 1910-11 crop year refers to 1910).

12. See Dominion Bureau of Statistics, *Handbook of Agricultural Statistics*. "Normal" production and value of 1910 prairie field crops were calculated by assuming that grain prices were internationally given, that the average yield per acre of the six main field crops for 1909–10 and 1911–12 give a representative yield for a normal 1910 field crop year, and that the seeded acreage of 1910 was unchanged from the actual recorded amounts. To the resulting 1910 "normal" value of field crops was added the 1910 value of all other farm products, which were assumed to be unaffected by the poor crop year, resulting in a "normal" estimate of $290,973,162.

13. Census and Statistics Office, *Census of Prairie Provinces* (1916), table 1, 290. The census classification omitted the category part owners–part tenants from cash tenants and share tenants, so that the census information is incomplete.

14. Computed from data on seeded acreage, yields, and farm price of field crops, Dominion Bureau of Statistics, *Handbook*. A one-third share arrangement was the practice mentioned most frequently in the literature.

15. Regarding Ontario, R.L. Jones, drawing from several commentaries, noted, "By 1860 three other arrangements were the prevailing ones, at least in Dundas County: (1) the tenant provided his own implements, stock, and seed, and gave the landlord one-third of the gross produce, including the hay and straw; (2) the tenant provided all his own implements and livestock, and gave the landlord half the produce;

(3) the landlord provided everything and got two-thirds of the gross produce. The second was the commonest practice." See Jones, *History of Agriculture in Ontario, 1613–1880* (Toronto, 1946), 68, n.4.

16. In the western Middle West of the United States, c. 1900, "Rental payments varied somewhat, but one-third of the crop or its value was the usual cost of rent. Share tenants were predominant over cash tenants in all the groups except Iowa. Twelfth Census, [1900] V, Agriculture, 48." See K.D. Bicha, *The American Farmer and the Canadian West, 1896–1914* (Kansas, 1968), 147, n. 27.

17. In 1926, computed on a number-of-tenants basis rather than by acres, 83 percent of prairie tenants rented on a share basis. See R.W. Murchie, *Agricultural Progress on the Prairie Frontier* (Toronto, 1936), 94, n.10. On farm management methods Murchie observed that ". . . it would appear that . . . it will be necessary to wait for the arrival of more stable agriculture before the cash-renting system can be widely adopted." Murchie also noted that "The major reason for the preference for share-renting probably lies in the fact that, under share-renting, part of the risk is passed on to the landlord" (p. 94). For a discussion of the economics of share tenancy which takes the view that share tenancy does not result in inefficient allocation of resources, see S.N.S. Cheung, *The Theory of Share Tenancy* (Chicago, 1969). Where there is no easily measured crop or product produced, such as in grazing, we conclude that tenant farming would likely be done on a cash basis. Rent estimates based on cash arrangements would reflect less productive land use and would therefore give a downward bias. A supporting observation of one economist who lived as a youth in rural Saskatchewan, c. 1910, is that share methods were the usual farm arrangements for renting land for crops, while farmers would often "turn out" their stock of cattle to graze on the natural cover ("prairie wool") for a small cash payment for a portion of an adjacent section (G. Reid Elliott, Professor Emeritus, University of Victoria).

18. The business cycle peaked in June 1920 and reached a trough in September 1921. See D. White, *Business Cycles in Canada* (Ottawa, 1967), table A1.2. In assessing the authenticity of the 1920–21 census rent estimates, it can be shown that, considering the timing of the business cycle, the date of enumeration of 1 June 1921 for the census, and the timing of price arrangements of farm agreements for rentals and shares, relatively lower cash prices were likely paid for the cash rentals recorded by the census. Presumably contracts for cash rentals were made in the spring of 1921 or in the contractions phase of the cycle. Agreements for shares, which the census recorded, were likely made in the spring of 1920 in the upswing of the cycle. The 1920 census value of share rentals was likely influenced by the favourable prices of the 1920 crop, relative to 1921. It appears that the 1921 census figures for rents per acre include both a downward and upward price bias. However, it can also be shown that the 1920 value of the output of a computed one-quarter acre share was considerably lower that its output value in previous or wartime years. We conclude that share values computed by the census on the 1920 crop basis did not contain the high price exaggeration of somewhat earlier years.

19. Improved prairie land increased from 5.5 million acres in 1901 to 23 million in 1911 and 44.9 million in 1921. See *Census of Canada*, vol. VIII (1931), table 1.

20. Wholesale market prices at Fort William for no. 1 Northern wheat rose, on trend, from $0.752 per bushel in 1901 to $1.0075 in 1911, while in the same period, the price of no. 2 oats at Fort William was about constant, on trend. Wheat and oats together account for most of the value of prairie field crops. Wheat freight charges, Regina to Fort William over the period 1901–11, fell from $0.12 to $0.108 per bushel. Wheat and oats prices and wheat freight cost are from Urquhart and Buckley, *Historical Statistics of Canada* (Toronto, 1965), 359, 548.

21. In computing hypothetical rent, Chambers and Gordon assumed, without explanation, that wage costs were 46 percent of total prairie farm output in 1901, while wage changes 1901–11 were given without citation as increasing at 2 percent per year.

22. The above calculations could be recomputed for both the Chambers-Gordon original rent estimate and the new 1911 estimate, each of them redone with a revised wage series, an upward revision of the value of farm products after 1901 in accord with the upward movement of farm prices through 1911, and a revised national income estimate for 1901 and 1911.

23. Taking the assumption again that the wage bill was 46 percent in 1901 of the value of total prairie farm products, or $17,402,000, we find from Urquhart and Buckley, *Historical Statistics*, 84, that money wages in the Canadian economy rose by 181.2 percent over the period 1901–20. The wage bill under these assumptions advanced to $31,532,000 and, without making an allowance for the rising prices of prairie agricultural products, this means that the Chambers and Gordon type of counterfactual adjustment becomes

irrelevant. The 1920 national income estimate of Firestone, *Economic Development*, 74, is used for this calculation since the sharp recession of 1921 was reflected in that year's GNP.

24. Caves, "Export-Led Growth and the New Economic History," 409.

25. Chambers and Gordon, "Primary Products . . .: An Empirical Measurement," 324.

26. See *Census of Canada* (1931). For example, change for the prairie provinces in improved acres of land 1901–11 was 17,377 acres and for the period 1911–21, 21,893 acres. While the change in gainfully employed was about half the size in 1911–21 as in 1901–11, the change in capital goods as recorded by implements and buildings was more than double in the later decade.

27. Chambers and Gordon, "Primary Products . . .: An Empirical Measurement," 326, 327.

28. Board of Inquiry into the Cost of Living, *Report* (Ottawa, 1915), I: 652–53.

29. *Census of Canada* (1911), table 45, lx. In another data source, the differential in favour of Saskatchewan relative to Ontario, 1910, is less at 27 percent for wages in the summer season. See Department of Agriculture, *Statistical Yearbook* (1911).

30. Limitations of space prevent the introduction of other evidence indicating absolute and rising urban wage differentials in favour of the prairie provinces. There is actually detailed wage data available for the period 1901–11. See, for example, on Toronto and Winnipeg carpenter wages, Department of Labour, "Wages and Hours of Labour in Canada, 1911–1920, Report 1," *Supplement to Labour Gazette* (Mar. 1921): 5.

31. Chambers and Gordon, "Primary Products . . .: An Empirical Measurement," 318.

32. Adapted from Fogel, "The Specification Problem," 299, and P. Temin, "Labour Scarcity and the Problem of American Industrial Efficiency in the 1850's, "*JEH* XXVI, 3 (Sept. 1966), 295.

33. Temin employs a two-factor framework of agriculture and manufacturing in his Mathematical Appendix to develop a model which that of Chambers and Gordon closely resembles. "Both functions are assumed to be homogeneous of degree one. . . . In other words, there are no economies or diseconomies of scale, factors of production are never redundant, and there are diminishing returns to any single factor" (Temin, ibid., 295). With respect to Temin's assumption that agricultural commodities were used only for consumption, Fogel noted that "This is certainly an unacceptable assumption. Firms employed in the processing of agricultural commodities accounted for more than 50 percent of the value added by the manufacturing section in 1860. . . . Thus Temin's exclusion of *T* [land] from the manufacturing production function is not justified by the observation that little land was directly employed in manufacturing" (Fogel, "The Specification Problem," 301).

34. In 1910, out of total value added in manufacturing, the food and beverage industry accounted for 17.1 percent, while the wood products industry accounted for 16.4 percent. While some outputs of the food and beverage industry are not relevant, the inclusion of the paper industry and non-ferrous metal industry would provide another 9.2 percent of value added for consideration. See G.W. Bertram, "Economic Growth in Canadian Industry, 1870–1915: The Staple Model and the Take-off Hypothesis," *Canadian Journal of Economics and Political Science* XX (May 1963): 176.

35. Chambers and Gordon, "Primary Products . . .: An Empirical Measurement," 325.

36. Ibid.

37. The number of salary and wage employees in the Chambers and Gordon appendix C group of industries totalled 143,000 while all manufacturing totalled 510,000 in 1910. In gross value of production, appendix C industries total $324 million out of a total of $1152 million. In both cases the proportions were 28 percent. As Chambers and Gordon indicate, the subset industries account for well over half the total employment in the group; that is, something more than 14 percent. Number of employees and gross value of production are from Urquhart and Buckley, *Historical Statistics*, 463.

38. An additional issue involves the reality of the gadget industry as a determinant of wages in the entire economy. According to the census of 1911, manufacturing industry accounted for 13.7 percent of the total gainfully employed in all sectors, while agriculture accounted for 34.3 percent. Dominion Bureau of Statistics, *Occupation Trends, 1891–1931* (Ottawa, 1939), 6–7. The mechanics of wage determination would make it appear highly doubtful that wage rates would be determined by as small an employment sector as the gadget (manufacturing) industry, particularly against a background of regional economic differences. "All urban employments are ultimately in competition with agricultural employment, and the level of agricultural income in a region provides a sort of base from which urban wage structure graduates upward. . . ." See L.G. Reynolds and C.H. Taft, *The Evolution of the Wage Structure* (New Haven, 1956), 181.

39. Chambers and Gordon, "Primary Products . . .: An Empirical Measurement," 326.

40. T. Scitovsky, *Papers on Welfare and Growth* (London, 1964), 74.

41. Chambers and Gordon drew their estimate from Denison's non-empirical estimate that the U.S. enjoyed a 10 percent increase in economies of scale, 1929–57. Denison's time period is, of course, much later than the 1901–11 Canadian experience. See E.F. Denison, *The Sources of Economic Growth in the United States* (Committee for Economic Development, 1962), 175.

42. See E.J. Chambers and G.W. Bertram, "Urbanization and Manufacturing in Central Canada, 1870–1890," *Conference on Statistics*, Canadian Political Science Association (Toronto, 1964).

43. See K.A.H. Buckley, "Review of O.J. Firestone, *Canada's Economic Development, 1867–1953*," *American Economic Review* XLIX, 3 (June 1959): 431–33. Buckley's concern was that Firestone's estimates of real national income per capita increased at a zero rate from 1910 to 1930 and he suggested that ". . . the Firestone bench mark estimate for 1910 may be too high."

44. See appendix A for Buckley's annual GNP estimates for 1900–27. In constant dollars, a comparison of Firestone's bench mark decennial percentage changes in GNP with Buckley's figures indicates the following: 1900–10, 166.96 to 155.14 percent; 1910–20, 124.52 to 134.93 percent; and 1900–20, 207.89 to 209.33 percent. In both above calculations in the text, the Chambers-Gordon figure for national income in 1911 was used. If the lower Buckley estimate for GNP in 1911 was used instead, the numerator of the ratio would be larger and the contribution of the wheat boom would be higher than shown.

45. Limitations of space permit only a mention of other factors that would, in total, also appear to indicate a Chambers and Gordon underestimate. M.C. Urquhart's criticism (see Chambers and Gordon, "A Rejoinder," 882), regarding the increase in tariff revenues that may be substituted for taxes is quantitatively underestimated in Chambers and Gordon's rejoinder estimate of $13 million, since this amount is restricted to imports that would have been generated by wheat exports. To be consistent with their use of all prairie agricultural products for wheat, the value of imports on which the tariffs is levied should be all prairie agricultural exports. While Canadian primary product experience does have relevance for other countries, the effects of Canadian tariff policy on such items as agricultural implements—which would reduce the value of agricultural land and thereby reduce rent imputed to land—would first have to be removed from the estimate. (This implication was suggested from reading an excellent paper of Kenneth Norrie on tariff and agricultural implements.) Two other factors, which may not be minor in assessing changes in per capita income due to the wheat boom, are that all the discussions so far have omitted an estimate of the change in urban rent that may have been attributable to the wheat boom, while an estimate is required of a possible decline in rural agricultural rents in the remainder of Canada.

46. Caves, "Export-Led Growth and the New Economic History," 417–18.

47. See appendix B for an analysis of Caves' estimate of $118.5 million.

48. Caves, "Export-Led Growth and the New Economic History," 410–11.

49. Nathan Keyfitz, "The Growth of Canadian Population," *Population Studies* IV (June 1950), 51, table 4.

SECTION 5

ECONOMIC GROWTH AND CHANGE IN THE TWENTIETH CENTURY

CANADIAN NEWSPRINT, 1913–1930: NATIONAL POLICIES AND THE NORTH AMERICAN ECONOMY†

TREVOR J.O. DICK

Early twentieth-century industrial expansion in Canada is typically characterized by the combination of U.S. technology and Canadian natural resources to produce quantities of output for a U.S. market far in excess of the Canadian market for the same output. The post–World War I expansion of Canadian newsprint production provides a leading illustration of this phenomenon. In less than two decades after 1913 annual output of Canadian newsprint grew from 402 to 2,985 million tons, while annual exports to the United States rose from 218 to 2,145 million tons. By 1930, only a trivial part of this output, 5.5 percent, was consumed in Canada. U.S. production of newsprint hardly changed over the same period, while U.S. consumption more than doubled.[1]

In this study, an economic model is used to help discriminate between two broadly different interpretations of Canadian newsprint expansion — interpretations that find implicit expression in a number of blended forms in the literature. At one pole, the development of the industry can be seen as an integrated North American phenomenon wherein firms are largely uninhibited in their response to market forces prompting the use of the latest technology and the most recently discovered resource abundance. At the other extreme, industrial expansion can be seen as the outcome of manipulative government policies. On the one hand, the producing provinces in Canada announced deliberate policies of industrialization by prohibiting the export of pulpwood logs from leased Crown lands, while on the other hand, the U.S. publishing industry persuaded its government

†*Journal of Economic History* XLII, 3 (Sept. 1982): 659–87. This study has been long in the making and has benefited from the helpful comments and suggestions of many persons. Robert Fogel and Stanley Engerman first sparked the author's interest in the topic and encouraged him to pursue it. Revision was aided by participants at various gatherings — the Seminar for the Application of Economics and Quantitative Methods to Canadian Economic History on two occasions, an annual meeting of the Western Economic Association, an annual meeting of the North American Economic Studies Association, and participants in the Harvard Economic History Workshop. Special thanks go to Jack Carr, Melvyn Fuss, Frank Lewis, Barry Eichengreen, Robert Zevin, Vivian Nelles, anonymous referees, and the co-editors of *The Journal of Economic History* at various stages in this article's evolution.

to reduce tariff duties against Canadian newsprint. There has been no attempt in the literature to specify a comprehensive explanation of this example of industrial expansion that would permit an accurate assessment of the scope of policy promotion.

The discussion is organized in four main sections. First, the historical background of the industrial expansion is reviewed, describing the main facts of the industry's growth, the emergence of integration across the international boundary, the interaction of trade policies in the two countries, and the issues raised by previous accounts of historians and economists. Second, a model is proposed and elaborated for organizing the discussion of these issues. Third, the data collected for testing this model and the estimation procedures and results are reported. Finally, these results are used to provide a new perspective on the scope available in retrospect for commercial and manufacturing policies to influence this industrial expansion. The main conclusion is that this scope was certainly less than perceived by those attempting to influence policy at the time, and probably less than most commentators have been prepared to concede since that time.

The Historical Setting of Twentieth-Century Newsprint Expansion

Early History of Pulp and Paper in the United States and Canada

The industry dates from about the mid-nineteenth century when it was discovered in both Europe and America that wood rather than rags could be used effectively to produce a pulp for paper making. The process involved both mechanical and chemical components using running water and supplies of soda and later sulphur. By the last quarter of the nineteenth century, the process was clearly a commercial success and well suited to the North American abundance of spruce forests and rivers. Newsprint quickly became the largest single output of the industry, and by 1900, patents on the critical elements in making pulp from wood had expired. The shift from rags to wood as the primary input of paper was facilitated by the invention of the Fourdrinier paper machine at the beginning of the nineteenth century and its introduction to the United States before the Civil War, gradually replacing the earlier Dutch cylinder machines. The manufacture of pulp and paper together in an integrated mill became the most common organization of newsprint production.[2]

In the nineteenth century, the industry grew to a much larger size in the United States than in Canada, although the rates of growth were similar in the two countries. United States pulpwood supplies were still readily available near to the largest growing urban centers in that country.[3] The first mills appeared shortly after the Civil War, and by the 1880s and the 1890s, the U.S. paper industry was growing at a rate as high or higher than any rate recorded before the 1920s.[4] The growth of U.S. newsprint proceeded nearly independently in North America almost to the end of the nineteenth century. Production rose from 100,000 tons a year in 1869 to over one million tons a year by 1914. As late as 1911, when the industry produced over 1,100,000 tons, imports were only 54,000 tons, less than 5 percent. Although the industry was less independent of external supplies of pulpwood, still 80 percent of the industry's requirements were met from domestic sources. Similarly, most of the pulp used by the industry was made in the United States around the turn of century. Only 142,000 tons of pulp were imported from Canada in 1909 compared with 1,179,500 tons produced in the United States. Trade with countries other than Canada was minuscule.[5]

Accompanying the nineteenth-century growth of the U.S. industry was a dramatic rise in the capitalization of pulp and paper mills. The technology of the pulp and paper industry increasingly implied large fixed capital investment. While the early years of U.S. papermaking accommodated a large number of independent firms, capital requirements progressively raised a barrier to entry and, in combination with substantial price declines in the late nineteenth century, created an incentive for concentration and merger activity.[6] This culminated in the creation of the International Pulp and Paper Co. in 1898 that absorbed many smaller firms. Together with its Canadian subsidiary, International retained its dominance, but suffered a progressive decline in its share of the North American market to about 10 percent by 1930. Whether and how such concentration was justified became matters of intense debate between producers and publishers after the turn of the century.[7] The number of mills producing newsprint in the United States had dropped to about seventy-five by the eve of World War I, most of the decline having occurred before 1900. The daily capacity of an average mill stood at about sixty-five tons in 1910 compared to less than ten tons only twenty years earlier.[8]

The Canadian pulp and paper industry, able to share in the same nineteenth-century technological breakthroughs as its U.S. counterpart, established its first mills at about the same time.[9] The first groundwood paper mill appeared in Valleyfield, Quebec, in 1869. Such mills served mainly local markets with their final products, but began to export some pulpwood and pulp before 1900 and eventually some paper before 1914.[10] This early market for Canadian products was much smaller than the total U.S. market, although it did exceed the Canadian market. By 1900, Canada was already producing more pulpwood and pulp than Canadian paper manufacturers could absorb, the difference being exported to the United States. By 1908, Canada produced 1.3 million cords of pulpwood and used only 0.5 million cords at home, while the United States was consuming at an annual rate of over 3 million cords, only 2.5 million of which were produced in the United States.[11] Similarly, while the United States absorbed 2 million tons of pulp in 1908, 0.5 million tons were imported. At the same time, Canada produced only 0.4 million tons and exported half of this, mostly to the United States.[12] Thus, almost from the beginning of the twentieth century, the Canadian industry, though much smaller than the U.S. industry, was starting to develop exports of pulp and pulpwood of a magnitude much more important relative to Canadian output than to U.S. consumption, while both countries remained nearly self-sufficient in newsprint.[13]

In the years leading up to 1900 and before exports of Canadian newsprint to the United States became important, the value of output from Canadian paper mills grew nearly tenfold and the number of mills doubled. The first mill with machines specially adapted to newsprint production appeared in 1899, although small amounts of newsprint had been made in Canada since the 1870s. On the eve of World War I, there were about twenty-five newsprint-producing mills in Canada with an average daily capacity of sixty-nine tons, quite similar in size to their U.S. counterpart at the same time.[14] The tendency toward concentration already evident in the U.S. industry before World War I was not yet a prominent feature of the Canadian industry, and there was as yet little involvement of either U.S. capital or U.S. enterprise with the financial organization of the Canadian industry.

The Emergence of North American Integration

The rapid growth of the pulp and paper industry in both the United States and Canada before World War I and the large size of the U.S. industry relative to the Canadian industry in 1914 are the appropriate background against which to view later developments. In the United States, newspaper circulation between 1870 and 1909 rose by 80 percent, more rapidly even than population. In the next two decades circulation rose another 50 percent and population by 30 percent.[15] It is hardly surprising that this sustained pressure on U.S. pulpwood supplies eventually spilled over onto Canadian forests. U.S. imports of pulpwood that began in the late nineteenth century rose to one million cords a year by 1914 and remained at that level into the 1930s.[16] There was a clear price incentive for these imports. From 1901 to 1909, for example, the manufacturing cost of newsprint in the United States rose from $25 to $35 per ton, directly attributable to a $10 rise in the cost of wood required to produce a ton of newsprint. All other elements of cost remained virtually unchanged over these years. In 1909, $26 of the total per ton cost went into the purchase of wood.[17] Expansion of the U.S. industry up to World War I also relied on imports of manufactured pulp, both mechanical and chemical, that rose from less than 100,000 tons a year in 1900 to 675,000 tons in 1914. Unlike pulpwood, imports of pulp continued to rise into the 1930s until they reached a level of about two million tons a year.[18]

The most dramatic aspect of growing integration between U.S. and Canadian pulp and paper production, however, was the development of the North American newsprint trade. Canadian newsprint exports to the United States began before World War I. Their value was $1,200,000 in 1910 and $2,000,000 in 1912, and rose dramatically to over $100,000,000 a year in 1930, accounting for 30 percent of Canada's total exports to the United States compared with only 1.2 percent in 1910.[19]

These changes amounted to a reorganization of the pulp and paper industry within North America such that Canadian plants, led by U.S. capital and enterprise, became the dominant suppliers of newsprint for a North American market while many U.S. facilities specialized in the non-newsprint products of the industry. The expansion of U.S. newsprint production was at an end, although production continued to 1930 at World War I levels. While the U.S. industry augmented its dwindling domestic supplies of raw materials with Canadian pulpwood and pulp, it relinquished all further newsprint expansion to the rapidly expanding Canadian plant and equipment financed in the United States. By the 1920s, subsidiary activities of U.S. firms were well entrenched. The leading participant was the International Pulp and Paper Co., which constructed its first Canadian mill at Three Rivers, Quebec, in 1921, and subsequently formed a Canadian subsidiary, the Canadian International Paper Co.[20]

Large-scale capital expansion was rapid, and by the late 1920s, Canadian output had become concentrated in three large mergers: The International Paper Co., Abitibi Power and Paper Co., and the Canadian Power and Paper Co.[21] While a few smaller groups and several smaller firms survived, there was a strong incentive to combination that went almost unresisted in Canada and was provided by the fall in prices following their boom level in 1920 and by the development of excess capacity in the late 1920s.[22] Yet the merger movement was less than a success. The Canadian Newsprint Co., formed in 1927, and its successor, the Newsprint Institute of Canada, formed in 1928, were unable to work out any consolidation to restrict output that would stem the price fall, and most of the newsprint companies in eastern Canada went into receivership in the 1930s. Canadian governments that had co-operated in the pulp and paper reorganization and newsprint expansion in Canada left newsprint producers almost entirely to market forces and to their own devices. Canadian financial mergers appeared more commonly in times of prosperity than depression and often were unsuccessful in their attempt to increase earnings.[23] The U.S. government, for its part, had been won over by the publishers and remained passive to the plight of subsidiary firms that overexpanded in Canada.

The movement toward integration had been underway for many years and there was a well established pattern of pulp and paper mills locating near to the source of their main input, pulpwood.[24] Nevertheless, the changes after World War I were of such a magnitude as to leave the impression that the long-run equilibrium of the industry had not been fully worked out by 1930.[25] The longevity of capital in the industry and the ongoing technological change that was given renewed impetus by expanding war and postwar demands give rise to this impression. Larger paper-making machines that could operate at faster speeds were the hallmark of new Canadian plant and equipment manufactured in the United States. The versatility of older machines in the United States meant that they could be adapted to other lines of paper output, while the continued production of substantial newsprint output in the United States implied modernization as well as some access to Canadian resources to compete in the long run with Canadian newsprint output.[26] The daily capacity of Canadian paper mills had risen to 285 tons by 1930 from under 100 tons during World War I. Because of the nature of capital already in place in the United States and the zero net expansion there, U.S. newsprint mills did not achieve this daily capacity until World War II. By that time the number of mills producing newsprint was only about ten, or one quarter the number of Canadian mills producing newsprint. In 1930, the number of producing mills was more nearly the same in both countries, but their average daily capacity was quite different.[27] It took the eventual post-1930 recovery of the North American market as a whole to see the integration process through to its logical conclusion.

The Growth of National Policies

The intervention of government in the U.S. pulp and paper industry and its newsprint sector in particular arose from a developing contest between publishers and producers. Except for a few isolated years, the industry after 1875 suffered from periods of price decline signalling a buyers' market.[28] The response of the paper producers took the form of corporate consolidation for price fixing and quantity restriction and efforts to obtain tariff protection. The publishers, unable to head off these industry initiatives before they won some success, mounted a progressively more effective campaign to attack the industry's pricing policies and tariff protection. Although the trend in concentration continued, particularly after the shift of newsprint expansion to Canada, the publishers did eventually succeed in eliminating the U.S. tariff on newsprint, a feat without parallel in the rest of the protected manufacturing sector.[29]

It was not until nearly the turn of the century that the struggle between the publishers and the paper industry began in earnest. Although a tariff of 15 percent *ad valorem* on unsized paper and 20 percent *ad valorem* on sized and glued paper appeared in 1883, annual paper production, including printing paper, was already 149,000 tons in 1879. Newsprint production alone expanded threefold in the 1890s to over a half million tons while the 1883 tariff was maintained in the McKinley legislation of 1890 and in the Wilson-Gorman tariff legislation of 1893. Although the beginning of newsprint production may not have required the tariff, the industry's spokesmen associated its subsequent expansion with protection. When the province of Ontario announced its manufacturing conditions, first against the export of logs destined for sawmills in 1898, and then against the export of pulpwood in 1900, by virtue of provincial ownership of Crown forest lands, the U.S. industry reacted strongly.[30] Anticipating such moves, the United States in 1897 had legislated the Dingley tariff, which contained a graduated tariff rate increasing with the unit value of the imported product. Additional duties were to be levied against paper imports from countries that taxed pulpwood exports. A duty of $1.57 a ton was also levied on pulpwood bound for the United States.

In the battle against protection, John Norris, the publishers' chief spokesman, was unable to overcome the producers' fears that the industry would be lost to Canada without the tariff. The industry continued to persuade the government that the tariff imposed no real hardship and made little difference to price. In 1909 preparatory to the Payne-Aldrich tariff legislation, the Mann committee made it clear that the United States wanted a special kind of reciprocity, namely, free trade in pulpwood, in return for any reduction in the newsprint tariff with the clear intention of using Canadian resources to help support a protected U.S. industry. In the end, the newsprint tariff was marginally lowered from $6 a ton to $3.75 plus a surtax of $2 and the amount of any export levy if Canada discriminated against the United States in the export of pulpwood. The existing duty on mechanical pulp of $1.67 a ton would be continued only where export restrictions on pulpwood were retained by Canada. Retaliatory duties were set at a maximum of 25 percent over the regular rates.

The key to the publishers' eventual success lay in the Canadian attitude. The Canadian response was to remain adamant since no U.S. legislation could save the U.S. industry if it could not obtain raw materials. The loophole in the wood export prohibition provided by Quebec forests and supported by her settlement interests was closed in 1910 by an export restriction matching the one already in effect in Ontario. As things stood, the Payne-Aldrich tariff was a hollow victory for U.S. producers wanting to remain and expand in the United States. Although Canada-U.S. trading relations were reaching a low ebb, the U.S. publishers won a partial victory in 1911 when they pointed out and the U.S. government conceded that not all Canadian forests were Crown lands, and that paper made from private wood should not be taxed since the provinces could not restrict the export of wood from private lands. Having won a tariff concession on at least some paper coming from Canada, the publishers went on to argue optimistically that this would soon lead to the removal of Canadian export restrictions altogether, particularly as the Canadian paper industry was already starting to expand rapidly. From then on the producers were on the defensive, and in 1913, the Underwood tariff reduced the duty on newsprint to a level that permitted free entry.[31] All retaliatory provisions in the tariff were removed. No other aspects of the Canada-U.S. trading relationship, however, were altered. The possibility of more general trading reciprocity died with the Canadian election result of 1911, and provincial restrictions on pulpwood exports remained on the legislative books. The future of the industry appeared to be where it had always been — near to the source of raw materials, notwithstanding the international boundary.[32]

From a public-policy standpoint the arena now shifted to industrial organization and pricing considerations. As the industry expanded in Canada, the size and importance of multinational enterprise grew. At the same time, antitrust sentiment increased in the United States, especially as Canadian law against combinations appeared to be less severe than U.S. law.[33] With the tariff issue resolved, the publishers focused their attack on the pricing policies of companies like International Paper. The coincidence of rising war and postwar demand, sharply rising prices, and Canadian expansion brought the industry under major investigation by the Federal Trade Commission (FTC) in 1916, and more or less permanent surveillance thereafter.[34] This marked the beginning of attempts, largely unsuccessful, by governments in both countries to regulate the industry.[35] Evidence of collusive activity among major producers was uncovered by the FTC in 1916, and the offending companies were required to dissolve their association and be subject to a price ceiling. But the FTC had no power to regulate prices, and the ceiling was only one part of more general wartime controls that were allowed to lapse after the war was over. Henceforward, the industry attempted to organize competition via price leadership in an effort to avoid antitrust action. Resort to price leadership was an understandable response by producers committed to heavy long-term fixed capital investment. Yet it is clear from the price history that competition so repeatedly broke this practice that serious questions can be raised about the feasibility of attempts to improve the industry's performance by regulation. Whether or not price stability or regulation would have improved the situation, there is no doubt that neither was achieved. Prices went up and down along similar paths in both countries. In the United States, the companies managed to escape prosecution under the Sherman Antitrust Act while ostensibly under the control of the FTC. In Canada, where the governmental response was to set up a regulatory Board of Commerce to control the industry, this body apparently had little more success with respect to sales to Canadian publishers, the only sales pertinent to its regulation. Such sales were, in any case, rapidly becoming a trivial part of Canadian production.

Historians, Issues, and Analyses

Scholarly attention to the history of the industry in North America has spanned a wide spectrum of approaches to political economy. Changes in U.S. tariff policy are most commonly discussed, though seldom in isolation from other factors such as comparative advantage, resource policies, and competition and its regulation. Resources, technology, and demand are not usually discussed without some reference to a policy context. Most studies treat a number of factors, but leave open any explicit integration of these factors within a coherent analytical framework.

All commentators on the tariff give some credence to the contemporary view of U.S. producers that removal of the U.S. import duty would remove the industry to Canada.[36] Some writers like Southworth, Smith, Stevenson, Weeks, Johnson and Percy, and Nelles imply that tariff removal was instrumental in shifting the center of newsprint production to Canada.[37] Others like Guthrie and Bladen believe the attraction of Canadian resources was overwhelming.[38] A few like Traves are more equivocal and believe that both resources and the tariff played some role.[39]

The fact that most Canadian pulpwood forests remained in the hands of Ontario and Quebec led many commentators to argue that the determination of these provinces to restrict the export of unprocessed logs was instrumental in bringing the newsprint industry's expansion to Canada.[40] Guthrie, however, believes that the attraction of Canadian resources would have operated overwhelmingly in any case, while Aitken and Nelles take an intermediate position that both resource pull and policy were effective.[41]

Commentary on the organization and performance of the industry, while admitting the presence of aspects of imperfect competition, also acknowledges frequent episodes of vigorous price competition. On the side of imperfect competition and oligopolistic structure are arguments incorporating price leadership,[42] the declining number of firms in the industry through merging activity,[43] the differentiated and multi-product nature of pulp and paper output,[44] the large fixed capital requirements,[45] and the common assumption that the industry enjoyed economies of scale.[46] On the other side of the argument in support of price competition, writers have pointed to the inelastic demand for newsprint,[47] the dominance of standardized newsprint among pulp and paper products,[48] the fact that many newsprint mills, especially in Canada, came to produce newsprint almost exclusively,[49] the persistence of a competitive fringe even when mergers occurred,[50] the variability of price in spite of the contract system of price making,[51] the temporary and incomplete nature of cartels and the tenuous ability of dominant firms to maintain price leadership,[52] the general failure of regulation to influence price and quantity,[53] and the appearance of excess capacity.[54]

The main difficulty with virtually all the political economy discussions of the early history of the newsprint industry is their inability to resolve the questions at issue beyond conjectures based on casual empiricism. It cannot be determined, for example, what the precise effect of trade restrictions may have been by simply arguing that these things influenced price. There must be a substantive, well specified and tested general hypothesis about how price was determined, formulated in such a way that the questions of interest can be examined. In the remaining sections of this paper one possible and plausible framework is chosen that allows the tariff and embargo questions in particular to be focused coherently.

Modelling the North American Newsprint Expansion

As a point of departure, the industry is assumed to have grown as a North American whole fundamentally in response to forces articulated in the marketplace. Insofar as policies had any effect, these effects are viewed as modifications of market price and quantity. There are two main aspects of this starting point for analysis. First, the market setting permits the use of the well established theory of supply and demand to organize important elements of the story that other writers have variously treated. Second, the emphasis on North America picks up the fact that the essential elements of this story from a market perspective cut across the boundary between Canada and the United States. Because it stresses the international competition facing producers in either country, and is supported by evidence from regression analysis that there was a single nominal newsprint price in North America, a competitive industry model is seen as the most reasonable first approximation to the framework within which the industry is hypothesized to have expanded.[55] The advantage of such a model is that it permits an examination of the impact of supply and demand forces on the growth of the industry. A formal model of imperfect competition is judged less appropriate because it would emphasize restrictions on competition whereas the issues to be examined clearly involved the exercise of competitive pressures.

For a competitive industry, price and output can be taken as determined by supply and demand specified by equations taking the general form of equations (1) and (2):

$$Q = DP^{-\epsilon} \tag{1}$$
$$Q = SP^{\gamma} \tag{2}$$

Solving this simple system for P and Q yields

$$Q = D^{\gamma/(\gamma+\epsilon)}S^{\epsilon/(\gamma+\epsilon)} \tag{3}$$
$$P = (D/S)^{1/(\gamma+\epsilon)} \tag{4}$$

By transforming (3) and (4) rates of growth,

$$\overset{*}{Q} = \frac{\gamma}{\gamma + \epsilon}\overset{*}{D} + \frac{\epsilon}{\gamma + \epsilon}\overset{*}{S} \tag{5}$$

$$\overset{*}{P} = \frac{1}{\gamma + \epsilon}(\overset{*}{D} - \overset{*}{S}) \tag{6}$$

it is immediately evident that demand factors become more important relative to supply factors the more elastic is supply relative to demand.[56]

In the empirical context of this study, the price, P, is taken to be the relative price of newsprint that would be obtained from deflating nominal price by an appropriate index of general price movement. Measured in terms of the same currency, it turns out that the nominal price of delivered newsprint in the two countries is highly correlated. Transportation costs are, therefore, conceptually included in P. This will facilitate an assessment of the claim made by some writers that transportation costs were an important factor in determining the location of newsprint production.[57]

Q is taken to refer to the combined newsprint output of Canada (including Newfoundland) and the United States, using the observation that one North American price prevailed for the industry's output, and that newsprint was the most important single output of the pulp and paper industry. The assumption is likewise made that the same technology is shared by producing units in the two

TABLE 1

Definition of Symbols

Q	= Output
D	= Shift term in the demand function for output
S	= Shift term in the supply function for output
S'	= Defined by equations (22) and (23)
P	= Price of output
A	= Index of productive efficiency
L	= Labor input
R	= Raw material input
K	= Capital input
w	= Wage rate
r, r_i	= Unit cost of raw materials; $i = 1, 2$.
C	= Newspaper circulation per capita
$\overline{P}$	= Population
m, b	= Constants
ϵ	= Elasticity of demand for output
γ	= Elasticity of supply of output
α_i	= Output elasticity of input; $i = 1, 2, 3$.
ϕ_1	= Elasticity of demand with respect to C
ϕ_2	= Elasticity of demand with respect to $\overline{P}$
ν, μ	= Uncorrelated random errors

NOTE: Asterisks (*) upon symbols denote time rates of change. Hats (∧) upon symbols denote point estimates. Ln preceding a symbol denotes the natural logarithm thereof.

countries, and that fundamental elements of newsprint demand, also partly technological and anchored in the production of and the demand for newspapers, were likewise similar in both countries. Newspaper circulation per capita was only slightly higher in the United States than in Canada, and there is no evidence that newspapers were produced differently. The plausibility of interpreting Q as combined Canadian and U.S. output is further supported by a close match between combined North American production and consumption. Canadian exports and U.S. imports are almost identical, and newsprint trade with third countries is trivial. Canadian production, moreover, is heavily dominated by U.S. investment and parent firms so that private profit maximization within each country independently is unlikely always to have been the case. Indeed, the possibility that some of the Canada-U.S. trade was intrafirm trade cannot be ruled out.

Another possible, though perhaps less plausible, interpretation of Q is the amount of newsprint traded between Canada and the United States. Within the period that can reasonably be investigated econometrically, and that sees the establishment of the industry in Canada primarily to serve the U.S. market, this trade grows to over 90 percent of Canadian production and to nearly 65 percent of U.S. consumption. Equilibrium in this market, given the virtually self-contained North American setting, must have reflected nearly the same forces that determined price and output as a whole.

In these supply and demand terms, North American newsprint production grew from 1913 to 1930 at a continuous annual average rate of 2 percent. Canadian production grew at 8 percent, U.S. production at -0.2 percent, and Canadian exports to the United States at 13 percent per annum. The real price of newsprint rose rapidly until 1920, and fell still more rapidly in the next ten years. These changes, in the context of the model, interpret the locational shift of the main source of supply within North America to new Canadian producing units as part of the adjustment to a new long-run equilibrium within a single industry. Lack of attention in the literature to the industry's expansion in these terms is not surprising. While newsprint was a star performer among Canadian manufacturing industries and Canada's principal export soon after World War I, it was of only minor importance to total U.S. trade, which was in turn much less important relative to U.S. output than was Canadian trade to Canadian output.

As a first approximation in modeling supply-side considerations, consider a Cobb-Douglas production function for a single output, Q, and three factors of production, labor, raw materials and capital, L, R and K.

$$Q = AL^{\alpha 1}R^{\alpha 2}K^{\alpha 3} \qquad (7)$$

The assumptions of competitive pricing and profit maximization subject to this production function make it possible to construct the supply function.[58] Because of the longevity and slow turnover of capital in the industry relative to the number of years included in the sample for this study, it is appropriate to consider the supply curve for the short run during which entrepreneurs do not increase their capital input.[59]

$$Q = [mA^{1/(1-\alpha1-\alpha2)}w^{-\alpha1/(1-\alpha1-\alpha2)}$$
$$r^{-\alpha2/(1-\alpha1-\alpha2)}K]P^{(\alpha1+\alpha2)/(1-\alpha1-\alpha2)} \qquad (8)$$

A further simplification results from assuming constant returns to scale, guaranteeing an upward sloping supply curve.

$$Q = [mA^{1/\alpha3}w^{-\alpha1/\alpha3}r^{-\alpha2/\alpha3}K]P^{(\alpha1+\alpha2)/\alpha3} \tag{9}$$

where $\alpha_1 + \alpha_2 + \alpha_3 = 1$.

Two issues are raised by these straightforward procedures. First, the average daily capacity of newsprint mills grew quite rapidly from 1913 to 1930, yet the largest mills were at most 1.5 percent of the total capacity of the industry by 1930. Economies of scale are ambiguous to define and still harder to document where a multi-product industry like pulp and paper is the setting. For the total paper component, as well as for total pulp and paper, factor shares were relatively constant over the sample years.[60]

Second, while the period under examination captures the main changes motivating the analysis, it deals with a span of years within which long-run competitive adjustment was not yet completed. As noted in the previous section, the same competition that was removing the industry to Canada was also leaving behind in the United States producing units that were slowly exiting the industry or modernizing to meet the scale and design efficiency of new plants in Canada. This is reflected in the country-specific functional shares derived from industry data for this period, and raises an issue about the working assumption of the model that technology was similar in the two countries. One way to handle this is to open the model to include two supply curves jointly facing a single demand. Another is to lengthen the sample period. Introducing an additional supply curve so alters the structure of the model that the testable implications of constrained maximization are weakened. Lengthening the sample period runs into the Depression and war years that severely disrupted the industry and have little to do with the forces that prompted resource re-allocation before 1930. Instead of adopting these "remedies," a compromise is offered by considering the sensitivity of the parameters in the model to different ways of extracting estimates of these parameters from the data that give rise to country-specific functional shares.

On the demand side, newsprint was the primary input into newspaper production. There were virtually no alternative sources of supply outside North America competitive with North American supply, and no technical substitutes for newsprint in newspaper production. The most appropriate variables for the demand function, therefore, are newspaper circulation per capita, C, and population $\overline{P}$, along with price, P.

$$Q = (bC^{\phi1}\overline{P}^{\phi2})P^{-\epsilon} \tag{10}$$

where b is a constant.

The complete model is the result of substituting the shift terms of (9) and (10) for S and D in equations (2) and (1).

$$Q = (mA^{1/\alpha3}w^{-\alpha1/\alpha3}r^{-\alpha2/\alpha3}K)P^{\gamma} \tag{11}$$

$$Q = (bC^{\phi1}\overline{P}^{\phi2})P^{-\epsilon} \tag{12}$$

By manipulating (11), total factor productivity, A, can be expressed as a function of prices, output, and capital.

$$A = m^{-\alpha 3}(w/P)^{\alpha 1}(r/P)^{\alpha 2}(Q/K)^{\alpha 3} \tag{13}$$

The reduced form of (11) and (12), analogous to (3) and (4), is obtained by solving for Q and P.

$$Q = [bC^{\phi 1}\,\overline{P}^{\phi 2}]^{\gamma/(\gamma+\epsilon)}[mA^{1/\alpha 3}w^{-\alpha 1/\alpha 3}r^{-\alpha 2/\alpha 3}K]^{\epsilon/(\gamma+\epsilon)} \tag{14}$$
$$P = [bC^{\phi 1}\,\overline{P}^{\phi 2}]^{1/(\gamma+\epsilon)}[mA^{1/\alpha 3}w^{-\alpha 1/\alpha 3}r^{-\alpha 2/\alpha 3}K]^{-1/(\gamma+\epsilon)} \tag{15}$$

Finally, transforming (14) and (15) into rates of growth yields

$$\overset{*}{Q} = \gamma/(\gamma + \epsilon)[\phi_1\overset{*}{C} + \phi_2\overset{*}{\overline{P}}] + \epsilon/(\gamma + \epsilon)[(1/\alpha_3)\overset{*}{A}$$
$$- (\alpha_1/\alpha_3)\overset{*}{w} - (\alpha_2/\alpha_3)\,\overset{*}{r} + \overset{*}{K}] \tag{16}$$

$$\overset{*}{P} = 1/(\gamma + \epsilon)[\phi_1\overset{*}{C} + \phi_2\overset{*}{\overline{P}}] - 1/(\gamma + \epsilon)[(1/\alpha^3)\overset{*}{A}$$
$$- (\alpha_1/\alpha_3)\overset{*}{w} - (\alpha_2/\alpha_3)\,\overset{*}{r} + \overset{*}{K}] \tag{17}$$

Equations (14) and (15) are the starting point for the statistical investigation.

Reinterpretation of the Growth of North American Newsprint

Econometric Specification and Estimation

Two general strategies are available to estimate the parameters of equations (14) and (15). First, to economize on data, particularly with respect to poorly measured capital stock and productivity, the supply elasticity may be estimated directly from factor shares.[61] It can be shown that under certain conditions the model is reduced to a single just-identified equation used to obtain a consistent estimate of the demand elasticity.[62] Second, using the best available proxies for the right-hand-side variables of (11) and (12), a more standard two-stage procedure can be used to estimate the parameters of these two overidentified equations. The first procedure has the advantage of avoiding the use of some highly questionable data, but involves making estimates whose consistency is problematic unless some tight conditions are met. The second procedure uses the data rejected by the first method, and is only clearly superior if these data provide suitable instrumental variables. Given the uncertainties of the data, therefore, neither method is obviously superior to the other, and both are used and their results compared.

According to the first method, equation (11) is simplified by replacing its term in parentheses with S. A random disturbance is added to the result and to equation (12) yielding

$$Q = SP^{\gamma}e^{v} \tag{18}$$
$$Q = (bC^{\phi 1}\,\overline{P}^{\phi 2})P^{-\epsilon}e^{\mu} \tag{19}$$

Taking logarithms, and solving for P and Q, yields the reduced form,

$$\ln P = \frac{1}{\gamma + \epsilon} \ln b + \frac{\phi_1}{\gamma + \epsilon} \ln C + \frac{\phi_2}{\gamma + \epsilon} \ln \overline{P}$$
$$- \frac{1}{\gamma + \epsilon} \ln S + \frac{\mu + \nu}{\gamma + \epsilon} \tag{20}$$

$$\ln Q = \frac{\gamma}{\gamma + \epsilon} \ln b + \frac{\gamma \phi_1}{\gamma + \epsilon} \ln C + \frac{\gamma \phi_2}{\gamma + \epsilon} \ln \overline{P}$$
$$+ \frac{\epsilon}{\gamma + \epsilon} \ln S + \frac{\gamma \mu + \epsilon \nu}{\gamma + \epsilon} \tag{21}$$

To estimate these equations requires data for lnS where, from (18)

$$\ln S + \nu = \ln Q - \gamma \ln P \tag{22}$$

From equation (9), and using data on factor shares to provide an estimate $\hat{\gamma}$ of γ

$$\ln S' = \ln Q - \hat{\gamma} \ln p = \ln S + \nu + (\gamma - \hat{\gamma}) \ln P \tag{23}$$

This procedure modifies the reduced form and implies (18) holds identically LnS' becomes an instrument for lnP, and the parameter estimates for (19), it can be shown, will be consistent only if $\hat{\gamma} = \gamma$ and μ and ν are uncorrelated.[63]

Canadian and U.S. data on factor shares yield, via equation (9), supply elasticities of 2.33 and 3.62, respectively.[64] The labor shares were similar, .21 for Canada and .16 for the United States. The raw material share was larger in the United States, .63, than in Canada, .49, reflecting higher costs in the United States. The capital share was larger in Canada, .30, than in the United States, .21, reflecting initially higher capital intensity in the newer part of the industry. The estimated short-run supply elasticities, $\hat{\gamma}$, implied by these shares may be taken as bounds on the average elasticity for the industry as a whole over the sample period. While some of the difference may be a function of different measurement concepts and errors associated with different statistical agencies, the supply elasticity might also be interpreted to have fallen as long-run adjustment in the industry proceeded.

To estimate the demand elasticity, e, either equation (20) or (21), appropriately modified to incorporate lnS' using $\hat{\gamma}$, is sufficient. The country-specific data for Q, P, C, and $\overline{P}$ are displayed in table 2.[65] North American aggregates are obtained for Q and $\overline{P}$ by simple addition, and for P and C by averaging using population weights. Since both reduced forms are exactly identified, OLS is applied, and since the data are times series, a correction for first-order serial correlation of the residuals is used. Using equation (20), for example, and $\hat{\gamma} = 2.33$,

$$\ln P = -16.0 \ln b - 0.9 \ln C + 3.89 \ln \overline{P} - 0.32 \ln S' \quad R^2 = 0.97 \tag{24}$$
$$(-4.7) \quad (-2.7) \quad\quad (5.7) \quad\quad (-9.6) \quad \text{D.-W.} = 1.21$$

Table 2

Newsprint Industry Data, 1913–1930

	(1)	(2)	(3)	(4)	(5)	(6)	(7)	(8)
	Q		P		C		$\overline{P}$	
	CAN	US	CAN	US	CAN	US	CAN	US
1913	402	1305	56.9	111.9	0.18	0.22	7.6	97.2
1914	470	1313	58.5	106.8	0.19	0.23	7.9	99.1
1915	549	1239	57.9	101.9	0.19	0.24	8.0	100.5
1916	662	1315	59.2	117.1	0.20	0.25	8.0	102.0
1917	726	1359	76.4	122.8	0.21	0.26	8.1	103.3
1918	770	1260	90.2	106.9	0.22	0.28	8.1	103.2
1919	841	1324	104.8	117.2	0.22	0.25	8.3	104.5
1920	938	1512	151.9	155.8	0.21	0.26	8.6	106.5
1921	849	1225	155.1	171.2	0.20	0.26	8.8	108.5
1922	1142	1448	108.1	114.7	0.20	0.27	8.9	110.0
1923	1315	1485	113.9	120.5	0.19	0.28	9.0	112.0
1924	1453	1481	111.5	118.0	0.20	0.29	9.1	114.1
1925	1633	1530	106.3	108.6	0.19	0.29	9.3	115.8
1926	2075	1684	100.0	100.0	0.21	0.31	9.4	117.3
1927	2286	1485	98.6	101.9	0.21	0.32	9.6	119.0
1928	2645	1417	98.1	97.2	0.21	0.32	9.8	120.5
1929	2981	1392	86.5	89.9	0.22	0.32	10.0	121.8
1930	2985	1282	85.3	91.7	0.21	0.32	10.7	123.1

Columns: (1) and (2) thousands of tons of newsprint; (3) and (4) newsprint price indexes,
1926 = 100; (5) and (6) newspaper circulation per capita; (7) and (8) millions of population.
NOTE: CAN = Canada, US = United States.
SOURCES: See note 65.

and for $\gamma = 3.62$,

$$\ln P = -11.7\ln b - 0.6\ln C + 2.82\ln \overline{P} - 0.24\ln S' \quad R^2 = 0.98 \quad (25)$$
$$(-5.3) \quad (-2.8) \quad (6.5) \quad (-14.3) \quad \text{D.-W.} = 1.12$$

where t-ratios are in parentheses under each coefficient estimate. These results
display goodness of fit and correctly signed point estimates of the coefficients
significant at the 5 percent level. Using these estimates, the values in table 3 are
derived. It is evident that the elasticity of demand is consistently less than unity
regardless of which supply elasticity estimate is used, with the consequence, by
equation (5), of assigning more weight to demand shifts vis-à-vis supply shifts in
explaining the evolution of quantity.

Under the alternative strategy, the starting point is equations (11) and (12).
Taking logarithms, adding random disturbances, and imposing the restriction of
constant returns to scale provides two overidentified estimating equations:

$$\ln Q - \ln K - \ln A = \alpha_3 \ln m + \alpha_1 (\ln Q - \ln w - \ln K)$$
$$+ \alpha_2 (\ln Q - \ln r - \ln K) + \alpha_3 \gamma \ln P + \nu \quad (26)$$

$$\ln Q = \ln b + \phi_1 \ln C + \phi_2 \ln \overline{P} - \epsilon \ln P + \mu \quad (27)$$

TABLE 3

Estimated Elasticities

Equation	γ	ϵ	ϕ_1	ϕ_2	$\epsilon/(\gamma + \epsilon)$	$\gamma/(\gamma + \epsilon)$	$1/(\gamma + \epsilon)$
(24)	2.33	.80	−.29	1.24	.26	.74	.32
(25)	3.62	.55	−.15	.68	.13	.87	.24
(30)	3.00	.45	1.6	6.8	.13	.87	.29

SOURCE: See text.

The variable, r, is interpreted as a vector of two inputs to incorporate both pulpwood and electricity. Labor accounts for about $1/5$, pulpwood from $1/2$ to $3/5$, electricity about $1/5$, and capital less than $1/5$ of total costs.[66] These equations are estimated by two-stage least squares with a correction for first-order serial correlation of the residuals. The data used are displayed in table 4.[67] Country-specific series on factor prices are averaged using population weights. Capital stock data is aggregated by addition and the productivity series is a single series of patents.

$$\ln Q - \ln K - \ln A = -3.38\ln m + 0.40(\ln Q - \ln w - \ln K)$$
$$(-5.5) \qquad\qquad (2.5)$$
$$+ 0.74(\ln Q - \ln r_1 - \ln K) - 0.19(\ln Q - \ln r_2 - \ln K) + 0.72\ln P \qquad (28)$$
$$(4.3) \qquad\qquad\qquad (-3.9) \qquad\qquad\qquad (5.4)$$

$$\ln Q = -51.0 - 2.32\ln C + 12.0\ln \overline{P} - 0.34\ln P \qquad (29)$$
$$(-6.3) \quad (-2.5) \qquad (7.4) \qquad (-1.2)$$

From (28) and (29), $\gamma = 18.6$, and $\epsilon = 0.34$. Now, the supply elasticity far exceeds the demand elasticity while the latter remains below unity, reinforcing the relative importance of demand shifts suggested by equations (24) and (25).

Finally, using the observation that Canadian exports and U.S. imports of newsprint were virtually equal to one another within North America during the sample period, equation (20) can be re-estimated employing the quantities traded and the prices that were equivalent for domestic and foreign buyers. To proceed with the estimation of (20) in this context requires prior information about γ to start the analysis, where γ is now interpreted as the elasticity of supply of exports rather than of exportables. Since the required elasticity is an elasticity of excess supply, there is a presumption that it is higher than the estimates used in equation (23) to provide a basis for (24) and (25).[68] Equation (20) is re-estimated using U.S. imports of newsprint from Canada for Q and a derivation of S' based on $\gamma = 3$.[69] The P used is as before, while U.S. series are used for C and $\overline{P}$.

$$\ln P = -6.15 + 0.45\ln C + 1.98\ln \overline{P} - 0.29\ln S' \qquad (30)$$
$$(-2.9) \quad (2.0) \qquad (4.9) \qquad\quad (-17.4)$$
$$R^2 = .99 \qquad\qquad\qquad\quad D.\text{-}W. = 1.68$$

TABLE 4

Supplementary Newsprint Industry Data

	w		r₁		r₂		K		A	
	CAN	US	CAN	US	CAN	US	CAN	US	CAN	US
1913	94.0	79.4	73.6	98.7	219.6	246.8	30.6	89.1	72.2	72.2
1914	99.7	81.4	75.7	97.9	211.6	229.8	36.2	92.2	74.4	74.4
1915	98.9	100.4	71.2	96.6	190.3	215.1	39.2	104.5	76.7	76.7
1916	87.5	111.2	64.7	88.9	152.1	187.0	40.1	108.8	78.4	78.4
1917	76.4	110.0	66.2	99.1	119.6	148.6	39.4	102.7	80.1	80.1
1918	72.3	108.3	75.4	109.3	109.3	127.8	46.6	97.4	81.5	81.5
1919	77.6	107.9	93.8	105.9	100.2	113.1	49.0	94.1	83.5	83.5
1920	83.7	112.2	105.5	118.4	90.3	105.8	55.9	89.8	85.6	85.6
1921	102.3	102.4	142.1	142.9	106.3	116.6	72.7	101.6	88.2	88.2
1922	98.4	94.6	106.5	112.7	110.3	113.0	76.5	100.4	90.5	90.5
1923	100.4	101.6	107.9	110.4	107.9	108.8	83.0	100.7	92.5	92.5
1924	104.4	101.8	108.4	109.4	104.8	107.8	91.4	101.5	94.9	94.9
1925	94.6	101.5	107.2	105.1	98.9	105.9	89.3	99.9	97.4	97.4
1926	100.0	100.0	100.0	100.0	100.0	100.0	100.0	100.0	100.0	100.0
1927	96.9	103.1	90.4	100.7	98.8	99.3	115.4	109.4	103.0	103.0
1928	97.9	103.2	92.7	101.1	96.3	98.0	136.1	104.8	106.0	106.0
1929	102.9	108.3	86.9	100.8	90.9	94.2	126.0	131.0	109.0	109.0
1930	93.2	104.6	86.7	100.0	89.0	91.5	141.7	136.8	112.7	112.7

SOURCE: See note 67.
NOTE: w = wage rate, r₁ = pulpwood price, r₂ = hydro-electricity price, K = capital stock, A = total factor productivity. All data are indexed to the base 1926 = 100.

Like the demand elasticities already estimated, the elasticity of import demand is less than unity. Experimentation showed that the import demand elasticity could be made to approach zero by raising the estimated supply elasticity no higher than 10. Again, these results reinforce the implications of the previous elasticity estimates.

Explaining Industrial Growth

Applying rates of growth transformations to equations (20) and (21), dropping the error terms, tells the main story.

$$\overset{*}{P} = \frac{\phi_1}{\gamma + \epsilon} \overset{*}{C} + \frac{\phi_2}{\gamma + \epsilon} \overset{*}{P} - \frac{1}{\gamma + \epsilon} \overset{*}{S}' \tag{31}$$

$$\overset{*}{Q} = \frac{\gamma \phi_1}{\gamma + \epsilon} \overset{*}{C} + \frac{\gamma \phi_2}{\gamma + \epsilon} \overset{*}{P} + \frac{\epsilon}{\gamma + \epsilon} \overset{*}{S}' \tag{32}$$

$\overset{*}{C}$, $\overset{*}{P}$ and $\overset{*}{S}'$ are obtained by regressing the log of C, $\overline{P}$, and S' on time, and $\overset{*}{D}$ is implied from a rate of growth transformation of (12).

$$\overset{*}{D} = \phi_1 \overset{*}{C} + \phi_2 \overset{*}{P} \tag{33}$$

Using the parameter estimates obtained in equations (24) and (25), equations (31), (32), and (33) can be implemented, and the resulting rates of change are reported in columns (1), (3), and (5) of table 5. In a similar manner, using the estimates from equation (30), the rates of change in columns (2), (4), and (6) of table 5 are derived. While equations (28) and (29) display some overall consistency with the elasticity results based on equations (24), (25), and (30), they incorporate weaknesses in detail too severe to permit any plausible extension and rates of change interpretation based on equations (16) and (17).

Two observations stand out in the results displayed in table 5. First, taking the period as a whole, supply was certainly more elastic than demand, but it was supply that advanced to the right more rapidly. Taking the elasticity weights into account, 58 percent of North American output growth and 84 percent of the growth in North American trade was attributable to demand influences in the newsprint market. The reliability of these results is enhanced by the fact that the growth rates predicted for Q and P are reasonably good proxies for the growth rates actually recorded. North American output and price for the period as a whole grew at average annual rates of 2.7 percent and −0.9 percent, while trade expanded at 13 percent per annum.[70]

Second, the experiences before and after 1921 differed sharply. Before 1921, price was rising and output was growing almost entirely because demand was shifting along nearly stationary supply curves. After 1921, price fell rapidly while output continued to increase, though much more rapidly than before. While the rightward shift in demand moderated slightly, supply shifted to the right much

TABLE 5

Average Annual Rates of Change

| Variable | | 1913–21 | | 1922–30 | | 1913–30 | |
		(1)	(2)	(3)	(4)	(5)	(6)
Q	(a)	0.63	10.59	4.70	15.28	1.98	13.36
	(b)	0.41		3.39		1.24	
P	(a)	0.29	4.60	−3.86	−4.79	−1.28	−1.15
	(b)	0.14		−4.51		−1.30	
D	(a)	0.85	12.00	0.47	13.44	0.94	12.87
	(b)	0.49		0.28		0.53	
S′	(a)	−0.04	3.82	12.53	28.0	4.93	16.49
	(b)	−0.08		19.09		5.97	
C		2.27	2.35	2.54	2.44	2.06	2.08
P̄		1.22	1.21	0.97	1.40	1.24	1.40

SOURCES: See text. For columns (1), (3) and (5) only (a) is based on regression (24) and (b) on regression (25). Columns (2), (4) and (6) are based on regression (30).

more rapidly. U.S. demand for Canadian newsprint grew steadily while Canadian supply suddenly exploded at twice the rate the demand for it was growing. The trade in newsprint had hardly begun in 1913 when the U.S. market was already substantial so that the growth in demand for Canadian exports after 1913 was many times more rapid than the growth rate of demand in North America as a whole. The supply response, however, was delayed until after 1921.

The behavior of newsprint price is easily explained by competitive market forces. During the years up to 1921, North American demand was expanding and supply actually retreated as some U.S. plants withdrew from production before Canadian expansion could compensate for the loss. Since supply was less than perfectly elastic, price rose. After 1921, when supply advanced over ten times more rapidly than demand, price fell. Since supply was more elastic than demand, the price rise before 1921 was more moderate than the decline thereafter, and the price fell overall.

The behavior of output reflects the same market forces. The slow output growth before 1921 results not only from a stagnant and marginally retreating supply curve but also from its low elasticity and the small rate of price increase despite an early one percent rate of rightward shift in demand. After 1921, when the rate of demand shift was slightly less, and given the inelasticity of demand, a massive supply shift was required to generate enough price fall for the large increases in output to clear the market.

It is possible, therefore, to explain the behavior of price and quantity during the pre-1930 expansion in these terms. It is not necessary to invoke explicitly any of the features of industrial organization traditionally alleged to detract from competitive performance. The difference between the behaviour of supply and demand before and after 1921 accords well with the process of lagged adjustment to a long-run competitive equilibrium under market stimulus suggested earlier in the discussion of the industry's history.

The Role of Commercial and Manufacturing Policies

United States Tariffs

The imposition of a U.S. tariff on Canadian exports would have distorted the market in traded goods assumed to lie behind regression equation (30). Had an *ad valorem* duty on Canadian newsprint of 15 percent been reimposed in 1913 and retained throughout the sample period, the supply curve of Canadian exports would have experienced a once-and-for-all shock equivalent to a 15 percent upward shift against the price axis. Given an elasticity of export supply of 3, this shift amounts to a 45 percent leftward shift against the quantity axis. Equation (30) and its equivalent for lnQ patterned on (21) imply that the price, inclusive of the tariff, would have been 13 percent higher and output for export 5.8 percent lower once-and-for-all. These changes are worth about three years of pre-1921 price advance and less than half a year of the export growth actually achieved. The price to the Canadian producer would also have been 13 percent lower once-and-for-all, and Canadian output, assuming a supply elasticity of 2.33 and a demand elasticity of −0.8, would have been 9.39 percent lower, or approximately a little under one year's setback to the growth of the industry based in Canada.

On the U.S. side, imports would, of course, have been reduced by the same amount as any reduction in Canadian exports. In addition, firms producing in the United States would have benefited from a 13 percent price rise. But they would have experienced a once-and-for-all increase in their output of about 7 percent, only half a year's growth in the output being imported from Canada, not enough to match the growth in U.S. demand.

It is clear, therefore, that the removal of the U.S. tariff by 1913 could not have been a factor of major importance to the development of the North American newsprint trade and to the expansion of the industry in Canada. Had it been otherwise, then superimposing the tariff on the events that actually took place after 1913 should have occasioned a major departure from recorded events by perpetuating the industry in the United States and preventing its removal to Canada.

The fact that the U.S. import demand for Canadian newsprint was inelastic, however, raises the curious possibility that Canadian non-newsprint tariffs might have contributed to Canadian newsprint expansion. The reason is that when a country facing an inelastic foreign demand curve for its exports attempts import substitution via tariffs on imports, the relative price of exportable goods rather than importable goods rises.[71] As Canada specialized in newsprint for a North American market, the U.S. pulp and paper industry tended to specialize in other non-newsprint products. At the same time, Canada erected tariff barriers to replace domestic consumption of these expanding lines of U.S. production with import substitutes. This is an area for future research that takes account of the multi-product nature of the pulp and paper industry as a whole.

Canadian Pulpwood Embargoes

The export embargo on Canadian pulpwood distorted factor markets by indirectly taxing U.S. producers where the delivered cost of U.S. pulpwood exceeded the delivered cost of Canadian pulpwood, thereby raising U.S. costs of production. This would have reduced U.S. supply and increased U.S. demand for exports of Canadian newsprint. Unlike the tariff, an effective embargo should have made the U.S. industry smaller and the Canadian industry larger.

In a comprehensive analysis where satisfactory estimates of production function parameters can be obtained, it would be appropriate to analyze this question taking into account all relative factor prices and technical elasticities of substitution. Since data for this are inadequate, the following analysis improvises by assuming Canadian and U.S. pulpwood to have been perfect substitutes, and the elasticities of substitution between pulpwood and other factors of production to have been zero. These plausible assumptions permit a first approximation to the effect of pulpwood trade embargoes to be calculated.

There are three pulpwood prices relevant to the analysis. The price of pulpwood to U.S. mills, given the Canadian embargoes, was a composite of the prices paid for domestic and imported pulpwood since not all Canadian wood was subject to the embargo. Wood sold from private Canadian lands could be exported without restriction, and upwards of one-fifth of U.S. pulpwood consumption was imported during the sample years.[72] At the U.S. mill, the reported price of imported wood consistently exceeded the price paid for domestic wood.[73] Given that wood at or near the cutting site was probably cheaper in Canada than in the United States, one must assume that Canadian wood did not bear higher delivery costs than U.S. wood to all U.S. mills, or else no U.S. mills would have been paying higher delivered prices for imported wood when some mills paid lower delivered prices for domestic wood. The delivered price of pulpwood to Canadian pulp and paper mills was consistently lower than the average delivered prices to U.S. mills over the sample period.[74] A number of factors might account for this, including the location of Canadian mills vis-à-vis wood supplies and the pricing policies applicable to wood cut from Crown lands.

The critical question in treating the impact of export embargoes is, of course, what the delivered price to U.S. mills would have been for wood cut on Crown lands that supplied Canadian mills. It is reasonable to assume that delivery costs from these lands to Canadian mills were probably lower than to U.S. mills. The price differential recorded in the prices actually paid by Canadian and U.S. mills, therefore, likely exaggerates the saving that might have been enjoyed by U.S. mills if they had purchased wood from Canadian Crown lands. This cost differential is used as an upper bound in deriving the price effect on the U.S. industry. The recorded differential varies from 10 percent to 20 percent in favor of Canadian pulpwood. Again, to establish an upper-bound cost saving from buying Canadian wood, the calculated price effect uses 20 percent. Pulpwood constituted at most three-fifths of the cost of newsprint. Removing the embargo would, therefore, offer a subsidy that would lower the supply curve of the U.S. industry by at most 12 percent against the price axis. Inasmuch as more of the U.S. newsprint market would be served from the United States, there is also an implicit saving in the transport costs of newsprint since Canadian mills can be assumed to be more remote to U.S. markets. This saving may have been as much as 50 percent, and with transport costs accounting for approximately 10 percent of the delivered price of newsprint, this factor could add another 5 percent of subsidy, bringing the total upper-bound subsidy to 17 percent.[75]

Taking the supply elasticity of the U.S. industry at 3.62, a downward shift of the supply curve by 17 percent is equivalent to a rightward shift against the quantity axis of 61 percent. Using equation (32) and the estimates from equation (25) to capture the impact on the U.S. industry, the implied subsidy leads to a once-and-for-all increase in U.S. output of at most 8 percent, barely more than the already calculated effect of the U.S. tariff and only a half year's growth in the output being imported from Canada. For such a subsidy it would hardly have been worthwhile for the bulk of the producing units of the industry to have remained in the United States.

Notwithstanding U.S. grumbles at the time, the U.S. industry lost little from the Canadian pulpwood export embargoes and would, therefore, have gained little by their removal. By the same token, these embargoes provided a slender fillip for the Canadian industry. The Ontario and Quebec manufacturing conditions clearly had little to do with the removal of the newsprint industry to Canada after World War I.

In retrospect it is significant that the U.S. tariff and the Canadian pulpwood export embargoes appear to have distorted the market by similar orders of magnitude. A consequence of this from the point of view of the U.S. industry is that the benefit derived from the tariff was just about offset by the hurt accruing to the pulpwood embargoes. And from the point of view of the Canadian industry, the removal of the tariff while continuing the embargoes gave a combined policy impetus to this industry of about two year's growth.

Conclusion

Notwithstanding the political controversies and government policies in Canada and the United States surrounding the expansion of the newsprint industry after 1913, this expansion appears to have been dominated by the operation of market forces on a North American scale. Relatively elastic supply combined with relatively inelastic demand explain well the observed behavior of prices and quantities within a competitive framework. The growth of U.S. demand accounts for more than half the expansion of Canadian industry and exports.

While the reimposition of the earlier U.S. tariff would have reduced this growth and protected U.S. production, the effect would have been small on the expansion that occurred in Canada. Similarly, "manufacturing conditions" in Canada based on the provincial ownership of pulpwood forests were of small consequence to the growth of the industry in Canada. The sustained relatively inelastic demand of the United States for Canadian newsprint leaves open the possibility that Canadian non-newsprint tariffs could have played some role in accelerating the Canadian newsprint expansion.

Notes

1. See sources of table 2, note 65.

2. The details of this story can be found in a number of places. See, for example, James D. Studley, *The United States Pulp and Paper Industry* (Washington, D.C. 1938), 1–7; Louis T. Stevenson, *The Background and Economics of American Papermaking* (New York, 1940), chap. 1; David C. Smith, *The History of Papermaking in the United States* (New York, 1970), chaps. 1–6.

3. See David C. Smith, "Wood Pulp and Newspapers 1867–1900," *Business History Review* 38 (Autumn 1964): 328–45, and John A. Guthrie, *The Newsprint Paper Industry* (Cambridge, Mass., 1941), chap. 2.

4. See Lyman H. Weeks, *A History of Paper Manufacturing in the United States 1690–1916* (New York, 1926), chaps. 12–14, and Studley, *The U.S. Pulp and Paper Industry*, 59.

5. See Studley, *The U.S. Pulp and Paper Industry*, 76–87.

6. See Stevenson, *The Background and Economics of American Papermaking*, chap. 4.

7. See Simon N. Whitney, *Anti-Trust Policies, American Experience in Twenty Industries* (New York, 1958), chap. 6, esp. 355–58, and J.G. Cummins, "Concentration and Mergers in the Pulp and Paper Industries of the United States and Canada 1895–1955" (Ph.D. dissertation, Johns Hopkins, 1960).

8. See R.S. Kellogg, *Newsprint in North America* (New York, 1948), 10–27.

9. See George Carruthers, *Paper-Making*, Part II: *First Century of Paper Making in Canada* (Toronto, 1947).

10. See Studley, *The U.S. Pulp and Paper Industry*, 79, 85.

11. See R.G. Lewis, "Development of the Pulp and Paper Industry from 1900 to 1925," *Pulp and Paper Magazine of Canada* (Feb. 1927): 187; Studley, *The U.S. Pulp and Paper Industry*, 60, and R.S. Kellogg, *Pulpwood and Woodpulp in North America* (New York, 1923), appendix, 230–32.

12. See Studley, *The U.S. Pulp and Paper Industry*, 70, 78; M.C. Urquhart and K. Buckley, *Historical Statistics of Canada* (Toronto, 1965), 334; and Kellogg, *Pulpwood and Woodpulp in North America*, 224–29.

13. A good historical summary of Canadian and U.S. production and consumption data is provided in Canadian Pulp and Paper Association, *Reference Tables* (Montreal, 1951).

14. Data on the early Canadian mills can be found in the Lockwood Trade Journal Co., *Lockwood's Directory of Paper and Allied Trades* (New York, annually from 1884–85), and in Carruthers, *First Century of Paper Making in Canada*.

15. See Guthrie, *The Newsprint Paper Industry*, 9.

16. See Kellogg, *Pulpwood and Woodpulp in North America*, 230.

17. See United States Tariff Board, *Pulp and News-print Paper Industry*, Senate Document no. 31, 62nd Congress, 1st Session (Washington, D.C., 1911), 77ff., and Guthrie, *The Newsprint Paper Industry*, chap. 9.

18. See Kellogg, *Pulpwood and Woodpulp in North America*, 226, and Studley, *The Pulp and Paper Industry*, 78.

19. See Canadian Pulp and Paper Association, *Reference Tables*, table 67: 24.

20. The developing interest of U.S. investors is recounted in H. Marshall, Frank A. Southard, and Kenneth Taylor, *Canadian-American Industry* (New Haven, 1936), 35–53, 330. About half the industry was U.S. owned by 1930. See also H.G.J. Aitken, *American Capital and Canadian Resources* (Cambridge, Mass., 1961), 37, 42–43, 70–71.

21. Growing concentration in Canada is described by Guthrie, *The Newsprint Paper Industry*, chap. 5; Lloyd G. Reynolds, *The Control of Competition in Canada* (Cambridge, Mass., 1940), 23ff.; V.W. Bladen, *An Introduction to Political Economy* (Toronto, 1944), 162–83, and Cummins, "Concentration and Mergers."

22. See Robert E. Ankli, "The Canadian Newsprint Industry, 1900–1940," in *Variations in Business and Economic History, Essays in Honor of Donald L. Kemmerer*, edited by Bruce R. Dalgaard (Greenwich, Conn., 1982), and Reynolds, *The Control of Competition in Canada*, 99.

23. See Reynolds, *The Control of Competition in Canada*, 173–75, and H.V. Nelles, *The Politics of Development* (Toronto, 1974), 443–64, and chap. 12.

24. See J.W. Birch, "The Changing Location of the Wood Pulp Industry in the United States and Canada: 1900–1956" (Ph.D. dissertation, Johns Hopkins, 1961).

25. See Reynolds, *The Control of Competition in Canada*, 100. Some of the considerations that weigh

heavily in the equilibration process are discussed in C.P. Fell, "The Newsprint Industry," in *The Canadian Economy and its Problems*, edited by H.A. Innis and A.W.F. Plumptre (Toronto, 1934), 40–53.

26. See J.G. Glover and W.B. Cornell, *The Development of American Industries* (New York, 1941), 145–50, and Stevenson, *The Background and Economics of American Paper Making*, chap. 4.

27. See sources noted in notes 8 and 14.

28. For prices from 1862 to 1939, see Bladen, *An Introduction to Political Economy*, 153–54, 159, and Kellogg, *Newsprint in North America*, 49.

29. For a detailed account of this progressive encounter, see L. Ethan Ellis, *Print Paper Pendulum* (New Brunswick, N.J., 1948), chaps. 1–5, and his *Reciprocity 1911* (New Haven, 1939), chap. 3.

30. See Ellis, *Print Paper Pendulum*, chap. 3.

31. Ibid., 88–89.

32. See Guthrie, *The Newsprint Paper Industry*, 179.

33. See John W.M. Bliss, "Another Anti-Trust Tradition: Canadian Anti-Combines Policies 1889–1910," *Business History Review* 47 (Summer 1973): 39–50, and Reynolds, *The Control of Competition in Canada*, 169–70.

34. See Federal Trade Commission, *Report on the News-print Paper Industry* (Washington, D.C., 1917), and O.E. Merchant, "The Government and the Newsprint Paper Manufacturers," *Quarterly Journal of Economics* 32 and 34 (Feb. 1918 and Feb. 1920): 238–56 and 313–28.

35. For accounts of regulation, see J.A. Guthrie, "Price Regulation in the Paper Industry," *Quarterly Journal of Economics* 60 (Feb. 1946): 194–218, and Tom Traves, *State and Enterprise, Canadian Manufacturers and the Federal Government 1917–1931* (Toronto, 1979), chap. 3.

36. See Ellis, *Print Paper Pendulum*, 51, 56–57.

37. See Constant Southworth, "The American-Canadian Newsprint Paper Industry and the Tariff," *Journal of Political Economy* 30 (Oct. 1922): 681–82; Smith, *The History of Paper Making in the United States*, 316, 347; Stevenson, *The Background and Economics of American Paper Making*, 195; Weeks, *A History of Paper Manufacturing*, 317; Richard Johnston and Michael B. Percy, "Reciprocity, Imperial Sentiment and Party Politics in the 1911 Election," *Canadian Journal of Political Science* (Dec. 1980): 715, and Nelles, *The Politics of Development*, 346.

38. See Guthrie, *The Newsprint Paper Industry*, 46, and Bladen, *An Introduction to Political Economy*, 155.

39. See Traves, *State and Enterprise*, 30.

40. See, for example, Southworth, "The American-Canadian Newsprint Industry and the Tariff," 694, and Smith, *The History of Paper Making in the United States*, 209.

41. See Guthrie, *The Newsprint Paper Industry*, 46; H.G.J. Aitken, "Defensive Expansion: The State and Economic Growth in Canada," in *Approaches to Canadian Economic History*, edited by W.T. Easterbrook and M.H. Watkins, Carleton Library no. 31 (Toronto, 1967), 212, and Nelles, *The Politics of Development*, 104.

42. See Guthrie, *The Newsprint Paper Industry*, chap. 8, and Guthrie, "Price Regulation in the Paper Industry," 198–200.

43. See Guthrie, *The Newsprint Paper Industry*, chap. 5.

44. See J.A. Guthrie, *An Economic Analysis of the Pulp and Paper Industry* (Pullman, Washington, 1972), chap. 2, and Guthrie, *The Newsprint Paper Industry*, chap. 7.

45. See Stevenson, *The Background and Economics of American Paper Making*, chap. 4.

46. See Guthrie, *The Newsprint Paper Industry*, 93–94; Guthrie, "Price Regulation in the Paper Industry," 197; Guthrie, *An Economic Analysis of the Pulp and Paper Industry*, 187; Bladen, *An Introduction to Political Economy*, 159–61, and Stevenson, *The Background and Economics of American Paper Making*, chap. 6. Despite the impressive growth in size of plant and the technological progress of the industry after 1910, the present writer is unaware of any study that attempts to establish scale economies on the basis of anything more than casual empiricism. To be successful, such a study would have to define scale in a way to take into account the multiproduct nature of the industry.

47. See Guthrie, *The Newsprint Paper Industry*, chaps. 1 and 6 and 122–24; Guthrie, "Price Regulation and the Paper Industry," 196, and Stevenson, *The Background and Economics of American Paper Making*, 139–40.

48. See Kellogg, *Newsprint in North America*, 7–9, and Studley, *The United States Pulp and Paper Industry*, 74–75.

49. See Glover and Cornell, *The Development of American Industries*, 147–48.

50. See Guthrie, "Price Regulation and the Paper Industry," 202.

51. See Guthrie, "Price Regulation and the Paper Industry," 214–15, and E.A. Forsey, "The Pulp and Paper Industry," *Canadian Journal of Economics and Political Science*, 1 (Feb. 1935): 506. All contract prices were made subject to a provision that the price shall not be higher than that charged to any customer by any mill with an annual capacity no less than 100,000 tons, a provision highly conducive to price cutting.

52. See Guthrie, *The Newsprint Paper Industry*, chap. 8. While International managed to hold onto its position as dominant firm, its share of the market was reduced over the sample period from about 25 percent to about 10 percent.

53. See note 35.

54. See note 22. The Newsprint Association of Canada's record of rated capacity is found in L. Ethan Ellis, *Newsprint Producers, Publishers, Political Pressures* (New Brunswick, N.J., 1960), table III, 240, 243. See also A.E. Safarian, *The Canadian Economy in the Great Depression* (Toronto, 1959), 44.

55. Price uniformity in the United States was an objective of the contract system. See C.R. Coughlin, "The Newsprint Industry in Canada" (M.A. thesis, McGill University, 1939), 105. A coefficient of correlation of .7 or better between Canadian and U.S. prices was obtained by regression.

56. An elaboration of this type of model in different contexts is pursued in Robert W. Fogel and Stanley L. Engerman, eds., *The Reinterpretation of American Economic History* (New York, 1971), 98–115. The symbols used in equations (1) to (6) and in all equations henceforward are listed and defined in table 1.

57. See Guthrie, *The Newsprint Paper Industry*, chap. 12.

58. Details of the derivation of the supply function can be seen in Fogel and Engerman, *The Reinterpretation*.

59. Some machines installed before 1900 were still in operation in 1930. See Glover and Cornell, *The Development of American Industries*, 145.

60. Factor shares can be computed for every year after World War I, and for every three or four years before then, from cost data assembled in the manufacturing censuses of Canada and the United States.

61. See equation (9).

62. See Paul L. Joskow and Edward F. McKelvey, "The Fogel-Engerman Iron Model: A Clarifying Note," *Journal of Political Economy* 81 (Sept./Oct. 1973): 1236–40. See also Gavin Wright, "Econometric Studies of History," in *Frontiers of Quantitative Economics*, edited by M.D. Intriligator (Amsterdam, 1970), 449–53.

63. See Joskow and McKelvey, "The Fogel-Engerman Iron Model," 1240.

64. See Canada, Dominion Bureau of Statistics, *Canadian Forestry Statistics Reference Paper* (Ottawa, 1959), table 18: 43, and United States, Bureau of Labor Statistics, *Census of Manufacturing* (Washington, D.C., 1919, 1920, and 1929), 433, 553, and 541 respectively.

65. Canadian and U.S. production data are obtained from the Canadian Pulp and Paper Association, *Reference Tables*, table 45: 19 and table 51: 20. Relative newsprint prices were obtained by deflating newsprint prices by general retail price movements and indexing to a Canadian dollar base of 1926 = 100. The underlying series are New York contract prices from Kellogg, *Newsprint Paper in North America*, 49–50, and Canadian retail prices from Dominion Bureau of Statistics, *Prices and Price Indexes 1913–25*, and *Prices and Price Indexes 1913–27* (Ottawa, 1925 and 1927), 88–89 and 66–67. The deflators used are Series E-135 from U.S. Bureau of the Census, *Historical Statistics of the United States*, vol. 1 (Washington, D.C., 1976), and a combination of Canadian Department of Labour index revised by Gordon Bertram and Michael Percy in their "Real Wage Trends in Canada, 1900–1926: Some Provisional Estimates," *Canadian Journal of Economics* (Feb. 1979): 306, and Series J-128 from Urquhart and Buckley, *Historical Statistics of Canada*. The exchange rate between Canadian and U.S. dollars is recorded in Series H-627 from Urquhart and Buckley, *Historical Statistics of Canada*. Newspaper circulation for the United States is from A. McC. Lee, *The Daily Newspaper in America* (New York, 1937), 726–27 and from the Canadian Pulp and Paper Association, *Reference Tables*, 22. Newspaper circulation for Canada is from Dominion Bureau of Statistics, *Canada Year Book* (Ottawa, 1935), 771, and A. McKim, *Canadian Newspaper Directory* (Montreal, 1909 and 1919), 258–60 and 307–09. Canadian population is Series A-1 from Urquhart and Buckley, *Historical Statistics of Canada*, and U.S. population is Series A-22 from *Historical Statistics of the United States*, vol. 1.

66. See Guthrie, *The Newsprint Paper Industry*, chap. 13.

67. All the data for wages, raw material prices, and capital stock are expressed in dollar values or index form in the sources used. The series in table 4 derived from these data are deflated to a Canadian dollar base

of 1926 = 100 using the same deflators employed in constructing the series in table 2. See note 65. The underlying series for Canadian wages is from Dominion Bureau of Statistics, *The Pulp and Paper Industry* (Ottawa, annual), and for U.S. wages, see Stevenson, *The Background and Economics of American Paper-making*, 62–63. For Canadian pulpwood prices, see Dominion Bureau of Statistics, *The Pulp and Paper Industry*, and Guthrie, *The Newsprint Paper Industry*, chap. 9. For U.S. pulpwood prices, see Kellogg, *Newsprint Paper in North America*, 64. For a Canadian hydroelectricity price index, see Series J-132 in Urquhart and Buckley, *Historical Statistics of Canada*, and for the United States, see Series S-116 in *Historical Statistics of the United States*. The capital series are, in principle, stock values from the U.S. manufacturing census and from Dominion Bureau of Statistics, *The Pulp and Paper Industry*. For productivity change, Canada and the United States are assumed to have followed the same path in the absence of discriminating studies. The benchmark figures provided by John Kendrick, *Productivity Trends in the United States* (New York, 1961), 471, were interpolated using times series of patents taken from Jacob Schmookler, *Invention and Economic Growth* (Cambridge, Mass., 1966), 225.

68. See Edward Leamer and Robert M. Stern, *Quantitative International Economics* (Boston, 1970), 8–17.

69. It might be argued that a domestic (United States) supply variable ought to be included in equation (30) on the grounds that it properly belongs in (19) under the current interpretation. In defense of the estimators sought in (30), it should be noted that they are designed mostly to deal with the problem of simultaneity raised by G.H. Orcutt, "Measurement of Price Elasticities in International Trade," *Review of Economics and Statistics* 52 (May 1950): 117–32. In this case, recognition is also given to the excess demand property of import demand by treating simultaneity within a closed North American economy where Canadian output and exports expanded for precisely the same reasons that U.S. output did not, namely, the substitution of a low- for a high-cost producer of newsprint. Deriving export supply and import demand curves using domestic elasticities presents a problem with the current sample since the consumption and production shares to be applied change radically over the years of the sample. Fortunately, a reasonably stable outcome can be obtained by this method for the Canadian export elasticity in the neighborhood of 3.

70. These actual rates of change are the result of regressing the logarithms of the variables on time.

71. If the foreign demand elasticity is too low, domestic protection protects the "wrong" industry. See Lloyd A. Metzler, "Tariffs, the Terms of Trade and the Distribution of National Income," *Journal of Political Economy* 57 (Feb. 1949): 1–29.

72. See Kellogg, *Pulpwood and Woodpulp in North America*, 230.

73. See Kellogg, *Newsprint Paper in North America*, 64.

74. See Guthrie, *The Newsprint Paper Industry*, 149, and Dominion Bureau of Statistics, *The Pulp and Paper Industry* (1917), table U. The reported average value per cord is inflated by a factor of 1.125.

75. See Guthrie, *The Newsprint Paper Industry*, chap. 12.

FINANCE AND FOREIGN CONTROL IN CANADIAN BASE METAL MINING, 1918–55†

ALEXANDER DOW

Two contrary interpretations seek to explain the history of Canada's extractive resources.[1] What may be termed the orthodox position considers the exploitation of Canada's non-renewable natural resources in the first half of the twentieth-century as a success story, in which foreign capital was married to Canadian materials to the benefit of all. Certainly this view prevails among those within the Canadian mining industry, as the following quotation illustrates:

> It is obvious that the proper development of the mining industry, and all the resource industries, requires capital. Like it or not, the internal sources of money are just not sufficient. Some foreign investment is absolutely necessary. In our reaction to the extent of American investment in our country, we tend to lose sight of the fact that this foreign capital is essential to us.[2]

Academic analysis stresses also the role of entrepreneurial talent and the latest U.S. technology which accompanied direct foreign investment in the development of Canadian resources. Hugh Aitken's writing shows this approach:

> American capital, entrepreneurship and technology have not merely exploited opportunities—they have also created them. Their function has been not merely to facilitate the doing of things that would have been done anyway, but also to get things done that might not have been done at all.[3]

Thus the orthodox position, presented both in popular and academic form, acknowledges the positive contribution of substantial foreign participation in the development of Canada's extractive industries. Seen as a corollary to a necessary drawing on the pool of foreign savings, particularly from the United States, foreign ownership also brought human capital, providing an entrepreneurial thrust otherwise lacking within the Canadian mining industry. In addition to the need for capital the orthodoxy indicates that U.S. ownership was promoted by the development of the technology of mining and mineral processing in the United States, and was stimulated by demand originating south of the 49th parallel which formed the greater part of the market for Canadian minerals.[4]

†*Economic History Review* XXXVII, 1 (Feb. 1984): 54–67.

An alternative, more sceptical, view of the benefits to the Canadian economy of foreign investment has been adopted by some revisionist staples theorists. Writers in the Canadian "staple" tradition insist that Canada's economic development has been distinctive and not simply an illustration of classical economic principles at work. They stress that natural resource exploitation, given an external demand, shapes the maturing of an economy dependent on relatively unprocessed "staple exports" and seems to explain this entire process.[5] Fish, fur, timber, and wheat were successive staples in Canada's historical experience, but in the early twentieth century, somewhat awkwardly, mining development has been interpreted by some as evidence that mining should also be regarded as a staple, and suitable for analysis in terms of the staples approach. In one version this approach has been seen as an export-led growth model, in which a particular staple influences economic development uniquely on account of the distinctive linkages it creates.[6] In another, the staples approach is recast in the framework of dependency theory, whereby emphasis is extended from linkage or multiplier effects to the distribution of the economic rents from staple production.[7] Foreign ownership and the leakage of economic rents from the domestic economy define a form of exploitation. With respect to extractive resources, including minerals and mineral fuels, these modern staples writers (sometimes called "Canadian Left Nationalists") argue that foreign ownership reflects the expansion of America's economic power.[8] One corollary of Britain's decline as imperial lodestar is the growing stock of U.S. investment in Canada, including the Canadian mining industry.

Echoing the dependency notion of a "comprador" bourgeoisie, this Left Nationalist or revisionist amalgam of staples and dependency thinking promoted the suggestion that Canada's indigenous capitalist class has been based to an unusual degree on commercial functions, rather than on manufacturing or any industrial activity requiring a long-term investment in fixed capital. As a result, investment in industries was neglected in contrast to involvement in, and financial support of, trades, transportation, and financial institutions;[9] Canadian savings were diverted from Canadian heavy industries. Though foreshadowed in the original staples approach of the 1930s, this assertion has proved contentious,[10] leaving the issue which this article seeks to illustrate as yet unresolved.

I

A corollary of both orthodox and revisionist positions appears to be that Canadian industries in the twentieth century were starved of Canadian capital. The orthodox view perceives an absolute shortage, whereas the revisionists identify and deplore a direction of capital away from industries towards other forms of economic activity. Moreover, an influential work in the Left Nationalist stream explained foreign ownership of Canadian industry as partly due to an absence of entrepreneurial initiatives among Canadians.[11] Surprisingly, this view is shared by both orthodox and at least some revisionist economic historians. There is a degree of consensus that Canada's development has been hindered by the inability of industries to obtain access to adequate investment funds from the pool of Canadian savings, and by the failure by Canadians to acquire the entrepreneurial skills and to undertake the risks upon which success under industrial capitalism depends.

The mining sector is a particularly interesting test of the staples-oriented approach for by the mid-1950s many mining enterprises were under foreign ownership. The orthodox interpretation regards foreign involvement as the inevitable outcome of the industry's need to seek foreign finance. The Left Nationalists, however, argue that foreign ownership was a result of the Canadian inheritance of an institutional structure ill-suited to industrial development.[12] The base metal mining industry in Canada was heavily dominated by the output of nickel, copper, lead and zinc in the period 1918–55. Military demands, along with the "new industrialism" based on electricity and the internal combustion engine, saw production of these four metals in Canada rise from $74 million in 1918 to $632 million in 1955. The maintenance of the momentum of expansion required exploration and development on an ever increasing scale. Consequently, the industry employed large amounts of fixed capital, and used a standard technology with high capital/labour ratios. The characteristic industrial structure was that of oligopoly. By 1954 the mining, smelting and refining of nickel-copper was conducted by only six firms of which the most dominant, the International Nickel Co. (INCO), was controlled from the United States. Other major producers were Falconbridge Nickel Mines and Sherritt Gordon Mines, which while initially developed as Canadian firms were subsequently sold into U.S. ownership.

For lead-zinc mining, smelting, and refining, the concentration was such that by 1954 the six largest firms contributed 86 percent of the net value added. In this case a Canadian firm, a subsidiary of the Canadian Pacific Railway Co., was dominant, the Consolidated Mining and Smelting Co. of Canada (COMINCO), at the heart of which was the Sullivan lead-zinc mine in south-eastern British Columbia. For copper-gold mining, both smelting and refining and concentration were similarly pronounced. About 88 percent of the net value added was created by the six biggest firms, of which the two largest were owned by respectively U.S. and Canadian investors. The Hudson Bay Mining and Smelting Co. in Manitoba was developed under U.S. patronage, but Noranda Mines in Quebec, initially a U.S. enterprise, became an entirely Canadian company from the late 1920s. By tracing the financial evolution of these large firms an assessment is possible of the validity of the orthodox and Left Nationalist views, though our analysis of a single sector is presented as no more than suggestive for the entire extractive industry. Similar work is needed on precious metals and the mineral fuels, especially oil, to complete a comprehensive evaluation of the contrasting interpretations.[13]

II

Nickel-copper deposits of a sulphide type are spotted throughout the Canadian Shield, but the area which has been unique in the richness and extent of its nickel-copper ores is the Sudbury basin in Northern Ontario.[14] A valley 37 miles long and 17 miles wide, the rim of the basin contained the various mines. When cutting in preparation for the transcontinental Canadian Pacific Railway revealed an ore body in 1883, the copper content had excited interest. Typically, the Ontario government concession, bought by local speculators for a nominal sum, was later sold to a larger business firm, H.H. Vivian and Co. of Swansea.[15] The

Murray Mine, as it was called, was worked unprofitably from 1889–94, the ore being smelted locally and shipped to Wales for refining. Later, during World War I, anxious to receive a reliable source of nickel for war purposes the British government bought the property, and formed the British American Nickel Co., which mined it temporarily.[16] Only one British firm survived in active production till 1928. The Mond Co. owned a nickel-refining method invented by Dr Lindsay Mond, which was used as the basis for designing a Welsh refinery supplied by ore from Sudbury.[17] However, it was American entrepreneurship which triumphed when the International Nickel Co. (INCO) was formed by the fusion of the American-led Canadian Copper Co. (owning properties in Sudbury) with the Orford Co., which had refining works in the U.S.A. The new company was incorporated in New Jersey in 1902.[18]

Although the initial experience of nickel-copper mining in Canada was of British and American impetus, with the formation and growth of INCO the American interests came to dominate. Almost all INCO's shares were held by U.S. residents in 1915, suggesting an influx of U.S. capital into Canada which was the consequence of the Sudbury activities of the American firm.[19] The merger and formation of INCO cost no more than $10 million, and by 1916 no less than $30 million had been distributed in dividends,[20] an indication of the very substantial return to American investors, which was achieved, in part, from economic rent from Sudbury ores. Such an exodus of Canadian mineral wealth has to be offset against the undoubted financial inflows required to establish the mining and smelting operation in Sudbury. Of course, new capital was required to finance the expansion of output during the First World War. Furthermore, the International Nickel Co. of Canada, a wholly owned subsidiary, was established in 1916 with a Dominion charter. This move represented the culmination of a long political struggle to have nickel refined in Canada, instead of shipping smelter matte overseas.[21] INCO had resisted such a suggestion for many years, but the pressure of the Royal Ontario Nickel Commission, a scandal over Sudbury nickel which had reached Germany by submarine, and the attraction of cheap Ontario hydropower, had broken the company's resistance. Investment in the new subsidiary took the form of building the refinery at Port Colborne, Ontario, for which, it was reported, the finance came from the American company.[22]

After a few lean years, the peacetime demand for nickel in automobiles and in specialty steels began to grow in the 1920s, and INCO's growth was described by contemporaries as follows: "In 1926 the company undertook a program of expansion, largely in Canada, which cost $52 million before its completion in 1933. Seventy-one per cent of the capital was provided by the sale of securities and the rest out of earnings and reserves."[23] This conclusion of Marshall and Southard was somewhat misleading, however, for the major part of a 1924 stock issue related to the takeover of the Mond Co., and thus involved a transfer of assets, with concomitant financial flow, between foreign principals. Once again, a capital inflow of impressive scale turns out to have been more modest on closer examination. By 1934, when the dust from complicated stock transactions had settled, Canadians owned 21 percent of the shares, British residents owned 33 percent, and U.S. residents owned 42 percent. Assets in Canada and abroad were valued at $200 million. The main source of capital propelling expansion came from ploughed back profits and economic rents. In every year from 1920 to 1934 profits were ploughed back into fixed capital formation, some $64 million in total over the years by one estimate.[24] In short, INCO represents a model of internally generated growth, supported by some occasional and modest infusions of U.S. capital. From 1930 to 1955 there were no further equity issues in INCO of Canada.

Mond having been absorbed, INCO's monopoly position in nickel was at its strongest in 1929. Though Le Nickel continued to mine New Caledonian ore, only one small competitor remained in Sudbury. Falconbridge Nickel Mines was a small and speculative concern when it was established with an Ontario charter in 1928 by Thayer Lindsley, an American engineer and mining promoter. Perhaps from fear of the anti-combine legislation in the U.S.A., or influenced by a report that the young company had obtained an independent nickel refinery in Norway, INCO seemingly allowed Falconbridge to develop the European market unchallenged. The small firm may have created a helpful illusion of serious competition. More than a simple producer, Falconbridge Nickel Mines became the flagship for a corporate empire dedicated to financing and developing new mines in Canada and abroad.[25] The Sudbury property, the surpluses from which were to fund so many new mines, was bought from Minneapolis owners for $2.5 million. Never before had so much been paid for a Sudbury property, and presumably the sum reflects a considerable element of economic rent. It seems likely that the realization of resource rent in this instance caused an outflow across the capital account of the Canadian balance of payments. The purchase was financed not by Thayer's own money, for he was not initially wealthy, but from a sale of shares (some through the Toronto Standard Stock and Mining Exchange) in two holding companies, Ventures Ltd. and Sudbury Basin Mines. Of course, to the extent that U.S. residents bought the shares, the capital outflow was mitigated. Falconbridge needed fresh capital in 1936 as the sales of nickel recovered from the depression. In the mid 1930s an extensive construction programme was initiated involving improvements to the Falconbridge mine and smelter and to the upgrading of the Norwegian refinery. Total expenditures for the construction were $2.1 million. Cash balances had been invested from 1932 in several Canadian gold-mining stocks, which reflected the buoyant gold market of the depression years. When the reserves were liquidated, a capital gain of about a half million dollars was realized[26] and applied to the expansion programme. Thus, through the mobilization of capital gains, equity shares in other mining companies contributed to finance nickel development.

Prior to World War II, Falconbridge was a comparatively small producer of nickel and copper. Only after the war, when it was still a Canadian company in the Lindsley empire, did Falconbridge start to challenge INCO. Anxious to increase nickel production and to build sources of supply separate from INCO, the U.S. government sponsored, among others, two Lindsley firms, Falconbridge and Sherritt Gordon Mines. In each case the chain of events leading to changed ownership can be traced to the strain placed on the financial capabilities of the firms as a result of attempts to increase sales dramatically to the U.S. government in the late 1940s and early 1950s.[27] A study of Falconbridge shows that ploughed back profits and economic rents were of major importance in financing growth.

Shareholders even complained, at times, about the small proportion of profits distributed as dividends. There was, indeed, an injection of American funds, less in the initial stages than one might suppose from a casual assessment, but more in the hidden form of bonuses on contracts in the 1950s,[28] and some in the growth of Falconbridge to multinational status. The Canadian equity and bond markets provided the funds at various stages, but throughout the company's history American entrepreneurial flair was instrumental to success.[29]

Incorporated under Ontario charter in 1927 as part of the Lindsley group of companies, the initial focus of Sherritt-Gordon Mines was on the Sherridon deposits of copper, zinc, gold, and silver in northern Manitoba. Production started in 1931, but the mine closed because of low metal prices from 1932 to 1936. Exhaustion of the Sherridon ore was complete by the late 1940s, when the company's focus switched to nickel mined from a new site at Lynn Lake, some 150 miles north of Sherridon. Most of the finance for Sherritt-Gordon Mines before 1946 came from equity shares issued in the booming stock market conditions of the late 1920s. Unusual for such a remote minesite, the proximity to the smelter and hydro-power supply of Hudson Bay Mining and Smelting, with which company appropriate contracts were signed, meant that neither power facilities nor smelter facilities had to be financed. A railway feeder line, 42 miles in length to the main Hudson Bay Railway, was supplied by Canadian National Railways (CNR) in 1929, with financial assistance from the Dominion.[30]

Sherridon's exhaustion was intimately tied to the eventual American takeover of Sherritt-Gordon. Lynn Lake was established as an alternative mine site in the years 1945–53, when the company became primarily a nickel, rather than a copper, producer. Such a transition required the building of new capacity to smelt and refine the nickel, and for technical reasons severing the hitherto convenient arrangement with Hudson Bay Mining and Smelting. A new reduction plant in Alberta was built, based on the experimental leaching technology (which proved considerably more expensive than envisaged in the initial budget), and a power site had to be developed on the Churchill River in Saskatchewan. In combination, these developments led the investment needs of the Sherritt-Gordon Mines to outrun the capacity (or willingness) of the existing shareholders to supply capital. Takeover by the Newmont Mining Corporation of the U.S.A. was the result. Even a five-year contract with the U.S. government beginning in 1950, and other contracts with American steel producers, proved inadequate to ensure sufficient financing within Canada.

How can the American takeover be explained? The immediate cause was the financial strain imposed by the development of Lynn Lake and the Alberta leaching plant. However, an explanation is also required for the inadequacy of Sherritt-Gordon's internal resources, as is an answer to the question why was Canadian capital not forthcoming when required? Bearing on both these issues is the operation of wartime price controls in Canada. Following the practice of all Lindsley companies, Sherritt-Gordon ploughed back a high proportion of gross profits into exploration. Lynn Lake represents one of the fruits of this policy. However, as shown in the Annual Report for 1951, the bulk of the firm's Sherridon ore was mined under conditions when its full value could not be realized. Together with other copper producers in the British Empire, in 1939 the company agreed to supply the British government "at a fair price."[31] About three-quarters of the output of Sherritt-Gordon was earmarked in this way, the balance being sold in Canada, but domestic prices were also controlled from between 1942 and 1947. Thus, after a period of closure during the depression, followed by price restrictions during the war, Sherritt-Gordon lacked reserves to provide for the postwar removal and expansion.[32] The lack of Canadian risk capital to finance Sherritt-Gordon's development is suggestive at a more general level. A plausible general conclusion might be that after Canadian business emerged from the depression, price controls and heavier taxation associated with World War II forced Canadian business into a disadvantageous position in comparison with its counterpart in the U.S. Is it plausible, therefore, to regard Canada's contribution to the war effort as explaining the relative absence of risk capital in the late 1940s and early 1950s?

III

Lead and zinc mining, smelting and refining comprised the main business of COMINCO. The Canadian Pacific Railway Company (CPR) built the southerly Crowsnest Pass route through the Rockies to Kootenay Lake, whence from 1898, by steamer and rail, shipments could be transferred north to the CPR main line. Engaged in a battle with American promoters of railroads and steamship lines for the traffic of south-eastern British Columbia, in 1898 the CPR purchased the recently completed smelter at Trail, the owner of which had had grand ambitions for railway development of his own. To ensure a steady supply of ore to the smelter the CPR was drawn gradually into the business of mining. COMINCO was incorporated under Dominion charter in 1906, by which time in addition to the original copper-gold smelter the Trail metallurgical works included a blast furnace to produce smelter lead and a small electrolytic lead-refining plant. Beyond the Trail complex COMINCO's operations extended to mines in nearby Rossland and along the tracks to Moyie in East Kootenay. In 1910 the company acquired the Sullivan Mine in East Kootenay, which contained a rich lead-zinc ore so complex that nobody could then economically separate it. A Canadian research effort located in Trail solved that metallurgical problem, first by subsidized electrolytic methods in 1916, then with increasing commercial success by a process of selective flotation started in 1920 and improved thereafter. The richness of the Sullivan Mine enabled the company to grow within three decades into a multinational corporation whose activities included mining and metallurgical operations and, via by-products of the Sullivan ore, fertilizer and chemical manufacture.[33]

The capital structure of the firm was straightforward. Bonds issued in 1918 to the amount of $3 million (later increased to $4 million) were retired in 1925, returning to a simple capital structure based on equity shares. Mine development and the expansion of reduction plants were financed to some extent by fresh stock issues, but relied most heavily on the re-investment of profits and economic rents.[34] Unusual for a mining company, COMINCO had a large bank overdraft with the Bank of Montreal. The security for this facility was inventory built up in expectation of sales to the Imperial Munitions Board, and credit amounted to just over $2 million in 1917 when the issued capital stood at almost $10.5 million. Over the next three years the amount of this bank lending increased and included a bridging loan in anticipation of funding, which reached a peak in excess of $5 million in 1920. Not until 1925 was this element of COMINCO's financing eliminated. Bank borrowing again occurred in 1930 which increased to a total of almost $3.9 million in 1932, the purpose of which was to finance increased inventories and to establish fertilizer production. It seems likely that COMINCO's favourable financial position resulted from the prestige of the CPR and its close links with the Montreal financial community, and that such connections were probably influential in securing substantial sums of capital at critical periods in the company's development in a form most unusual for a mining company. The major source of finance was ploughed back profits and economic rents, and in this respect the basis for COMINCO's growth resembled that of INCO. Financing was available from Canadian sources when needed. Of course, since the CPR was a stock widely owned in Britain (though control of the company rested in Canada), an appreciable percentage of the COMINCO stock and bond financing may have involved an inflow of British portfolio capital. No bonds were issued between 1936–55, nor was any new finance raised by stock issues during these years.

A legal quirk caused Noranda Mines Ltd. to become incorporated in Ontario.[35] An American syndicate, headed by Samuel Thomson and Humphrey Chadborne, had been formed in New York in 1922 with a view to buying and developing promising mineral properties. Soon after its formation the syndicate took an option on the Tremoy Lake property in Quebec staked by Ed Horne and owned by the Tremoy syndicate in which he held an interest. A Canadian lawyer, James Murdoch, who represented the Thomson and Chadborne syndicate noticed that under Ontario law the members of the syndicate were personally liable for the mining interest they held in Ontario. To remove this potential embarrassment, for small mining ventures were prone to fail, Noranda Mines Ltd. was incorporated in Ontario in 1922, and the shrewd Canadian lawyer became interim president of what was still a small concern. He remained, however, after the Noranda smelter was built at Rouyn and even when the locus of control shifted to Canada in 1927 continued as president. He retired in 1952, having been intimately involved in the pace and direction of the company's expansion and its emergence as a multinational company.

The general manager in charge of mine development, including the erection of the Rouyn smelter, was Ernest Hibbert, a British immigrant. For assistance Hibbert employed two men who had worked with him in the defunct British American Nickel venture at Sudbury. These men, H.L. Roscoe and R.V. Porritt, were responsible for the underground development of the new mine. Porritt was a McGill University graduate in mining engineering who rose within the company to become president in 1964; Roscoe, an American, became senior vice-president in 1956. Also involved in the Noranda mine site and smelter construction was J.R. Bradfield, another McGill University graduate, who, having worked in the U.S., joined the New York designers in 1926 with a view to becoming on-site civil engineer at Rouyn. He became company president in 1956 and chairman of the board in 1964. The managerial personnel of Noranda, therefore, provides no support for those who argue that a lack of entrepreneurial or technical skill explains the U.S. presence in Canadian mining. But was this case exceptional?

Three features of the case explain the success of Noranda as a Canadian mining corporation. First, Murdoch was something of a nationalist. Second, and more important, fortuitous and unique circumstances affected Noranda, for the Lower H ore body found in 1929 which proved to be the lode, rich in copper and gold on which Noranda's prosperity in the 1930s depended, occurred two years after advance in Canadian ownership in the company had taken place. The original development had occurred on the basis of a supply of ore assured for only three years. Yet in the late 1920s the price of Noranda Mines stock soared. The New York interests decided to unload Noranda at a substantial premium on the original investment. The Annual Report for 1927 recorded a change in share ownership since 1926, the result of which was that a majority of the issued shares were registered in the names of shareholders resident in Canada, and a new Toronto office soon replaced that in New York, which closed. Two years were to pass before the discovery of the Lower H ore body transformed a small and speculative enterprise into a rich and burgeoning corporation based on Canadian enterprise, technical skills, and capital. For the final circumstances that explain Noranda's Canadianization was the ready availability of Canadian capital. A factor here was the coincident occurrence of gold as well as copper in the Noranda ore deposits. Successful gold mining in Ontario had built up reserves of capital in Porcupine and Kirkland Lake since before World War I, and investment tended to be attracted into similar activity. Consequently, some of these funds were deployed through the equity market to finance Noranda. Further strength derived from the flexibility of the company's output mix resulting from the existence within the Noranda property both of gold- and copper-rich ores.

One of the major figures in the Canadianization of Noranda was Noah Timmins, owner of the Hollinger Mines, whose wealth, accumulated from gold mining, enabled him to invest in Noranda and to join the board in 1925. A $3 million issue in 1927 of 7 percent first mortgage sinking-fund gold bonds was taken up exclusively by Hollinger, which received as part of the deal a bonus of 30,000 Noranda shares. Two years later the entire Noranda 1927 bond issue was repaid from an equity issue. However, the bonus shares, added to shares obtained earlier by Noah Timmins in exchange for claims held beside the Horne property, perpetuated his influence as a major stockholder in Noranda. From 1930 Noranda's growth was financed by internally generated profits and economic rents which accrued to the enterprise. The refinery built for Noranda in Montreal in 1931 was owned by Canadian Copper Refiners, a joint venture. Nichols Copper (an American concern linked with Phelps Dodge) and British Metals, a marketing organization, joined with Noranda as senior participant in the share subscription of the new company which combined within a single organization refinery, technology, and market outlets. Over and above equity funding for the refinery's construction, Noranda guaranteed a $2.5 million bond issue of Canadian Copper Refiners to ensure adequate finance. The origins of Noranda's capital, therefore, are clearly identified. In the long run it came mainly from Noranda's successful exploitation of its Quebec deposits. The crucial early financing came from the United States. Thereafter, a combination of the booming market in Noranda shares, the backing of funds accumulated from gold mining profits at the Hollinger

Mines, and the fortuitous timing of the discovery of the richer ore lodes, enabled Canadian entrepreneurs to assume control of the corporation.

The Dominion Charter of the Hudson Bay Mining and Smelting Company was granted in 1927. A technology having been found to separate the Flin Flon (Manitoba) copper-zinc ores by research in Denver and by field experimentation, the Whitney group of New York exercised an option on the property and launched what was then a massive investment in the north of Manitoba. Not surprisingly, American entrepreneurship, capital, and technology played prominent parts in this development. Perhaps most striking is the willingness of an American entrepreneurial group to experiment with a flotation method, which in the 1920s was coming into widespread commercial use.[36] It was the successful application of this method which transformed the ore deposits, known since 1915, into a commercial success involving mining and smelting operations. Refining was carried out by Canadian Copper Refiners in Montreal, in whose refinery Noranda possessed an interest. Funding for Hudson Bay Mining and Smelting came from the sale of shares which Canadian investors appeared eager to acquire when the company was first formed. The purpose of initial financing was to raise $15 million to $20 million in cash to bring the enterprise into commercial operation. In January 1928, however, the *Northern Miner* reported that few shares of Hudson Bay Mining and Smelting were available to the Canadian public, since the New York interests were keeping nearly all their stock;[37] moreover, share listing on the Toronto Standard Exchange was not yet achieved. The New York share distribution was private, but reportedly widespread;[38] nonetheless, at his death in 1930 Harry Payne Whitney owned 30 percent of the company's $5 million bonds issue in addition to 30 percent of the common stock.

While most of the capital to launch this enterprise was obtained in New York, this seems to have been the result of rationing, at least in part. Canadians were eager to purchase equity but the conditions under which the company was launched initially frustrated their intentions. We conclude, therefore, that even in this case, which might seem at first glance to be unambiguous, shortage of risk capital does not explain the American ownership of a major new deposit; the explanation is to be found in the mode of operation of American financiers when the company was floated. Thereafter, apart from the bond issue of 1930, the financing of Hudson Bay Mining and Smelting depended entirely on ploughed back profits and economic rents. The $5 million bond issue took the form of convertible debentures, all of which were retired before July 1935 by purchase or conversion into capital stock. Control remained in U.S. hands until 1955.[39]

IV

A comparison of the total assets of those companies whose histories we have examined provide a wider perspective (table 1). First, the relative importance of INCO is apparent in both 1935 and 1955; the rich Sudbury deposits and the world monopoly achieved by the 1920s rendered INCO a unique phenomenon in Canadian mining history. We have remarked already that a limited infusion of U.S. capital seems to have been necessary for INCO's success. COMINCO and Noranda both grew faster than INCO from 1935 to 1955, in each case using

TABLE 1

Total Assets of Leading Companies in Canadian Base Metal Mining, 1935 and 1955

| | ($ million) | |
	1935	1955
Inco	210.6	519.6
Cominco	49.9	200.8
Noranda	34.0	113.6
Hudson Bay M and S	34.6	74.1
Falconbridge	9.6	68.8
Sherritt-Gordon	8.6	58.2

SOURCE: *Survey of Mines* (*Financial Post*, 1936, 1957).

primarily Canadian capital. At the same time, Falconbridge and Sherritt-Gordon grew to become multi-nationals in their own right. The former relied throughout mainly on Canadian capital, while not until the early 1950s was Sherritt-Gordon acquired by American funds. Hudson Bay Mining and Smelting did employ American capital to become established in the late 1920s, but not, apparently, because of a lack of Canadian investment interest. The histories of leading firms suggest that any notion that there was heavy involvement of foreign firms in the Canadian base metal mining industry due to a shortage of Canadian capital in their development stages is quite false.

The main source of development finance for base metal mining between the wars was the reinvested surplus generated within each of the major concerns. From the original gold mines of Ontario, too, a certain surplus which had accumulated was attracted to the related copper-gold mining industry in Quebec. For the mass of speculative small concerns, which accounted for but a small part of output, the Toronto Standard Stock and Mining Exchange provided a channel into mining, for Canadian risk capital until its absorption in 1934 by the Toronto Stock Exchange, which continued the tradition. Montreal also served as a market for some small mining stocks. That there was American investment in Canadian mining is not surprising, given the opportunities; but it would be incorrect to conclude that this investment by its size was the critical factor which propelled the Canadian mining industry. Canadian economic rents, rather than the American capital, are to be seen as the motive force of the industry from 1918–39. Only in the 1950s did bonus contracts and capital injections create a situation where there may be some truth in Hugh Aitken's aphorism that American capital got things done that might not have been done at all. However, it seems likely that American policies supporting high base-metal prices may have been more significant than were direct capital injections, even in the 1950s. After World War II the dynamic seems to have resulted from market manipulation rather than from vigorous inflows of U.S. capital. Furthermore, the view that Canada could not develop necessary technologies but required American "packages," including technical expertise, entrepreneurship, and capital, seems to be invalidated by the historical experience of base metal mining. Sometimes, indeed, this was the reality, for example at Flin Flon where the Whitney group of financial interests possessed the expertise to devise in Denver, Colorado, a commercial production technique on which Hudson Bay Mining and Smelting flourished. At Trail, by contrast, a Canadian research effort supported by Canadian financial backing solved the problem of separating the Sullivan ore by a commercially successful process. The Noranda Mines in Quebec employed Canadians who proved to be extremely effective entrepreneurs. Market access and technical needs were solved in that case by establishing bilateral links with American and British concerns in the joint financing of the Montreal refinery. In short, the reality was much more diverse, and is more difficult to explain than the easy generalization of the orthodox school would have us believe.

The Left Nationalist view should be seen in the light of the history of COMINCO. Twice at crucial points in the company's development injections of capital were received from the sphere of commerce. As it was owned by Canadian Pacific, COMINCO's connections with Canadian commercial capital were of the best. Yet bank lending was available in these instances for essentially long term purposes: for the launching of the selective flotation technique of separation in 1920, and for the establishment of fertilizer operations from waste sulphur in 1930. In certain circumstances it seems as if Canadian commercial and financial capital could penetrate the production sphere, which raises the possibility that examples might be found in other sectors of the Canadian economy. The Noranda and the Lindsley companies were able to tap a variety of sources of Canadian capital to finance their growth, which also suggests that while no direct assistance was provided the dominance of commercial capital in Canada was not such as to inhibit the flow of indigenous finance for productive industry. Furthermore, Canadian entrepreneurship was in evidence throughout the industry during the entire period. There is little support, therefore, for either orthodox or revisionist interpretations from the experience of base metal mining from 1918 to 1955. The history is one of considerable Canadian achievement combined with U.S. involvement, and suggests that foreign domination of the industry must be explained in terms other than a shortage of Canadian capital or a lack of Canadian entrepreneurship.

Notes

1. A version of this paper was presented to the Annual Meeting of the Canadian Historical Association in Montreal (June, 1980). The author would like to thank Dr P. Phillips (University of Manitoba), I. Spry (University of Ottawa), Dr I.M. Drummond (University of Toronto), and members of the University of Toronto Economic History Workshop for helpful comments. All references to $ are to Canadian dollars, unless otherwise indicated.

2. R.M. Longo, *Historical Highlights of Canadian Mining* (Toronto, 1973), 164.

3. H. Aitken, *American Capital and Canadian Resources* (Cambridge, Mass., 1961), 104.

4. Only a few writers note, as does Hugh Aitken, the importance of re-invested earnings to the growth of foreign ownership. See Aitken, *American Capital.*

5. The "staples approach" identifies the work of a group of scholars in Canada in the 1920s and 1930s. W.A. Mackintosh of Queen's University and Harold Innis of the University of Toronto led this group. See D.G. Creighton, *Harold Adams Innis: Portrait of a Scholar* (Toronto, 1957), 105.

6. M.H. Watkins, "A Staple Theory of Economic Growth," *Canadian Journal of Economics and Political Science* XXIX (1962): 14–58. For linkages see A.O. Hirschman, *The Strategy of Economic Development* (1958).

7. M.H. Watkins, "The Staple Theory Revisited," *Journal of Canadian Studies* 12 (1977): 83–95.

8. This approach is found in the work of economists, political scientists, sociologists, and historians. A recent review of this literature was presented by D. McNally, "Staple Theory as Commodity Fetishism: Marx, Innis and Canadian Political Economy," *Studies in Political Economy* 6 (1981): 35–63. See also D. Drache, "Rediscovering Canadian Political Economy," *Journal of Canadian Studies* 11 (1976): 3–18.

9. R.T. Naylor, "The Rise and Fall of the Third Commercial Empire of the St. Lawrence" in *Capitalism and the National Question in Canada*, edited by G. Teeple (Toronto, 1973), 1–41. R.T. Naylor, *The History of Canadian Business* (Toronto, 1975), I: 2–18.

10. L.R. McDonald, "Merchants Against Industry: An Idea and its Origins," *Canadian Historical Review* 56 (1975): 263–81; C. Pentland, "Marx and the Canadian Question," *Canadian Forum* (Jan. 1974): 26–8.

11. K. Levitt, *Silent Surrender: The Multinational Corporation in Canada* (Toronto, 1970), 40.

12. Successful historical interpretations must explain adequately, or survive "testing" by confrontation with events. The evolving Canadian base metal mining industry offers such a possibility of assessing the orthodox and revisionist schools of mining history described above. Information sources include company annual reports, the *Financial Post Survey of Mines* (various years), the *Financial Post Corporation (Yellow Card) Service*, and contemporary newspaper reports.

13. Comparatively little has been written on the extractive industry of Canada by economic historians, though anecdotal publications are plentiful. Still unchallenged in scope is H.A. Innis, *Settlement and the Mining Frontier* (Toronto, 1936). More recently, for Ontario, there has appeared H.V. Nelles, *The Politics of Development: Forests, Mines and Hydro-Power in Ontario, 1849–1941* (Toronto, 1974). A specialized bibliography is W.G. Richardson, *A Survey of Canadian Mining History* (The Canadian Institute of Mining and Metallurgy, Special Vol. 14, 1974).

14. See D.M. LeBourdais, *The Sudbury Basin* (Toronto, 1953).

15. The British North America Act (1867) of the Westminster Parliament established the Canadian constitution, by which property rights over natural resources were vested in the provinces.

16. See T.W. Gibson, *Mining in Ontario* (Toronto, 1937), 78.

17. Royal Ontario Nickel Commission (hereafter RONC), *Report* (Toronto, 1917), 59.

18. For details on INCO see O.W. Main, *The Canadian Nickel Industry* (Toronto, 1955), 76–123. J.F. Thomson and N. Beasley, *For the Years to Come* (Toronto, 1960), 139–90. D.M. LeBourdais, *Metals and Men* (Toronto, 1957), 119–26.

19. RONC, *Report*, 73.

20. A.C. Dow, "The Canadian Base Metal Mining Industry (Non-ferrous) and its Impact on Economic Development in Canada, 1918–55" (PhD thesis, University of Manitoba, 1980), 138–43.

21. The ore removed from a mine would contain less than 4 percent of recoverable metals. By milling and smelting the mineral, for example, nickel matte was made 95 percent pure. Refining improved the purity to over 99 percent. See J.R. Boldt and P. Quesneau, *The Winning of Nickel* (Toronto, 1967), 350–5.

22. H. Marshall and F. Southard, *Canadian-American Industry* (Toronto, 1976), 98.

23. Ibid.

24. A. Skelton, "Nickel" in W.Y. Elliot et al., *International Control in the Non Ferrous Metals* (New York, 1937), 191.

25. For details on Falconbridge see D.M. LeBourdais, *The Sudbury Basin* (Toronto, 1953), 138; J. Deverall, *Falconbridge* (Toronto, 1975), 39–51. F.S. Moore, *American Influence in Canadian Mining* (Toronto, 1941), 35. R.M. Longo, ed., *Historical Highlights of Canadian Mining* (Toronto, 1973), 63–5.

26. Falconbridge Nickel Mines, *Annual Report* (1936).

27. In fact, McIntyre Porcupine Mines, a Canadian gold producer, bought Falconbridge in 1957 when cash-flow problems emerged. Not until 1967 did a U.S. company, Superior Oil, take over.

28. Falconbridge signed the first five-year contract for nickel with the U.S. government in 1948. During the Korean conflict in 1951 the U.S. Defence Materials Procurement Agency agreed to a ten-year contract at market prices for each year along with $6 million advance. Then the U.S. government, in the biggest order of the three, contracted to buy large quantities of refined nickel over nine years at market prices plus a premium of 40 cents a pound. At that time (1953) the market price for nickel was 60 cents a pound. With an expected

sale of 100 million pounds of refined nickel, the bonus amounted to an anticipated $40 million. These bonuses, which allowed a substantial expansion to be undertaken, represent capital inflow of an unusual sort.

29. However, another Falconbridge career is noteworthy. Born in Saskatchewan, Horace Fraser graduated from the University of Manitoba in 1924 with a B.Sc. in chemistry. After a Harvard Ph.D. in geology, he worked briefly for INCO before accepting a university teaching position in California. During World War II he worked in Washington, D.C., in the area of minerals procurement. Sought out by Lindsley, Fraser joined Falconbridge after the war rising to become president and managing director in 1957. His success is a reminder of the part played by Canadians in the entrepreneurial function within firms such as Falconbridge.

30. Canada, *Debates of the House of Commons*, 82nd Session, 17th parliament, 21 May 1931, 1858–60.

31. Sherritt-Gordon Mines, *Annual Report* (1939).

32. Considering that exhaustion loomed, it is remarkable that over two-thirds of the company's profits from exploiting the Sherridon deposits came in the period from 1947 to 1951.

33. See "The Story of COMINCO," *Canadian Mining Journal* 75 (1954): 151–393.

34. T.W. Bingay, "A Brief History of The Consolidated M and S Co," *Miner* 9 (1936): 49–51.

35. L. Roberts, *Noranda* (Toronto, 1956), 52.

36. Selective flotation is a method of separating metal-bearing ore from crude rock based on the principle that a substance will tend to stick to an air bubble, if the surface is not wetted by water. In flotation tanks the desired minerals are made hydrophobic by the addition of suitable chemicals to a liquid ore pulp. See J.R. Boldt and P. Quesneau, *The Winning of Nickel* (Toronto, 1967), 199–204.

37. *Northern Miner*, 19 Jan. 1928.

38. "Flin Flon Deal Outlines," *Northern Miner*, 26 Jan. 1928.

39. Subsequently in the 1960s the company was sold to South African interests.

FURTHER READING

The introduction, its footnotes, and notes for the articles themselves offer a substantial list of references, which it is not intended to recapitulate here. This note is meant to offer further starting points from which interested researchers can pursue their work, with a particular emphasis on recent sources that in turn give access to earlier material.

Good general bibliographies for Canadian economic history can be found in Trevor J.O. Dick, *Economic History of Canada: A Guide to Information Sources* (Detroit: Gale, 1978) and William Marr and Donald Paterson, *Canada: An Economic History* (Toronto: Gage, 1980). Each issue of the *Canadian Historical Review* (hereafter *C.H.R.*) includes in its "Recent Publications" pages a section focussing on economic history. The Canadian Historical Association's *Register of Post-Graduate Dissertations in Progress in History and Related Subjects* can also be helpful.

Indispensable to all students is *Historical Statistics of Canada*; its second edition (F.H. Leacy, ed.) was published by Statistics Canada in 1983. Because some pertinent early historical series are not included in this edition, the original edition (M.C. Urquhart and K.A.H. Buckley, eds.) is not entirely superseded.

Several of the articles published here prompted direct responses. Le Goff's article was not the start of the debate it surveyed, but it did provoke a further round: see Gilles Paquet and Jean-Pierre Wallot, "The Agricultural Crisis in Lower Canada, 1802–12; mise au point. A Response to T.J.A. Le Goff," *C.H.R.* LVI (1975): 133–61; and Le Goff's response, ibid.: 162–8. For the article by Isbister, see Donald Kerr and William J. Smyth, "Agriculture, Balanced Growth, and Social Change in Central Canada since 1850: Some Comments toward a More Complete Explanation," *Economic Development and Cultural Change* XXVIII (1979–80): 615–22; and Isbister's reply, ibid.: 623–5. For the article by Peter George, see L.J. Mercer, "Rates of Return and Government Subsidization of the Canadian Pacific Railway: An Alternative View," *Canadian Journal of Economics* (hereafter *C.J.E.*) VI (1973): 428–37; and George's "Rates of Return and Government Subsidization of the Canadian Pacific Railway: Some Further Remarks," *C.J.E.* VIII (1975): 591–600. For the article by Norrie, see K. Gary Grant, "The Rate of Settlement of the Canadian Prairies, 1870–1911: A Comment," *Journal of Economic History* (hereafter *J.E.H.*) XXXVIII (1978): 471–3; and Norrie's reply in ibid.: 474–5; see also, for a more general review of the literature here, Norrie's "The National Policy and the Rate of Prairie Settlement," *Journal of Canadian Studies* XIV, 3 (Fall 1979): 63–76. For the Chambers and Gordon article, besides the Bertram article reprinted here (and the earlier criticism and responses it notes), see especially Richard E. Caves, "Export-Led Growth and the New Economic History" in *Trade, Balance of Payments and Growth: Papers in International Economics in Honor of Charles P. Kindleberger*, edited by J. Bhagwati, et al. (Amsterdam: North Holland, 1971), 403–42.

On the economic history of Quebec, Robert Armstrong's recent *Structure and Change: An Economic History of Quebec* (Toronto: Gage, 1984) offers a starting point; its chapter notes also offer convenient bibliographies. Paul-André Linteau, René Durocher, and Jean-Claude Robert, *Quebec: A History, 1867–1929* (Toronto: Lorimer, 1983), a translation of their 1979 *Histoire du Québec contemporain: De la Confédération à la crise (1867–1929)* pays careful attention to economic themes; a volume carrying the story forward from 1929 is in preparation. Two older works are still of fundamental importance: Fernand Ouellet's *Economic and Social History of Quebec, 1760–1850* (Toronto: Macmillan, 1980), a translation of his *Histoire économique et sociale du Québec, 1760–1850: structures et conjoncture* (Montréal: Fides, 1966); and Jean Hamelin and Yves Roby's *Histoire économique du Québec, 1851–1896* (Montréal: Fides, 1971). The excellent bibliography of Canadian history published in every issue of the *Revue d'histoire de l'Amérique française* (hereafter *R.H.A.F.*) offers best access to continuing work in the field.

No other province has had as much attention paid to its economic history as has Quebec. A three-volume economic history of Ontario is currently in progress, however. Its third volume is the first to appear: K.J. Rea, *The Prosperous Years: The Economic History of Ontario, 1939–75* (Toronto: University of Toronto Press, 1985). Ian Drummond's *Progress without Planning: The Economic History of Ontario, 1867–1941* will be the next to be published.

Rea's volume also offers a starting point for those interested in the modern economic history of Canada. Another access point to the recent past is Robert Bothwell, Ian Drummond, and John English, *Canada Since 1945: Power, Politics, and Provincialism* (Toronto: University of Toronto Press, 1981), which pays considerable attention to economic matters.

Of the themes not centrally treated in articles included in this collection, some have been more researched than others. The study of historical demography in Canada has been relatively active, as can be seen in the bibliographies of new work in Canadian population history frequently included in *Histoire sociale/Social History* (hereafter *H.S./S.H.*) since 1979. Here too Quebec has the richest tradition, and the richest sources (though far from a monopoly on the subject). For a glimpse of this work in English, see J. Henripin and Y. Peron, "The Demographic Transition of the Province of Quebec" in *Population and Social Change*, edited by D.V. Glass and R. Revelle (London: Arnold, 1972). For examples of much more recent work, see Christian Pouyez, Yolande Lavoie, et al., *Les Saguenayens. Introduction à l'histoire des populations du Saguenay, XVIe–XXe siècles* (Sillery: Presses de l'Université du Québec, 1983); and Lorraine Gadoury, Yves Landry, and Hubert Charbonneau, "Démographie differentielle en Nouvelle-France: villes et campagnes," *R.H.A.F.* XXXVIII (1984–85): 357–78 (this entire issue focusses on "population et histoire").

Crucial building blocks to any wider understanding of Canadian economic history are evidence on the trade cycle and on prices. On the former, see E.J. Chambers, "Late Nineteenth-Century Business Cycles in Canada," *Canadian Journal of Economics and Political Science* (hereafter *C.J.E.P.S.*) XXX (1964): 391–412; and K.A. Hay, "Early Twentieth Century Business Cycles in Canada," *C.J.E.P.S.* XXXII (1966): 354–65. See also L. Blain, D.G. Paterson, and J.D. Rae, "The Regional Impact of Economic Fluctuations during the Inter-war Period: The Case of British Columbia," *C.J.E.* VII (1974): 381–401. On prices in the pre-1914 era, much work is still to be done. The best recent examples of work in the field are E.J. Chambers, "New Evidence on the Living Standards of Toronto Blue Collar Workers in the pre-1914 Era" (paper presented to the 14th Conference on the Use of Quantitative Methods in Canadian Economic History, Montreal, October 1985); and Fernand Ouellet with Jean Hamelin and Richard Chabot, "Les prix agricoles dans les villes et les campagnes du Québec d'avant 1850: aperçus quantitatifs," *H.S./S.H.* XV (1982): 83–127. See also Gordon Bertram and Michael Percy, "Real Wage Trends in Canada 1900–26: Some Provisional Estimates," *C.J.E.* XII (1979): 299–312.

On monetary issues, see Angela Redish, "Why Was Specie Scarce in Colonial Economies? An Analysis of the Canadian Currency, 1796–1830," *J.E.H.* XLIV (1984): 713–28; and her "The Economic Crisis of 1837–1839 in Upper Canada: Case Study of a Temporary Suspension of Specie Payments," *Explorations in Economic History* XX (1983): 402–17. There is also useful material, including a bibliography, in A.B. McCullough, *Money and Exchange in Canada to 1900* (Toronto and Charlottetown: Dundurn, 1984). For examples of recent work on industrialization, see Kris Inwood, "The Decline and Rise of Charcoal Iron: The Case of Canada" (Ph.D. thesis, University of Toronto, 1984) and his brief note on "Productivity Growth in Obsolescence: Charcoal Iron Revisited," *J.E.H.* XLV (1985): 293–8; and Peter Wylie, "Electrification and Technological Adaptation in Canadian Manufacturing 1900–1929" (paper presented to the 14th Conference on the Use of Quantitative Methods in Canadian Economic History, Montreal, October 1985).

A number of sources already mentioned pertain to the "pre-statistical" era, though the selection problem becomes more difficult still here, because economic issues are even less distinguishable from wider social history than in later periods. See, both for context and for some treatment of Canadian issues, the outstanding book by John J. McCusker and Russell R. Menard, *The Economy of British America 1607–1789* (Chapel Hill: University of North Carolina Press, 1985). Louise Dechêne, *Habitants et marchands de Montréal au XVIIe siècle* (Paris: Plon, 1974) is a justly acclaimed volume. Other sources embodying challenging approaches include Allan Greer, *Peasant, Lord, and Merchant: Rural Society in Three Quebec Parishes 1740–1840* (Toronto: University of Toronto Press, 1985); and A.J. Ray, *Indians in the Fur Trade* (Toronto: University of Toronto Press, 1974). See also Douglas McCalla, "The 'Loyalist' Economy of Upper Canada, 1784–1806," *H.S./S.H.* XVI (1983): 279–304; and "The Internal Economy of Upper Canada: New Evidence on Agricultural Marketing before 1850," *Agricultural History* LIX (1985): 397–416.

For some recent discussion in the staples tradition, see John Richards, "The Staple Debates" in *Explorations in Canadian Economic History: Essays in Honour of Irene M. Spry*, edited by Duncan Cameron (Ottawa: University of Ottawa Press, 1985); John McCallum, *Unequal Beginnings: Agriculture and Economic Development in Quebec and Ontario until 1870* (Toronto: University of Toronto Press, 1980); and many of the titles listed in *The New Practical Guide to Canadian Political Economy*. A pioneering article, K.A.H. Buckley, "The Role of the Staple Industries in Canada's Development," *J.E.H.* XVIII (1958): 439–50, should not be overlooked.

For approaches to economic history in general, see Donald McCloskey, "The Achievements of the Cliometric School," Jon S. Cohen, "The Achievements of Economic History: The Marxist School," and Robert Forster, "Achievements of the Annales School," three lively, personal, yet authoritative accounts that, with David Landes's "On Avoiding Babel" and a discussion by Douglass C. North, can be found in *J.E.H.* XXXVIII (1978): 1–80. Also recommended is J. Morgan Kousser, "Quantitative Social-Scientific History" in *The Past Before Us*, edited by Michael Kammen (Ithaca: Cornell, 1980), 433–56.

An honest attempt has been made to secure permission for all material used, and, if there are errors or omissions, these are wholly unintentional and the Publisher will be grateful to learn of them.

T.J.A. LeGoff, "The Agricultural Crisis in Lower Canada, 1802–12: A Review of a Controversy," *Canadian Historical Review* (March 1974): 1–31; Eric W. Sager and Lewis R. Fischer, "Atlantic Canada and the Age of Sail Revisited," *Canadian Historical Review* (June 1982): 125–50. Reprinted by permission of the authors and University of Toronto Press.

Marvin McInnis, "Marketable Surpluses in Ontario Farming, 1860," *Social Science History* VIII, 4 (1984): 395–424. Reprinted by permission.

John Isbister, "Agriculture, Balanced Growth, and Social Change in Central Canada Since 1850," *Economic Development and Cultural Change* XXV (1976–77): 673–97; Edward J. Chambers and Donald F. Gordon, "Primary Products and Economic Growth: An Empirical Measurement," *Journal of Political Economy* LXXIV, 4 (Aug. 1966): 315–32. © by The University of Chicago Press. Reprinted by permission of the authors and the publisher.

Richard Pomfret, "The Mechanization of Reaping in Nineteenth-Century Ontario: A Case Study of the Pace and Causes of the Diffusion of Embodied Technical Change," *Journal of Economic History* XXVI, 2 (June 1976): 399–415; K.H. Norrie, "The Rate of Settlement of the Canadian Prairies, 1870–1911," *Journal of Economic History* XXXV, 2 (June 1975): 410–27; Trevor J.O. Dick, "Canadian Newsprint, 1913–1930: National Policies and the North American Economy," *Journal of Economic History* XLII, 3 (Sept. 1982): 659–87. Reprinted by permission of the authors and the Economic History Association.

Paul Craven and Tom Traves, "Canadian Railways as Manufacturers, 1850–1880," Canadian Historical Association, *Historical Papers 1983*: 254–81. Reprinted by permission of the authors and the Canadian Historical Association.

Peter J. George, "Rates of Returns in Railway Investment and Implications for Government Subsidization of the Canadian Pacific Railway: Some Preliminary Results," *Canadian Journal of Economics* I, 4 (Nov. 1968): 740–62; Gordon W. Bertram, "The Relevance of the Wheat Boom in Canadian Economic Growth," *Canadian Journal of Economics* VI, 4 (Nov. 1973): 545–66. Reprinted by permission of the authors and the Canadian Economics Association.

A.G. Green and M.C. Urquhart, "New Estimates of Output Growth in Canada: Measurement and Interpretation." Published by permission of the authors.

Alexander Dow, "Finance and Foreign Control in Canadian Base Metal Mining, 1918–55," *Economic History Review* XXXVII, 1 (Feb. 1984): 54–67. Reprinted by permission of the author and the review.